The Cambridge Companion to the Brontës

The extraordinary works of the three sisters Charlotte, Emily and Anne Brontë have entranced and challenged scholars, students and general readers for the past one-hundred-and-fifty years. This *Companion* offers a fascinating introduction to those works, including two of the greatest novels of the nineteenth century – Charlotte's *Jane Eyre* and Emily's *Wuthering Heights*. In a series of original essays, contributors explore the roots of the sisters' achievement in early nineteenth-century Haworth, and the childhood 'plays' they developed; they set these writings within the context of a wider history, and show how each sister engages with some of the central issues of her time. The essays also consider the meaning and significance of the Brontës' enduring popular appeal. A detailed chronology and guides to further reading provide further reference material, making this a volume indispensable for scholars and students, and all those interested in the Brontës and their work.

D0223950

THE CAMBRIDGE
COMPANION TO
THE BRONTËS

EDITED BY
HEATHER GLEN

CAMBRIDGE
UNIVERSITY PRESS

PUBLISHED BY THE PRESS SYNDICATE OF THE UNIVERSITY OF CAMBRIDGE
The Pitt Building, Trumpington Street, Cambridge CB2 1RP, United Kingdom

CAMBRIDGE UNIVERSITY PRESS
The Edinburgh Building, Cambridge, CB2 2RU, UK
40 West 20th Street, New York, NY 10011-4211, USA
477 Williamstown Road, Port Melbourne, VIC 3207, Australia
Ruiz de Alarcón 13, 28014 Madrid, Spain
Dock House, The Waterfront, Cape Town 8001, South Africa

http://www.cambridge.org

First published 2002

Printed in the United Kingdom at the University Press, Cambridge

Typeface Sabon 10/13 pt.   *System* LATEX 2$_\varepsilon$ [TB]

A catalogue record for this book is available from the British Library

Library of Congress cataloguing in publication data
The Cambridge companion to the Brontës / edited by Heather Glen.
p.   cm. – (Cambridge companions to literature)
Includes bibliographical references and index.
ISBN 0 521 77027 0 (hardback) ISBN 0 521 77971 5 (paperback)
1. Brontë family – Handbooks, manuals, etc.   2. Brontë, Charlotte, 1816–1855 – Criticism
and interpretation – Handbooks, manuals, etc.   3. Brontë, Emily, 1818–1848 – Criticism
and interpretation – Handbooks, manuals, etc.   4. Brontë, Anne, 1820–1849 – Criticism
and interpretation – Handbooks, manuals, etc.   5. Women and literature – England –
Yorkshire – Handbooks, manuals, etc.   6. Yorkshire (England) – In literature –
Handbooks, manuals, etc.   I. Title: Companion to the Brontës.   II. Title: Brontës.
III. Glen, Heather.   IV. Series.
PR4168 .C29   2002
823'.809 – dc21   2002067052

ISBN 0 521 77027 0 hardback
ISBN 0 521 77971 5 paperback

CONTENTS

ILLUSTRATIONS

NOTES ON CONTRIBUTORS

JULIET BARKER was curator and librarian of the Brontë Parsonage Museum, Haworth, from 1983 to 1989. She is the author of *The Brontës* and *Wordsworth: A Life*, and editor of *The Brontës: Selected Poems*; *Charlotte Brontë: Juvenilia 1829–35*; *The Brontës: A Life in Letters* and *Wordsworth: A Life in Letters*.

CAROL BOCK is Associate Professor of English at the University of Minnesota, Duluth. Her publications include *Charlotte Brontë and the Storyteller's Audience* (1992).

STEVIE DAVIES taught English Literature at Manchester University before becoming a full-time author in 1984. She is currently the Royal Literary Fund's Writing Fellow at the University of Swansea. She has published a number of volumes of literary criticism, including two studies of Milton, one of Virginia Woolf, and four of Emily Brontë. Her first novel, *Boy Blue*, won the Fawcett Prize in 1989; two other novels have been longlisted for the Booker Prize. Her most recent novel is *The Element of Water*.

KATE FLINT is Professor of English at Rutgers University, New Brunswick. She is author of *The Woman Reader, 1837–1914* and *The Victorians and the Visual Imagination*, as well as numerous articles on Victorian and twentieth-century fiction, painting and cultural history. Her current research is on Victorians and Native Americans.

HEATHER GLEN is a Senior Lecturer in English at the University of Cambridge, and a fellow of New Hall, Cambridge. She is the author of *Vision and Disenchantment: Blake's Songs and Wordsworth's Lyrical Ballads*, and editor of *'Jane Eyre': New Casebook*. She has also edited Emily Brontë's *Wuthering Heights* (1988) and Charlotte Brontë's *The Professor* (1989). Her most recent book is *Charlotte Brontë: the Imagination in History*.

ANGELA LEIGHTON is Professor of English at the University of Hull. She is the author of *Shelley and the Sublime, Elizabeth Barrett Browning*, and *Victorian Women Poets: Writing Against the Heart*, as well as articles and essays on nineteenth- and twentieth-century literature. She is currently writing a book about aestheticism, and a collection of essays on poetry.

JOHN MAYNARD is Professor of English at New York University. He is the author of a number of books on Victorian subjects, including *Charlotte Brontë and Sexuality*. He is co-editor of *Victorian Literature and Culture*.

JILL MATUS is a Professor of English at the University of Toronto. She is the author of *Unstable Bodies: Victorian Representations of Sexuality and Maternity* and *Toni Morrison*; and has written articles on George Eliot, Charlotte Brontë, Charles Dickens, Mary Elizabeth Braddon, Angela Carter, African American fiction and literary theory.

RICK RYLANCE is Professor of Modern English Literature and Dean of the School of Arts and Letters at Anglia Polytechnic University, Cambridge. His most recent book is *Victorian Psychology and British Culture 1850–1880*. He is presently writing volume 11 of the Oxford English Literary History, *1930–1970: Literature Among the Wars*.

PATSY STONEMAN is a Reader in English at the University of Hull. Her publications include *Elizabeth Gaskell* and *Brontë Transformations: The Cultural Dissemination of 'Jane Eyre' and 'Wuthering Heights'*. Her other work on *Wuthering Heights* includes editing the Macmillan New Casebook (1993) and the Icon Critical Guide (1998) and writing the Introduction to the Oxford World's Classics edition (1995).

ABBREVIATIONS

Except in the case of the following abbreviations, full details of works referred to are given after each chapter, either in the notes or in a list of works cited.

ABP   *The Poems of Anne Brontë: A New Text and Commentary*,
        edited by Edward Chitham (Basingstoke: Macmillan, 1979)
AG   Anne Brontë, *Agnes Grey*, edited by Robert Inglesfield and
        Hilda Marsden (Oxford: World's Classics, 1992)
CBL   *The Letters of Charlotte Brontë*, edited by Margaret Smith, 3
        vols. (Oxford: Clarendon, 1995, 2000; vol. 3 forthcoming)
CBP   *The Poems of Charlotte Brontë: A New Annotated and
        Enlarged Edition of the Shakespeare Head Brontë*, edited by
        Tom Winnifrith (Oxford: Blackwell, 1984)
CH   *The Brontës: The Critical Heritage*, edited by Miriam Allott
        (London: Routledge & Kegan Paul, 1974)
EBP   *Emily Jane Brontë: The Complete Poems*, edited by Janet Gezari
        (Harmondsworth: Penguin, 1992)
EEW   *An Edition of the Early Writings of Charlotte Brontë*, edited
        by Christine Alexander (Oxford: Basil Blackwell, vol. 1, 1987;
        vol. 11, parts 1 and 2, 1991)
JE   Charlotte Brontë, *Jane Eyre*, edited by Margaret Smith, with an
        introduction and revised notes by Sally Shuttleworth (Oxford:
        World's Classics, 2000)
P   Charlotte Brontë, *The Professor*, edited by Margaret Smith and
        Herbert Rosengarten, with an introduction by Margaret Smith
        (Oxford: World's Classics, 1991)
PBBP   *The Poems of Patrick Branwell Brontë: A New Annotated and
        Enlarged Edition of the Shakespeare Head Brontë*, edited by
        Tom Winnifrith (Oxford: Blackwell, 1983)

S	Charlotte Brontë, *Shirley*, edited by Herbert Rosengarten and Margaret Smith (Oxford: World's Classics, 1981)
SHCBM	*The Miscellaneous and Unpublished Writings of Charlotte and Patrick Branwell Brontë*, edited by Thomas James Wise and John Alexander Symington, 2 vols. (Oxford: Blackwell, 1936–8)
TWH	Anne Brontë, *The Tenant of Wildfell Hall*, edited by Herbert Rosengarten, with an introduction by Margaret Smith (Oxford: World's Classics, 1993)
V	Charlotte Brontë, *Villette*, edited by Margaret Smith and Herbert Rosengarten, with an introduction and notes by Tim Dolin (Oxford: World's Classics, 2000)
WH	Emily Brontë, *Wuthering Heights*, edited by Ian Jack, with a new introduction by Patsy Stoneman (Oxford: World's Classics, 1995)

CHRONOLOGY OF THE BRONTË FAMILY

1777 Patrick Brontë born at Emdale, County Down, Ireland.
1783 Maria Branwell born at Penzance, Cornwall.
1802 Patrick Brontë enters St John's College, Cambridge.
1806 Patrick Brontë ordained as a clergyman in the Church of England.
1812 Patrick Brontë married to Maria Branwell.
1814 Maria Brontë born.
1815 Elizabeth Brontë born.
1816 Charlotte Brontë born.
1817 Patrick Branwell Brontë born.
1818 Emily Jane Brontë born.
1820 Anne Brontë born.
      Brontë family move to Haworth, where Patrick Brontë becomes Perpetual Curate.
1821 Mrs Brontë dies.
      Her sister, Elizabeth Branwell, comes from Penzance to live with the family.
1824 The four eldest Brontë daughters sent to the Clergy Daughters' School at Cowan Bridge.
1825 Maria and Elizabeth Brontë return home to die.
      Charlotte and Emily removed from school.
1826 Branwell given the toy soldiers from which the 'Young Men's Play' develops.
1829 Charlotte writes 'The History of the Year'.
1831 Charlotte goes to Margaret Wooler's school at Roe Head, where she meets her lifelong friends Ellen Nussey and Mary Taylor.
1832 Charlotte leaves Roe Head.
1835 Charlotte returns to Roe Head as a teacher.
      Emily briefly at Roe Head as a pupil; returns home ill and Anne takes her place.

1838   Branwell set up as a portrait painter in Bradford.
Emily goes to teach in Miss Patchett's school at Law Head, near
Halifax, where she remains six months.

1839   Branwell returns home in debt.
Charlotte and Anne employed as governesses: Charlotte by the
Sidgwicks at Stonegappe, Lothersdale, Anne by Mrs Ingham at
Blake Hall, Mirfield.
Emily at home.

1840   Branwell employed first as tutor by the Postlethwaites at
Broughton-in-Furness, then as clerk on the new Leeds–Manchester
railway at Sowerby Bridge, Halifax.
Anne employed as governess by Mrs Robinson, at Thorp Green
Hall, near York. Emily at home.

1841   Charlotte employed as governess by the Whites, Upperwood
House, Rawdon.
Branwell becomes clerk-in-charge at Luddenden Foot, near Halifax;
publishes some poems in the *Halifax Guardian*. Charlotte, Emily
and Anne plan to start a school of their own, and ask their aunt
Elizabeth Branwell for financial help.

1842   In February, Charlotte and Emily go to study at Pensionnat Heger,
Brussels, with a view to improving their qualifications as teachers.
Elizabeth Branwell dies, and they return home in November.
Branwell dismissed from Luddenden Foot.

1843   Charlotte returns to the Pensionnat Heger.
Branwell joins Anne at Thorp Green, where he becomes tutor to
Edmund Robinson.

1844   Charlotte returns to Haworth. Writes a series of unanswered letters
to her beloved teacher, M. Heger.
Emily begins to transcribe her poems into notebooks.
The 'Misses Brontë' unsuccessfully advertise their school.

1845   Arthur Bell Nicholls appointed curate at Haworth.
Branwell dismissed from his employment at Thorp Green because
of a liaison with his employer's wife.
Charlotte discovers one of Emily's poetry notebooks.

1846   *Poems by Currer, Ellis and Acton Bell* published at the sisters'
expense.
The Professor, Wuthering Heights and *Agnes Grey* all completed
by the middle of the year.
Charlotte accompanies her father to Manchester for a cataract
operation, and begins writing *Jane Eyre*.

1847   *Wuthering Heights* and *Agnes Grey* accepted for publication by
        Thomas Newby; no publisher found for *The Professor*.
        Jane Eyre published by Smith, Elder & Co. on 19 October, and
        Wuthering Heights and *Agnes Grey* by Thomas Newby in
        December. Charlotte writes to her publisher in December that she is
        planning 'another venture into the three-volume novel form'.

1848   *The Tenant of Wildfell Hall* published in June by Thomas Newby.
        First volume of *Shirley* completed and copied by the end of
        September.
        Branwell Brontë dies on 24 September, aged 31. Emily Brontë dies
        of consumption on 19 December.

1849   Anne Brontë dies of consumption on 28 May, in Scarborough.
        Shirley published by Smith, Elder & Co. in October.
        Charlotte visits London in December, staying with her publisher
        George Smith and his family.

1850   Charlotte pays visits to the Smiths in London, to the
        Kay-Shuttleworths in Windermere (where she meets Elizabeth
        Gaskell), and to Harriet Martineau in Ambleside.
        Publishes a new edition of *Wuthering Heights* and *Agnes Grey* with
        a 'Biographical Notice' of her sisters.

1851   Charlotte visits London, going to the Great Exhibition and to
        Thackeray's lectures; and goes to stay with Elizabeth Gaskell at
        Plymouth Grove, Manchester.

1853   *Villette* published by Smith, Elder & Co. under the pseudonym of
        Currer Bell.

1854   Charlotte Brontë marries Arthur Bell Nicholls.

1855   Charlotte Brontë Nicholls dies on 31 March, in the early stages of
        pregnancy, aged 38.
        In June, Patrick Brontë writes to Elizabeth Gaskell suggesting that
        she should write Charlotte's biography.

1857   *The Life of Charlotte Brontë* by Elizabeth Gaskell published by
        Smith, Elder & Co. in March.
        The Professor, Charlotte's first novel, published for the first time by
        Smith, Elder & Co., with a preface by Arthur Bell Nicholls, in June.

1861   Patrick Brontë dies, aged 84.
        Arhur Bell Nicholls leaves Haworth and returns to Ireland. Sale of
        the household effects of Haworth Parsonage.

1893   The Brontë Society founded at a meeting in Bradford Town Hall on
        16 December.

1894　The Brontë Museum opened in the upper floor of the Yorkshire Penny Bank, Haworth.

1906　Arthur Bell Nicholls dies at Banagher, Ireland, aged 88.

1928　Haworth Parsonage opened to the public as the Brontë Parsonage Museum on 4 August.

HEATHER GLEN

Introduction

The Brontë sisters are not obviously difficult writers. Indeed, they may seem all too easily accessible. Generations of readers have thrilled to the passion of Cathy and Heathcliff, identified with the sufferings of Lucy Snowe and Agnes Grey, succumbed to Mr Rochester's dark allure. These are not texts which seem to require elucidation, but stories which millions have urgently, if often incoherently, felt to be speaking of and to their own most intimate concerns. And if – as Charlotte Brontë acknowledged, in the Biographical Notice with which, in 1850, she prefaced her sisters' novels – their strangeness has needed explanation, explanation has seemed readily to hand. Since the publication of that Notice, and of Elizabeth Gaskell's *Life of Charlotte Brontë* seven years later, the key to the Brontës' works has been found – straightforwardly or more indirectly, both by ordinary reader and professional academic – in the peculiar circumstances of their authors' brief and tragic lives. The story of those lives has, indeed, assumed an almost mythic place in the English cultural imagination: after Shakespeare's Stratford, Haworth Parsonage is England's most visited literary shrine.

Yet this passionate appropriation, this confident biographical interpretation, have in some ways been a barrier to understanding. Readers of Jane Austen have long been aware of the distance between her culture and their own, of the ways in which scholarship can bridge that distance and enable them to grasp nuances and significances which might otherwise go unremarked. Readers of the Brontës – compelled, perhaps, by those apparently universal themes of childhood suffering and romantic love, of hunger and deprivation and yearning desire – have not, on the whole, felt this distance. Yet even universal themes have particular historical inflections. A central premise of this *Companion* is that to see the Brontës clearly we must see them in their cultural difference, not simply as speaking of that which we already know, or of subjective experience easily assimilable to ours, but from and of a world as foreign as it is familiar, one whose preoccupations and discourses are tantalisingly different from ours.

What is to be gained by looking at 'the Brontës' not as three (or five) individual, and very different, writers, but together, as a group? The simplest answer is that from the time of the sisters' first venture into publication, as 'Currer, Ellis and Acton Bell', the Brontës *have* been thus seen: that even as they have drawn distinctions between them, common reader and academic critic alike have been sharply or confusedly aware of those shared characteristics which set their writings apart from other writings of their time. As Charlotte Brontë's 1850 preface to her sisters' works indicates, theirs are regional novels: self-consciously different from such metropolitan works as those of Dickens and of Thackeray. Their protagonists are not, centrally, the privileged classes, but men and women who must make their own way in the world – unconnected, poor and plain. The concentration is less on a world of social interaction than on intense subjective experience; less, it sometimes seems, on culture than on nature – on what Charlotte Brontë called, in a discussion of Jane Austen, 'what throbs fast and fully, though hidden, what the blood rushes through, what is the unseen seat of Life' (*CBL* II, 383). And if in this the Brontës are somewhat different from other Victorian novelists, they are different too in their passionate individualism, their defiance of social and moral convention, their focus on rebellion and desire. 'Coarse', each was labelled by her contemporaries: 'blasphemous', Charlotte and Emily were called. It is clear that in their dealings with sexuality and with religion all three are more searching, more exploratory than most of their contemporaries were prepared to be. Such qualities as these in their writings have led to their grouping both in popular consciousness and in literary histories: it seems not unreasonable to try to understand those writings by exploring the cultural influences and life experiences which all three sisters shared.

Yet as this *Companion* will suggest, there are rather more interesting reasons for considering the Brontës together than this. If any literary works might be said to issue from the same context, these are they. Most of the surviving juvenilia, much of the poetry, five of the seven published novels, were written, literally, together: by three women living in close proximity, in the confined space of an early Victorian household and the emotional intimacy of an extraordinarily devoted family, bound together by common interests and experiences, accustomed from earliest childhood to discussing the process of literary composition, even to sharing a fantasy world. Yet the differences between their works are radical, and striking: arguably far more so than the similarities which their closeness might explain. To consider these differences is to gain an unparalleled insight into the complex and creative and unpredictable ways in which a writer may not merely reflect, but imaginatively reflect upon her world. Indeed, it is arguable that one can trace within the works of the Brontë sisters not just three quite distinctive modes of engagement with what may from a distance seem common preoccupations, but a complex, creative dialogue with one another: a dialogue which began in childhood and which for the survivor continued even in the last of her works.

This volume both draws upon and questions that long tradition of biographical reading which has dominated discussion of the Brontës, especially of Charlotte and Anne. (The difficulty of reading *Wuthering Heights*, with its multiple narrators, in this way, has led to a different kind of fascination with Emily's enigmatic life.) Chapters 1 and 2 sketch in that common matrix of place, of family history, of shared imaginative 'play', out of which the sisters' creative achievement grew. Each of these chapters considers some of those facts of the Brontës' lives which have fascinated generations of readers; but each shows also how those facts themselves might point beyond narrowly biographical interpretations of their works.

The myth of the Brontës as isolated individual geniuses has partly depended on a firm belief in Haworth's remoteness from the world. But as Juliet Barker suggests in the first essay in this volume, Haworth in the early nineteenth century was not the 'remote moorland village' which Charlotte Brontë once called it, but an industrialising town. Many of its problems, as inescapable to those who lived there as the stench which pervaded its streets, were the problems of the nation at large: poverty, insanitary housing conditions, no safe water supply. But Haworth had also a small but growing number of middle-class families, and a lively social and cultural life of which the Brontës partook. Their world, indeed, was not confined to Haworth, even in their early years. Each, as Barker shows, went elsewhere for education of various kinds. Moreover, there were always books and journals in the parsonage, whether purchased by their father or borrowed from elsewhere. In the 'History of the Year', which the child Charlotte wrote at thirteen, the periodicals she reads and the opinions of those who write for them are as vividly present to her as that which actually happens in 'the kitchin of the parsonage house'.[1]

From childhood, each of the Brontës was not merely a reader but a writer; and a highly self-reflexive one. Their surviving childhood manuscripts evince a sharp awareness of the literary culture of their day: a culture not merely of romantic expressiveness but of ironic self-presentation, of debunking, sardonic humour, and of lively controversy. It was in imitation of this culture that their earliest 'books' were produced. These tiny 'printed' volumes are not autobiographical outpourings but, as Carol Bock demonstrates, sophisticated works of art. They display an acute and often comic consciousness of their own status as fictions, in their joking and wondering references to the great creating Genii (the Brontë children themselves), whose fiat has made possible the existence of all the 'plays'. The multiple narrators of Glass Town, with their competing versions of events, give evidence of the children's aware-ness, from the beginning of their writing lives, of the ways in which fiction enables something quite other than a monologic perspective on the world. And in this, they point suggestively forward to that in the later novels which perhaps most sharply questions any attempt to read them as disguised au-tobiography: their sophisticated use of a variety of narrative personae, their play with different voices and narrative points of view.

The Brontë sisters' poetry has its root in those youthful plays. In chapter 3, Angela Leighton considers these poems and that first, joint attempt at pub-lication, *Poems by Currer, Ellis, and Acton Bell*. These are simple, unadorned lyrics, in the simple 'plain-song' language – as Swinburne was later to call it (*CH*, 412) – of romantic lyric and Wesleyan hymn. Here, surely, if any-where, one hears directly the accents of each sister's intimate voice, speaking of personal experience in a straightforward confessional way. Yet the truth, as Leighton suggests, is very different from this. The original speakers of many of these poems were the characters of Gondal and Angria, their stories of heroism and passion, of adultery and betrayal, very far from anything that happened in their creators' actual lives. For the purposes of publication the sisters removed all reference to the melodramatic sagas out of which their verses had sprung. Thus decontextualised, these spare, 'abstract' lyrics (as Charlotte Brontë called Emily's) have an enigmatic quality which even con-temporaries noticed: 'No preface introduces these poems to the reader', be-gan the volume's first review (*CH*, 59). Drawing on that 'web' of childhood, yet emptied of narrative cues, they demand a more rigorous reading than their surface simplicity might suggest. And such a reading discloses, in Emily Brontë's poetry, a strenuous engagement with metaphysical questions – of time, of change, of embodiment, of mortality, of imaginative transcendence – quite different from that of any other poetry of the nineteenth century. 'The tone of all these little poems is certainly uniform', wrote a reviewer of the first edition (*CH*, 63), but the modern reader is more likely, Angela Leighton sug-gests, to concur with Charlotte's awed sense of Emily's absolute originality, and of the very different nature of their powers.

There follow three essays on the novels; not, as has been customary in discussions of 'the Brontës', considering the work of each sister separately, but grouping them together in the order in which they were composed. In chapter 4, Stevie Davies discusses the three novels with which the three sisters hoped to make their debut as professional novelists. *The Professor, Agnes Grey* and *Wuthering Heights* were sent out together in 1846 as 'three distinct and unconnected tales' which might, Charlotte suggested, be published 'as a work of 3 vols. of the ordinary novel-size' (*CBL* 1, 461). The last two novels *were*, of course, published as just such a 'work of 3 vols.': it is suggestive to reflect on how different both novels might have appeared to readers turning straight from the 'purposeless power' of *Wuthering Heights* (*CH*, 228) to Anne's 'more acceptable' tale (*CH*, 219) of virtue rewarded and happiness won. If *The Professor* remained unpublished until after its author's death, it was conceived and written at the same time as the other two. Each, as Stevie Davies shows, presents a quite distinctive face to the reader. In each one hears the accents of a clear individual voice. Yet if they are thus 'distinct' they are not exactly 'unconnected'. As contemporary reviewers registered, in speaking of the likeness between 'the brothers Bell' – by some they were thought to be possibly 'a single personage' (*CH*, 230) – they seem to be differently inflecting the same subject-matter, imagery, concerns.[2] Setting them side by side one catches tantalising hints of a dialogue – 'snatches' of that 'conversation' in the dining-room of Haworth Parsonage, when the sisters, at the peak of their creative collaboration, read aloud from and debated 'the stories they were engaged upon'.[3]

Chapter 5 deals with the novels which followed this first attempt at fiction for publication, both apparently written between the summers of 1846 and 1847, Charlotte's *Jane Eyre* and Anne's *The Tenant of Wildfell Hall*. Each rather differently evokes that Regency world of aristocratic sexual profligacy which, depicted in such works as Thomas Moore's *Life of Byron* (1830), had fascinated the youthful Brontës: each offers a scathing portrait of the celebrated masculinity of that world – the chastened Rochester; the dependent, helpless Huntingdon. Each also evokes the Protestantism in which the sisters had been reared: its defensive, triumphant individualism, its pressing sense of the immanence of heaven and hell. Each has at its centre a woman caring for herself – earning her own living, learning to resist passion and preserve her integrity in a world of patriarchal power. And in each, that heroine is a visual artist: not simply a moral exemplar, but one whose expressiveness is celebrated in suggestively subversive ways. Yet as Jill Matus suggests, the 'strong family likeness' which contemporary reviewers discerned is also revelatory of difference – like 'the eyes... of Catherine Earnshaw' gazing disquietingly at Heathcliff from the different faces of her daughter and her brother's son (*WH*, 322). To set these novels side by side is to see the strengths of each more sharply: *Jane Eyre*'s innovatory reworking of melodrama and romance into a psychologically acute, historically specific new realism; *The Tenant of Wildfell Hall*'s powerful, reflective exposure of the implications of contemporary marriage laws and social mores. It is also to see more sharply how each writer transforms and reworks the materials she draws upon, in order to articulate her own characteristic vision of individual and social possibility in the England of her time.

Chapter 6 deals with the surviving sister's two final, very different works. *Shirley*, too, is set in the early years of the century. But it seems at a far greater remove from the stirring romanticism of Scott and Byron than do *Wuthering Heights, Jane Eyre*, or *The Tenant of Wildfell Hall*. Its world is the 'real, cool, and solid' world of early industrial Yorkshire, 'unromantic as a Monday morning' (*S*, 5); if it does, despite this disclaimer, present romantic aspiration, it is aspiration ironically seen. Alone among the Brontës' published novels, it uses an impersonal, uncharacterised narrator, who maintains a sardonic, and sometimes elegiac, distance from the striving, competing, desiring characters who populate the fictional world. *Villette*'s is a more sombre, and apparently more constricted, narrative, of loneliness, depression, despair. It might seem to mark a return to the first-person narratives of the sisters' earlier years, albeit in a darker key. But the world which 'passe[s] before' its narrator 'as a spectacle' (*V*, 175) is also quite unlike that of any of the sisters' previous novels: not a place of violence and death and hunger, of distant horizons and desolate moors, but of solid, unromantic bourgeois comfort and prosperity. These novels were both completed when their author

> almost despaired, because there was no one to whom to read a line, or of whom to ask a counsel. *Jane Eyre* was not written under such circumstances, nor were two-thirds of *Shirley*.[4]

Yet as Kathleen Tillotson puts it, 'some part of the web was still weaving, even in Charlotte's latest, loneliest works'.[5] In my essay I argue that these two final Brontë novels participate no less than the others in that extraordinary creative dialogue which all the sisters shared; that the narrative strategies developed in those early childhood 'plays' still here seem to be shaping their author's imaginative understanding of a rapidly changing world.

In the seven short years between 1846 and 1853 the scribblers who had created Glass Town and Angria and Gondal became professional writers. They produced, between them, some of the finest poetry in the language, and seven extraordinary novels. For them, it seems, from childhood, the fictive provided a space within which they could articulate a developing understanding of the society in which they lived. And if their writings are more self-reflexive, more disinterestedly intelligent, than biographical readings have tended to suggest, they are also far more wide-ranging in their intellectual power and reach. They do not simply speak, narrowly, of the sisters' personal concerns: they can be seen to reflect and reflect upon some of the most pressing issues of their day. Chapters 7, 8 and 9 discuss some of those issues, and explore the ways in which each of the Brontës, very differently, engaged with them in her work.

A central concern, in all of the Brontës' novels, is with the struggles of their protagonists to survive and to make their way in the world. 'Mary Ann could scarcely read a word, and was so careless and inattentive, that I could hardly get on with her at all', says Agnes Grey, of one of her attempts to succeed as a governess (*AG*, 21). 'I shall get on', insists Crimsworth to his brother, as the latter taunts him with his poverty (*P*, 16). 'I cannot get on. I cannot execute my plans', cries the frustrated entrepreneur, Robert Moore (*S*, 25). In chapter 7, Rick Rylance discusses what it meant in the early nineteenth century to speak of 'getting on'. The term, much used in the period – Ruskin was later to devote a whole section of *The Crown of Wild Olive* (1866) to 'the Goddess of Getting-on'[6] – primarily signified making one's way in the world. This was a constant pressing concern for the educated children of an impoverished clergyman – a father whose rise from humble beginnings provided a striking example of the possibility of getting on. 'Who ever rose in the world without ambition?' asked Charlotte, appealing to her aunt for money to go to school in Brussels in 1841, so that she and her sister Emily might be better equipped to start a school and gain 'a footing in the world'. 'I want us *all* to get on. I know we have talents and I want them to be turned to account.'[7] Rick Rylance considers the ways in which the Brontë sisters' novels explore a whole constellation of issues raised in early nineteenth-century England by the rhetoric of 'getting on': the relation between private self and public self-image, the meaning of 'character' and of individual 'independence', the repellence and the fascination of the figure of the 'self-made man'. Within this analysis, features of the novels which might have seemed to reflect merely private concerns begin to appear as sharply, provocatively interrogative of the ideology of their time.

Questions of character and social mobility were, as Rylance suggests, bound up with questions of gender. In early nineteenth-century England, a woman was hardly expected to 'get on' in the same way as a man. 'Literature cannot be the business of a woman's life, and it ought not to be' wrote Southey to Charlotte Brontë in March 1837, when she asked for his advice on pursuing a literary career (*CBL* 1, 166). Yet, as Kate Flint points out, women were in the Brontës' lifetimes entering the literary marketplace in increasing numbers. Currer, Ellis and Acton Bell were all acutely aware that the subject of the woman writer was one of the issues of the day. But literature for them was not merely a career. It was a space of possibility – a 'free place', Mrs Gaskell called it – within which they could explore and play with the constraints and conditions of their world.[8] Woman's relation to literature appears within their novels as appropriative, empowering, subversive: Jane 'draw[s] parallels in silence' (*JE*, 11), Shirley takes issue with Milton (*S*, 320); 'Miss Cathy's riven th'back off "Th' Helmet uh Salvation"', Joseph shouts, appalled (*WH*, 19). 'He that runs may read', says Joe Scott, arguing with Shirley over Genesis. 'He may read it in his own fashion', tartly replies Caroline (*S*, 329).

Each of the Brontës' novels in a different way interrogates the gender stereotypes of its time. Anne and Charlotte begin unobtrusively, with *Agnes Grey*'s quietly devastating exposure not merely of the exploitation of the governess but of the violence at the heart of polite family life; *The Professor*'s exploration, through the ironised figure of Crimsworth, of the construction and the cost of masculinity in the society through which he moves. But the following novel of each – as their respective prefaces suggest – more directly challenges convention; for each deals more overtly with passion and sexuality. In *The Tenant of Wildfell Hall* Anne Brontë offers a stark anatomy of a patriarchal society, and an eloquent argument against that 'unarmed' ignorance which was judged woman's proper state (*TWH*, 31); Helen's story raises disturbing, and unanswered, questions not merely about the position of woman within a society whose mores and laws are those of a debased masculinity, but also about what such a woman might do with 'the serious part of myself' (*TWH*, 190). In *Jane Eyre* Charlotte Brontë presents an even more disquieting heroine, angry at injustice, and longing for 'incident, life, fire, feeling' (*JE*, 109), who insists on her own integrity, pursues her own career, and virtually proposes to a man. Here, once again, there is a central concern with what marriage means for a woman within the depicted society; the tension between passionate longing for relationship with another and passionately defended 'independence' is urgent, suspenseful, compelling; and perhaps, as Kate Flint suggests, remains unresolved to the end. In *Wuthering Heights*, however, such issues are differently inflected. Emily Brontë seems to have been far less concerned than her sisters with the gender specific constraints of early nineteenth-century society. Rather, her novel presents a powerful challenge to the notion, inscribed most insistently in romantic fiction for women, that desire can indeed be fulfilled. Its first, haunting image of its heroine as a child at the window forever unable to get in stands in suggestive contrast to the more usual novelistic image of a girl dreaming of romance. And its final, fended-off suggestion of the possibility of 'unquiet slumbers' works against such resolution as is offered through the younger Catherine and Hareton's more conventional story of happy requited love.

In her two final novels, Charlotte Brontë, now a famous 'woman writer', seems to be continuing that questioning of contemporary assumptions about gender begun in these earlier works. Some of the themes of Anne Brontë's novels are explicitly debated in *Shirley*: the lack of opportunities for women in the chapter called 'Old Maids'; the position of the governess, and also of the mismatched woman, in Caroline's conversations with her mother, whose maiden name was Agnes Grey (*S*, 376). Emily Brontë's scorn of contemporary stereotypes of gender is picked up in the novel's questioning of gender identity,[9] especially through the figure of Shirley, with her masculine name and independence, who, Charlotte told Mrs Gaskell, was a 'representation of . . . what Emily Brontë would have been, had she been placed in health and prosperity'.[10] But if, as I suggest in my essay,[11] there is a ghostly dialogue with her sister in the novel's final paragraphs, Charlotte Brontë's part in that dialogue is bleaker than her sister's was. Her heroines are, as Kate Flint puts it, 'swallowed up' in marriage; they do not live on in their passion, haunting the places they loved, as Cathy and Heathcliff perhaps do. Indeed, at the ending of *Shirley*, even those places have gone. In *Shirley*, Charlotte Brontë does try to imagine different possibilities for women: her eponymous heroine has the freedoms conferred by wealth and beauty; the theme of friendship between women, adumbrated in *Jane Eyre*, is here more extensively explored. But Jane Eyre's ambiguous withdrawal into married bliss at Ferndean is replaced in this following novel by a far more desolate vision of phallic triumph and a ruined landscape – 'a mill mighty as the tower of Babel'; of a world which has no place for women's aspirations and dreams. *Villette*, with its scathing references to 'the narratives of women and girls', offers a rather different kind of challenge to the conventions of romance. Here the expected happy love story is that which the heroine watches between another and the man she has loved; here, as Thackeray complained, she goes on from this disappointment to a very different kind of love.[12] Lucy Snowe's tormented account of her loneliness and survival is in some ways, as Kate Flint argues, 'the most subtle, most triumphant portrayal' in all the Brontës' novels 'of woman's growth into self-recognition and self-sufficiency'. Yet Kate Flint points, too, to that in the novel which troubles such a reading, and allows one also to see it as a narrative of blank despair. For *Villette* is perhaps most subversive in its insistence (deplored by contemporary reviewers) on the acknowledgement of a 'pain' at the heart of a woman's experience which undermines all possibility of a coherent self.

The subject of chapter 9 may seem rather more remote than are questions of class and gender from present-day concerns. But religion, as John Maynard points out, shaped every aspect of the Brontë sisters' lives. It was within the discourse of religion that much of their thinking was framed. More than any other aspect of the Brontës' mental universe, this one is foreign to the twenty-first century reader, to whom, all too often, any invocation of the Bible signifies unquestioning belief. In his essay on this subject, John Maynard takes a rather different view. In each of the Brontës' novels he finds a searching engagement with the religious discourse of its time. *Agnes Grey*'s sober narrative of an obscure but virtuous life may seem straightforwardly illustrative of the clash between religious values and the values of the world. But its quiet depiction of the unassuming governess as the religious arbiter of her society has a potentially subversive edge. *The Tenant of Wildfell Hall* may appear more luridly orthodox. Its depiction of the dreadful end of the dissipated Arthur Huntingdon is entirely seriously evocative of Brocklehurst's warning tracts; Helen's diary quite realistically conveys how fundamental to the experience of many in early nineteenth-cenutury England was belief in a life beyond. But its framing romantic narrative raises, Maynard suggests, questions that are not considered in straightforward puritan discourse, and provides a thought-provoking counterpoint to its heroine's certainties. The other two sisters' novels are rather more overtly questioning of the religious thought and mores of their time. *Shirley*'s satiric portrait of irrelevant, disputatious clergy is not marginal but central to its vision of hunger unsatisfied. *Jane Eyre* is a secular heroine, with a secular destiny. Within her narrative of pilgrimage, religion figures more as threat than promise; if its ending speaks of the certainty of a 'sure reward', an 'incorruptible crown' (*JE*, 452), it is in the third person, of another; a strangely disquieting alternative to her own insistence on married bliss. Emily Brontë's poems and novel, with their very different imagery of straining at mortal bounds, pose a far less ambiguous challenge to conventional orthodoxy. Yet these too are framed within familiar religious discourses of earthly limitation and of spiritual transcendence, discourses which they rework and reinflect to powerful and disconcerting effect. Charlotte Brontë's final novel, with its prominent biblical imagery, has been seen by some recent critics as a more orthodox providentialist narrative.[13] But it was found 'half atheistical and half religious' by more than one contemporary reviewer;[14] and its vision of the meaning of the experience it presents might, as John Maynard argues, equally be seen as a bleakly secular one.

For a hundred and fifty years, the Brontës have been perhaps the most popular writers in the English literary canon. Their works have been commodified and adapted, imitated and rewritten; their home is a centre of tourism; their lives have the status of myth. Some of these phenomena may seem to have little to do with the Brontës' actual achievement, and certainly to have no place in an academic volume like this. In the final chapter, Patsy Stoneman, however, argues that they should not simply be dismissed. In a powerful, subtle argument, which draws upon some of the most recent developments in historical and literary theory, she points to the indeterminacy of the boundary between 'fiction' and 'fact'. The 'myths' which have circulated about the Brontës' lives, inaccurate as they often are, might, she suggests, tell more about the history of which their writings speak than perhaps at first appears. And the differing kinds of readings which these texts have evoked over time raise thought-provoking questions not merely about the processes whereby literary texts survive but also about the bases of more academic criticism.

The primary aim of this *Companion* is to point to the ways in which historical contextualising or careful critical analysis can lead to a sharpened understanding of these ostensibly well-known texts. But Patsy Stoneman's essay provides a salutory reminder that the continuing cultural life of the Brontë sisters' writings has arguably consisted less in academic interpretation than in the passionate desire of generations of readers to make these works their own. The child Jane Eyre in the window-seat, dreaming over a book; Shirley and Caroline repeating verses to one another; the young Catherine Earnshaw's 'library', in which 'scarcely one chapter had escaped a pen-and-ink commentary' (*WH*, 18) – such images and others like them speak in their different ways both of the appropriation of the text and of acknowledgement of its otherness, both of excited self-recognition and encounter with that which is strange. It is something of this experience, both of intimacy and of difference, that the novels of their creators have offered to generations of readers; and it is to the enhancement of that experience that this *Companion* is addressed.

NOTES

1. 'The History of the Year', in *Charlotte Brontë, Juvenilia 1829–1835*, edited by Juliet Barker (Harmondsworth: Penguin, 1996), 2.
2. For examples of such reviews, see *CH*, 217, 218, 227, 234, 247.
3. Virginia Woolf, *Women and Writing*, edited by Michèle Barrett (London: Women's Press, 1979), 75; Elizabeth Gaskell, *The Life of Charlotte Brontë* [1857], edited by Alan Shelston (Harmondsworth: Penguin, 1985), 307.
4. Charlotte Brontë to George Smith, 30 October 1852, quoted in Juliet Barker, *The Brontës* (London: Weidenfeld & Nicolson, 1994), 705.
5. Kathleen Tillotson, *Novels of the Eighteen-Forties* (Oxford University Press, 1954), 263.
6. John Ruskin, 'Traffic', in *The Crown of Wild Olive: Four Lectures on Industry and War* (1866); in *The Library Edition of the Works of John Ruskin*, edited by E. T. Cook and Alexander Wedderburn, 39 vols. (London: Allen, 1903–12), vol. 18: 448, 452, 507–8.
7. Thus Gaskell, reflecting current usage, in *Life*, 220; Margaret Smith reads this as 'I want us all to go on' (*CBL* 1, 269).
8. Gaskell, *Life*, 308.
9. On this aspect of *Shirley* see Patricia Ingham, *The Language of Gender and Class. Transformation in the Victorian Novel* (London: Routledge, 1996), 49–54.
10. Gaskell, *Life*, 379.

11. Chapter 6, below, pp. 131–2.
12. '*Villette* is rather vulgar', he wrote in a private letter. 'I don't make my *good* women ready to fall in love with two men at once' (*CH*, 198).
13. See, for example, Barry Qualls, *The Secular Pilgrims of Victorian Fiction: The Novel as Book of Life* (Cambridge University Press, 1981) and Thomas Vargish, *The Providential Aesthetic in Victorian Fiction* (Charlottesville: University Press of Virginia, 1985).
14. *The Observer*, 7 February 1853, 7. See also *Christian Remembrancer*, in *CH*, 204.

I

JULIET BARKER

The Haworth context

Most biographies begin, as Dickens in *David Copperfield* famously said they should, at the beginning: that is, with the birth of their subject. Elizabeth Gaskell, however, took a different view, dedicating the first two chapters of her *Life of Charlotte Brontë* not to Charlotte, nor even to her ancestry, but to the place where she grew up and spent most of her adult life. In this way, Gaskell set Haworth at the forefront of the Brontë story, deliberately linking place and subject in an exceptionally emphatic way. She explained why she did so quite candidly.

> For a right understanding of the life of my dear friend, Charlotte Brontë, it appears to me more necessary in her case than in most others, that the reader should be made acquainted with the peculiar forms of population and society amidst which her earliest years were passed, and from which both her own and her sisters' first impressions of human life must have been received.[1]

The reason why it was so necessary to do this is not immediately apparent to the modern reader, though it was obvious to Gaskell's contemporaries. *Jane Eyre* had taken the literary world by storm when it appeared in 1847, but it was regarded in the terminology of the day as 'a naughty book'. Polite society was shocked at the notion of Rochester's attempt at bigamous marriage, his casual discussion of his former mistresses with his daughter's teenage governess and the improper behaviour of both master and governess during their courtship. Even Gaskell, the most ardent of Charlotte's champions, would not allow her unmarried daughters to read *Jane Eyre* for fear that they might be tainted by what one reviewer called its 'total ignorance of the habits of society, a great coarseness of taste, and a heathenish doctrine of religion'.[2]

Speculation about the identity and, more especially, the sex of the author of *Jane Eyre* had been rife from the first. This increased to fever pitch with the publication of Emily's *Wuthering Heights* (1847) and Anne's *The Tenant of Wildfell Hall* (1848), which were widely presumed to be works from the same hand. As G. H. Lewes put it, the Brontë novels were 'coarse even for men, coarse in language and coarse in conception' (*CH*, 292). Once Charlotte's identity became known, the speculation became positively prurient. How was it possible for a spinster living a life of complete obscurity and seclusion in a remote Yorkshire village to have written such shocking books? The reviewer in the *Christian Remembrancer* spoke for many when he hinted darkly that there must be sinister reasons for what seemed like a deliberate withdrawal from society (*CH*, 203).

It was therefore no accident that Gaskell placed so much emphasis on Haworth in the opening chapters of her *Life of Charlotte Brontë*. What she was trying to prove was that there was nothing inherently evil, perverse or even odd about Charlotte and her sisters. Morally flawless themselves, they had attracted the world's opprobrium only because they had innocently, but accurately, reproduced the harsh realities of life in Haworth in their novels, unaware that it differed significantly from society at large. Gaskell's magnificent opening sequence, with its evocation of the journey from Keighley to Haworth, was thus invested with massive symbolism: it was a passing from the comparative civilisation of a thriving commercial town, which Gaskell's readers would recognise as typical of the industrial West Riding of Yorkshire, to a strange moorland village, cut off from the ordinary world by the 'monotonous and illimitable barrier' of the surrounding hills. Every page of her description is peppered with carefully chosen adjectives such as 'wild', 'bleak', 'oppressive', 'lonely' and 'isolated',[3] which reinforce the idea that Haworth was physically remote; a place not only difficult to get to, but also, more significantly, difficult to leave.

Not unnaturally, the people who lived in this solitude were, according to Gaskell, as strange and inhospitable as the landscape: curt and harsh of speech, rude to the point of 'positive insult' to strangers, 'independent, wilful, and full of grim humour'. With much colourful quotation from the life of an earlier rector of Haworth, William Grimshaw, Gaskell draws a picture of a savage, lawless population, delighting in bull-baiting, cock-fighting and drunken funeral feasts, which literally had to be horse-whipped out of the inns and into church on Sundays. The exploits of Heathcliff and Arthur Huntingdon seem tame by comparison.

Gaskell succeeded triumphantly in vindicating the Brontë sisters' reputation. Reviewers of her biography agreed that 'the knowledge that the authors painted life as it lay around them in their daily path is sufficient refutation of the charge, that they revelled in coarseness for coarseness' sake, and drew pictures of vice in accordance with their own inherent depravity'.[4] What she failed to do, quite deliberately, was to paint an accurate picture of Haworth in the time of the Brontës. It was unrecognisable not only to its inhabitants, but even to the tourists who flocked to see it in the wake of her book. The reaction of two visitors to Haworth in August 1857 (only five months after the publication of *The Life of Charlotte Brontë*) was typical.

> Our previous conceptions of the locality had been formed entirely from Mrs Gaskell's description and the frontispiece to the 'Memoirs of Charlotte Brontë'; and we found all our expectations most gloriously disappointed. We had supposed Haworth to be a scattered and straggling hamlet, with a desolate vicarage and a dilapidated church, surrounded and shut out from the world by a wilderness of barren heath, the monotony of the prospect only broken by the tombstones in the adjacent graveyard. Our straggling hamlet we found transformed into a large and flourishing village – not a very enlightened or poetical place certainly, but quaint, compact, and progressive, wherein, by the bye, we observed three large dissenting chapels and two or three well-sized schools.[5]

The problem with Gaskell's description of Haworth was that it was almost a hundred years out of date. Haworth was not a small rural village but a busy industrial township. Even though the Brontës themselves pandered to the idea that they lived in rural and social isolation,[6] this was simply not the case.

Haworth stands 314 metres (1,031 feet)above sea level in the South Pennines, close to the Yorkshire–Lancashire border. It is surrounded by swelling hills which are riven with pastoral, wooded valleys and crowned with unenclosed moorland, stretching as far as the eye can see. The hillsides are dotted with small farmsteads and the valley bottoms with little mills which once harnessed the power of the abundant springs and streams pouring off the moors. Between one and three miles further south along the Worth valley is Oxenhope, which was in the early nineteenth century divided into two settlements, Near and Far Oxenhope; to the west, a mile away over the moors, lies Stanbury. Both villages belonged to the old Haworth township and formed part of the sprawling and ill-defined chapelry of Haworth, which the gazetteers of the day described as covering an area of precisely 10,540 acres; effectively it encompassed all the villages, hamlets, farms and cottages lying outside the parameters of the nearest towns.[7]

These towns, none of them more than a dozen miles away, included some of the most important manufacturing areas of northern England: Bradford to the east and Halifax to the southeast were pre-eminent in the woollen industry of the West Riding of Yorkshire; Burnley to the west, just over the border into Lancashire, was a centre of the cotton trade. The moors round Haworth were covered with a network of packhorse trails which, since medieval times, had linked these places together. The last three decades of the eighteenth century had seen an exponential growth in traffic as the cottage industries of washing, combing, spinning and weaving locally produced wool had given way to the insatiable demand of the new water-driven and increasingly mechanised mills. Haworth's position was crucial in this development, for it straddled the main route between Yorkshire and Lancashire and much of the commercial traffic between the two counties passed along the turnpike roads and through the centre of the town. The large number of public houses, including the three clustered at the top of Main Street, the White Lion, King's Arms and Black Bull, were there to serve this passing trade rather than the local population for, despite Gaskell's colourful accounts of drunken revellry, an independent survey in 1850 found that the consumption of beer and spirituous liquor in Haworth was 'very much' below the average of other places.[8]

Haworth was not merely a conduit for the wool trade but played an important role itself in the manufacture of worsted and woven cloth. Even when the Brontës first arrived, in 1820, the town already contained some thirteen working mills, which increased rapidly in size and number over the forty-one years of the Reverend Patrick Brontë's incumbency. By 1850 there were three worsted spinning and weaving mills in Haworth itself: Mytholmes mill was modestly sized, employing only thirty-nine hands, but Sugden's employed 134 and Butterfield's, which was newly built, was expected to employ between 900 and 1,000 men, women and children once it became fully operational.[9] Of all the cottage industries which had been so important in the previous century, only wool-combing and, to a lesser degree, hand-loom weaving, survived into the middle of the nineteenth. Quarrying also continued to employ a considerable number of inhabitants: the great hollows and spoil heaps at the top of Penistone Hill, behind the town, marked the quarries where flagstones and masonry blocks were cut ready for transportation by cart to all parts of the surrounding area. Only in the wider township was farming a common occupation. The land was too high and arid to sustain a wide variety of agriculture but hay and oats were grown, principally for animal feed. Though Haworth had two annual livestock fairs, sheep and pigs (which were frequently prize-winners at the Keighley agricultural show) were more in evidence than cattle. Most of the farmers simply scratched out a living from a few acres of inhospitable land, though some of the larger landowners, like the Taylors of Stanbury and the Heatons of Ponden Hall, had become wealthy by judicious investment in property, rents and smallscale manufacturing.

The fact that Haworth was principally a working-class manufacturing town was readily apparent in its appearance. The mills lay in the valley bottom, the church of St Michael and All Angels at the top of the hill. Between them snaked Main Street, famously described by Mrs Gaskell as having its cobbles (or setts, to use the Yorkshire word) laid endwise 'in order to give a better hold to the horses' feet; and even with this help, they seem to be in constant danger of slipping backwards'.[10] Main Street was lined with eighteenth- and early nineteenth-century terraced cottages, some displaying the long row of mullioned windows on an upper storey which indicated that hand-loom weaving was carried on inside. Like the neighbouring Pennine towns of Heptonstall and Hebden Bridge, Haworth literally was built into a hillside so steep that cottages which appeared to be only two storeys high from the front were actually five or six at the back, creating over- and under-dwellings inhabited by different families. Most of the working population lived at the top of Main Street, however, close to the brow of the hill and within the cramped confines of a triangle bounded by three roads, of which at least one, West Lane, was tarmacademised. The houses here were a rabbit warren of small, ramshackle back-to-backs, built round cobbled or earthen yards and accessible only by narrow alley-ways. Even here many of the cottages were home to several different families.

When, at Patrick Brontë's request, an investigation was carried out by Benjamin Herschel Babbage on behalf of the General Board of Health in 1850, the report identified twenty-five cellar dwellings which had been created as separate houses out of the cellars of the cottages above. They therefore lay several feet below the level of the street outside and were inevitably damp and airless. Many of the inhabitants were wool-combers who carried out their trade from home. A skilled and therefore highly paid occupation – when work was available – wool-combing was carried out in conditions that were pernicious to health. To minimise the risk of breaking fibres, the wool was combed in rooms without ventilation, where iron stoves were kept alight day and night to maintain the right degree of heat and humidity. As many of the combers lived and slept with their families in the rooms where they also worked, it was not surprising that the incidence of infective lung diseases, especially tuberculosis, was exceptionally high amongst them.[11]

A typical example of this type of working-class accommodation was found by the inspectors in Gauger's Croft: 'consisting of two rooms, one of them a wool-comber's shop, the other a living-room and kitchen; the family, seven in number, slept in two beds in the shop, which was very hot and close even in the day-time, and must have been very bad at night'. Conditions were often little better in the upper dwellings. In the upper portion of a cottage in Back Lane, the inspectors discovered three rooms opening into each other: in the largest room, which was less than 7 feet wide and 24 feet long, eight quarry men slept in four beds; in the second, smaller room, slept six men and boys who worked the wool-combing business which was carried on in the third room where a fire was lit constantly day and night.[12]

These unhealthy working and living conditions were made worse by primitive sanitary arrangements. Even in 1850 there was not a single water-closet in the town and the entire population was served by sixty-nine privies, an average, as the inspector pointed out, of one to every four-and-a-half houses. Lacking any other means of disposal, the contents of these earth closets were emptied into midden heaps adjoining the houses, where, mixed with household refuse and the offal from slaughter-houses, they festered for months on end, creating a major hazard to public health. As there were no sewers, surface drainage was carried away in open channels and gutters. Most seriously of all, the water supply which served almost everyone in the town by means of nine pumps and two public wells (five other wells were in private hands, including the one belonging to the Brontës) was polluted by these effluents; one spring even ran through the churchyard. In the circumstances, it is not surprising that ill-health was endemic.

The grim statistics of the Babbage Report of 1850 reveal that Haworth shared the same mortality rates as some of the most unhealthy districts of inner-city London: 41.6 per cent of the population died before they reached their sixth birthday. Viewed in this local context, the deaths within the Brontë family seem far less unusual and tragic than would otherwise be the case. All survived beyond their seventh year and only the two eldest daughters, Maria and Elizabeth, who died aged eleven and ten respectively, did not exceed the average age at death. However, the mortality rate in Haworth was 10.5 per cent higher than the maximum rate set by Parliament as the level at which 'special remedies' were required. Ironically, the reasons identified for these unacceptably high mortality rates were those typical of the new industrial towns: overcrowding, the tainted water supply and primitive sanitation.[13]

The Babbage Report makes morbidly entertaining reading but, taken in isolation, it creates a picture of Haworth which is just as misleading as that painted by Mrs Gaskell. The fact remains that, poor as sanitary conditions were in the town, they were not unique, nor even unusual in the nascent industrial society of the first half of the nineteenth century. Despite the threat to public health identified by the inspector appointed by a newly conscious and increasingly interventionist Victorian government, the population of the town increased dramatically in line with its manufacturing activity. Census returns reveal that in the half century between 1801 and 1850 it more than doubled, rising from 3,164 to 6,848; in 1821–31, the first decade of the Brontës' residence, it increased by 25 per cent. As the only clergyman covering the entire chapelry at that period, Patrick Brontë was kept immensely busy. On average he baptised 290 children and carried out 111 burials a year.[14] The impression that Haworth was a thriving and populous town, rather than the isolated rural village of Brontë legend, is unavoidable.

It would also be a mistake to see the Babbage Report as confirming the popular hypothesis that the Brontës were socially and culturally isolated in Haworth. Babbage's remit necessarily confined him to the condition of the working classes, amongst whom it was indeed unlikely that the Brontës would find kindred spirits. It did not extend to their own middle class, whose existence is therefore undocumented in his report. Yet it is clear from the directories and local newspapers of the period that there was a small, but growing and influential number of professionals and people of independent means living within the area. William White's 1837 *History, Gazetteer and Directory of the West Riding of Yorkshire*, for instance, lists twenty-nine people who might be placed in this category, as distinct from the tradesmen and craftsmen who otherwise merit inclusion. In addition to the mill-owners, the list includes three clergymen (including Patrick Brontë himself), three heads of local schools, two quarry owners, a surgeon, a wine and spirit merchant and five men whose occupation is given as 'gentleman'. By 1843, this last category had risen to eleven, and two members of the Greenwood family, Joseph and William, were defined for the first time simply as 'Esquire'.[15]

The existence of these people is significant for two reasons: firstly, they and their families were the natural social peers of the Brontës and, secondly, they had an impact on the cultural and intellectual life of the Haworth. The first point is only relevant because Mrs Gaskell and subsequent biographers have placed great emphasis on the supposed fact that the Brontë girls grew up 'bereft, in a singular manner, of all such society as would have been natural to their age, sex, and station'. Mrs Gaskell identified only one family, the Greenwoods of Bridge House, as the exception to the general rule. Despite being dissenters, they had been 'remarkably kind and attentive' to Mrs Brontë in her last illness and 'had paid the children the attention of asking them occasionally to tea . . . At this house, I believe, the little Brontës paid their only visits; and these visits ceased before long.'[16] Whilst it suited Mrs Gaskell's purposes to suggest that the Brontës had no normal social contacts outside their own close-knit family circle, this was clearly not the case. Their father's occupation made this impossible. Not only was he on close personal terms with many of the local clergy, including Theodore Dury of Keighley and Thomas Crowther of Cragg Vale, and also his own relation by marriage, John Fennell of Cross Stone: these friendships extended to their respective families. Charlotte's first letter was written during a family visit to Cross Stone in 1829, Caroline Dury was a friend of Charlotte's, and the Crowther daughters were at the Clergy Daughters' School at Cowan Bridge at the same time as the Brontë girls.[17] Moreover, visiting clergymen, invited to preach fund-raising sermons on behalf of the Sunday school or missionary and Bible societies, were a constantly recurring feature of life at Haworth Parsonage.

Like the church trustees and officials, the ever-increasing band of curates, the bell-ringers and Sunday-school teachers, even the occasional visiting bishop, had to be received and entertained by the parson's children, whether they wished to do so or not.[18]

Beyond the formal performance of their parochial duties, there is evidence that the Brontës did enjoy more voluntary social contact. Though such correspondence is of its very nature ephemeral, a few of their replies to invitations from Ann Greenwood of Spring Head and the Taylor family of Stanbury are extant, couched in language which suggests that these were not isolated instances.[19] Charlotte's school friend, Ellen Nussey, too, when she stayed at the parsonage, casually records paying social visits as if they were nothing out of the ordinary. Her diary of 1844, for example, includes references to 'plenty of fun & fatigue' with the Heatons of Ponden Hall and a walk 'under umbrellas' in the Greenwoods' garden at Oxenhope.[20] These visits were reciprocated, for there are references in the Brontë correspondence to friends and neighbours being invited to tea on a purely social basis. The family of Ebenezer Rand, master of the new National School which opened in Haworth in 1844, seems to have been on particularly friendly terms with the Brontës.[21]

Whilst none of this is evidence of actual intimacy between the Brontë sisters and their neighbours, it is conclusive proof that they were part of, and on familiar terms with, a social circle centred on their father's profession. In that respect, at least, they were far more normal than Mrs Gaskell or her followers have allowed. That none of these friendships – nor even, it should be stressed, Charlotte's lifelong friendship with Ellen Nussey – ever approximated the intensity of the relationship between the Brontë siblings tells us more about the Brontës than about the society in which they lived. Like all large families they had no need actively to seek companionship from other children and it is significant that the only time they did so was when they were away at school. It is unlikely that Charlotte would have made friends with Ellen Nussey or Mary Taylor had she not been separated from her siblings and alone at Roe Head. Similarly, Anne's only known friendship outside the family was formed when she was a pupil at the same school.[22] Sharing the same interests and enthusiasms, and bound together by the joint creation of their secret imaginary worlds, the young Brontës had no need to look outside their own home for emotional or intellectual sympathies.

What Haworth did have to offer, however, was a cultural life which, if it could not match that of the great cities, was still valuable and important. Far from being the philistine and barbarous place of Brontë legend, Haworth in the period from 1820 to 1861 was a community with cultural aspirations and, perhaps more surprisingly, a venerable musical tradition. As one of its inhabitants, Benjamin Binns, later remembered, 'Haworth in those days was remarkable for its cultivation of music, and the goddess was wooed for herself rather than for any pecuniary gain.' The Haworth Philharmonic Society, one of the oldest in the country, had been established in or around 1780. It held regular concerts in the town, usually in the large room of the Black Bull, which was then the closest thing to an Assembly Room that Haworth possessed.[23] The Haworth Choral Society, which met and performed four times a year at various venues, was less ancient. Under the aegis of Thomas Parker, an 'almost matchless' local tenor who was in great demand throughout Yorkshire and Lancashire and was even invited to sing at the Crystal Palace, the society was highly ambitious and successful in the 1840s and 1850s. Its speciality was sacred music, and oratorios such as Haydn's *Creation* and Handel's *Samson* and *Judas Maccabaeus*, made regular appearances on its programme.[24] According to Benjamin Binns, Patrick Brontë was 'passionately fond of oratorio' and 'often attended concerts and other meetings of an elevating tendency in the village, taking with him the members of his family'. It was undoubtedly for this reason that he initatated a public subscription in the township to build an organ in his church, personally supporting the campaign with fund-raising sermons. The public performance of Handel's *Messiah* on 23 March 1834 which inaugurated the successful installation of the organ was such a milestone in the musical life of the town that it even found its way into the Brontë juvenilia, in the form of a sardonic description by Charlotte of Branwell's rapturous response to John Greenwood's playing.[25] The installation of the organ transformed the possibilities for public performance and Haworth Church thereafter became a popular venue for concerts.

With music of such calibre a regular feature of Haworth life, it was perhaps not surprising that these skilled amateur musical societies attracted professional musicians as soloists. John Greenwood himself, Abraham Sunderland, his replacement as organist of Keighley (who taught the Brontë children music), Mrs Sunderland, 'The Yorkshire Queen of Song', who often partnered Thomas Parker in oratorios, were only some of many, though perhaps the most remarkable performer was the German violinist, G. F. Hoffman, who in the Sunday school in December 1842 'astonished a numerous audience by his extra-ordinary abilities as a musician' and earned himself their 'unbounded applause'.[26] The concerts of neighbouring towns also attracted musical talent of the highest international standing. Halifax, less than a dozen miles away and well known to all the Brontës, played host in the 1830s and 1840s to such notables as Nicolo Paganini, Johann Strauss 'The Waltz

King', Franz Liszt and Felix Mendelssohn.[27] In the light of all this, it is not surprising that, as we shall see, at least three of the young Brontës were talented musicians in their own right.

The visual arts were not as well represented as music. But in addition to Branwell Brontë Haworth is said to have boasted its own resident artist, James Constantine, a favourite of the Ferrand family who held the lordship of the manor.[28] Four miles away, in Keighley, the Brontës had an inspirational figure in John Bradley, a founder member of the Keighley Mechanics Institute, who was both its first secretary and architect of its new building. Though apparently not a professional artist, Bradley exhibited regularly at events sponsored by the Royal Northern Society for the Encouragement of the Fine Arts and chose to have his own portrait painted with his brushes and palette in hand. William Dearden, a schoolmaster of Keighley and friend of the Brontë family, later remembered meeting Patrick and his children 'many times' in Bradley's studio, 'where they hung in close-gazing inspection and silent admiration over some fresh production of the artist's genius'. It was to Bradley that Patrick turned when he wished to appoint a drawing-master for his children and many of their earliest sketches were executed under his guidance.[29]

When Branwell decided to become a professional portrait painter, however, he had to look further afield for tuition. Leeds, some twenty-five miles away, had been home to the annual exhibition of the Royal Northern Society for the Encouragement of the Fine Arts since 1808. The exhibitions, which the Brontës visited, were a curious mixture of old masters on loan from private collections and new works by contemporary artists which were for sale. In 1834 Charlotte, who at the time harboured ambitions to be an artist herself, exhibited two of her own drawings, 'nimini-pimini' pencil copies of engravings of Bolton Abbey and Kirkstall Abbey. As neither picture found a buyer and Charlotte's eyesight was already beginning to fail under the strain of such detailed work, these were probably factors in her determining to abandon any hope of an artistic career.[30] One of the regular exhibitors was the Leeds-based portrait painter, William Robinson, who had been trained by Sir Thomas Lawrence and was widely regarded as one of the most distinguished artists of the day. In securing lessons with Robinson in 1834–5, Branwell could claim to be part of an eminent artistic tradition, centred on the Royal Academy, the metropolis and the court: the kind of high art which the Brontës had idolised since childhood, far removed from the limitations of the provincial art world. Nevertheless, it did not augur well for Branwell's own future as a professional artist that when Robinson died in 1838, he left his widow and children destitute.[31]

Like most other industrial townships of the period, Haworth also had its philanthropic, educational and self-improvement societies. The Masons and the Foresters each had a large membership and enjoyed the patronage of Patrick Brontë. Branwell became a Master Mason and was an active member of the Three Graces Lodge, particularly in 1836 and 1837.[32] The Brontë sisters were excluded by reason of their sex, though this did not prevent them attending the public lectures sponsored by the Foresters, and by the various religious societies in Haworth and the Mechanics' Institute. Until the Haworth branch of this latter was established in 1848–9 (too late for Branwell, Emily and Anne), the Brontës had to walk the four miles to Keighley to attend its lectures on politics, religion, science, history and literature and to borrow books from its library. On at least one memorable occasion, in 1840, when the likeable Haworth curate, William Weightman, was invited to lecture on the classics there, all three Brontë sisters and their guest, Ellen Nussey, turned out in force to hear him, even though it meant that they did not return home till midnight. It was a measure of the importance Charlotte attached to the Mechanics' Institute as an educational facility that she not only became a life member of the Haworth branch at its commencement but, according to her obituary pronounced by its chairman, 'ever evinced a deep interest in its welfare and prosperity', presenting copies of her books to its library, presiding at the tea-tables on the annual soirée and honouring its meetings with her presence.[33]

Books of every kind were readily available to the Brontë children through the library of the Keighley Mechanics' Institute and, more importantly, the circulating libraries of the town, which stocked the more congenial periodicals, histories, poetry and fiction. Robert Aked, who printed two of Patrick Brontë's pamphlets, *The Signs of the Times* (1835) and *A Brief Treatise on the Best Time and Mode of Baptism* (1836), had established a circulating library at his shop as early as 1822, and the bookseller, Thomas Hudson, also kept a lending library. Surprisingly, there was even a subscription library in Haworth itself, though its existence (which may have been short-lived) is only documented because its contents were put up for sale in 1844. According to the local people, the Brontë sisters were familiar figures 'trudging down to Keighley' to change their books.[34] As their father could not afford to subscribe to a wide range of newspapers and periodicals, these had to be borrowed from friends. *Blackwood's Magazine*, for instance, was lent to them by the Reverend Jonas Driver, who lived in Haworth until his death in December 1831. Aunt Branwell, Patrick's sister-in-law, who came to look after the young Brontes when their mother died, was then persuaded to subscribe to *Fraser's Magazine*. Patrick's subscription to the Keighley Mechanics'

Institute eighteen months later may also have been an attempt to supply the deficiency caused by Driver's death.[35]

Newspapers played a hugely important role in the Brontë household, and were regarded as a necessary expense. In March 1844 Patrick Brontë informed the editors of the Whig *Leeds Mercury* that he had been a subscriber for 'more than thirty years'. He also subscribed to the rival Tory paper, the *Leeds Intelligencer*. As this suggests, he was far more liberal in his views than has generally been supposed. Indeed, he regularly lent newspapers to John Winterbottom, the Baptist Minister of Haworth, who was his vocal and active opponent on the vexed question of Church Rates.[36] His children, who were less tolerant, incorporated the proprietor and editor of the *Leeds Mercury*, Edward Baines, into their juvenilia, turning him and his three sons into the villains of their imaginary worlds.[37] A third newspaper, the *John Bull*, which even the twelve-year-old Charlotte considered 'High Tory very violent', was lent to them by the same Jonas Driver who lent them *Blackwood's Magazine*.[38]

The Brontës' own library was very small. It included the books their father had acquired for his own classical studies, such as his editions of the works of Horace and Homer's *Iliad*, both of which bore his proud inscription that they had been awarded to him as prizes 'for having always kept in the *first Class*, at St John's College – Cambridge'. His interest in the natural world (which must have been a personal passion, as it was not a subject included on the Cambridge syllabus) was represented by at least three valuable books bought principally for their illustrations: the famous American ornithologist John James Audubon's *Ornithological Biography, or An Account of the Habits of the Birds of the United States of America*, Thomas Bewick's *A History of British Birds* and *The Gardens and Menagerie of the Zoological Society delineated*.[39] His liking for romantic literature was evident in his purchase of an early edition of Walter Scott's *The Lay of the Last Minstrel*. Other works by Scott in the parsonage included *Tales of a Grandfather*, bought by Aunt Branwell as a new year's gift for her nephew and nieces in 1828, and *The Vision of Don Roderick* and *Rokeby*, a present to Charlotte from her headmistress, Margaret Wooler, when she left her post as teacher at Dewsbury Moor on 23 May 1838.[40]

Though Scott's influence on the imaginative and literary development of the young Brontës was to be profound, there was another section of the family bookshelves which was to be equally important, if for different reasons. The largest collection of books by one author had a familiar name on the title-page – that of Patrick Brontë himself. Scholarly clergymen had always published sermons, religious commentaries and didactic works, and it was not uncommon for those of the Evangelical persuasion, like Patrick, to attempt to reach a wider audience by preaching a moral message in the more accessible form of simple tales and poems. Most of Patrick's efforts fell within these latter categories and were written in the first flush of enthusiasm after his relocation to Yorkshire: *Winter Evening Thoughts: A Miscellaneous Poem* (1810), *Cottage Poems* (1811), *The Rural Minstrel* (1813), *The Cottage in the Wood* (1815) and *The Maid of Killarney* (1818) were all firmly in the Evangelical tradition. They were, Patrick claimed, 'chiefly designed for the poorer classes of society' and intended 'to convey useful instruction, in a mode not unacceptable'.⁴¹ What was unusual about Patrick's books was that he clearly wrestled with his conscience in writing them. As he disarmingly confessed in the introductory advertisement to *Cottage Poems*, he had been occupied in writing them 'from morning till noon, and from noon till night' whenever his clerical duties permitted. What is more, 'his employment was full of real, indescribable pleasure, such as he could wish to taste as long as life lasts'. That 'could wish' was significant. As a clergyman, Patrick could only justify his excursions into fiction on the grounds that they had a spiritual and moral purpose, yet the creative act had become a consuming passion for him and an end in itself, thereby threatening the proper fulfilment of his clerical duties. He acknowledged this danger in his preface to *The Cottage in the Wood* in words which are probably so harsh because they were self-applicable: 'The sensual novelist and his admirer, are beings of depraved appetites and sickly imaginations, who having learnt the art of *self-tormenting*, are diligently and zealously employed in creating an imaginary world, which they can never inhabit, only to make the real world, with which they must necessarily be conversant, gloomy and insupportable.' Having tasted the seductive delights of creating an imaginary world for himself, Patrick understood the same compulsion in his children. His advice to them, as Charlotte later told Robert Southey, was to channel their energies into the performance of their daily duties and to reserve the pleasures of the imagination for their leisure hours. In this he was simply recommending what he himself had done. But his children, lacking his willpower and motivation and spurred on by each other, were unable to break the spell.⁴²

It will have become apparent that the Reverend Patrick Brontë was a remarkable man, whose influence on his children was of crucial importance in their development as individuals and as novelists. Mrs Gaskell's *Life of Charlotte Brontë* depicts him as a misanthropic eccentric, given to violent rages in which he destroyed furniture and clothing, a man of 'strong and vehement prejudices',⁴³ who, after the death of his wife, shut himself away from his young family and declined even to eat meals with them. As with her portrayal of Haworth, Gaskell drew this caricature of Patrick in order to explain what contemporaries saw as unfeminine in his daughters' attitudes and opinions: they had been deprived of a 'normal' upbringing and had been brought up in a loveless and repressive home. Her portrait of Patrick was as unrecognisable to his friends as her description of Haworth had been to its inhabitants and many of them publicly leapt to his defence. It says much for Patrick that he declined any public refutation of what amounted to a serious libel of his character, fearing that to do so would be to undermine the credibility of Mrs Gaskell's work. Instead, he contented himself with a mild reproof in a private letter, dismissing the wilder anecdotes with quiet humour and dignity. 'I never was subject to those explosions of passion ascribed to me', he informed her publisher, George Smith, 'and never perpetrated those eccentric and ridiculous movements, which I am ashamed to mention'.[44]

But, as Patrick was the first to admit, he was not an ordinary man. 'I do not deny that I am somewhat excentrick [sic]', he told Gaskell. 'Had I been numbered amongst the calm, sedate, *concentric* men of the world, I should not have been as I now am, and I should, in all probability, never have had such children as mine have been.'[45] His own career had been a personal vindication of his passionate belief in the power of education to transform lives. The eldest of ten children born to a poor Irish tenant farmer, he had taught himself to read and write, set up as a village schoolmaster at the age of sixteen, and, nine years later, won a sizar's place[46] at St John's College, Cambridge. There his single-minded determination to pursue his studies so that he could enter the Church of England attracted the attention of the Evangelicals and the personal patronage of one of the most influential lay members of that movement, William Wilberforce. Ordained on leaving university, he found a ready welcome in Evangelical circles and became a conscientious and committed clergyman. In 1809 he left the south of England for the West Riding of Yorkshire where the traditional, rural parish structure had been overwhelmed by the rapid growth of the new industrial towns, leaving whole populations bereft of spiritual guidance. Patrick's mission was to reclaim these lost souls for the Anglican Church and he dedicated his entire life to achieving it by every means possible: baptising, preaching, educating, but also working indefatigably for the material welfare of his parishioners. He laboured ceaselessly on behalf of individuals – one of his earliest successes was to secure the release of a young man wrongly arrested for desertion from the army[47] – and for the wider needs of the community. In Haworth this led him to set up not only a Sunday school but also adult literacy classes. Both his active support for those seeking to reduce the working hours of factory children and his fourteen-year campaign to improve the public water supply and sanitation brought him into conflict with the mill-owners who were the most powerful members of his congregation. Nevertheless, he made his opinions known and did not shrink from voicing them in the many letters he wrote to the local newspapers and in the petitions he organised to Parliament. Occasionally, as in his vocal opposition to the Poor Law Amendment Act of 1834, which ended the old system of outdoor relief and made charitable assistance to the unemployed, infirm and elderly dependent on residence in workhouses, he even found himself quoted in the national newspapers.[48]

Patrick's rise through the ranks of the church hierarchy had been steady rather than meteoric and in 1820, aged forty-three, he accepted what was to become his final appointment as rector of Haworth. The post was technically a perpetual curacy, which gave him security of tenure for life: he could not be evicted legally from either the living or the parsonage that came with it. This was crucially important for Patrick who, unlike most clergymen of the time, had no source of income other than his clerical salary to support himself and his growing family. As all the Brontës were uncomfortably aware, however, when he died they would have nothing. His salary of around £170[49] was too small to enable them to acquire any savings during his lifetime and on his death their home would pass to the next incumbent. In the circumstances, Patrick's anxiety about his health and his insistence that his children should be capable of earning their own livings were entirely understandable.

The now-famous parsonage to which Patrick brought his wife, Maria, his six children, Maria, Elizabeth, Charlotte, Branwell, Emily and Anne, the eldest of whom was six years old, the youngest only three months, and two young maidservants in April 1820 was elegant and commodious by comparison with most houses in Haworth.[50] The Brontës were fortunate too in that their home stood in one of the healthiest locations on the outskirts of the town and at the very top of the hill. They had their own well, supplied by moorland springs unsullied by the twin unspeakables of farmyard or churchyard effluent, and they were one of only two dozen households in the town to have their own privy.[51] The parsonage, which had been built in 1779, had a small garden to the front and a paved yard to the rear. On two sides it was enclosed by churchyard, on the third by Church Lane, a quiet cobbled byway which ran at a tangent from the top of Main Street, past the church, the sexton's cottage and yard and the National School, built by Patrick in 1832. It stood at the top of Church Lane, and literally was the last house in the town. Beyond it lay only the moors, which were to become the creative inspiration for so much of the Brontës' writings.

The house itself was solid and uncompromising, the only concession to ornament being a pilastered and pedimented central doorway. Like all the houses in Haworth, it was built of local stone, hewn out of the quarries on the hillside behind, and roofed with stone flags to withstand exposure

Figure 1 Haworth Parsonage in the 1850s. From an ambrotype in the Brontë
Parsonage Museum.

to the winds. Downstairs there was a dining room, which was the family
living room, and, across the passageway, Patrick's study, where all the official
business of the chapelry was conducted. Behind the study was the kitchen,
where the children would gather round the fire to while away the long, dark
winter evenings with their imaginary games and to listen to the tales of their
much-loved servant, Tabby Aykroyd, who stayed with the family for thirty
years. A small storeroom behind the dining room and a back wash kitchen
completed the ground floor. Upstairs, there were three double bedrooms, a
tiny bedroom for the servants over the storeroom, and an even smaller room,
over the hall passage, which was used as a playroom and sewing room, but
grandly designated the 'children's study'.

When the children were young, the house must have seemed austere and
bare. Patrick had to support himself, a wife, six children and two maidservants. There was no money for luxuries. 'There was not much carpet
anywhere', one of Charlotte's schoolfriends, Ellen Nussey, remarked on her
first visit in 1833,

> except in the Sitting room, and on the centre of the Study floor. The hall floor
> and stairs were done with sand stone, always beautifully clean as everything

about the house was, the walls were not papered but coloured in a pretty dove-coloured tint, hair-seated chairs and mahogany tables, book-shelves in the Study but not many of these elsewhere. Scant and bare indeed many will say, yet it was not a scantness that made itself felt.[52]

With its stone-flagged floors throughout the ground-floor rooms and its curtainless windows (having buried so many women and children who had been burnt to death in household accidents, Patrick was justifiably afraid of fire, so internal wooden shutters supplied the place of curtains until the children were grown) the parsonage must indeed have seemed bleak and poverty-stricken to the relatively wealthy Ellen. To the young Brontës, however, it was a much-loved home, where the lack of creature comforts was more than compensated for by the abundance of intellectual stimuli.

For most such stimuli, the children were indebted to their father. His profession and, more especially, his active engagement in the political and social, as well as religious, issues of the day profoundly affected his children. Not only did he take them to the local concerts and lectures, but he dedicated a considerable portion of his limited income to educate them in the liberal arts. Abraham Sunderland, the Keighley organist, was employed to give them music lessons and a five-octave cottage piano was purchased so that they could practise at home. Emily's diary paper of 24 November 1834 records that Mr Sunderland was expected and 'Anne and I have not Done our music excercise which consists of b majer.' Charlotte's short-sightedness apparently prevented her learning the piano but both Emily and Anne became proficient enough to teach others. Emily, in particular, who played 'with precision and brilliancy' was considered so talented that when she went to the Pensionnat Heger in Brussels in 1842 one of the best professors in Belgium was engaged to give her lessons. Branwell, in addition, learnt to play the flute.[53] Drawing lessons for all the children were provided by John Bradley of Keighley, who encouraged them to develop their skills by copying Thomas Bewick's engravings. Drawing skills were a prerequisite of a genteel education at the time, and would be essential to Patrick's children if they were to earn their livings as teachers and governesses. But he was supportive of his children's artistic ambitions to the point of allowing affection for them to blind him to their limited abilities. Charlotte could not have exhibited her drawings at the age of eighteen without his approval. Although plans for Branwell to enter the Royal Academy were never realised, Patrick paid for at least two courses of expensive lessons (at the modern equivalent of more than £90 a lesson) with William Robinson of Leeds, as well as supporting his son financially in his ill-fated attempt in 1839 to set up a professional portrait painting studio in Bradford.[54]

During their early years the young Brontës were educated by their father. Formal instruction was supplemented by afternoon walks on the moors, which were an opportunity for practical lessons in natural sciences, and evening sessions when, according to the servant, Sarah Garrs, Patrick gathered his children around him 'for recitation and talk, giving them oral lessons in history, biography or travel'. They were expected to write out the stories he told next morning; this, it has been suggested, gave rise to a lifelong habit of thinking out their stories in bed.[55] Such methods of instruction, far removed from the dull parrot-learning and recitation of grammar and lists of geographical and historical facts which were the staple diet of early nineteenth-century education, were calculated to appeal to the young Brontës' imaginative faculties, even if they did not prepare them for the rigours of school life. When Charlotte entered Roe Head school in January 1831, her schoolfellows 'thought her very ignorant, for she had never learnt grammar at all, and very little geography', but 'She would confound us by knowing things that were out of our range altogether.'[56]

Unlike most parents of the period, Patrick made no effort to censor his children's reading and encouraged their impassioned discussion and debate on the political and religious issues of the day. The newspapers he took also provided the young Brontës with rich material for their imaginative play. Charlotte's vivid portrayal of the arrival of the special edition carrying the terms of the Roman Catholic Emancipation bill, interrupting her 1829 novelette 'Tales of the Islanders', portrays father and children equally caught up in the excitement of the moment: 'with what eagerness papa tore off the cover & how we all gathered round him & with what breathless anxiety we listen[e]d ...'[57] Given such passionate interest in issues of this kind, and their equally emotional identification with heroes both living and dead, it is not surprising that, on occasion, when play-acting, the young Brontës were carried away by their enthusiasm and had to call in their father to act as arbiter in their quarrels.[58]

In her *The Life of Charlotte Brontë* Mrs Gaskell portrayed the Brontës as victims of an abnormal childhood and upbringing, suffering an involuntary exile from civilisation, society and friendships in the barbarous isolation of Haworth, and the loveless, repressive atmosphere of a home ruled with a rod of iron by a tyrannical and egocentric parent. She could not have been more wrong. The young Brontës certainly had an unconventional childhood, but this proved to be a liberation for them. Their father's passion for politics, literature and nature and his unorthodox methods of educating them were inspirational to such clever, imaginative children. A more 'normal' middle-class upbringing would probably have suffocated their budding talents. Far from being the gloomy place of Brontë legend, Haworth Parsonage was a vibrant powerhouse of intellectual activity. As they grew older, the Brontës were sometimes frustrated by the limitations of small-town, provincial existence, but this was because, since childhood, they had learnt to dream and to nourish ambition. It is, however, significant that forays into the world beyond rarely lived up to their expectations. Each of the Brontë sisters was unhappy away from home and always anxious to return there. Ironically, Mrs Gaskell was right to place such emphasis on the formative influence of the Brontës' childhood in Haworth. Though she did so on false premises and for all the wrong reasons, it was indeed the key to their future success as novelists.

NOTES

1. Elizabeth Gaskell, *The Life of Charlotte Brontë* [1857], edited by Angus Easson (Oxford University Press, 1996), 15.
2. Elizabeth Rigby in the *Quarterly Review* 84, December 1848 (*CH*, 111).
3. Gaskell, *Life*, 9–11, 20–2.
4. *North American Review*, October 1857 (*CH*, 379).
5. Juliet Barker, *The Brontës* (London: Weidenfeld & Nicolson, 1994), 811. See also p. 814.
6. See, for example, Branwell Brontë to William Wordsworth, 10 January 1837 and Charlotte Brontë to Ellen Nussey, 23 January 1844 (*CBL* I, 160–1, 341); Charlotte Brontë to W. S. Williams, 24 August 1849 (*CBL* II, 240).
7. William White, *History, Gazetteer and Directory of the West Riding of Yorkshire 1837–8* (Sheffield, 1838), II, 433. The boundaries of the chapelry were not precise and Patrick Brontë was sometimes called upon to officiate in the hinterlands which fell between his own and neighbouring parishes.
8. B. H. Babbage, *Report to the General Board of Health on a Preliminary Inquiry into the Sewerage, Drainage, and Supply of Water, and the Sanitary Condition of the Inhabitants of the Hamlet of Haworth, in the West Riding of the County of York* (London: HMSO, 1850), 11–12.
9. *Ibid*, 6.
10. Gaskell, *Life*, 11.
11. Babbage, *Report to the General Board of Health*, 6, 11.
12. *Ibid*, 12, 14; William White, *History, Gazetteer and Directory of the West Riding of Yorkshire 1842–3* (Sheffield, 1843), 516.
13. Babbage, *Report to the General Board of Health*, 11–13, 16–17, 9–10, 12.
14. *Register of Baptisms, 1813–29* and *Register of Burials, 1813–1836*, Haworth Church.
15. White, *History, Gazetteer and Directory of the West Riding of Yorkshire* (Sheffield, 1838), 439; White, *History, Gazetteer and Directory of the West Riding of Yorkshire* (Sheffield, 1843), 370–1.
16. Gaskell, *Life*, 46, 472–3.
17. *CBL* I, 105; Barker, *The Brontës*, 167, 339, 183, 546, 802–3.
18. See Barker, *The Brontës, passim*. For Ellen Nussey's entertaining description of the annual visit by the Sunday-school teachers see *CBL* I, 602.

19. For examples dating from 1836 and 1842 see *CBL* I, 149, 305, 305–6.
20. Barker, *The Brontës*, 438.
21. *CBL* I, 351, 393–5, 442–3; *CBL* II, 184–5. See also Barker, *The Brontës*, 430, 437.
22. Barker, *The Brontës*, 172, 181. Anne's friend, Ann Cook, died within a year of leaving Roe Head (*CBL* I, 209 n.1).
23. [Benjamin Binns], 'The Brontës and the Brontë Country: A chat with one who knew them', *The Bradford Observer*, 17 February 1894, 6.
24. For oratorios performed in Haworth by the Haworth Choral Society see, for example, *The Halifax Guardian*, 12 November 1842, 8, *The Bradford Observer*, 8 February 1844, 8, and 24 October 1844, 6. For Thomas Parker, see his obituary in *The Keighley News*, 14 April 1866.
25. [Benjamin Binns], 'The Brontës and the Brontë Country', 6; Barker, *The Brontës*, pp. 210–11; Charlotte Brontë, 'My Angria and the Angrians', 14 October 1834 (*EEW* II: 2, 251–2).
26. *The Bradford Observer*, 5 January 1843, 5; *Keighley Saturday Observer*, 31 December 1842, 8; *The Leeds Intelligencer*, 10 December 1842, 7.
27. Barker, *The Brontës*, 212, 877.
28. [Benjamin Binns], 'The Brontës and the Brontë Country', 6.
29. Barker, *The Brontës*, 150; Christine Alexander and Jane Sellars, *The Art of the Brontës* (Cambridge University Press, 1995), 22–4, plate 5; William Dearden, letter to *The Bradford Observer*, 27 June 1861, 7.
30. Barker, *The Brontës*, 14; Alexander and Sellars, *The Art of the Brontës*, 25–6, 228–9.
31. Barker, *The Brontës*, 214.
32. *Ibid.*, 230, 247, 320.
33. *Ibid.*, 636, 725, 777; Ellen Nussey, 'Reminiscences, 1871', in Juliet Barker, ed., *The Brontës: A Life in Letters* (London: Viking, 1997), 74.
34. Barker, *The Brontës*, 148–9; *The Bradford Observer*, 28 March 1844, 5.
35. Barker, *The Brontës*, 149; *CBL* I, 112.
36. Patrick Brontë to the Editors of the *Leeds Mercury*, n.d. (*Leeds Mercury*, 16 March 1844, 6); Charlotte Brontë, 'The History of the Year', 12 March 1829, in Juliet Barker, ed., *Charlotte Brontë: Juvenilia 1829–1835* (Harmondsworth: Penguin, 1996), 2; [Benjamin Binns], 'The Brontës and the Brontë Country', 6.
37. See, for example, Charlotte's first volume of *Tales of the Islanders*, in Barker, ed., *Charlotte Brontë: Juvenilia*, 9–12.
38. Charlotte Brontë, 'The History of the Year', 12 March 1829 (Barker, ed., *Charlotte Brontë: Juvenilia*, 2).
39. Patrick's prize books are in the Brontë Parsonage Museum (HAOBP: bb207 and bb208). For examples of the Brontës' drawings copied from Bewick's *A History of British Birds* see Alexander and Sellars, *The Art of the Brontës*, passim. The first volume of *The Gardens and Menagerie of the Zoological Society delineated* (London: John Sharpe, 1830) is at the Brontë Parsonage Museum (HAOBP: bb69): it bears Patrick's inscription, in mixed Latin and English, that it was bought in May 1831 at the cost of one guinea on the advice of John Bradley and the comment 'The wooden cuts, in this Book, are excellent – Being done by the first of living engravers, on Wood – .' The Brontë copy of Audubon was

item 6 in Sotheby's 1907 sale catalogue of books and manuscripts belonging to Charlotte's widower, Arthur Bell Nicholls.

40. Patrick's *The Lay of the Last Minstrel* (London: Longman & Co., 1806) and Charlotte's presentation copy of *The Vision of Don Roderick; Rokeby* (Edinburgh: John Ballantyne & Co., 1811 and 1813) are at the Brontë Parsonage Museum (HAOBP: bb54 and bb214); the Brontës' inscribed copy of *Tales of a Grandfather* is mentioned in a footnote to the 1905 edition of Gaskell, *The Life of Charlotte Brontë* (London: Smith, Elder & Co., 1905), 125.

41. J. Horsfall Turner, ed., *Brontëana: The Reverend Patrick Brontë's Collected Works* (Bingley: T. Harrison & Sons, 1898), 19, 71.

42. *Ibid.*, 21, 102; Charlotte Brontë to Robert Southey, 16 March 1837 (*CBL* 1, 169).

43. Gaskell, *Life*, 45.

44. Barker, *The Brontës*, 803–5.

45. Patrick Brontë to Mrs Gaskell, 30 July 1857 (*Brontë Society Transactions* 8: 44 (1932), 129–30).

46. A sizarship was a form of scholarship for poor but able students entitling them to pay reduced fees and get free dinners, in the expectation that they would win high academic honours for their college.

47. 'Sydney' [Patrick Brontë] to the Editor of the *Leeds Mercury*, n.d., *Leeds Mercury*, 15 December 1810, 3; Barker, *The Brontës*, 37–8.

48. *The Times*, 27 February 1837, 6. For a summary of Patrick's career see Barker, *The Brontës, passim*.

49. *Ibid.*, 105.

50. The two maidservants were the sisters, Nancy and Sarah Garrs, whom the Brontës had taken into service when living at Thornton on the outskirts of Bradford.

51. Babbage, *Report to the General Board of Health*, 12.

52. Ellen Nussey, 'Reminiscences of Charlotte Brontë...reprinted by permission from "Scribner's Monthly," May 1871', *Brontë Society Transactions* 2: 10 (1899), 76–9.

53. *Ibid.*, 79; Constantin Heger to Patrick Brontë, 5 November 1842 (*CBL* 1, 299); Barker, ed., *The Brontës: A Life in Letters*, 29. The cottage piano, Branwell's flute and his handwritten book of music for the flute are at the Brontë Parsonage Museum.

54. Barker, ed., *The Brontës: A Life in Letters*, 31–4. Patrick Brontë paid 2 guineas for each lesson with Robinson. For Bewick see note 39 above.

55. Barker, *The Brontës*, 855 n. 90.

56. Mary Taylor to Mrs Gaskell, 18 January 1856, in Barker, ed., *The Brontës: A Life in Letters*, 18.

57. Gaskell, *Life*, 43, 46; Charlotte Brontë, 'Tales of the Islanders Volume II' [6 October 1829], in Barker, ed., *Charlotte Brontë: Juvenilia*, 17.

58. Patrick Brontë to Mrs Gaskell, 24 July 1855, in Barker, ed., *The Brontës: A Life in Letters*, 10.

2

CAROL BOCK

'Our plays': the Brontë juvenilia

'Once upon a time four gifted children built themselves a dream world, magnificently wrought and marvellously beautiful.' So begins the first serious study of the Brontës' juvenile writings, Fannie Ratchford's *The Brontës' Web of Childhood*, published in 1941.[1] Ratchford's description of the juvenilia as 'a dream world' where the children 'found escape from the discipline and restraints of ordinary life' seems apt when one reads the journal Charlotte kept as a young teacher at Roe Head School. After one particularly tedious day in October 1836, she complained:

> I am just going to write because I cannot help it. [Branwell] might indeed talk of scribblemania if he were to see me just now, encompassed by [students] . . . all wondering why I write with my eyes shut – staring, gaping – hang their astonishment! . . . Stupidity the atmosphere, school-books the employment, asses the society! What in all this is there to remind me of the divine silent unseen land of thought, dim now, and indefinite as a dream of a dream, the shadow of a shade? . . . Now I should be agonized if I had not the dream to repose on.[2]

The dream Charlotte refers to is, of course, the romantic saga of love, war, passion, and revenge that she and her siblings had been writing together for nearly a decade. Clearly, writing *was* a refuge from reality for Charlotte, and we have good reason to believe that it served the same purpose for Branwell, Emily and Anne as well. But this tells only half the story, for the other striking feature of the Brontës' early writing is its stunning representation of the culture of their times. Many of the characters are based on well-known public figures such as the popular painter John Martin; the prime minister of England Arthur Wellesley, Duke of Wellington; and the eminent physician John Robert Hume. The plots are informed by detailed knowledge of actual military campaigns and scientific expeditions, while the gorgeous settings owe as much to contemporary descriptions published in newspapers and magazines as they do to either the children's imaginations or to the standard geography textbook which they owned. The tales demonstrate a

34

familiarity with current parliamentary debates, as reported in the periodical press, and with reviews of contemporary theatrical productions, musical performances and art exhibitions. Most remarkable, however, is the way in which these writings appropriate and respond to the print culture of early nineteenth-century England. Profoundly influenced by their reading of books and contemporary periodicals, the young Brontës filled their imaginative world with authors and critics, publishers and printers, poets, pamphlet writers, playwrights, editors, booksellers and, of course, that key component of the modern literary economy, the reading public. Escapist as these 'dream' stories may have been, they show remarkable fidelity to the public realm of authorship, reading and publishing in which each of the Brontës later sought to construct a professional identity and earn a living.

The Brontës began their apprenticeship in the profession of literature early, and the story of that beginning is well known. On 5 June 1826, their father, the Reverend Patrick Brontë, returned from a clerical conference in the city of Leeds with presents for his four young children, aged from five to ten: a dancing doll for Anne, a toy village for Emily, a box of wooden soldiers for Branwell, and a set of ninepins for Charlotte. There is no record of the children playing with the doll or the toy village, and the ninepins may never have been put to their proper use; but the toy soldiers were another matter. On the morning after their father's return, each child selected a particular soldier as his or her own, naming it after an admired public figure and identifying with it as a character in the plays they began to make up together. As the older children, Charlotte and Branwell took the lead in this game, immediately claiming the identities of the two great political rivals of their time, the Duke of Wellington and Napoleon Bonaparte. Emily and Anne hastily selected the childish appellations 'Gravey' and 'Waiting Boy', which were soon replaced by the heroic names of Parry and Ross, Arctic explorers familiar to the children from accounts of their expeditions printed in *Blackwood's Magazine*, a much-read periodical in the Brontë household. The ninepins were used to represent the African characters in an elaborate story about European expansion and empire building. 'Our plays', as Charlotte called these games of dramatic make-believe (*EEW* 1, 5) quickly evolved into written stories, poems, plays and magazines; by 1829 the children were immersed not only in an imaginative world, known as the Glass Town Saga, which they had created around these characters but also in the activity actually of making the books and magazines that were a central feature of that imaginary realm. The earliest juvenile writings are consequently tiny, handsewn booklets containing nearly microscopic print (or rather the children's handwritten imitation of print), their diminutive size being intended to reflect their origin and authorship in the fictitious world of the children's toy heroes.

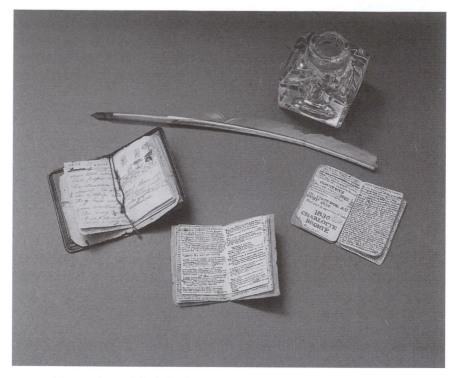

Figure 2 Some of the little Glass Town volumes. Brontë Parsonage Museum.

By 1831, Emily and Anne had broken away from their older siblings in this game of make believe to write their own stories about 'Parry's Land' and 'Ross's Land', which they soon transformed into the kingdom of Gondal. None of Emily's or Anne's early manuscripts survive, so we know relatively little about their content or about the younger siblings' working relationship as collaborating writers. Fortunately, this is not the case for Charlotte and Branwell, whose separate kingdom of Angria seems to have been founded in 1833. Most of their juvenilia remains extant and provides a fascinating view of this sister–brother team of apprentice authors and of the fictions they together produced. It is only recently, however, that the manuscripts have been collected and made available in reliable, scholarly editions which make sustained analysis possible. The publication history of the Brontë juvenilia is itself a story filled with scandal and betrayal, as befits Charlotte and Branwell's early tales. It has a happy ending, however, and can be quickly recounted.

After Charlotte's death in 1855, Elizabeth Gaskell gained access to a large packet of Charlotte's juvenile writing, which she found 'extraordinary' but of limited use to her as a biographer bent on securing Brontë's reputation with the Victorian public. 'They are the wildest & most incoherent things', she wrote to Charlotte's publisher, George Smith, 'They give one the idea of creative power carried to the verge of insanity.'[3] Having quickly skimmed these voluminous manuscripts densely packed with 'indescribably fine writing', Gaskell returned them to Charlotte's husband, Arthur Bell Nicholls, who took them with him to Ireland when he left Haworth after Patrick Brontë's death in 1861. In 1895, the journalist Clement Shorter visited the now elderly Mr Nicholls and purchased this packet, along with Branwell's manuscripts, all of which had lain untouched 'in the bottom of a cupboard tied up in a newspaper' for thirty years.[4] Through Shorter, they came into the possession of Thomas J. Wise, the villain of this story. Wise privately printed abridged and inaccurate editions of some of these manuscripts; he removed the original covers from a number of the booklets and had them rebound for his own personal library; and others he took apart page by page, selling the fragments to friends and acquaintances. Portions of manuscripts were bound and titled as if they were separate volumes; sheets from different volumes were removed from their original bindings and rebound together. Signatures and other small parts of pages were literally cut out of manuscripts and sold or given away. Titles were fabricated, attributions of authorship were deliberately falsified, and signatures were forged. As a result, Charlotte and Branwell's books, so carefully 'printed' and handbound by the child-authors themselves, were dismembered, mis-collated, misidentified and dispersed in pieces, mostly across the United States and Britain. For many years, the most complete collection of their juvenile writings was that published in 1936–8 by Wise himself and his co-editor, John Alexander Symington; obviously this edition was not accurate or, complete and, when the truth became known, was not respectable as a work of scholarship.[5]

The mutilation and dispersal of the juvenilia has, of course, had a negative impact on Brontë criticism, which until recently necessarily depended on unreliable editions of the early work and limited access to the original juvenile manuscripts in their authentic forms. Thanks largely to the efforts of two scholars, Christine Alexander and Victor A. Neufeldt, that situation is now entirely changed. Alexander has compiled a dependable bibliography of Charlotte's manuscripts and is editing a scholarly, multi-volume collection of her juvenile writings; Neufeldt has done the same for Branwell.[6] Now that the juvenilia has been released from the restricted purview of textual scholars and bibliographers and made widely available in reliable editions, we can study these extraordinary writings in their entirety and with confidence in the authenticity of the texts we are examining. We can, therefore, begin to reassess the imaginative venture that Ratchford called – or perhaps miscalled – the 'druglike Brontë dream' (*Web*, 5). Such a reassessment will result from a variety of critical tasks, some innovative and some traditional to Brontë studies. For example, now that it is possible to conflate Charlotte's and Branwell's manuscripts, we can more effectively study the Glass Town and Angrian sagas as they were actually written, that is, as one highly collaborative and inter-responsive text, in episodic form and of epic proportion. It is also now time to reconsider how the juvenilia anticipates the mature work and reflects Charlotte and Branwell's development as authors, a critical effort that has been hampered in the past by our partial and inaccurate knowledge of their early texts.

Since the publication of Ratchford's seminal work on the juvenilia, the critical consensus has been that Charlotte's growth as a writer was delayed, and Branwell's fatally arrested, by the tangled 'web of childhood' they had wrought around themselves in making up 'our plays'. It is true that Charlotte continued to write about the imaginary world she and Branwell had created together until she was at least twenty-three, but late juvenile stories like 'Henry Hastings' (1839), 'Caroline Vernon' (1839), and the fragmentary 'Ashworth' (1840) demonstrate that she had made significant advances as a writer of realistic fiction even at that time, seven years before she wrote her first published novel, *Jane Eyre*. Branwell's early death and the fact that, unlike Emily and Anne, he published no book before dying, have made it easy to depict him as a professional as well as a personal failure. But the quality of his poetry is easily as good as much that was being published in the 1830s, and his success in placing his poems (fifteen between 1841 and 1847) in papers such as the *Halifax Guardian* and the *Leeds Intelligencer* suggest that, given more time and greater acumen as a literary businessman, Branwell might have had a respectable, perhaps even an impressive, career as an author.

But analysis of Charlotte and Branwell's management or mismanagement of their literary careers lies beyond the scope of this chapter. Here, I propose to focus on the pre-professional years of their literary apprenticeship and to contribute to the reassessment of the early writings by demonstrating how they both reflect and helped to construct the young Brontës' relationship to print culture of their time. The precision with which their tiny manuscripts imitate the material form and textual content of contemporary publications suggests that the dream-like kingdoms which the Brontës imagined were inspired by actual literary life, or rather by the 'real' culture of print as the children knew it. Drawing on the representations of that culture in periodicals from the 1820s and 30s, Charlotte and Branwell appropriated the personae, places, plots and controversies of contemporary literary life into narratives that were, in no inconsequential way, about the problems of authorship, professional recognition and earning a living. The juvenilia thus reveal much about the Brontës' youthful aspirations and anxieties regarding their potential for careers in authorship.

But authorship was not only a topic to be written about; it was also a role the Brontës enthusiastically played. In making up 'our plays', Charlotte and Branwell created a stage on which they could imaginatively act out their aspirations and anxieties, scripting parts for each other and for themselves in the personae of contemporary literary figures – authors and editors, printers and publishers, ingenues and mentors, patrons and poets, readers and reviewers. Through narrative play, they both wrote and enacted a serial drama about the potentials and pitfalls, the rewards and dangers of authorship in the England of their day.

While no one would deny that the Brontës were imaginative writers, it is also true that the little books they wrote in childhood were made quite literally from what lay close at hand in their home. A scrap of wallpaper, lined music sheets, fragments of book advertisements, a used Epsom salts bag – these were the homely materials from which the future authors fashioned their first literary productions. The blue sugar bag from which nine-year-old Branwell cut the cover for his 'Battel Book' in 1827, for example, was no doubt requisitioned from the parsonage kitchen after it had been emptied and tossed aside. This reliance on household leftovers was dictated in part by a scarcity of paper, as was the diminutive size of their books. But such economy gains new significance when we consider that the contents of Branwell's first manuscript were similarly appropriated. The 'Battel Book', which recounts the battle of Washington in a charmingly inaccurate and abbreviated fashion (the text of this illustrated eight-page booklet is only thirty words long), is Branwell's childish imitation of an anonymous book reviewed in the April 1821 issue of *Blackwood's Magazine*. The Brontës had access to *Blackwood's*, as Charlotte explained in 1829, because Jonas Driver, a neighbour, lent his back issues to the family when he had finished reading them (*EEW* 1, 4). The parallels between the sugar bag and *Blackwood's* are obvious. Without discounting the originality of the young Brontës' minds, one must acknowledge that theirs was an art of appropriation: as children and even as young adults, they took material – ideas, images, names, plots, conventional forms and actual facts – from available cultural sources, and made imaginative use of it. What they assimilated from their culture and how they used it is the subject of the following discussion.

Though the Brontës are popularly associated with images of wind-swept moors and billowing heather, in fact, culture rather than nature is prominent in Charlotte and Branwell's early works. Both wrote narrative accounts of imaginary imperialistic expeditions into foreign lands, of the founding of new nations and the growth of new cultural centres. Their stories depict mighty cities, complete with palaces, government buildings, military installations, hotels, libraries, schools, museums, club rooms, salons, restaurants and taverns. Their characters are politicians, soldiers, artists, authors, antiquarian scholars, bluestockings, socialites, tutors, students, lawyers, criminals, jailors, spies, physicians, governesses and grave-robbers. But no zone of culture is represented more fully or with more complexity in their writing than that of print production and reception.

Glass Town, the principal city of their imaginary kingdom (later renamed Verreopolis, and then Verdopolis) is served by two rival printer–publisher–booksellers, Sergeants Bud and Tree (their names derive from 'their ligneous nature', according to Ratchford, *Web*, 7); both are shrewd, 'lawyer-like' characters who are not above lying in order to promote themselves or discredit each other. This rivalry is apparent in the Glass Town authors as well. Young Alexander Soult is presented as a 'celebrated poet' whose 'end will be great' though 'his beginnings are small' (*EEW* 1, 127); yet he is also satirised by both Charlotte and Branwell as a 'hare-brained' author beset by romantic notions about poetic inspiration and neglected genius (*WPBB* 1, 457). His sometime friend and patron, Arthur Wellesley, the dashing Duke of Zamorna, on the other hand, is portrayed as a respected minor poet in the romantic tradition. Arthur's younger brother, Charles, begins his literary career as a writer of delightful songs and tales, but soon develops into a social commentator and author of political satire; like other Glass Town writers, he is not above committing libel, particularly against his brother and his rival, the respected prose writer Captain Tree. Arthur Wellesley remains an aristocratic amateur, writing romantically inspired poems when not occupied in military conquest, parliamentary debate, or amorous dalliance; but Charles, having disenfranchised himself from his wealthy family, writes out of economic necessity, to pay his rent and keep a shirt on his back. In one particularly amusing scene from Charlotte's 'The Return of Zamorna' (1837), Charles writes a story in his underwear as his landlord stands over him, waiting to take the completed manuscript directly to the publisher for cash.

Glass Town abounds with political writers, including Captain Bud, father of the printer–bookseller of the same name, and the numerous politicians whose speeches and letters are published in Glass Town newspapers. During times of intense political upheaval, politicians like Branwell's Rogue, Duke of Northangerland, flood the city and surrounding countryside with cleverly written pamphlets and public notices to sway public opinion and further their causes in Parliament. Branwell makes a point of showing that Northangerland and his associates read few books but daily consume all the news and gossip from papers and journals such as the *Verdopolitan Magazine*, the *Monthly Intelligencer*, the *Northern Review*, the *Verdopolitan Intelligencer*, and 'all the tremendous et cetera' that Glass Town produces by way of periodical and ephemeral publications (*WPBB* 1, 299).

A more refined reader, Charlotte's Zamorna owns the finest and largest library in Africa but keeps only the most select books for his own personal use in his private apartments. Scholarly writers in Glass Town include historians such as John Leaf and antiquarians such as John Gifford ('Professor R.A.S.'), the latter probably based on William Gifford, the first editor of the *Quarterly Review*. Such authors appeal to serious-minded readers like Mary Henrietta Percy, a lover of poetry (especially Byron, a favourite in the Brontë household) and profoundly philosophical conversation. Livelier debates occur regularly at Lady Zenobia Ellrington's salon, where intellectuals and literati discuss classical writers whom this alarming bluestocking reads 'in the original' (*WPBB* 1, 450).

Livelier still are the discussions depicted in the 'Conversations' series in Branwell and Charlotte's *Young Men's Magazine*. Based on the popular 'Noctes Ambrosianae' series in *Blackwood's Magazine*, these dramatic scenes depict bibulous meetings of well-known (male) Glass Town literati who discuss the latest publications and current events over food and (too much) drink in 'Bravey's Inn', the Glass Town version of 'Ambrose's Tavern', the actual Edinburgh public house where the 'Noctes' dinners supposedly took place. Perhaps the most interesting depiction of an author in the juvenilia is that of Henry Hastings, a young 'unknown' who achieves celebrity early in life only to degenerate suddenly into a murderous drunkard, apparently having been corrupted by the very milieu into which his literary fame has brought him.

As this brief survey of characters reveals, authorship as presented in the early writings is an exciting but problematic career. Facility with the printed word is a means to power in Charlotte and Branwell's juvenile stories, but it does not guarantee success, for with it comes the decided possibility of professional failure, public humiliation and sometimes worse. This can be seen not only in the career of Henry Hastings, whose story unfolds in the late juvenile narratives by both Branwell and Charlotte, but also in several of their early stories. Charlotte's 'The Poetaster', written in 1830, is a good example. Supposedly written by Charles Wellesley, 'The Poetaster' is a satirical drama that makes fun of romantic poets in general and of the 'hare-brained' Glass Town poet, Alexander Soult, in particular. Since Charles Wellesley is one of Charlotte's favourite narrators and 'Young Soult' is one of Branwell's pseudonyms, the play is also Charlotte's way of mocking her younger brother's literary pretensions. The principal characters of the play are Henry

Rhymer, a fictitious character based on the 'real' poet Soult (in turn based on Branwell); Arthur Wellesley, the play's representative true poet (and one of Charlotte's heroes); his younger brother Charles; and Captain Tree, a famous Glass Town author and father of the publisher–printer–bookseller of the same name. Rhymer presents himself at the Wellesleys' palace, poems in pocket, to try to 'interest [Arthur and Charles] in [his] favour' and gain the patronage of their father, the powerful and wealthy Duke of Wellington (*EEW* I, 182). But after reading a few of Rhymer's truly awful poems, Charles and Arthur refuse to use their influence on his behalf and dismiss him with the warning to seek 'any employment, whether honest or dishonest, and think no more of blotting white paper with unmeaning hieroglyphics' (*EEW* I, 191). Having been thrown out of the Wellesleys' palace, Rhymer proceeds to the home of Captain Tree, 'to request [his] patronage and support' (*EEW* I, 192). Again, Rhymer's effort to gain an influential friend among the Glass Town literati is rebuffed, not only because his poems are so bad, but also on the grounds of class: 'What', gasps Tree, 'could induce you, a linen-draper's apprentice, to think of writing!' (*EEW* I, 192). Offstage, the exasperated Rhymer murders Tree in retaliation and is tried, convicted and sentenced to death by hanging. The final scene of the play takes place on a scaffold where, predictably, Rhymer is pardoned at the last moment on the 'condition that [he] should write no more but immediately take to some useful employment' (*EEW* I, 195). In the end, Rhymer accepts a post as Charles' secretary, 'a perfect sinecure with a salary of £200 a year' (*EEW* I, 196) – a position that, ironically, will give him the time and financial security necessary to keep writing, though he risks his life to do so.

While Rhymer discovers that authorship can be fatal, Edwin Hamilton experiences another sort of death when he attempts the pen in 'The Tragedy and the Essay', written three years later, when Charlotte was seventeen. An architect by profession, Hamilton hesitates to show his first play to any of his fellow Angrians, and when he finally works up the courage to confide in his patron, Arthur Wellesley, we can see why. 'Blushing to the temples', Hamilton announces that he has written a tragedy: 'At these words, the spirit of criticism began to sparkle in Arthur's eye and the smile of sarcasm to curl his scornful lip. Poor Hamilton actually shrunk together as he saw his noble patron gazing on him with that cool, keen, and composed aspect of contempt which he sometimes assumed in order to torture the wretches dependent on his favour' (*EEW* II, 1, 236). It turns out, however, that Arthur actually likes his protégé's drama and arranges to have it produced at the Theatre Royal, where it is well received on opening night until 'a preconcerted signal for an indiscriminate attack on the tragedy' is given by someone in the audience. Easily swayed by one loudly cracked joke, the theatre-goers begin to hiss, groan and shout their disapproval until the manager is forced to placate them by cancelling the rest of the performance. Confronting his patron with a 'corpse-like countenance', Hamilton moans, 'All hope of fame is gone and I desire to live no longer!' (*EEW* 11, 1, 239). As an experienced Verdopolitan author, Arthur takes this all in his stride. Showing Hamilton how to play the game of literary politics by encouraging the instigator of the attack on the play to 'turn author' himself, he urges Sir Frederic Lofty to write an essay on 'the art of the laundress', an entirely original theme which, he insists, will bring him 'renown of such a nature and extent as would satisfy the ambitions of most men' (*EEW* 11, 1, 241). Lofty takes Arthur's ridiculous advice seriously and duly composes the piece for publication. Not surprisingly, the publisher Tree coolly rejects the piece as 'not in [his] way': 'You have probably mistaken me for Mrs Bleachum, the washerwoman', Tree drily observes as numerous bystanders convulse in laughter at Lofty's expense. Left gaping 'more like a statue than a living man', Frederic Lofty, like Henry Rhymer and Edwin Hamilton, finds that authorship can be an 'annihilating' experience (*EEW* 11, 1, 243).

Branwell's narratives present literary life in Glass Town and Angria as no less vicious. Captain Bud's introduction to 'The Liar Detected', written in 1830 when Branwell was thirteen, is representative:

> It has always been the fortune of eminent men in all ages and every country to have their lives, their actions, and their works traduced by a set of unprincipled wretches who, having no character of their own to support and being too indolent to work, vilely employ their days in spitting their venom on every author of reputation within their reach. Homer had his Zoilus, Virgil his Meavius, and Captain Tree his Wellesley. All these were and are alike contemptible in character and influence, and, like vipers, can do no more than bite the heels of their enemies. (*WPBB* 1, 92)

Bud then proceeds to expose Charles Wellesley as a 'little reptile' whose literary reputation rests on the publication of numerous books of verse that appeal to 'ladies of fashion' and 'young misses' (a hit clearly aimed at Charlotte as well as her pseudonymous character) and on his editing a short-lived literary magazine – part of the vulgar 'tremendous etcetera' of Glass Town print ephemera. The purpose of Bud's introduction is, of course, to discredit Charles in the eyes of the reading public. Like Charles' 'enemy', Captain Tree, Bud intends to 'quash...the little Author' for good – an interesting development given that Bud is both a friend of Charles' and Captain Tree's literary rival (*WPBB* 1, 93). Such disloyalty, not to say outright treachery, is commonplace among the Glass Town literati.

The squabbling, backbiting and betrayal among Glass Town literary figures is, of course, partly a result of sibling rivalry between their creators. The subtext of the Glass Town and Angrian stories is a game of good-natured if sometimes rather earnest one-upmanship between Branwell and Charlotte, the two oldest of the four surviving Brontë children. If we think of sibling rivalry as instinctive behaviour allowing offspring to compete for a nurturing parent's attention, then the fact that Mr. Brontë was himself a minor author may help to account for Charlotte and Branwell's struggle to outdo each other in their game of mock authorship. As his children knew, Patrick Brontë had raised himself from obscurity in rural Ireland to a position of greater status in England through his facility with print: first as a serious-minded young reader who caught the eye of a patron, then, with his patron's assistance, as a student at Cambridge, and eventually as a teacher, a curate of the Church of England, and a published author. What better way to gain such a father's approval than to excel at writing? There is more than a grain of truth in this explanation, but an analysis of the Brontës' family dynamic, and its relation to Charlotte and Branwell's development as authors, must be made within the larger context of the culture in which it worked itself out. Charlotte and Branwell's depiction of literary life as intensely political, as fraught with risk as well as opportunity, derived, in part, from sibling rivalry; but that rivalry was given cultural authority and particular form by ideas about writing and authorship that they absorbed through their reading. This can be seen if we consider the representations of the author provided to them in the works to which they had access in their home.

The Brontë children read widely and attentively from the books and periodicals available to them, which included much of the usual fare for literate middle-class families of the time: the Bible and prayer books, John Bunyan's *Pilgrim's Progress*, Hannah More's *Moral Sketches*, Aesop's *Fables*, *The Arabian Nights' Entertainments*, *Gulliver's Travels*; major English writers such as Shakespeare and Milton; poetry by Wordsworth, Cowper, Scott, Byron, Moore, and others; standard educational texts including J. Goldsmith's *A Grammar of General Geography* and Rollin's *History*, the novels of Sir Walter Scott, and much more. They found the most compelling and direct representations of contemporary literary experience not in books, however, but in the two periodicals the family received: *Blackwood's*, which they began reading almost as soon as they had learned to read, and *Fraser's Magazine for Town and Country*, which they received in place of *Blackwood's* after 1831. The influence of *Blackwood's* on the Brontës' earliest writings has long been recognized, though the nature of that influence has perhaps not been adequately understood; the influence of *Fraser's* has been barely acknowledged. Recent work on the history of authorship and reading audiences suggests that we should now consider more seriously the cultural work performed by *Blackwood's* and *Fraser's* in the hands of these four brilliantly literate children, who responded so eagerly to their effects.

Periodicals like *Blackwood's* and *Fraser's* played a key role in the formation of the middle-class reading audience during the early nineteenth century. Through their letterpress, illustrations, advertisements, prefatory and back matter, such magazines textually constructed a hypothetical group of readers – an imagined community of like-minded consumers of print – with which actual readers of the periodical learned to identify through the process of reading itself. At the same time, these literary magazines strenuously engaged in the process of defining authorship within their pages: they repeatedly confronted readers with verbal and visual images of popular authors of the day; they discussed the nature of various authorial types in reviews and 'original papers'; they dramatised supposed authorial experiences in skits and 'conversations' between real and imaginary writers; and, not least of all, the producers of these magazines inscribed their own print personalities and practices within each issue published. In an important sense, then, such magazines directed a massive game of 'making-up' literary culture in the 1830s, and in that respect they were fundamentally similar to the 'plays' about literary life that the Brontë children were writing at the same time.

Each issue of *Blackwood's* and *Fraser's* invoked particular authorial personalities (for example, the 'neglected author', the 'literary lion', the well-known 'bluestocking', and her newer counterpart the 'she-author'); they assigned roles to members of the reading audience (the 'ingenuous pupil of the muse' or the 'blockhead' reader); and they dramatically rendered a world of relationships through the medium of print. Actual authors and other figures associated with these magazines were represented through personae which were sometimes pseudonymous; for example, John Wilson, the most prolific contributor to *Blackwood's* in the 1830s, appeared in the character of the periodical's fictitious editor, 'Christopher North', and William Maginn adopted several different print personae ('Ensign Morgan O'Doherty', 'the Doctor', and 'Oliver Yorke') during his tenure first at *Blackwood's* and later as editor of *Fraser's*. Sometimes the names of actual authors were appropriated for use in the performance: Coleridge, for example, appears as a member of 'The Fraserians' group though he had virtually no contact with this supposed club of tippling literati and certainly never joined in drunken meetings like those dramatised in the magazine. Though the representations of literary life purveyed in *Blackwood's* and *Fraser's* were, unquestionably, a distortion of the actual experiences of real literary professionals in early nineteenth-century England, these magazines nevertheless played a crucial role in forming public conceptions about literary life; and they did so precisely at the time when the middle-class reading audience was rapidly expanding and when the profession of authorship was opening up to many who had previously been excluded. In other words, magazines like *Blackwood's* and *Fraser's* mediated authorship and readership simultaneously, interpellating a willing audience into an ideology of print that encouraged consumers to identify themselves as both literate and literary – that is, both as readers and, at least potentially, as professional authors.

Not merely were the Brontës particularly susceptible to the influence of these periodicals, they were also precociously aware that this cultural development was taking place, as another passage from Charlotte's 'The Poetaster' reveals. Having kicked the presumptuous poet and underclass upstart Henry Rhymer out of his house, Captain Tree laments the changes that were transforming the profession of authorship at the time at which Charlotte was writing:

> Oh, how that noble profession is dishonoured! I could weep for very misery. Alas, alas, that those days would come again, when no one had even a transitory dream of putting pen to paper except a few choice spirits set apart from and revered by all the rest of the world; but it cannot be hoped for, it cannot be hoped for. And some years hence, perhaps, these eyes will see, through the mists of age, every child that walks along the streets, bearing its manuscripts in its hand, going to the printers for publication. I am unable to abide these thoughts. But I will go to my friend Cowal's house and we will both drown our manifold sorrows in a glass of wine. (*EEW* 1, 192–3)

The reference to mere children boldly coming forward as published authors is, of course, Charlotte's way of laughing at herself and her siblings for their childish literary pretensions: for being self-described 'scribblemaniacs' who assiduously composed, printed, bound and distributed their own manuscripts to the eager young readership of Haworth Parsonage. Those familiar with *Blackwood's Magazine* as it appeared in the 1820s and early 30s will also recognise that 'The Poetaster' points back to its origins, not only in Ben Jonson's play of the same name, but also in 'Maga', as *Blackwood's* was affectionately known. The play's satirical attack on a romantic literariness which it paradoxically also endorses (for example, in Tree's reference to the 'few choice spirits' who are true poets, like Arthur Wellesley) is very much like *Blackwood's* brand of criticism, a lively if inconsistent mix of late-Augustan satire and romantic sentiment about 'original genius'. More famously, the passage's closing evocation of authors as drinking companions derives from *Blackwood's* popularising of this trope in the 'Noctes Ambrosianae' series, an image of male literary camaraderie that continued to be evoked in *Fraser's* under William Maginn's editorship in the 1830s and 40s, and later in the immensely popular magazine, *Punch*. The main point of this passage from 'The Poetaster' – that, like it or not, authorship was becoming a viable occupation for an increasingly broad segment of the population in the 1830s – was a truth apparent to anyone who read the literary periodicals of the day, and Charlotte's response to that cultural shift – an ironic lament that humorously energises the very thing it supposedly regrets – closely approximates the way in which the magazines themselves reacted to this development. Officially committed to conserving public taste and saving 'the profession' from the lowering influence of a new and inferior breed of writers (supposedly inferior not merely as writers but also by virtue of class and gender), magazines like *Blackwood's* and *Fraser's* nevertheless provided employment opportunities for such would-be authors at a time when book publishers were notoriously reluctant to support writers whose names were unknown. Moreover, in spite of their stated intent to arrest the careers of mediocre authors, these magazines paradoxically tried to encourage literary ambition in their young readers, who increasingly formed an important market for literary periodicals in the nineteenth century. Written mostly in the 1830s, when the cultural influence of these magazines was at its peak, Charlotte and Branwell's juvenile stories can help us to understand better the process by which young readers were interpellated into the ideology of authorship current in this particular decade. And, more to the purpose of this volume, they can show how cultural influences combined with personal and familial circumstances to make the Brontës especially susceptible to the solicitations of that ideology.

As is well known, some of Charlotte and Branwell's earliest manuscripts are diminutive versions of *Blackwood's Magazine*, which thirteen-year-old Charlotte called 'the most able periodical there is' (*EEW* 1, 4) and which Branwell remembered, at age seventeen, as 'the chief delight' of his childhood.[7] In writing their stories, the Brontës drew on back issues of *Blackwood's* from as early as 1818, just one year after the magazine was established as a Tory rival to the *Edinburgh Review*. Directed and published by William Blackwood, an acute literary businessman, the magazine was collaboratively edited by a group of brilliantly reckless young men who served as its primary contributors during its early years, John Gibson Lockhart and William Maginn being perhaps the most daring, and offensive, of the group. *Blackwood's* quickly gained notoriety, and a huge readership, through its outrageous satirical attacks on public figures, many of them authors. On more than one occasion, people came to blows over *Blackwood's* cruelly personal, if funny, satirical attacks. In 1821, for example, John Scott, editor of a rival magazine, was actually killed by a close friend of Lockhart's in a duel that resulted from Scott's public objections to the style of *Blackwood's* reviews. Repeatedly appearing in court on charges of libel, William Blackwood usually settled such charges quietly and allowed his irresponsible but very funny writers to continue their work. As a result, the magazine sold so well that William Blackwood could congratulate himself on his success at a time when the book trade, and the economy as a whole, was in a prolonged slump.

Like many of their adult contemporaries, Charlotte and Branwell were delighted by the slashing humour and wild energy of the *Blackwood's* writers, who presented literary life as ruthlessly competitive but also immensely entertaining. We do not know if the Brontës read either the 'Chaldee Manuscript', published in *Blackwood's* in 1817, which pilloried most of the Edinburgh literary world in its allegorical account of the rivalry between Blackwood and Constable, owner of the *Edinburgh Review*; or the infamous series of class-motivated attacks 'On the Cockney School of Poetry' begun in October of the same year – though the assault on Keats continued even after his death in 1821, and it is certain that the Brontës had issues from that time. In any case, *Blackwood's* remained notorious for its attacks on literary figures at least until the beginning of the next decade, that is, during the entire time the Brontë family received the magazine. It is surely owing to the influence of *Blackwood's* that Charlotte, at age fourteen, was able to write passages such as the following, from the personal 'Advertisements' in the October 1830 issue of *The Young Men's Magazine*, which she and Branwell wrote together in imitation of *Blackwood's*:

> LORD CHARLES WELLESLEY hereby challenges that impudent braggadocio, who boasted of being able to manage forty such as the above whom he denominated 'a slender weed that ought to be rooted up'. The Advertiser was then incognito, at a small tavern, named The Flame of Fire, and he requests his insulter to meet him in the great croft behind Corporal Rare-lad's barn, thirty miles east of the Glass Town, with seconds, etc., to try a match at fisty-cuffs. LCW.
> (*EEW* I, 240)

As is generally the case with the juvenile writing, there is more than one source for the content and style of this passage: certainly Branwell's well-documented interest in boxing is one of the reasons for the little joke Charlotte is playing here. Branwell's ideas about boxing, like his understanding of authorship, were partly derived from print representations of the sport, especially in *Blackwood's* itself. 'Christopher North' (in reality, John Wilson) was depicted as an energetic pugilist, and boxing was frequently mentioned favourably in the issues the Brontës read; for example, the article on which Branwell based his 'Battel Book' refers familiarly to the 'fight betwixt Black

Sam and Chicken, lately fought at Ravelrig Toll', thereby implying that the *Blackwood's* reader would, of course, be 'in the know' about this recent match. But, as we have seen, pugilism was more than a mere topic of interest in *Blackwood's*: it was an activity in which its readers and writers both literally and metaphorically engaged. The dominant mode of its writers was an especially aggressive form of satire, a mode of authorship which assumes, as Jane Tompkins notes, 'that literary production and reception are the moral equivalents of physical combat'.[8]

We do not usually think of the Brontës as satirical writers. But their first and arguably most formative conception of literary life was drawn from a magazine which constructed its readers according to the contextual assumptions of satire: their juvenilia, like the early *Blackwood's*, addresses a known, coterie audience; is self-reflexively concerned with the members of that readership; and has the aim of 'hitting' well-known targets (public figures in general and, in particular, other authors, critics, editors, reviewers, and so on). Thus, in the advertising section of her magazine, Charlotte constructs a model of literary experience that mirrors the literal and metaphorical representations of authorship in *Blackwood's*. The magazine served not merely as a generic model for Charlotte and Branwell's writing; more importantly, it provided a model of authorship and reading that was compatible with their actual situation. As an analogue for the sibling rivalry which helped to fuel Charlotte and Branwell's joint efforts, *Blackwood's* satiric model of literary production and reception met the personal needs of these two competitive young writers: it validated their rivalry by giving it expression and cultural authority at the same time that it displaced their competition from the problematic context of family to the safer arena of public life and professional experience.

Shortly before the Brontës stopped receiving *Blackwood's* in 1831, William Maginn left Edinburgh to establish a new, and similarly popular, magazine based on the *Blackwood's* model: *Fraser's Magazine for Town and Country*. Charlotte and Branwell's aunt, Elizabeth Branwell, who had lived with the family since Mrs. Brontë's death, began subscribing to *Fraser's* in 1832. In this way, the Brontës continued to be exposed to the kinds of ideas about authorship with which they had already grown familiar from reading and imitating *Blackwood's*. But the issues of *Fraser's* that they read in the 1830s added a new feature to the representation of authorship, one that was to be of increasing importance as Charlotte and Branwell grew older. Although, like *Blackwood's*, *Fraser's* was known for its harsh satirical assaults on popular contemporary authors, it also often turned away from such targets to invoke a more sympathetically rendered view of the author in the persona of the talented young writer, who was often addressed as part of the magazine's reading audience. This author-cum-reader was encouraged to persevere in the effort to become a successful writer but at the same time cautioned against the difficulties of 'coming forward' properly as a public figure. Ambitious young writers were repeatedly warned against the fatal error of 'authorial vanity' and, through savagely satirical commentary on authors such as Byron, Bulwer Lytton and Robert Montgomery, they were shown the negative consequences of overly aggressive careerism. At the same time, however, they were also frequently reminded of immensely talented writers who had failed to secure the fame and fortune they deserved because they were too reticent or too naive about the ways in which literary business is conducted and authors' careers are managed. What every young author needed, *Fraser's* announced, was 'a kind, compassioning adviser... [to instruct] these inexperienced mariners how to trim their vessels, avoiding all the shoals and quicksands of a siren-thronged world; how to repair into the tranquil haven, how to produce their freight, and deal in an advantageous traffic with the inhabitants on shore, thereby gaining uncountable riches!' (March 1830, 226).

Repeatedly, *Fraser's* offered its services in just this capacity. For example, in one issue, Oliver Yorke, the magazine's fictitious editor, announced his intent 'to take [Letitia Landon] under our special protection' in order to save her career from mismanagement by another editor and to bring her work to the notice of influential critics. Landon will profit from the support and advice of his wise counsel, Yorke confidently asserts, and so attain 'a yet loftier and firmer station among the living authors of England' (December 1832, 656). (Actually, Landon was an established author by this time, and not much younger than Maginn, but her public persona as the sweet, romantic 'L.E.L.' made it easy for him to represent her as a literary ingénue and thereby reinforce the cultural construct of the naive but gifted writer in need of protection.) Landon is the most famous of the young authors that *Fraser's* adopted in this fashion, many of the others being true 'unknowns' with whom Charlotte and Branwell might identify. In representing the novice author as dependent on an older and wiser counsellor for protection and guidance, *Fraser's* constructed a professional relationship that, by analogy, validated Charlotte and Branwell's early dependence on their father's support and approval. The magazine thus allowed them to transfer personal insecurities from their originating context in family life and individual psychic experience to a public context of cultural discourse about professional careers. It allowed them to translate childhood anxieties into adult terms and to express them in fictional narratives about professional success and failure. This transformation can be seen in the plotting and re-plotting of some of their early stories.

In the very early juvenilia, both by Charlotte and by Branwell one particular plot is repeated numerous times. A child or children are abandoned or become lost; they enter a dark, subterranean place; emerge in a relatively lighted area where they are threatened by actual or anticipated danger; and are eventually rescued by their father or by a father figure. The repetition of this plot obviously expresses the ontological insecurity which all children experience to some degree, and which the Brontës, because of the early deaths of their mother and two older sisters, are likely to have felt more acutely than most. It also clearly emphasises their reliance on their father to supply the security and guidance of which they had been deprived. Well into their adult years, they continued to retell this story; but gradually they changed the terms in which the basic plot was worked out. The lost child became an ambitious young adult, the journey underground was turned into departure from the homeland (usually England, though sometimes a British colony such as India) and voyage to an exotic land of opportunity (Africa) where 'rising talent' was quickly recognised and encouraged by powerful patrons. The history of Robert Pelham, given in summary form by Branwell is representative:

> 'Sir Robert Weever Pelham was by birth an Englishman . . . On his [father's] death . . . Sir Robert . . . finding himself unfettered and aware of his own great ability and knowledge, looked about for some place, some method by which to signalize himself, exert his ambition and employ his mind, but alas, England affords no field for such. He saw that and determined to embark for the widely celebrated and magnificent regions of Africa where he felt that his talent would find its way. (*WPBB* 1, 348)

Almost as soon as he arrives in the city of Verdopolis, Pelham meets the influential Lord Ellrington, who sees 'in a moment his vast ability', takes him immediately under his protection and puts him on 'the road to power'. Pelham becomes a politician rather than an author, and the other young protagonists in these stories pursue a variety of careers. All of them, however, involve leaving home and 'coming forward' as a public figure under the protection of a powerful friend or patron in a cultural milieu that allows the individual to 'unfold [his] character' to full advantage (*WPBB* 11, 26). This is of course a young person's fantasy, but it also is precisely the *bildung* that *Fraser's* mapped out for aspiring young authors; and a romantically exaggerated version of the story of Mr Brontë's own rise from obscurity. Moreover, it is an adaptation of the myth of empire by which Britain was constructing its national identity during the Brontës' lives. Charlotte and Branwell's narrative of development and identity formation was taken quite directly from both private and public sources: from their father, who provided a form of male nurturing through his example of social and professional advancement; from print sources which reinforced that example through depictions of authorial experience that were compatible with the lesson his example taught; and from the expansionist project by which their country itself was constructing and imposing its national identity throughout the world. In this way, *Blackwood's* and *Fraser's* made it possible for Charlotte and Branwell to appropriate the myths and representations of their culture and to put them to use as they began to construct their future adult identities as literary professionals.

NOTES

1. Fannie Elizabeth Ratchford, *The Brontës' Web of Childhood* (New York: Columbia University Press, 1941), xiv.
2. Quoted in Ratchford, *The Brontës' Web of Childhood*, 108.
3. J. A. V. Chapple and Arthur Pollard, eds., *The Letters of Mrs Gaskell* (Manchester University Press, 1997), 398.
4. Clement Shorter, *Charlotte Brontë and Her Circle* (London: Hodder and Stoughton, 1896), 25.
5. Tom Winnifrith, *The Brontës and Their Background* (New York: Barnes & Noble, 1973), 7–27.
6. Christine Alexander, *A Bibliography of the Manuscripts of Charlotte Brontë* (Keighley: The Brontë Society, 1982); *EEW*; Victor A. Neufeldt, *A Bibliography of the Manuscripts of Patrick Branwell Brontë* (New York: Garland Publishing Inc., 1993); and Victor A. Neufeldt, ed., *The Works of Patrick Branwell Brontë*. 3 vols. to date (New York: Garland Publishing Inc., 1997–1999). Hereafter cited within the text as *WPBB*.
7. Quoted in Margaret Oliphant, *Annals of a Publishing House: William Blackwood and His Sons, Their Magazine and Friends*. 2 vols. (Edinburgh: W. Blackwood & Sons, 1897), II, 187.
8. Jane P. Tompkins, 'The Reader in History', *Reader-Response Criticism From Formalism to Post-Structuralism* (Baltimore: Johns Hopkins University Press, 1980), 212.

3

ANGELA LEIGHTON

The poetry

And I must now conclude this Introduction already too long with saying, that what is contained in this History is a statement of what Myself, Charlotte, Emily and Anne really pretended did happen among the 'Young Men' (that being the name we gave them) during the period of nearly 6 years. (SHCBM I, 63)

Thus the thirteen-year-old Branwell recorded, with an acute sense of historical momentousness, his acquisition of various sets of toy soldiers, the 'Young Men', who were destined to have such an adventurous afterlife in the Brontë children's writings. The first set was given to him in 1824, the year in which four of his sisters, Maria, Elizabeth, Charlotte and Emily, left home for school. If the soldiers were meant to keep him company in the absence of all except the four-year-old Anne,[1] the acquisition of three more sets in the following two years may have retained a connection with more traumatic losses: the deaths, in 1825, of his older sisters, Maria and Elizabeth. When, in 1826, Charlotte, Emily and Anne pounced with delight on a new set of soldiers and each chose for herself the one who would become the projection and object of her special 'genius', the children had lost not only their mother, Maria Branwell, in 1821, but also these two sisters. The history of what the survivors 'really pretended did happen' to those toy soldiers carries the intensity of a story won, in part, from the harsh facts of childhood bereavement. Both a writing network and an imaginative safety net, the sagas of Angria and Gondal were the product of a collaborative sibling creativity which also included, like a ghostly memory, the ones who were dead. The poetry of the four Brontë children took root in those narratives.

At the age of twenty, and in her first year of teaching away from home, Charlotte recalled with nostalgia the power of those fantasies. So real did they still seem that one of them turned up, large as life, in her schoolroom. The Duke of Zamorna, her Byronic, demonic adulterer and cynic, appeared before her one day, 'leaning against that obelisk, with the mute marble Victory above him, the fern waving at his feet' (*CBP*, 190). The memory of that apparition inspired the long poem beginning 'We wove a web in childhood' (*CBP*, 184–90). The speaker starts by wondering if childhood's fancies are dead: 'Are they blighted, failed and faded, / Are they mouldering back to clay?' (lines 9–10). But far from being swallowed up in the earth, those fancies revive. Imagining the past and the 'old familiar faces' (line 62), she finds that the 'bright darling dream' (73) can still call her 'home' to them (line 78). To prove the fact, the poem launches into an exotic tale, like the ones Charlotte and Branwell invented for their shared fantasy-land of Angria. A 'master' in a grand hall embraces his child the night before a battle. The poem then cuts to a graveyard where memorial tombstones mark the plain:

> That waste had been a battle-plain,
> Head-stones were reared in the waving fern.
> There they had buried the gallant slain
> That dust to its own dust might return,
> And one black marble monument
> Rose where the heather was rank and deep,
> Its base was hid with the bracken and bent,
> Its sides were bare to the night-wind's sweep.
>
> A Victory carved in polished stone,
> Her trumpet to her cold lips held . . .
> (lines 165–74)

This is the landscape of Zamorna's 'live' apparition. The same fern, moonlight and funerary monuments, the same mute Victory, appear in both. What arrested Charlotte in the schoolroom was the sight of Zamorna leaning against a tomb, as if acknowledging his dusty provenance. The 'bright darling dream' of the poem similarly rounds back to the graveyard's 'clay' – a short circuit of association which runs through all the Brontës' work. 'We wove a web in childhood' thus searches for the homeground of dreams and finds it, characteristically, not far from 'head-stones'.

In 1826 it was Branwell, the owner of the toy soldiers, who assumed leadership of the writing inspired by them. Twenty years later, however, it was Charlotte who set about finding a publisher for a collection of poems by herself and her sisters. She later recalled how she came upon Emily's poems accidentally and, being struck by their difference from 'the poetry women generally write' (*WH*, 361), conceived the idea of a joint volume. *Poems by Currer, Ellis and Acton Bell* was published in 1846. The omission of

Branwell – who had in the preceding year been ignominiously dismissed from his post as a tutor because of an affair with his employer's wife – suggests the extent to which he had become morally and imaginatively excluded from the group.[2] Thus *Poems*, by default, became a collection of women's poems – a fact which, in spite of the pseudonyms, is quietly flagged by the prominent first place of Charlotte's monologue, 'Pilate's Wife's Dream'. In commercial terms, the venture was a failure. After a year, and in spite of some sympathetic reviews, only two copies had been sold, and Charlotte disposed of a few more to prominent authors, including Wordsworth, De Quincey and Tennyson. The failure of *Poems* meant that the sisters turned their attention to more marketable prose.

Yet the Brontës' poetry is in no sense either just a trial-run for novels or an accidental by-product of Angria and Gondal, though it retains links with both of those. Its formal clarity and simplicity were won, paradoxically, from the murky sensation sagas of adultery, politics and murder inspired by the beloved toy soldiers. Though much of the poetry was written in the context of those sagas, it was then altered for publication. Proper names and initials were excised, titles changed and lyrical passages taken out of context. This inevitably raises a problem of interpretation. To try to return the poems to their original context – a reconstructed context in the case of Gondal – is to hear in them the characters and events of a larger drama. To take them out of that context, as the sisters themselves did for publication, is to turn them into universal lyrics, subtly bound to the author-person of the poet. The difference, as Barbara Hardy has pointed out, affects the status of 'metaphor'.[3] Read as a dramatic event, death is specific, closed and conclusive. Read as an elegiac condition, it is open, unfinished and uncanny. Emily's famous poem 'Cold in the earth – and the deep snow piled above thee!' points up the difference. It was originally a lament spoken by Rosina Alcona to one of her many lovers, Julius Brenzaida, now long dead. The Gondal context of Rosina's faithlessness, cruelty and Byronic appetite for power gives an extra dimension to the poem's ironies. Far from being a monotone of grief for a dead lover, this is a very twisted elegy. Rosina's forgetting and remembering is the self-dramatising struggle of one who has hardly given up life to mourn the dead. At the same time, to locate the poem in Gondal and ignore Emily's published title, 'Remembrance', is to lose a sense of the poem's elegiac anonymity, its carelessness of character and motive, its technical virtuosity. Without names and their histories, the perspectives of being in or out of the grave, dead or alive, become ambiguously interchangeable. Emily's decision to shed references to Gondal in her published work is a decision to give the poem free standing-room; to let the play of literal and metaphorical

'THE NORTH WIND', drawing by Emily Brontë

Figure 3 Watercolour known as 'The North Wind', by Emily Brontë. Copied from William Finden's engraving of Richard Westall's 'Ianthe', published as the frontispiece to Thomas Morre's *Life of Byron* (London: John Murray, 1839).

meanings remain unfinished. In the best of her work, death thus ceases to be a narrative fact and becomes a poetic figure. In particular, it becomes a figure for writing itself: a monument to the 'darling' dreams – those shared sibling inventions – which might still be summoned, live and entrancing, from the past. It becomes, to put it simply, less a theme than a form.

The two major influences on all the Brontës' poetry were Byron and Wordsworth. Their love of Byron was fuelled by the general 'Byroniana'[4] of the age, and particularly of the annuals – those fashionable gift-book anthologies of stories, poems and engravings, of which we know the Brontës owned at least three.[5] The annuals promoted a highly gendered, story-bound, death-bound poetry, rich in Byronic betrayal and reproach. 'Remember me – Oh! pass not thou my grave / Without one thought whose relics there recline',[6] calls the hapless Medora in Byron's *The Corsair*. Being remembered is the one compensation for being, otherwise, as good as dead to him. Byron gave the Brontës a *dramatis personae* of roving men and dying women which Charlotte and Branwell reproduce with relish. In Angria women die and men, sometimes, remember them. The influence of Wordsworth, however, particularly the Wordsworth of the Lucy poems, is less focused on sexual conflict and more on an exchange between poet and nature. If Lucy is 'in her grave',[7] the earth at least is full of her. Something is thus recovered by the poet, as the dead pass productively into nature's beauty. This Wordsworthian exchange, which is rich in imaginative compensations, runs through the poetry of Emily and Anne. To be 'in the earth' is in a sense to be in poetic, as well as literal, homeground.

There is one way, however, in which the Brontës differ from their Romantic predecessors: their stories draw on an imagery of the grave which is also, communally, touched by real life. Their elegies, whether Byronic or Wordsworthian, home in on a specific place:

> Speak, O speak, and say to me
> I am not come too late to thee!
> Oh tell me that my arm can save
> Thy spirit from the hideous grave!
> Maria! O my only love
> Tell me thou wilt not die…
>
> (*PBBP*, 12–33, lines 335–40)

Branwell's long poem, 'Misery', tells the story of a horseman racing through the night to reach his dying wife. True to innumerable models, in the annuals and in the Brontës' own sagas, Maria dies. Over her dead body the poem runs its course of exclamations. The name, however, is resonant. The sister spirit from the grave who cannot be rescued ensures that the poem goes circling, against its own narrative impulse, around the same obsession. The sensation story of 'Misery', which should drive it forward, is thwarted by the counter-gravity of elegy. The Byronic specifics of characterisation and context: a castle, a horseman, a night journey, a dying lady, are halted by a more general memory that already calls from beyond 'the hideous grave'. It is that movement downwards, out of narrative and into the productive metaphors of earth, which will mark the best of the Brontës' poetry.

One of Charlotte's earliest prose fragments, interestingly, starts with a poignant memory of her sister:

> Once papa lent my Sister Maria A Book it was an old Geography [?one] and she wrote on its Blank leaf papa lent me this Book. the Book is an hundred and twenty years old it is at this moment lying Before me while I write this I am in the kitchin of the parsonage house Haworth.[8]

It is curious to note how the twelve-year-old Charlotte orientates her own place in the world in relation to a sister and a book. The act of writing 'this' becomes a carefully calculated historical event in relation to the puzzling timescale of 'an hundred and twenty years' and the look of a dead sister's writing. The present, being in 'the kitchin', is assessed against that historical backdrop of time and loss. It also takes the form of a copying of the past. Twice a book is 'lent' by 'papa' and twice something is written. Charlotte self-consciously repeats the actions of her sister, and writes, if not in, at least in the consciousness of, a book.

Stevie Davies has persuasively argued how much 'the art of memory'[9] shapes the Brontës' sense of narrative. In their poetry, remembering may sometimes be an easy sentimental formula which, as in the poetry of Hemans and L.E.L., is mainly a bid for emotional attention. Charlotte and Branwell, who once battled over the death of another Mary, the wife of Zamorna,[10] enjoy the appeal of dying women. 'O say that when I'm cold and dead / Thou wilt Remember Me!' cries another of Branwell's innumerable Marys (*PBBP*, 239, lines 15–16). Charlotte's betrayed speaker in 'Stanzas' (*CBP*, 59–61) asks: 'One moment – think of me!' (line 8). Many of Charlotte's longer poems turn on unremembered, unrewarded female faithfulness. 'The Wife's Will', 'Frances' and 'The Letter' all feature long-suffering women whose note of reproach or longing rarely changes. 'I to him will still be true!' ('Preference', *CBP*, 56–8, line 72) is the Hemansesque refrain which runs through Charlotte's verse, tying its imagination to a popular moral agenda.

However, the curiously hybrid poem, 'Mementos' (*CBP*, 8–15), hints at another trend. Although it too turns into a story like those of the annuals, in which a faithful wife dies and a villainous husband, in a roundabout way, kills himself ('Death's axe...lopped his desperate days', (lines 243–4)), the relaxed and urbane tone of the opening promises a different kind of poem:

> Arranging long-locked drawers and shelves
> Of cabinets, shut up for years,
> What a strange task we've set ourselves!
>
> (lines 1–3)

This suggests a scene of cheerful domesticity, as if Charlotte were writing a poem about housework. She lists the oddments found in those cabinets: books, portraits, jewels, shells. Such 'Keepsakes', a word resonant of the annuals, have in fact not been in anyone's keeping for years. It is as if they come drained of emotional resonance. 'Keepsakes' and 'mementos' have forgotten what they were meant to keep or commemorate. They merely witness to the dust and mould of locked-up closets:

> I scarcely think, for ten long years,
> A hand has touched these relics old;
> And coating each, slow-formed, appears,
> The growth of green and antique mould.
>
> (lines 17–20)

These drawers and shelves are graves full of 'relics'. Echoing Tennyson's 'Mariana', the whole house seems to turn into a mouldering closet of its own: 'All in this house is mossing over' (line 21). Charlotte seems to have forgotten the companionable 'we' of the opening, as the poem becomes a receptacle of what is dead and past, 'ten long years'. A few stanzas later the timescale is extended: 'I fear to see the very faces, / Familiar thirty years ago' (lines 41–2). The idea of the past, measured in exact dates, is then connected with a specific figure: 'Too much the buried form resembling, / Of her who once was mistress here' (lines 49–50). Among the other relics is this 'buried form'. As in 'We wove a web in childhood', the familiarity of home and its companionably shared dreams opens into a graveyard. Some deep-set logic drives the poem back through the present, through the homeliness of 'Arranging long-locked drawers', to a past which has long locked its own treasured secret. The 'buried form' is the real object of this casual-sounding search among forgotten mementos. What the poem remembers, at the centre of all its chambers, cells, closets and caskets, at the centre of the house itself, is a 'buried form'. At this point, however, the eerie form becomes a character in a story. The ironic distance collapses, the casual tone disappears, and we are swept into another sensation saga of faithfulness, betrayal and death.

'Mementos' is interesting, however, not only for its strain of ironic realism, which Charlotte will later employ as a novelist, but also for the way in which it presents the poem itself as a memento. Its imagery of boxes closes in on the hidden object, locking it from sight, and even from memory. This dusty bric-a-brac may have no significance at all. Nonetheless, it is noticeable that memory, home and poem are all figured in terms of enclosure, of spaces which might contain something. The idea of a 'buried form' at the heart of the poem, of a forgotten content, is one which recurs with the force of an obsession in the more quietly elegiac work of Anne and Emily.

Gondal inspired a number of narrative poems by Anne, but she is uneasy with the high tragic tone. 'Alexander and Zenobia' (*ABP*, 52–9) keeps up its mournful longings and the usual call to 'think of me' (line 64) until the very last line when, quite unexpectedly and almost impatiently, it opts for a happy ending: 'And they are met at last!' (line 274). Anne's real gifts lie with the hymn, which retains the lovely simplicity of the lyric but invokes the saving presence of a 'Thou' who turns mourning and misery into comfort (see 'A Hymn', 91–2; 'A Prayer', 105; 'Confidence', 114). Her poems often answer Emily's more tormented visions with a plea for faith and cheerfulness. 'The Three Guides', for instance, which insists on the supremacy of Faith over Wisdom and Pride, responds to Emily's 'The Philosopher', where the internal struggle of three streams, golden, bloody and sapphire, is the churning mix which characterises the self's 'inky sea' (*PEB*, 7–8; *ABP*, 37). The poem entitled 'Memory' is a gentle, Wordsworthian evocation of memory's sweetening effects on nature, particularly on 'the slight bluebell, / My childhood's darling flower' (lines 26–7). But if Anne's work is marked by cheerfulness and faith, however hard-won, she too is roused by calls from the grave. 'Then awake! Maria, wake!' cries the speaker in 'The Student's Serenade' (line 29). In 'Severed and gone, so many years' (*ABP*, 141–3), the dead are invoked, not in fact but in memory: 'And, while I cannot quite forget, / Thou, darling, canst not quite depart' (lines 55–6). Memory holds the dead like a last container, before nature diffuses their spirit anywhere. Anne, too, seeks her darlings in the past, as presences which the poem tries to save from oblivion. But unlike Wordsworth, whose influence otherwise pervades the poem, she cannot 'quite forget' her 'darling' for all the beauties of nature.

The reason becomes clear in a poem which echoes a number of Emily's: 'Night' (*ABP*, 110). Here Anne invokes the 'blissful dreams' of night (line 2), not for themselves, but for the sake of the voice they might release:

> And then a voice may meet my ear
> That death has silenced long ago;
> And hope and rapture may appear
> Instead of solitude and woe.
>
> Cold in the grave for years has lain
> The form it was my bliss to see,
> And only dreams can bring again
> The darling of my heart to me.
>
> (lines 5–12)

Like all her siblings, the inspiration Anne seeks takes her back in time, 'long ago', to hear a 'voice' from the grave. This, however, is a curious elegy because, like many of Emily's, it is rapturous rather than mournful. It marks, not the end, but the potential beginning of a love story. 'The darling of my heart' might still be drawn out of the past, the grave and the night to cheer the 'solitude and woe' of the living speaker. It is just such a hope which drives Heathcliff to call wildly out of the closet window: 'Oh, my heart's darling! hear me *this* time' (*WH*, 27). That whole story starts with the return of the dead after 'twenty years' (*WH*, 24) of ghostliness – the measure of time, as David Daiches points out, between the year of writing and the death of Maria in 1826.[11]

The emotional logic of desire is measured by the Brontës, often with narrative precision, in terms of the past: 'fifteen wild Decembers', 'ten long years', 'an hundred and twenty years'. Their elegies are specific, not general, and their memories of the past carry, beside the 'blissful dreams' of childhood, the real and local memory of a grave. The ghosts and forms which emerge from that grave do not therefore readily transmute into Romantic muses or nature spirits. They are awkward Lucys, not easily exchanged for a tranquil nature poetry. When it came to dead sisters, the Brontës, unlike Wordsworth, felt the tug of fact in what they 'really pretended'.

Anne's use of the word 'form' signals this trouble. In 'Severed and gone', for instance, she writes: 'I know that in the narrow tomb / The form I loved was buried deep' (lines 5–6). Like Charlotte's 'buried form' in 'Mementos', Anne's forms for the dead express both the shadowy outlines of a memory and the fact of a bodily presence. The word equivocates between emptiness and fullness, death and life, present and past. It also equivocates between being in and out of the grave. 'Cold in the grave for years has lain / The form it was my bliss to see' audibly pivots two things on the word 'form': the cold dead and the blissful living, the present and the past, the unseen and the seen. The 'heart's darling', whether dream, ghost or writing in a book, is met as just such an equivocation between here and there, now and then, life and death. Such a form will not settle in nature and the grave. It stirs in the earth, and in the poem's earthbound memory.

Esther Schor has argued that the tradition of elegy undergoes a subtle change between high Romanticism and the mid-Victorians. Instead of preserving the difference between living and dead and drawing a salutary moral from that difference, the Victorians 'lay emphasis on all manner of interpenetration'[12] between them. The grave walls are down, and the Victorian ghost story emerges from the ruins. In Victorian poetry such 'interpenetration' rarely takes the form of active ghosts. Instead, it affects perspectives. Emily Brontë is one of the first to take the elegy in this new direction. Her poetry rejects both enlightenment consolatory moralising on the one hand and sensationalist Gothic on the other. Her elegies offer no wisdom about death and no macabre thrills. Yet they are obsessed with the grave and with penetrating the earth's cover. For her, the Wordsworthian sense of earth as an inspiriting presence is deepened and troubled by presences *in* the earth. Those cannot quite be forgotten. Like Anne's, Emily's longing for the 'buried form' not only takes her across the divide of life and death, but also affects the form of the poetry in which she does so. Her limpidly memorable elegies, taken out of the context of Gondal, close in on themselves, replacing the narrative event of death with a sense of its cold, formal conditions. Unlike Anne's, these elegies also have a rootless, impersonal quality, as if, in spite of the personal pronouns, they retained a strange inner distance:

> Cold in the earth – and the deep snow piled above thee,
> Far, far, removed, cold in the dreary grave!
> Have I forgot, my only Love, to love thee,
> Severed at last by Time's all-severing wave?
>
> (*EBP*, 8–9, lines 1–4)

The first lines of 'Remembrance' insist on memory, even while admitting forgetfulness. The repetitions, of cold, far, love and sever, convey a haunting not of ghosts, but of language. The more Emily repeats words which should seal the grave and sever its ties, the more does language seem to penetrate to the thing it has lost. 'Cold in the earth – and the deep snow piled above thee', for instance, doubles not only the fact but also the sensation of cold. The line gets colder. It probes the buried source of coldness, making cold *felt*. By piling on snow as well, the poet tranforms the sensation of cold, as Robin Grove points out, into a literal 'weight',[13] as if to force or hold something down. Snow buries the dead doubly 'deep', as if earth itself were not deep enough: 'they may bury me twelve feet deep, and throw the church down over me, but I won't rest', Cathy declares in *Wuthering Heights* (*WH*, 126). 'Remembrance' is troubled by a similar restlessness. However cold, deep and far the object, the words dig down to it. The poem's 'thee' is all the more intensely present for being in that very Brontëan memory-hold: 'Cold in the earth'.

Far from being a poem of 'Remembrance', then, in the Victorian tradition of proven emotional faithfulness, Emily's poem ironically admits that the passing of 'fifteen wild Decembers' is a good reason to forget – particularly if the wildness is not only nature's but also the speaker's: 'Sweet Love of youth, forgive, if I forget thee' (line 13). Forgetting, however, does not square either with this loving address or with the poem's circling fascination with its object:

> All my life's bliss from thy dear life was given,
> All my life's bliss is in the grave with thee.
>
> (lines 19–20)

C. Day Lewis has called the rhythm of 'Remembrance' 'the slowest...
in English poetry'.[14] However, Emily's characteristically alternating feminine and masculine rhymes also suggest movement thwarted. The feminine
rhyme gets out, especially in the tri-syllabic 'Decembers'/'remembers', 'forget
thee'/'beset thee', while the masculine, monosyllabic rhyme reins in. That
movement in and out sets up the verse form itself as a box, which contains
but also releases its rhythm. The stress between them matches the poem's
struggle of perspective in and out of that grave. 'All my life's bliss', for instance, is a phrase which twins with its double, 'thy dear life', like a Shelleyan
epipsyche, till 'life' becomes a figure which swings freely between dead and
living, thee and me, above and below ground. 'They who have been our
life – our soul / Through summer-youth, from childhood's spring', Emily recalls elsewhere (*EBP*, 103–4, lines 21–2). Whatever its biographical origins,
'Remembrance' confuses desire for life with desire for death. The grave, for
all its coldness and depth, is a mere formality of difference between them,
which the imagery, like the rhyme scheme, keeps crossing.

The tension between remembering and forgetting is then suddenly resolved
in the last line:

> And, even yet, I dare not let it languish,
> Dare not indulge in memory's rapturous pain;
> Once drinking deep of that divinest anguish,
> How could I seek the empty world again?
>
> (lines 29–32)

This is a new kind of memory. Far from being the sign of faithful and chaste
mourning, it is the sign of such 'bliss' indeed, such 'rapturous pain', that it
would become a consuming passion – rather like the poem's. That last line
silently throws into relief the poem's consistent corollary: that the grave is
full, and full of bliss and rapture – words also used by Anne to describe
the dream of meeting the 'darling of [her] heart'. Emily's poem ends up
confirming that what lies 'Cold in the earth' so completely fills memory,
grave and poem that there is nothing else outside it in the 'world'. Her elegy
sheds all that context in order to turn in on its own, enclosed place.

Thus, like her siblings, Emily draws on childhood's web of associations
between the past, the grave and the dead from which to win her lyric voice.
But she goes further than they in emptying her poems of narrative props.
As Elfenbein points out, memory in her work is 'eerily without content'.[15]
Her poetry seems to have cut loose from story, character, event, and all their
motivating emotions. Summarising the strengths of Emily's poetry, Charlotte
once described it as 'condensed and terse, vigorous and genuine' (*WH*, 361).
Often she uses the word 'abstract', as if to explain the way in which the poems

seem to have been abstracted from context or intention. All that remains is what she calls, quoting a negative review of Emily's work, the '*labor limae*' (*CBL* 11, 140), the work of the file, the polishing of the hard matter of form itself. Monumentally sparing, these are poems which 'empty' themselves of all merely extraneous distractions of plot or context. Their object lies within, not outside, themselves.

This empty quality also has something to do with Emily's peculiar use of personae. Her poems are both prolific in pronouns and oddly impersonal. The more presences she invokes, the less present in any human sense do they seem. 'The linnet in the rocky dells' (*EBP*, 11–12), entitled 'Song' for publication, strongly recalls Wordsworth's 'Three years she grew'. It suggests a scene of tranquil nature feeding almost literally – 'The wild deer browse above her breast' (line 5) – on the buried dead. But where Wordsworth keeps Lucy's whereabouts unspecific, sensing only the general spirit of death in nature, Emily's imagination homes in on the usual place:

> I ween, that when the grave's dark wall
> Did first her form retain;
> They thought their hearts could ne'er recall
> The light of joy again. (lines 9–12)

The word 'retain' beautifully differs from the expected 'contain'. It allows for the possibility that 'her form' could still go, with a will, unless restrained. The hint of force, of being detained, is gentled however by the artistocratic politeness of 'retain'. 'Did first her form retain' also carries the suggestion of an imprint, as if the grave were a memory-box stamped with an unforgettable figure. That meaning is briefly underlined by the next rhyming word 'recall'. Like Anne's and Charlotte's ambiguous forms, this one is both a body and a figure, a literal thing and an outline of that thing, retained, like writing, on the 'wall'. The 'form' in the grave thus moves between person and memory, object and cipher, suggesting, as a result, something that might still meet or resist the pressure of 'retain'.

That suggestion is heard again in the last stanza:

> And, if their eyes should watch and weep
> Till sorrow's source were dry,
> She would not, in her tranquil sleep,
> Return a single sigh!
>
> Blow, west-wind, by the lonely mound,
> And murmur, summer-streams –
> There is no need of other sound
> To soothe my lady's dreams.
>
> (lines 21–8)

That there is 'no need' implies that the dream is soothed by the Wordsworthian sounds of wind and streams. But the fact remains that only something unsoothed needs soothing. The last line contains a catch. The 'lady's dreams' turn out to be, not a consolatory euphemism but a quietly dramatic disturbance. Those ongoing 'dreams' carry into the quiet beyond the end of the line the idea of something in need of soothing – the idea of a still unquiet sleeper.

This poem strikingly refuses either emotional or narrative explanation. Without Gondal to specify who is dead and who speaks, the poem's pronouns, 'I', 'she', 'they', remain anonymous. Although the speaker refers to 'my lady', it is unclear whether she was, or is, his, or hers. But mourners are 'they' – the ones, elsewhere, who grieve and then forget. The speaker, by contrast, is cool and careless, like the wind and streams of nature which are in full possession of both the form and dreams of 'my lady'. Although this closely recalls Wordsworth's poem, there is one crucial difference. Where Wordsworth sets nature's voice against the narrator's, effectively creating a love triangle, Emily sees no competition. 'There is no need of other sound', the speaker asserts, thus dehumanising the story of desire and leaving only the tiny trouble of 'dreams' at the end.

It was the poet Mary Robinson who remarked, in her early biography of Emily (1883), that her poetry has 'no personal note'.[16] Ghosts, siblings, lovers, dreams, pass through names and situations without being rooted by those names or situations. It is of no importance why, in 'Song' for instance, the lady died or the speaker speaks of her. The possessive 'my' does not identify a relationship, an emotion or even, necessarily, a person. Only the formula remains, of the dead in their grave, and the living who speak about them. The love story between those two things drives Emily's imagination across the divide which should keep them apart: the earth itself. Her short fragment, 'When days of Beauty' (*EBP*, 84), suggestively accounts for this condensation of purpose. Of the poetic spirit, she writes:

> It seeks the consecrated spot
> Beloved in childhood's years
> The space between is all forgot
> Its sufferings and its tears.
>
> (lines 5–8)

That 'spot', in spite of its Wordsworthian overtones of childhood bliss, is really the grave. Emily's imagination returns to it, as to a place simplified of the noisy 'sufferings' and 'tears' of human life, those things which lie 'between', like an obstacle separating lovers. Her poetry's loose fit of pronouns, its emotional anonymity and 'abstract' aloofness result in an elegiac voice which almost has nothing to mourn. Instead, it hones its attention on that small literal and literary plot: 'in the earth'. Beside that 'spot,' and its haunting, elusive content, the narratives of life are nothing but empty 'space'.

'To A.S. 1830' (*EBP*, 146), a Gondal poem never revised for publication, shows the same arrangement of protagonists: a dead woman, a cool speaker and a distraught mourner:

> From morning's faintest dawning
> Till evening's deepest shade
> Thou wilt not cease thy mourning
> To know where she is laid;
>
> But if to weep above her grave
> Be such a priceless boon
> Go, shed thy tears in Ocean's wave
> And they will reach it soon.
>
> (lines 17–24)

These human presences are, however, characteristically supplemented by nature, with its waves and rains. Since the whole earth is a recycling of tears, the grave will be found by them eventually. Such large-scale mourning has lost all human reference. A metaphysical pun of tears and rain ensures, instead, that grief will penetrate the grave in a natural, if inhuman, contact between living and dead. The embedded love story, of the one who mourns 'To know', is thus dispersed into various forces of nature, which will go, where so many of Emily's poems go, grave-breaking eventually.

The anonymity of all these personae means that gendered readings of Emily's work are often difficult to sustain. Certainly, the buried form is more often female than male. But this need not reflect on the sex of the speaker. Claims, like Margaret Homans' and Irene Tayler's, that Emily's muse figures are male often assume that the speaker is female.[17] A sexual struggle is thus mapped onto a struggle for poetic identity. Camille Paglia's thesis, that the poetry betrays 'a delicate lesbian eroticism focusing on the night approach of angelic female spirits', similarly relies on a pre-prepared plot, about power, poetic identity and sexual eroticism.[18] But the heterogeneous crowd of pronouns in Emily's verse, along with its suppressed Gondal origins, is resistant to foundational plots. Her language remains unsettlingly open, exchanging freely between living and dead, natural and human, literal and metaphorical. To root her poems in gendered interests is to close down that exchange, or limit it to a love story of coupled protagonists which ignores the pull of impersonal place. If anything, Emily's poems can only be grounded in the ground, the place which holds, literally and metaphorically, so much of her attention.

'In the earth, the earth thou shalt be laid' (*EBP*, 152), for instance, seems to be a poem about lost human love. But as in many of Emily's poems, that perspective is reversed, so that the grounds for loss are taken away: 'Earth never misses thee' (line 20). Whether this is mother-earth or lover-earth does not matter much. What matters is the pun on missing. Earth 'never misses' the dead because it has no human feelings, or else because it would not miss what is permanently lodged within it. Earth is either ignorant or fully cognisant of their presence, either careless or careful. It is the equivocation rather than the resolution which matters, along with the usual supplanting of any human speaker with earth's point of view.

Even when Emily appears to give voice to characters, as in 'The Night-Wind' (*EBP*, 126), those characters remain elusive. Homans reads this poem as a drama of influence: the male, seducing wind attempts to steal the female speaker's 'linguistic powers'.[19] But Emily's wind is neutral, and its 'wooing voice' (line 18) set specifically against what is 'human':

> 'Play with the scented flower,
> The young tree's supple bough –
> And leave my human feelings
> In their own course to flow'
>
> The Wanderer would not leave me
> Its kiss grew warmer still –
> 'O come,' it sighed so sweetly
> 'I'll win thee 'gainst thy will –
>
> 'Have we not been from childhood friends?
> Have I not loved thee long?
> As long as thou hast loved the night
> Whose silence wakes my song?'
>
> (lines 21–32)

The slight mismatch of love objects here – the speaker loves the night, the wind loves the speaker – already starts to free the poem of purely sexual intention. As in so many of Emily's lyrics, the love story is a little crowded. There is not just the wind and its object, the speaker, but also the night, the silence and the song. The wind's tactics are not in competition with all those, but include them. Moreover, the terms of the invitation are slightly different from the lover's usual 'Come to me' motif. ' "O come," it sighed so sweetly' is more like the wheedling colloquialism of a child. The invitation is to play, not to love. If the speaker is being seduced, it is only to go out. 'Have we not been from childhood friends?' is reason enough to play again the game of going out in the dark:

> 'And when thy heart is laid at rest
> Beneath the church-yard stone
> I shall have time enough to mourn
> And thou to be alone'–
>
> (lines 33–6)

This warning, however, suddenly collapses the distance between childhood and the grave. 'The space between is all forgot'. An uncanny connection darkens Emily's *carpe diem* motif. The night-wind, after all, comes from the same outside as 'the church-yard stone'. Nature, with its lovely songs, contains the spot where, even in childhood, the 'heart is laid'. The child who wants to play has, at some level of connection, some knowledge of that spot and a gravitational pull towards it. 'I'll win thee 'gainst thy will', it cries, betraying the smallest undercurrent of menace in this delightfully winning ploy.

Between wind, child, lover and spirit from the grave, the fantasy of what lies outside circulates. The point of the poem is not ultimately to identify that fantasy, but to feel the stress of its invitation. The wind's winning ways will indeed 'win' over human 'will', though in a future which lies outside the poem. *Inside* the poem, the unfinished love story, with play, song, night or death, goes on. The drama of that love story concerns form, not content. This is not so much a struggle *for* poetry, in Homans' sense of finding 'poetic identity', but a struggle *of* poetry, in which identity is the thing lost in the game. The 'will' of the speaker, in this poem, carries no humanist or ethical charge.[20] Instead, it is a playful force of resistance, barely human, and in any case destined to be won over by, and to, nature.

The sense of poetry as a forgetful form runs through Emily's work. Although the grave may be out there, in the earth, it is also, as suggested by 'the dungeon-crypts' of 'The Prisoner' (*EBP*, 14–15, line 1), in here, in the condition of life itself. If the grave is a figure for both life and death, both being in here, closed in, and being out there, closed out, for being both a full space and an empty one, it becomes a rich metaphor for poetry itself. Emily's close-set verse forms, with their metrical ins and outs, impersonal pronouns, unfinished desires and ungrounded metaphors, mimic the place which haunted the childhood fantasies of all the Brontës. The grave is the place where a buried content might just come and go. So too is a poem.

This connection becomes clear in a last, minimalist verse, which yet sums up much of Emily's genius:

The night is darkening round me
The wild winds coldly blow
But a tyrant spell has bound me
And I cannot cannot go

The giant trees are bending
Their bare boughs weighed with snow
And the storm is fast descending
And yet I cannot go

Clouds beyond clouds above me
Wastes beyond wastes below
But nothing drear can move me
I will not cannot go

(*EBP*, 56, lines 1–12)

This unpunctuated fragment, perhaps part of a longer dialogue, is almost completely 'abstract'. Like 'The Night-Wind', it is a poem of intense desire which will not resolve into a human drama. The reason for being 'bound' is never given. The place is unspecifically vast. The speaker may be living or dead, inside or out, high up or low down. There is almost nothing in the poem to tell where, when, who or what this is. Instead, there is the power of a structure of words, a set of repetitive verse-boxes, which themselves embody the conflict of purpose and perspective being played out. Emily's feminine/masculine rhyme-scheme again enacts the struggle of the whole poem between getting out (a foot out), and staying in. But apart from the verse form, there is no other obstruction. The experience, for the reader, is almost that of being shut nowhere but in a poem.

At first, the problem seems simple. Going is a matter of going against the 'tyrant spell', though whether it means into or out of the storm is unclear. The evidence of Emily's other work suggests that the storm is the temptation. But the third stanza disproves this. We are already outside, or at least in a place open to both 'clouds above' and 'wastes below'. This ought to be a sublime Romantic scene, of the solitary on a mountain top. But Emily is not interested in such assertions of 'poetic identity'. There is no identifiable person, no mention of scenery, and the standpoint is bafflingly open. This literal groundlessness then becomes unnervingly metaphorical. 'Wastes beyond wastes below' suggests that the ground, instead of being a place on which to stand, opens up under our feet.

At this point, Emily turns everything on a pun: 'nothing drear can move me'. The juggling of two meanings of 'move' – budge and affect – only adds to the sense of battling stress. There are no clues in the poem to help ground 'move' in either meaning: outer or inner, transitive or intransitive. However, the last line then tricks our expectations: 'I will not cannot go.' The 'will', that capricious agent, suddenly sets itself against a new form of coercion, which is to be forced to go. But where we are going from or to, or for what reason, remains lost in the storm conflicts of this poem. In the end, there is only raw, irrational power, and a verse form which goes pushing and shoving against invisible obstacles.

If this is a reduction to the absurd, it is one that typifies Emily's work. The elementals of words, shorn of narrative, humanist or even just human content, are the essence of her lyrics. Something may be buried in a poem, an equivocal, ghostly memory or form, recalled from the past and woven from a web of sibling fantasies, half real, half pretended. However, in her best work, that object cannot be extracted and identified. It is not a person, a story or a content. Instead, it is a figure for the 'darling dream' of writing itself – the 'form' which makes form worth having in the first place. The figure of the grave, with all its varied passionate associations, with the past, dead sisters, memory and place, is a figure also for that formal constriction and 'spell' of poetry which, of all the Brontës, Emily alone perfectly achieves.

NOTES

1. Christine Alexander, *The Early Writings of Charlotte Brontë* (Oxford: Basil Blackwell, 1983), 29.
2. Juliet Barker, *The Brontës* (London: Weidenfeld & Nicolson, 1994), 462–90.
3. Barbara Hardy, 'The Lyricism of Emily Brontë', in Anne Smith, ed., *The Art of Emily Brontë* (London: Vision Press, 1976), 94–118, 99.
4. Andrew Elfenbein, *Byron and the Victorians* (Cambridge University Press, 1995), 81.
5. Christine Alexander and Jane Sellars, *The Art of the Brontës* (Cambridge University Press, 1995), 15.
6. *Byron: Poetical Works*, edited by Frederick Page, corrected by John Jump (Oxford University Press, 1970), 277–303.
7. William Wordsworth, *Poetical Works*, edited by Thomas Hutchinson, revised by Ernest de Selincourt (Oxford University Press, 1969), 86.
8. Alexander, *The Early Writings of Charlotte Brontë*, 20.
9. Stevie Davies, *Emily Brontë: The Artist as a Free Woman* (Manchester: Carcanet Press, 1983), 163.
10. Barker, *The Brontës*, 260–1.
11. Emily Brontë, *Wuthering Heights*, edited by David Daiches (Baltimore University Press, 1965), 20–21.
12. Esther Schor, *Bearing the Dead: The British Culture of Mourning from the Enlightenment to Victoria* (Princeton University Press, 1994), 234.
13. Robin Grove, '"It Would Not Do": Emily Brontë as Poet', in Smith, ed., *Art of Emily Brontë*, 33–67, 58.
14. C. Day Lewis, 'The Poetry of Emily Brontë', *Brontë Society Transactions* 13 (1965), 83–95, 91.
15. Elfenbein, *Byron and the Victorians*, 134.

16. A. Mary F. Robinson, *Emily Brontë*, 3rd edn (London, 1890), 134.
17. Margaret Homans, *Women Writers and Poetic Identity* (Princeton University Press, 1980); Irene Tayler, *Holy Ghosts: The Male Muses of Emily and Charlotte Brontë* (New York: Columbia University Press, 1990).
18. Camille Paglia, *Sexual Personae: Art and Decadence from Nefertiti to Emily Dickinson* (Harmondsworth: Penguin, 1990), 456.
19. Homans, *Women Writers and Poetic Identity*, 125.
20. See Matthew Campbell, *Rhythm and Will in Victorian Poetry* (Cambridge University Press, 1999), 31.

4

STEVIE DAVIES

'Three distinct and unconnected tales': *The Professor, Agnes Grey* and *Wuthering Heights*

In September 1841, Charlotte Brontë wrote an audacious letter soliciting funds for a European venture:

> Who ever rose in the world without ambition? When [Papa] left Ireland to go to Cambridge University, he was as ambitious as I am now. I want us *all* to go on. I know we have talents, and I want them to be turned to account. I look to you, aunt, to help us.[1]

The eldest Brontë daughter proposed a living narrative of self-improvement, attainable by those who, like the hero of *The Professor*, direct their energies towards an ambitious goal: 'Hope smiles on Effort!' She requested cash: "the needful", as it is characterised in the northern industrial idiom of Charlotte's first novel: 'I must live, and to live I must have what you call "the needful"; which I can only get by working' (*P*, 44). *The Professor* is a narrative of self-help, like Mrs Craik's *John Halifax, Gentleman* (1856). Pulling oneself up by one's own bootstraps, the practice of frugality and business probity, taking careful initiatives in pursuit of financial independence and security, were major themes in Charlotte's life. Her managing mind initiated the idea of a school, further education in Belgium and the submission of the sisters' first novels in June 1846: a three-volume work comprising 'three distinct and unconnected tales', Charlotte's *The Professor* (then entitled *The Master*), Emily's *Wuthering Heights* and Anne's *Agnes Grey* (*CBL* 1, 461). The aim was the generation of 'the needful' in both senses, economic and spiritual.

'Bread is bread, and a salary is a salary', states the narrator-hero of *The Professor*; but the biblical axiom that 'Man shall not live by bread alone' is also intrinsic to the novel. Like Charlotte's mature works, it treats the hunger of the heart, denied and underfed. 'A competency was what I wanted; a competency it was now my aim and resolve to secure', relates Crimsworth. The word 'competency' articulates the conflicts of *The Professor* and of Charlotte's life: its roots lie both in the idea of competition and that of sufficiency. The world of work, as Charlotte experienced it, was a site of

72

struggle and mutual antagonism for seekers after financial independence. And without having striven to secure 'the needful', emotional needs could not be assuaged. In life and art, Charlotte was canny enough to divine the superimportance of a bank balance.

Because her first novel (completed in June 1846) was nine times rejected, never appeared in her lifetime, and is a strangely dissonant work, it tends to be excluded from appraisal of the Brontës' first attempt at publishing fiction. She withdrew it from the joint venture in September 1846, and Emily may have expanded *Wuthering Heights* to fill the three-volume format demanded by publishers.[2] Analogies between *The Professor* and her sisters' first novels are skewed also by the perspective through which Charlotte mediated her subject. Like *Agnes Grey*, *The Professor* is a first-person narrative, the lonely testament of a fledgling entrepreneur in a world inhospitable to society's have-nots. Compelled both by financial straits and the 'wish for wings', Charlotte's teacher and Anne's governess move beyond their immediate community. Both authors use fictional autobiography, whose generic roots lie in Victorian confessional narrative, with its high valuation of authenticity, the work ethic, and first-hand experience. Whereas Emily Brontë constructs an intricate system of narratives bound by irony and multiple perspective, both *The Professor* and *Agnes Grey* confine narrative viewpoint. In a loveless world, their protagonists seek and, after harrowing misadventures, find earthly love.

Both were written from the stress of female experience in a marketplace which held cheap middle-class women's work. A conservative journal, *The Saturday Review*, wrote of governesses:

> Married life is woman's profession; and to this life her training – that of dependence – is modelled. Of course by not getting a husband, or losing him, she may find that she is without resources. All that can be said of her is, she has failed in business; and no social reform can prevent such failures...[3]

Failed in business: such callous cynicism hones our perception of the position of the Brontë sisters, heading for obloquy as 'old maids'. To earn one's own bread was vital. But Charlotte and Anne Brontë's first novels show a feminist appropriation of the work ethic that reaches beyond the pragmatic. Labour carries quasi-sacramental significance, according to the parable of the talents, cited in Charlotte's letter to Aunt Branwell ('I know we have talents'), a biblically authorised prohibition on the wasting of innate gifts, whether by man or woman. A woman's duty to earn the 'needful' is treated in *The Professor* as an expression of dedication to the 'yoke-fellow' ideal of Protestant marriage: 'our course ran side by side...we marched hand in hand' (P, 230). The tradition of honest God-sanctioned gain, computing profits, helping Providence to help oneself, is presented as a legitimate passion of the Protestant wife. *The Professor* has its married heroine, within a page of the bridal trip, express 'serious ardour' while computing francs:

> 'I am not satisfied...you are now earning eight thousand francs a year... while I am still at my miserable twelve hundred francs. I *can* do better, and I *will*.' (P, 228)

> Duties she must have to fulfil. and important duties; work to do – and excit-ing. absorbing, profitable work; strong faculties stirred in her frame, and they demanded full nourishment, free exercise... (P, 224)

As in the puritan work tradition of Defoe, the amatory involves the eco-nomic. However, if the quoted lines imply a feminist insistence on equal working status within marriage, an opposite tendency echoes Charlotte's romantic yen for a dominant male whom one can call 'master', who will 'punish' naughtiness delectably. Mutually contradictory fantasies of equal-ity and subjection create an unstable ending, in keeping with the fascinating volatility of the whole novel, a duality which Crimsworth can only focus by suggesting that he 'seemed to possess two wives' (P, 230).

The Professor has in common with *Wuthering Heights* themes of the alter ego, mother-loss and a dark violence in the heart of human affairs. It shares Emily's saturnine sense of the fratricidal relations bonding society, her cri-tique of so-called 'civilised' behaviour as collectively legitimised hypocrisy. In bitter letters from Brussels, Charlotte had expressed unapologetic misan-thropy. To Branwell she had written that people there are 'nothing – I don't hate them – hatred would be too warm a feeling...one wearies from day to day of caring nothing, fearing nothing, liking nothing hating nothing – being nothing, doing nothing' (*CBL* 1, 317). This *anomie* was poured into *The Professor,* in solution with humiliated despair at Heger's rejection of her love. Whereas Emily's misanthropy was focused as reclusive philosophy and an aesthetic of detachment, Charlotte's novel is compulsive, vengeful, spasming with a conflicted pain whose sources the text seems anxious to conceal.

The Professor's raw materials are incoherently transmuted into art. While Emily's novel masters with an iron hand the technique of the unreliable nar-rator, Charlotte's Branwellish, ill-tempered, gauche and often preposterous hero squirms in her grip, at times seeming little more than an inflamed ner-vous system. Fuming, costive, he exhibits infantile petulance one moment, and carries Charlotte's most cherished themes the next. In racist and anti-Catholic ebullitions, he manages to do both, as in his denunciations of Popish perfidy and fleshy, vacuous Brussels schoolgirls: 'Aurelia Koslow, a German fraulein, or rather a half-breed...somewhat Tartar features...slovenly... dirty'; 'Juanna Trista...of mixed Belgian and Spanish origin...precisely the same shape of skull as Pope Alexander the Sixth...she made noises with her mouth like a horse' (P, 91–2). A painful mingling of racism and sexual envy vents itself under cover of her male narrator's spleen against the degenerate maidens of Europe. Only the half-English Swiss Protestant Anglophile, Frances, a 'plain Jane' with a sterling spirit, is spared. Yet Charlotte's narrative looks forward to *Villette*, using Crimsworth's pathology to explore extreme emotion under extreme constraint: a hot heart in the 'snow-sepulchre' of unyielding winter.

A reader of the first three Brontë novels is impressed by the diversity of the sisters' talents. If books have faces, *The Professor*'s is set in hectic strain; *Agnes Grey* shows an expression of grave directness, attentively looking affliction in the eyes; *Wuthering Heights* turns from personal striving to get a living (a topic of no interest to Emily), to an epic imaginative world of inner drama in a working Yorkshire community. This latter novel has in common with *The Professor* a theme of aggressive misanthropy and a homesick lament for mother-loss. In *The Professor*, the portrait of Crimsworth's dead mother stands for all the steadiness, wisdom and tenderness absent in his world. A softly shaded lamp sheds a glow on a face with a 'thoughtful, yet gentle expression. The serious grey eye possessed for me a strong charm, as did certain lines in the features indicative of most true and tender feeling. I was sorry it was only a picture' (P, 11). The final sentence has a moving elegiac simplicity, diagnostic of the condition of turbulent lack prevailing in Crimsworth's world, which can never be wholly remedied.

The picture, sold in the process of the story, is restored to Crimsworth towards the end, when he observes not only the wisdom and benevolence of the face but also 'alas! the sadness...of those fine grey eyes' (P, 194). In a nomadic world without bearings, inheritance or sanctuary save what is self-made, the novel's major characters, awash in a Babel of European languages, experience not only atrophy of bondings but severance from what Frances venerates as 'associations'. Like Emily and Anne, Charlotte records the primacy of the homing instinct. When the market price of 'associations' is queried, Frances flashes back, 'your portrait, to anyone who loved you, would, for the sake of association, be without price' (P, 219): 'association' links man to Heaven. Love of home is not only the foundation and justification of patriotism but the deepest bond the characters of *The Professor* possess: however, in the world of mother-loss, only a painted image remains, bearing witness to the mortality of origins.

Superficially, the tale told in *The Professor* is simple. The narrator charts four phases: Eton, work in his brother's mill at X-, Belgium and marriage, with an eventual return to England. But the narrative technique is at once guileful and naive, casuistical and cloven.

From its outset, the novel records an abortiveness in human affairs and mimes that condition by abortive structures and off-key characterisation, dialogue and tone. The whole novel is set out of true, which, paradoxically, creates a fascination, like a succession of false chords, achromatic, bereft of harmony. If a novel may be said to suffer from mood-swings, *The Professor* does. It is highly wrought, subject to abrupt swerves of diction and register, deviating into paranoia on the one hand and rhapsody on the other, undercut by sarcastic reminders of life's banality. The narrator staggers along burdened by a weight of authorial emotion the plot will hardly bear.

In a preface to *The Professor* written after the publication of *Shirley,* Charlotte insisted on the essentially humdrum character of the story, its abdication of the 'imaginative and poetical...highly wrought fancy... pathos' (*P*, 1). In reality, *The Professor* was written in a whirlwind of emotions, covering the nakedness of its fevered inspiration in rags of irony. The author's nerves were shot by years of strain, longing and the tension of a conscientious woman suppressing a tormented conscience. Charlotte's letters during the years leading up to composition betray a conflicted, repressed character on the edge of breakdown: 'estrangement from one's real character', 'the adoption of a cold frigid – apathetic exterior' (*CBL* I, 266) culminating in separation from her beloved teacher:

> Monsieur, the poor do not need a great deal to live on – they ask only the crumbs of bread which fall from the rich men's table – but if they are refused these crumbs – they die of hunger...there are some cold and rational people who would say on reading [this letter] – "she is raving" – My sole revenge is to wish these people a single day of the torments I have suffered for eight months.
>
> (*CBL* I, 379)

In the years of sadness and gall which succeeded Charlotte's second period in Brussels is planted the forked root of *The Professor;* its insecure ironies and its camouflaged agenda. The author hunkers down behind a narrator who, as she wrote in a discarded Preface in the person of an old friend of Crimsworth, has 'to an impartial eye – in the midst of his good points little defects and peculiarities...of which he was himself excusably unconscious'.[4]

Crimsworth is no mere eccentric but a florid case of neurosis. The novel opens with a feint at the epistolary form, in a letter to a certain Charles. The two had been inseparable friends at Eton: but 'What animal magnetism drew thee and me together I know not': the letter writer cannot remember that they had anything in common. Charles' 'sardonic coldness' inspired in Crimsworth a feeling of superiority, then as now. Why then is he writing to Charles? The epistolary mode is dropped after one chapter, in the course of which antipathy ('mutual disgust') has been evinced towards both Crimsworth's uncles, representing the aristocracy and trade, his cousin and all her sisters, his brother Edward and his bride: that is to say, every living person with whom contact is made. All comers are 'alien to what I like' (*P*, 9). We learn later that Edward beats his wife, who leaves him.

Patrick Brontë owned a copy of Sir Humphrey Davy's *Elements of Chemical Philosophy* (1812), detailing the principles of magnetism and chemical combination, the attraction of affinities and the repulsion of disaffinities. Whereas *Wuthering Heights* founds a dialectical world on the psyche's affinities *and* disaffinities, Charlotte creates a context of near-universal recoil, where the narrator's ego endures perpetual siege by hostile eyes and discharges itself in fear and hostility. All relations are power-relations.

In *Wuthering Heights*, Lockwood sees Heathcliff's 'black eyes withdraw...his fingers shelter[ed] themselves, with a jealous resolution', a surly retreat echoed in the paranoid architecture of a house whose 'deeply set' windows, recessive vistas and guard-dogs deny right of entry (*WH*, 1–2). Lockwood, that human snail who 'shrunk icily into myself' when a young lady made eyes at him, frames and focuses this behaviour through unconscious parody, downright incomprehension and (in chapter 3) becoming sucked into a vortex of nightmare. Emily Brontë beckons us into a realm combining the comedic and the uncanny, mediating a mysterious network of unknown relationships. Charlotte Brontë's ironies are jittery, tenuous, in comparison. Suspicion and watchfulness prevail, and the field of vision is electric with aghast surmise and calculating, predatory watchfulness. Faces are masks. Eyes are weapons which seek out one's weak point, to get 'in'. Once character is penetrated, control is lost. There is little possibility of empathy or insight but a nightmarish feud of espionage and counter-espionage. In its way, the world of *The Professor* is as violent as that of *Wuthering Heights*. Here, as in Hindley and Heathcliff's fratricidal struggle over the pony, the elder brother takes the whip to the younger, but the calm disinterest of Emily's telling is absent. The adult antagonists of *The Professor* bawl puerile abuse like characters from Branwell's and Charlotte's juvenilia: 'you are my servant; obey me! Hypocrite and twaddler! Smooth-faced, snivelling greasehorn!' yells mill-owner Edward (*P*, 36) as he lambasts his brother.

Charlotte Brontë suffered from chronic shyness. In company she would gradually swivel in her chair, until she sat at a forty-five degree angle. She had pondered her own panic, using her self-consciousness to view herself being looked at. *The Professor* interrogates the transactions of people's eyes in social situations, where they guard inner and secret territory and repel the manoeuvres of would-be invaders. Crimsworth remarks, when giving his first class, that he:

> regarded them all with a steady and somewhat stern gaze; a dog, if stared at hard enough...will show symptoms of embarrassment, and so at length did my bench of Belgians. (P, 57)

Eyes are instruments not only of perception but of control. Zoraïde Reuter and Crimsworth engage in optical battle:

> her eyes reverted continually to my face. Her glances were not given in full, but out of the corners, so quietly, so stealthily, yet I think I lost not one. I watched her as keenly as she watched me; I perceived soon that she was feeling after my real character, she was searching for salient points, and weak points, and eccentric points...hoping in the end to find some chink, some niche, where she could put in her little firm foot and stand upon my neck... (P, 80)

The watcher is watched, and knows herself watched: she in turn observes the watcher of her watchfulness. In these optical battles, which centre around the politic, vigilant figure of Mdlle Reuter, an outward icon of female quiet as she nets her green silk purse, Charlotte Brontë's writing achieves an experimental, proto-modernist, quality. 'I watch very vigilantly', Mdlle Reuter acknowledges, 'I knit on still, and still I hold my tongue' (P, 18). In this image of the decorously silent female, Charlotte at once subverts the icon of woman's passivity; takes covert revenge on Madame Heger's vigilance; and presents tiny, coded dramas of optical interactions.

Symmetrically with this theme runs the novel's preoccupation with withholding and guardedness. Surrounded by competitors and foreigners, the hero strains to avoid giving himself away. The language of *The Professor* is a lexis of repression and strain at once chronic and acute. A body-language of tension, fear and self-hiding is minutely observed, with detachment and objectivity: 'my hand, so utterly a stranger to the grasp of a kindred hand, clenched itself to repress the tremor with which impatience would fain have shaken it' (P, 7). The hand that yearns to open in love convulses to a fist. It hurts itself. Crimsworth carries around with him a deadly anxiety, manifested in rigid posture combined with compulsive behaviour. A finely observed instance occurs after an acrid conversation with his 'friend' Hunsden:

> I found out that I was walking very fast, and breathing very hard, and that my nails were almost stuck into the palms of my clenched hands, and that my teeth were set fast; on making this discovery, I relaxed both my pace, fists and jaws. (P, 33)

Each detail of this anatomy of nervous strain, from panting to clenched jaws, is an authentic testament of tension which has become a way of life. Hypersensitive but void of empathy, the narrator-hero's sardonic self-dislike echoes others' distaste: he overreacts to everything, in extreme metaphors which show a nature thin-skinned to a pathological degree. The quest narrative originating in Bunyan's *Pilgrim's Progress* becomes a nervous ordeal to be toiled through in a fallen materialistic world.

The 'self-help' story is conceived as a fantasy of success, both economic and libidinal, but a bleak, wretched tone which darkens the telling of even the happier episodes implies the author's dissatisfaction with the fruits of fantasy. A fatal sterility sours the novel, which inhabits the landscape of the curse, the working world outside Eden, where Adam was condemned to till the wilderness. Crimsworth seeks an Eden in Mdlle Reuter's garden, where she walks, her cheek 'like the bloom on a good apple'(*P*, 71); but the apple is bad, the spring garden a fraud, and the *directrice* a serpent. The trauma of the fall and the curse is built into the novel. Mrs Gaskell disliked *The Professor*'s tendency to quote Scripture 'profanely'. Reading the novel against Anne Brontë's work, one is struck by a cynicism which strips the Bible of aphorisms to transplant them in the soil of its own jaded disappointment. In *The Professor*, matter is forlorn of spirit. Scripture shrivels in the marketplace free-for-all.

Lockwood's second nightmare in *Wuthering Heights* culminates in fisticuffs: 'each man's hand was against his neighbour'. The saturnine Heathcliff presides over a household of belligerent saturnalia. In *The Professor*, absence of fellowship represents the biblical condition of God's alienation from sinful man:

> For before these days there was no hire for man, nor any hire for beast; neither was there any peace to him that went out or came in because of the affliction; for I set all men every one against his neighbour.   (Zechariah 8: 10)

Blight lingers even when the novel rewards its striving hero with the love of Frances Henri. In a world of magnetic oppositions, Frances is represented as the '*Professeur*'s' one true counterpart.

Half-English, Protestant, small, plain and needy but proud, industrious and honourable, Frances re-enacts Charlotte's outsiderliness in the Brussels Catholic world. In the wooing and union of Crimsworth and Frances, the author seeks double gratification by splitting herself between two personae, consummating on the page her barren passion for Heger. But the strategem adulterates its own heady wine. Crimsworth discovers his pupil's uniqueness in her essays. Through writing, Frances first kindles attention. Her eyes become transparent windows into the soul: 'transfigured, a smile shone in her eyes…a frank and flashing glance…glow…radiance' (*P*, 125–6). Frances too has noticed that 'every room in this house, monsieur, has eye-holes and ear-holes' (*P*, 134). Her anxieties match his; her poverty salutes his; her shyness mirrors his; and when he meets her in the Protestant cemetery, he finds his treasure in the place of loss.

Yet one can hardly speak of a happy ending. No sooner is the troth plighted than Crimsworth pitches into a fit of 'Hypochondria', black depression of biblical dimensions:

> when my desires, folding wings, weary with long flight, had just alighted on the very lap of fruition, and nestled there warm, content, under the caress of a soft hand – why did hypochondria accost me now? I repulsed her as one would a dreaded and ghastly concubine coming to embitter a husband's heart toward his young bride; in vain…   (*P*, 211)

The hidden author, a homing dove cheated of repose in the 'lap of fruition', seems to sicken of phantasmal compensations. The reference to the uncanny bride gestures toward Bertha Rochester in *Jane Eyre*, which may be said to have hatched the egg laid by *The Professor*. The Crimsworth marriage, a narcissistic bonding of two Charlottes in twin personae, has confounded readers by a sado-masochistic oddness. Its child, Victor (named perhaps after the Hegers' youngest child, Victorine) recoils from his father and will be despatched to Eton, Crimsworth's first exile. The familial hearth, haven of the working man, seems obscurely awry.

The Brussels experience had been violently self-contradictory for Charlotte, arousing her by a taste of travel and the testy charisma of her 'Master', permitting knowledge beyond anything she could have sampled in England. But it also balked that arousal. Retrospectively, we see seeds of all Charlotte's future works in *The Professor*; most obviously of *Villette* but also (in the theme of the young single governess, her master's 'one ewe lamb' and counterpart) *Jane Eyre,* and (in the factories of northern England, wage-slavery, teacher-pupil romances and the 'old maid' issue) the 'industrial' novel, *Shirley*. But Charlotte's first novel coils around itself, generating obscured and coded meanings. In 1844 she had told Heger she practised French so that, 'when I pronounce the French words I seem to be chatting with you'; her secret ambition is to write a book and dedicate it to her 'master'. Having often praised him in French, she 'would like to tell you for once in English'. By 1846, the spate of letters, each a more anguished *cri de coeur*, had ceased: Monsieur was silent. Charlotte despaired. The 'hypochondria' Charlotte ascribes to Crimsworth had been tasted in all its bitterness by the author: 'I am in a fever – I lose my appetite and my sleep – I pine away'.[5] This last surviving letter to M. Heger was written, in French of course, in November 1845, eight months before completion of *The Professor*, whose hero records feverish insomnia, nausea and suicidal inclination. Charlotte had promised her 'master' a literary message in English: an intimate love-letter. But since then, she had despaired, knowing no message would be welcome. Her first literary excursion in the public realm resembles Hopkins' 'cries like dead letters sent / To dearest him, that lives, alas, away'.[6] A dead letter is one which is never opened by its recipient.

But Heger's language she kept. French for Charlotte was the language of Eros, in which her mouth could taste the communion of souls whose sweetness was denied to her life. *The Professor* is partly written in French. Probably she would have been ashamed to write her letters to Heger as passionately in English. Her native language declared its meanings too transparently. But, in the delicious accents of French, whose syllables she had taken from her 'master's' tongue on to hers, copying his voice's intimate music, she allowed her passion to express itself without bridle. In French she had wooed him in her '*Devoirs*', and he had responded with approbation. French carried that exotic sheen which foreign languages may cast on the most lacklustre objects.

The Professor is concerned with translation and its frustration. Crimsworth confesses himself at a loss to supply English words for experiences which seem ineluctably foreign: he describes Pelet's face as '*fine et spirituelle*. I use two French words because they define better than any English terms' his intelligent quality (*P*, 56). All translation is forgery: origins are cryptic, unreconstructable, truths hidden. Some chapters have a macaronic character, oscillating between English and French, as if the author cannot relinquish the gratification of its bitter-sweetness on the tongue:

'Où donc est Mdlle Henri?' I said one day ...
'Elle est partie, monsieur.'
'Partie! et pour combien de temps? Quand reviendra-t-elle?'
'Elle est partie pour tourjours, monsieur; elle ne reviendra plus.'

(*P*, 140)

The word *partie*, meaning 'departed', expresses for Charlotte a depth of personal sadness for which no English duplicate existed. The language of Eros was for her, by the time of *The Professor*, also the tongue of separation, severance, loss. To write in French, however, was a gesture of reinstatement of the hopes forfeited when Charlotte left Heger and, more terribly, Heger abandoned her, *parti*, by ignoring her letters. The language of recovery is also that of loss; incantation involves valediction.

Author and personages play games of *trompe l'oeil* with this duality. The most obvious is the title, *The Professor*. When offered a position as 'professor', young Crimsworth replies, 'I am not a professor.' The reply is, 'Oh...professor, here in Belgium, means a teacher, that is all' (*P*, 54). The novel's English title elevates the self-made hero beyond his (English) position and renders ambiguous all transactions. Language as subterfuge is a running theme. Crimsworth's first business-task is to translate English into German; but his own face is illegibly 'written in Greek' (*P*, 17). English is acclaimed as the language of plain speech, the mother-tongue:

'Speak English, if you please.'
'Mais – '
'English –...Answer me in your mother-tongue.'
(*P*, 128)

Just as Charlotte had taken delight in Heger's bossy banter, surrendering her paralysing anxiety, so Frances is comparably rewarded by an author who doesn't seem to wonder whether 'punishments' for talking French (*P*, 233) might pall on a wife of many years.

Experimental writing reminds us of the author's prodigious gifts: for instance, her use of the 'photographic scene'. The 1840s were the decade of that early form of photograph, the daguerreotype. Charlotte Brontë was not slow to appropriate techniques of photographic realism into her fiction, in a consciously stylised manner. Crimsworth ends chapter 5 by taking a mental photograph of the industrial landscape: 'I desired memory to take a clear and permanent impression of the scene, and treasure it for future years' (*P*, 39). Charlotte attempts to reproduce in language the photograph's authenticity not only as a keepsake but, in its immediate mingling of light and chemicals, authentic traces of recorded reality.

The Professor, constantly aware of its own narrative procedures, 'frames' its rhetorical devices, emphasising both matter and manner. This produces a baroque quality (typical of Charlotte's later work) in stressful dialogue with documentary realism. The narrator borrows from the visual arts a technique of static portraiture, inviting readers to 'just look here while I open my portfolio and show them a sketch or two' (*P*, 88). Word-painting renders ecstatic effects, as when Crimsworth views the rainbow: the sky is 'like opal; azure immingled with crimson: the enlarged sun, glorious in Tyrian tints, dipped his brim already...' (*P*, 165). Into the biblical material of God's covenant with Noah Charlotte introduces a language suggestive of a painted world, using verbal artifice such as circumlocution ('Tyrian tints'), personification ('dipped his brim'), high-register words with a touch of archaism ('immingled') and visionary afflatus ('methought'):

in a dream were reproduced the setting sun, the bank of clouds, the mighty
rainbow. I stood, methought, on a terrace ... [a visionary form] hovered as on
wings; pearly, fleecy, gleaming air streamed like raiment round it: light, tinted
with carnation, coloured what seemed face and limbs; a large star shone with
still lustre on an angel's forehead ... a voice in my heart whispered – 'Hope
smiles on Effort!'   (*P*, 165–6)

The prolix and gilded effusion leads to deliberate bathos. *The Professor*
inhabits a world of effortful secularity. In countless provincial art galleries
we come across Victorian allegories of Hope, a winged maiden with blindfold
and lyre, gauzy against a blue heaven. Victorian 'Hope' iconography suggests
less God's covenant than subjection to fortune's caprice. Hope must be blind
to exist at all, a blurred figure crooning lullabies.

Charlotte's yen for epic-heroic stylisation and polysyllabic Latinate diction
('my imagination was with the refulgent firmament beyond') has its root in
James Thomson's eighteenth-century Miltonics, and a visual source in the
heroic pictures of John Martin. But context is generally mock-heroic. Often
a free, spontaneous English of simple, energetic, pithy description preludes
the lucid intimacy of *Jane Eyre*, with its characteristic short clauses strung
on semi-colons. The description of the journey to Belgium is particularly
engaging: 'I was young; I had good health; Pleasure and I had never met ...
at that epoch I felt like a morning traveller' (*P*, 50). The felicitous image of a
'morning traveller' and the bounding rhythms capture the buoyancy of new
beginnings.

Other narrative modes include letters and Frances' verses – 'I gave, at
first, attention close' (*P*, 200) – which transiently yield the telling to Frances.
Charlotte was no poet (except in prose) and the quatrains are sentimental and prosaic; but they declared her heart's deepest longings. Nearly a
decade before the composition of *The Professor*, Southey had admonished
Charlotte: 'Literature cannot be the business of a woman's life: & it ought
not to be' (*CBL* 1, 166–7). In the novel, Mdlle Reuter echoes the prohibition:
'*literary* ambition especially, is not a feeling to be cherished in the mind of a
woman' (*P*, 139). But it is through literary success, the reading aloud of her
essay (a form of 'publication') and the claim to the 'laurel-wreath' (*P*, 204)
that Frances gains her heart's desire.

In *Agnes Grey*, Anne Brontë turned from the glamour of Gondal. 'Passages
in the life of an Individual', which she says she is writing in her diary paper
of 31 July 1845,[7] is perhaps the embryo of *Agnes Grey*. It belongs to the everyday prose of life, its grind, embarrassments, hopes. Anne's story concerns
a young, impoverished woman's struggle to cope as a governess. It uses a

plain style of intimate confession. *Agnes Grey* is a more candid analogue to the author's own experience than *The Professor* is to Charlotte's. Its style of thoughtful sincerity keeps faith with the tradition of Protestant spiritual autobiography. Nothing is hectic or abstruse. Anne writes from the perspective of a believing Christian, with Evangelical affiliations and a commitment to self-examination and veracity. Her heroine, a plain person without distinguishing features save a clear, intelligent and just voice of personal witness, is as 'grey' as her name, a recessive figure, a 'nobody' to the families who exploit her services. To readers of Agnes' story, this 'greyness' assumes its own beauty, composed of pathos and integrity. Grey, traditionally worn by Quakers and quietists to express radical dissociation from gaudy worldliness, expresses Agnes' sobriety and inwardness. The name 'Agnes' derives from the Latin 'agnus', 'lamb', with its reference to the Christian path of sacrifice.

Charlotte described *Agnes Grey* as a near-transcription of Anne's 'own experiences as a governess', and told Mrs Gaskell that

> none but those who had been in the position of a governess could ever realise the dark side of 'respectable' human nature' ... [whose] conduct towards those dependent on it sometimes amounts to a tyranny of which one would rather be the victim than the inflicter. (*AG*, ix)

However, Anne worked *from* autobiographical material rather than in servitude to it, shaping her tale as a love story, with its own symmetries and artistic structure. The genuineness of texture and dialogue in *Agnes Grey* is the product of minute observation, focused by a fine authorial irony and delicate power of understatement.

Agnes Grey is one of the undervalued works of Victorian fiction. At the time it was cursorily noticed, often with a kind of itchy condescension on the part of male reviewers, for 'Acton Bell' was readily detectable as a woman, detailing 'the minute torments and tediums' of a female world. 'We do not actually assert that the author must have been a governess himself ... but he must have bribed some governess very largely, either with love or money', quipped a reviewer (*CH*, 227). Charlotte's acuity in insisting on male pseudonyms was amply justified: whereas no one guessed that *Wuthering Heights* could have been created by a woman, *Agnes Grey*'s subject matter and perspective were recognisably female. The 'minute torments and tediums' of a governess' life were considered beneath the attention of the manly reader, and Anne's careful verisimilitude received mild praise and yawning levity.

This devaluation of 'women's' experience as trivial obscured the veracity of Anne's narrative. The novel, read sympathetically, has the beauty and sadness of music scored in the minor key. Its heroine is also minor, having the subdued tenor of the day-to-day world. Tone and manner remain resolutely low-key; there are no histrionics, and if *Agnes Grey* fails in sublimity, this is because it never seeks it. The novel offers careful readers the insights of a vigilant, no-nonsense mind, a subversive eye-witness hidden at the heart of the quotidian world of family respectability. *Agnes Grey* is the work of a protesting Protestant: its feminism and radical insistence on the God-given significance of any life, however 'grey', derive from Anne's strenuously lived Christian principles. The first shall be last, the meek shall inherit the earth: Anne's tenets are those of the Beatitudes. She voices witty contempt for the arrogant elite and a worldly clergy. Ecclesiastical satire in *Agnes Grey* is directly in the tradition of Reformation radicalism.

Anne Brontë extends sympathy beyond the human species: one of her novel's most heartfelt themes is man's inhumanity to animals. From the cruelty of the hunt to the maltreatment of pets, the novelist tracks down a viciousness in human nature, which it both analyses and rebukes, questioning what is meant by 'civilised behaviour'. Violations of reason and good feeling constitute a norm in a patriarchal system of education which scorns 'petticoat management' and alienates men from their tender instincts. *Agnes Grey* draws attention away from the limelit centre of Victorian society to the perspective at its shadowed rim. From the 'grey' area of the nursery, the servants' quarters and impoverished cottages, the view is of a shallow, showy elite, a vicar who 'kicked my poor cat right across the floor' (*AG*, 90) and lonely women whose only creaturely fellowship is provided by a pet. Like Emily Brontë, Anne had studied animal behaviour, and saw fit to include careful description of their expressiveness:

> Presently, I heard a *snuffling* sound behind me, and then a dog came *frisking* and *wriggling* to my feet...When I spoke his name, he *leapt up* in my face, and *yelled* for joy. (*AG*, 189; my italics)

A cluster of verbs records the dog's rapturous commotion as it rediscovers its mistress: an unmediated fervour culminating not in the expected 'barking' but in 'yelling for joy'. Darwin noted in manuscript jottings of the 1830s that man and animals share a spectrum of emotion and a gestural vocabulary: 'a dog *whines*, & so does man. – when opening his mouth in romps he [the dog] smiles'. Darwin's luminous statement that 'animals [are] our fellow brethren in pain, disease death & suffering...we may be all netted together' would certainly have been welcomed by Anne and Emily Brontë.[8]

While in the elemental context of *Wuthering Heights*, humanity and creaturely life inhabit one continuum, in *Agnes Grey* animals are fellow beings with an ethical claim on human protection. Tenderness towards animals is a major index of moral worth, elevating the curate above his 'superior', Agnes above her employer. Every reader wincingly remembers Tom Bloomfield's vivisectionist sadism with the baby birds, a boyish pastime socially sanctioned as natural behaviour. 'Sometimes', boasts the swaggering lad, 'I give them to the cat; sometimes I cut them in pieces with my penknife; but the next, I mean to roast alive' (*AG*, 18). Pulling off sparrows' legs, wings and heads is acceptable to father and uncle, provided no mess stains the lad's trousers.

The scene in which Agnes mercy-kills a brood of chicks Tom intends to torture gains a harrowing power from the 'quiet' matrix of Anne's narrative. Exact observation intensifies horror and pathos, while gesturing to the social pressures that create a child like Tom, a boy without empathy, whose hectic power-urge is never curbed. Tom at once exemplifies original sin and 'spoiling' by an indulgent education which sets no limits to male behaviour. The theme of boys' privileged, yet stunting, education looks forward to *The Tenant of Wildfell Hall*. Tom is less a child than a miniature man, who apes the offensive manners of adult males:

> exultantly [he laid] the nest on the ground, and standing over it, with his legs wide apart, his hands thrust into his breeches-pockets, his body bent forward, and his face twisted into all manner of contortions in the ecstacy of his delight. 'But you shall see me fettle 'em off. My word, but I *will* wallop 'em! See if I don't now! By gum! but here's rare sport for me in that nest.' (*AG*, 44)

The characterisation of Tom's behaviour as 'exultant', 'ecstacy', 'delight' expresses a manic quality of compulsive gratification. His body language – straddled legs, bent torso, hands-in-pockets – declares exhibitionism, a display of learned, imitative behaviour. The 'twisting' of the facial muscles into a sequence of 'contortions' codes unconscious horror in his own pleasure. Anne's careful description, withholding revulsion, permits a distance from the figure of the child, across which we can read and interpret. At once ludicrous, ugly and pitiful, the child (an only boy in a family of girls) is a sadder figure than the innocent creatures he abuses. Dialogue is forensic: for Tom's cant is the language of the field, sportsmen's bragging. The verb 'to fettle', associated with the stables, has the meaning 'to do for, beat', suggesting an infantile desire to inflict punishment. Body and speech articulate an attitude, deride it through parody and diagnose its pathology.

When 'manly' Mr Robson, that 'scorner of the female sex' who 'was not above the foppery of stays' (*AG*, 42) arrives, he repeats a version of the same behaviour by 'pausing to kick his dog' (*AG*, 45). Here is the source of the boy's malady. The sportsman reinforces Tom's arrogance by congratulating him on his 'spunk' and on being 'beyond petticoat government already'.

Finally, Tom's mother reprimands Agnes for upsetting her child. With caustic irony focused in the nuances of dialogue, the narrator exposes the casual assumptions which underlie normative cruelty, a brew of sentimentalism and haughty moral blindness.

> 'You seem to have forgotten,' said she, calmly, 'that the creatures were all created for our convenience.'
>   I thought that doctrine admitted some doubt, but merely replied –
>   'If they were, we have no right to torment them for our amusement.'
>   ... 'I think *you* have not shewn much mercy,' replied she, with a short, bitter laugh; 'killing the poor birds by wholesale, in that shocking manner, and putting the dear boy to such misery, for a mere whim!'
>
> (*AG*, 45–6)

In this threefold dialogue (with boy, uncle and mother) Anne Brontë explores social sanctioning of male violence: of the three, the abdication of reason, love and Christian values by the mother is climactic and decisive. With such a mother, Tom is in effect motherless. Her light-brained appeals to Scripture exhibit anthropocentric and androcentric assumptions which privilege man above all beings, and one's own son, however obnoxious, above criticism. Her 'short, bitter laugh' expresses defensive recoil, while her recourse to sentimental cant in adjective-noun clichés like '*poor* birds' (she has just called them 'soulless brutes'), '*shocking* manner', '*dear* boy' indicate a heart empty of moral content.

Agnes Grey describes children in two privileged families who lack mothering, though nominally they have mothers. Mrs Bloomfield's arrogance is succeeded by Mrs Murray's callous neglect of her two daughters. She marries off the thoughtless Rosalie to Sir Thomas Ashby, 'with his betting book, and his gaming table, and his opera girls' (*AG*, 184): Rosalie grows to abhor him. The younger daughter, in a hair-raising echo of Tom's killing of the chicks, appears 'with the lacerated body of [a] young hare in her hand', sadistically relishing its death-throes: 'didn't you hear it scream? ... It cried out just like a child.' Control belongs to mother-love: Anne exposes a nightmare of family life which fails to embrace and guard its young by setting boundaries.

Through it all, Agnes watches, intervenes, suffers. The novel focuses on the constancy of an inconspicuous soul who is rarely looked at, never interesting to her employer, save as a pair of hands. Anne captures the experience of shyness, the attempt to save face when hot and bothered in a social situation – 'doubting whether to keep waiting, or go to bed, or go down again' (*AG*, 57). Loneliness is mediated with pathos, both in the novel's attention to minutiae of events and in symbols: 'like a thistle-seed borne on the wind' (*AG*, 58). Biblical allusion lends depth and universality to affliction: 'working as a hireling among strangers' (*AG*, 168). But the tenor returns insistently to the humdrum and the routine.

In a 'quiet, drab-colour life', banked round with 'dull, grey clouds', Agnes seeks to be seen for the person she is: someone rare and special. Drab cloth was the undyed wear of the lower orders. Agnes' reference to 'drab' evokes homespun ordinariness in a world of bright, expensive silks, together with the struggling integrity of a tacit spirit. Shrewd touches display this mortifying effacement of 'inferiors' by 'superiors'. Strolling back from church, 'they talked over me or across, and if their eyes, in speaking, chanced to fall on me, it seemed as if they looked on vacancy – as if they either did not see me or were very desirous to make it appear so'. The invisibility of social subordinates is a running theme: to the vicar, handing the gentry into their carriage after church, Agnes owes 'a grudge for nearly shutting me out of it ... though I was standing before his face' (*AG*, 80). In a world of such stint, Agnes sees herself degenerating: 'Already, I seemed to feel my intellect deteriorating, my heart petrifying, my soul contracting' (*AG*, 98). This vision of personal atrophy prefigures *The Tenant of Wildfell Hall*'s demolition of the myth of woman as redemptive agent in a sullied world. *Agnes Grey* presents an implicated, striving heroine, susceptible to bitterness, envy and despair.

Enlightenment rationalism in Anne Brontë coexists both with Evangelical fervour and confessional realism. The novel's love story involves a pilgrimage towards Grace. Anne, who had suffered spiritual crises in which she despaired of God's existence or love, associates Mr Weston with renewal. Grace embodied in a tender-spirited person attests to the reality of divine love:

> The gross vapours of earth were gathering round me, and closing in upon my inward heaven; and thus it was that Mr Weston rose at length upon me, appearing like the morning star in my horizon, to save me from the fear of utter darkness; and I rejoiced that ... human excellence was not a mere dream of the imagination. (*AG*, 98)

This passage shows biblical and Miltonic antecedents. By her 'inward heaven' Agnes means that 'inner light' by which the Protestant spirit negotiates a wilderness of temptations. Fear of 'utter darkness' is Miltonic, 'utter' meaning both 'absolute' and 'outer', the final exile of damnation. Like her favourite poet, Cowper, Anne was subject to a Calvinist fear of predestination to hell. Prosaic tribulations therefore enact a spiritual drama of momentous consequence. The pregnant comparison of Mr Weston with Agnes' 'morning star' echoes the Book of Revelation, in which Christ's messenger testifies, 'I am ... the bright and morning star' (22: 17). The marriage of Agnes to

Mr Weston is a modest human equivalent of the mystical Marriage of the Lamb.

The appearance of Mr Weston on Agnes' horizon presents a point of light which bears witness to God's indwelling presence in believers. As the callow Rosalie waylays Mr Weston, Agnes is driven back upon her own spiritual resources. Out of silent grief, she composes her lyric poems:

> I still preserve those relics of past sufferings and experience, like pillars of witness set up, in travelling through the vale of life, to mark particular occurrences. The footsteps are obliterated now; the face of the country may be changed, but the pillar is still there to remind me how all things were when it was reared.
>
> (*AG*, 146)

Simple quatrains, between ballad and Wesleyan hymn, offer to the reader a deeper form of that intimacy of address which characterises the whole novel, compiled, Agnes says, from a diary (*AG*, 197). Poetry's witness is biblical, nomadic, a retrospect across the wilderness of Exodus. The inner landscape is barren and our human imprint soon annihilated. Only the written word prevails against time. The narrator lays primary emphasis on the ethical value of autobiography, promising to 'lay before the public what I would not disclose to the most intimate friend' (*AG*, 1). The novel's considerable artistry is subordinated to this duty of the plain style to verisimilitude. Mendacity is the great transgression, with frivolity a close second, since truth is sacred, and a woman's word observes a duty to echo God's Word.[9] In the minor key, *Agnes Grey* prizes humble details of beauty in the natural world, the tender ephemera of primroses, which focus the 'associations' binding Agnes to home and roots. There is a microscopic lens, a Wordsworthian attachment to a 'violet by a rocky stone / Half hidden from the eye'.[10]

But there is also panoramic focus: the 'wide white wilderness' of a snow scene; seascape and sunset of the concluding chapters; a profound symbolism of shadow that moves across the magnificent gardens of Rosalie's stately home:

> The shadow of this wall soon took possession of the whole of the ground as far as I could see, forcing the golden sunlight to retreat inch by inch, and at last take refuge in the very tops of the trees. At last, even they were left in shadow – the shadow of the distant hills, or of the earth itself.   (*AG*, 181)

As day progresses, shadow deepens: motion is all recessional, as an eye-witness too poor to own the cheapest watch sits through hours, registering the gradual failure of light in the world outside the window, the high wall like a sundial telling that the time is late. This long paragraph records the reduction of Agnes' own prospects to the sombre, 'workaday hue of … my world within'. For a little, the birds soaring high 'might still receive the lustre on their wings . . . at last, that too departed'. It is in the sombre, patient truthfulness of the novel's witness that its peculiar beauty lies.

Whereas in *Agnes Grey* the wilderness is marked retrospectively by 'pillars of witness', steadfast in their testament to the pilgrim's journey, Emily Brontë's *Wuthering Heights* embraces the wilderness as homeland, the soul's origin and its quietus. To the needy, mutinous children of the first generation, the moors are sanctuary, play-space but also the surface of the underworld. Nelly hums a primitive Danish–Scots ballad above the sleeping orphan, Hareton:

> It was far in the night, and the bairnies grat,
> The mither beneath the mools heard that.
>
> (*WH*, 76)

The earth ('the mools') is the mothers' burial chamber, spectrally alert to the keening of neglected children. In *Wuthering Heights*, the mothers die, leaving humanity to 'an infernal house' (*WH*, 65), from which the open moors offer refuge. Heath stealthily crosses the church wall to cover the first Catherine's grave, taking her body home; as children, she and Heathcliff run wild across its forbidden spaces. Peaty swamps preserve bodies in the burial ground, confounding the process of time and decay. Treacherous but beautiful, the moorlands at once beckon and threaten. Agnes can look back with certainty through the markers established by her lyrics, across a biblical wilderness alien to the exiled wanderer. The 'pillars of witness' are stable and definitive. But the terrrain of *Wuthering Heights*, 'the barren', is its own cryptic memorial.

Catherine Earnshaw, later estranged from her roots and identity as the married 'Catherine Linton', voices the poetry of the novel. She is a 'marred child', a 'wild, wick slip', a dictatorial, self-willed lass whose first recorded desire is for a whip, and whose natural affinity is for a man whose name compounds 'heath' and 'cliff', described by herself as 'an arid wilderness of furze and whinstone' (*WH*, 102). Whereas *The Professor* and *Agnes Grey* describe the struggle to tame the 'barren' in humanity, recoiling from ruffianly children and neglectful parents, *Wuthering Heights* places literate values in doubt, holding nature and culture in constant dialogue. Only in the second generation, with Hareton's acculturation, when 'the red firelight glow[s] on the two bonny heads' of teacher and pupil, does culture tame and nourish nature: the second Cathy cultivates Hareton's mind in reading-lessons (*WH*, 322).

But such reclamation fails to kindle the reader as does the devil-daring, godforsaken energy of the first generation. We are magnetised by wicked little heathens hell-raising on the moors, a bereft, headstrong and brilliant girl-child scrawling her transgressive diary over the margins and blank sheets of a pious tome. The narrator, taking her place in the boxbed, pokes his nose into her book, and reads how she took her 'dingy volume by the scroop and hurled it into the dog-kennel, vowing I hated a good book'. Catherine's attitude to books is vehement and appropriative: she would rather be a writer than a reader. Cathy disputes the canon – for it is certainly an expression of literary judgement to assert you hate a 'good book', in whatever sense. The Author of all is mocked. The diary-snippet, framed by Lockwood's commentary, is handwritten down the margins of a 'good' book. Nodding off, Lockwood has a double nightmare, of unforgivable sin, begotten by a girl's diary-secrets and scratched names on a ledge: '*Catherine Earnshaw... Catherine Heathcliff... Catherine Linton*' (*WH*, 17). The narrator is textually initiated into the cryptic drama of multiplying and divided identity: having perused Catherine Earnshaw's testament, he is subjected to hair-raising siege by an exiled Catherine Linton. For both narrator and reader, 'the air swarms with Catherines'. Catherines that are inside want to get out; and outsiders want to come in. This two-way flux of desire is the novel's dynamic.

Catherine's speeches have a poetry that magnetises the reader into imaginative embrace of her heresies. Just as her dreams go 'through and through me, like wine through water' (*WH*, 79), so her poetic voice dissolves its colours into our reading minds:

> ...heaven did not seem to be my home, and I broke my heart with weeping to come back to earth; and the angels were so angry that they flung me out, into the middle of the heath on the top of Wuthering Heights, where I woke sobbing for joy. (*WH*, 80)

The pulse of this speech is driven by the alliterating words that ground Emily's great novel: *heaven, home, heart, heath, Heights*. These 'H' words, forming a beguiling pattern with the names of Heights characters (Hindley, Hareton, Heathcliff), increase the aura of strangeness, each seeming like a shadow or reflection of the others, beckoning, mirroring, as if every name, person, event or thing were a ghost of every other. The names *Catherine, Heathcliff, Hareton* and *Earnshaw* recycle letters from *earth, heath, hearth, heart*. The key to such riddles is never confided. 'The secret truth of *Wuthering Heights*', said Hillis Miller, 'is that there is no secret truth.'[11] But that too is a matter of speculation. A secret, by its very nature, cannot be known. Emily Brontë brings language close to the condition of music, with its pattern of exposition, recapitulation and resolution. Music's enigmas cannot be 'solved'.

Catherine's dream derides and inverts the rigid irrationality of Christian (and matrimonial) law, which severs a woman from her deepest roots. How can the Father's 'heaven' which confounds its own logic by obligatory happiness and self-righteous angels tempt allegiance? Catherine prefers 'earth... the middle of the heath', as her original home. Her affinity with Heathcliff is 'the eternal rocks beneath', as against Linton's deciduous and perishable attraction, like 'the foliage in the trees'. Both are vital, but only one is necessary, for the one is the condition of the other. The dualism of the novel founds itself on the stressful interaction of binary oppositions – rocks/trees; heaven/earth; Grange/Heights; identity/opposition; chemical attraction/repulsion. For every 'rapping', there is a 'counter-rapping', as in Lockwood's first dream (*WH*, 22). Earth is the strife-giddy novel's destination and last word: 'that quiet earth'. The ending has the tone of that 'quiet consummation' in Shakespeare's *Cymbeline*; and, for all its ambivalence, echoes the desire in many of Emily's poems for 'the time when I shall be without identity'. In a Brussels essay, 'The Butterfly', Emily had viewed creation as 'meaningless', nature as 'a vast machine constructed solely to produce evil'.[12] A nihilistic strain coexists with a deep compassion for creaturely life condemned to savage impairment in a predatory chain of being.

Under snow, the moors are illegible. Storm and 'atmospheric tumult', the realm of the unconscious mind, which characterise these uplands, soon turn from the spectacular to the forbidding, awakening in the naive, unnerved narrator, Lockwood, an answering tumult. His nightmare of terror and cruelty as he dreams of the spirit at the window whose wrist he drags on the broken pane 'to and fro till the blood ran down' (*WH*, 23) also grasps the reader with its cold hand, and awakens a shocked thirst for elucidation. The narrator is astray in this *terra incognita*, where guideposts lie. Landmarks are all in doubt:

> ...the whole hill-back was one billowy, white ocean, the swells and falls not indicating corresponding rises and depressions...a line of upright stones [continued] through the whole length of the barren: these were erected and daubed with lime on purpose to serve as guides in the dark...but excepting a dirty dot pointing up here and there, all traces of their existence had vanished...
>
> (*WH*, 29)

The 'upright stones' reduced to 'dirty dots' mime our common disorientation as the author (hidden behind, between, or within a succession of discrepant narrators)[13] leads us into a terrain of doubt, in which little is sure save the dubiety of surfaces. *Wuthering Heights* observes a duty to chart, measure, count, in meticulous detail (the 'upright stones' are 'at intervals of *six* or *seven* yards', 'daubed with lime'): verisimilitude is not mocked, but the novel declares the limitations of realism, where guideposts can only be relied on as 'not indicating' truths hidden beneath. The deviant text is, if not illegible, then haphazardly legible. It has kicked literary convention into the kennel and vowed that it 'hates a good book', refusing its responsibility to account for itself politely to the reader.

Authorial irony makes the novel's meaning a forcefield of ambivalence, through canny use of the uncanny and terse description which constantly turns to symbol. Landscape is artfully personified and character assimilated to nature. A 'range of gaunt thorns all stretching their limbs one way, as if craving alms of the sun' (*WH*, 2) implies the exposure of life at altitude weathering it out against northerlies sweeping over the edge. The hawthorns with their beggars' 'limbs' suggest skeletal paupers condemned to famish for a charity the sun withholds. The suggestion of stint and distortion as an inevitable result of adverse conditions roots in a symbolic landscape close to Burke's idea, in *A Philosophical Enquiry into the Sublime and the Beautiful*, of the 'sublime' in art, which transmutes 'pain and danger [and] terror' into fascination.

Whereas Emily Brontë's sisters' novels registered spirited determination to secure a place in the adult world, to live fruitful and respected lives, *Wuthering Heights* demolishes the assumptions of the given world. The church decays in the course of the novel; God is mocked; gender-norms reversed. The novel is not radical but recidivist; uninterested in social protest, it exhibits an extremist's scepticism. It is one of the great prose poems in our language. Turning to *Wuthering Heights* from *Agnes Grey* and *The Professor* involves ascent from minor to major; from the personal and linear to the sublime and cyclical. A tale of hectic children and feuding adults also ponders quintessential mysteries of human experience, addressing the Faustian realm of a secret 'other world', through narrative language whose directness is only equalled by its reticence; dark, wicked mirth and soaring scenes of dramatic poetry. The anomalous love between Catherine Earnshaw and Heathcliff discharges rebellious energy against norms and laws, the self's boundaries: 'What were the use of my existence if I were entirely contained here?' Catherine meditates. But the metaphysical dimension is earthed in patiently observed psychology. The hubristic revolt of Catherine and Heathcliff masks neediness and damage. These orphaned children, whose passion awes readers with its power, are bonded in panic-stricken symbiotic dependence. Violence of speech and action, which so offended early critics,[14] expresses trauma. These children too crave alms of the sun.

Whereas Anne Brontë's vision of nature focuses on its gentler details, the face of primrose and harebell, Emily's novel has an epic sweep which marries (a marriage of constant stress) beauty and violence; extremes of desire with the grave; the demonic and the animal with the human: with dispassionate calm it ponders strife and fratricidal conflict within the human family and the mortal world. Yet *Wuthering Heights* too brings its gentler gifts: 'a handful of golden crocuses' laid by Linton on Catherine's pillow (*WH*, 134); 'the last bud from the multitude of blue-bells' (*WH*, 230); 'moths fluttering among the heath and hare-bells' in the incomparable conclusion. The author, unlike either of her sisters, had the rare gift of saying little, and the rarer gift of not needing to make herself understood. Taciturn in life, her eloquence in art attained a relentless economy, supporting her plot's withholding of vital facts (Where did Heathcliff originate? Where does he abscond to? How does he acquire his polish? What is the status of the 'ghost' of Catherine? Do the lovers rest in the 'quiet earth'?). The novel, by refusing us the pleasure of gratified curiosity, affords the sharper pleasure of perpetual arousal, an arousal which also constitutes a major theme. Heathcliff gazes into the space of his desire 'with such eager interest that he stopped breathing, during half a minute together', 'his eyes pursued it with unwearied vigilance'; his 'absorbed attention' cannot be distracted from his 'engrossing speculation' (*WH*, 331). Our intense curiosity is the literary equivalent of the character's straining desire, whose symptoms we perhaps palely emulate in reading.

Catherine's story is one of exogamy, change of name, movement away from origins; the normal pattern for women, but a norm her nature cannot endure. Her aberrant mind homes to childhood freedom, from the stifling gentry comfort of Thrushcross. The novel criticicises neither woman's lot in society nor Catherine's resistance to gender norms: it criticises nothing. It brings everything into dispute, tearing open consensus norms to reveal their subterfuges and casuistry. In her delirium, Catherine 'tore the pillow with her teeth ... seemed to find childish diversion in pulling the feathers from the rents she had just made', arranging them on the sheet according to different species:

> 'That's a turkey's ... and this is a wild-duck's; and this is a pigeon's ... And here is a moor-cock's; and this – I should know it among a thousand – it's a lapwing's. Bonny bird; wheeling over our heads in the middle of the moor. It wanted to get to its nest, for the clouds touched the swells, and it felt rain coming. This feather was picked up from the heath, the bird was not shot – we saw its nest in the winter, full of little skeletons. Heathcliff set a trap over it, and the old ones dare not come. I made him promise he'd never shoot a lapwing, after that, and he didn't. Yes, here are more! Did he shoot my lapwings, Nelly? Are they red, any of them? Let me look.'

'Give over with that baby-work!' I interrupted, dragging the pillow away, and turning the holes towards the mattress, for she was removing its contents by handfuls. 'Lie down and shut your eyes, you're wandering. There's a mess! The down is flying about like snow!'   (WH, 122–3)

What Nelly dismisses as 'childish diversion' and 'baby-work', furnishing only more chaos and chores, is, however, forensic and revelatory. The tug-of-war about a pillow is also a struggle over truth: whether to collude with society's hypocrisy or to face the terror of what it conceals. Nelly turns the ripped side face-down. For Catherine's pillow, part of the comfort padding her life at Thrushcross, is full of death. Killing and dismemberment are the price of the pillow. This is no 'diversion' but a literal and unpalatable fact. As its innards are drawn out and analysed by a pregnant woman engaged in deeper 'baby-work', 'civilised' life is anatomised as founded on disorder and destruction.

The vista of bleak beauty is fraught with desolation. Heathcliff's trap, delivering a 'nest of little skeletons' is a product of the blood-sports mentality like Tom's in *Agnes Grey*, but whereas in Anne's novel man's cruelty to fellow creatures is a sign of human disobedience to the divine command to love our neighbours, in Emily's it marks an orphaned universe, threatening the young of all species. The tender tone of the meditation beginning 'Bonny bird...' expresses endeared affinity with 'my lapwings', as if Catherine wished them under her wing against her companion's rapacity. Hurt passes on as hate: this behavioural law drives the plot. Catherine's wandering mind is only superficially disorderly. It eviscerates the assumptions of the social order.

Wuthering Heights is a novel of extraordinary intellectual power. It bears affinities to Shakespeare, Milton, Scott and the works of the English Romantic poets, especially Byron's dramatic poem, *Manfred* (1817), with its solitary outcast hero and its image of a love which reaches beyond the grave. In Belgium, Emily Brontë had had the chance to come into contact with German Romantic philosophy and art. While *The Professor* is cosmopolitan in its Brussels setting and addiction to the French tongue, *Wuthering Heights* has deeper European affiliations, with Goethe (especially *Faust*), with Novalis (the subjectivist 'world within'), with Schlegel (the unconscious, romantic irony), and with Hoffmann (the demonic *Doppelgänger* or double, and split personality). Schlegel's idea of irony as 'jest and yet seriousness, art-less openness and yet deep dissimulation', containing and inciting 'a feeling of the insoluble conflict of the absolute and the relative, of the impossibility of total communication' fits Emily Brontë's novel exactly, as does his notion of the 'synthetic writer' who provokes the reader into creative dialogue with double-bound ironies and polyphonic narrative.[15]

Wuthering Heights shows a unique grasp of dialectical philosophy. Dualism functions as irony, both in detail (Heathcliff's "walk in" means "Go to the Deuce!") and in dramatic irony. Whereas irony in *The Professor* is volatile, and in *Agnes Grey* self-deprecating and socially critical, in *Wuthering Heights* it constitutes the work's deep structure. Just before Catherine unforgettably identifies herself with Heathcliff ("Nelly, I *am* Heathcliff"), her own words have driven this 'other self' away. 'He had listened till he heard Catherine say it would degrade her to marry him, and then he staid to hear no farther.' The climactic moment of supreme dedication and poetic grandeur therefore marks a void. As in Greek and Shakespearean tragedy, every sublime claim Catherine utters predicts her doom: 'He quite deserted! We separated!... Who is to separate us, pray? They'll meet the fate of Milo!' (*WH*, 81). At this moment, Heathcliff has understood himself to be deserted; the two are separated; and the transgressor who will 'meet the fate of Milo' is Catherine herself. Catherine's attempt to unite with her 'other self' divides her: the schismatic self in the surface of the mirror, as she disintegrates, seems a terrifying other. Later, Heathcliff, in a nightmare of multiplied and dispersed identities, will view a universe of mirror-images of the lost Catherine.

The tragic clovenness of the first generation modulates in the second into tragi-comic harmony, as the Heathcliff element is bred and starved out and the second Catherine and Hareton unite. The plot divides to conclude. Heathcliff's plot against both dynasties aborts itself in irony. His degradation of the moving figure of Hareton arouses his own unwilled sympathy. 'It is a poor conclusion, is it not... when everything is ready, and in my power, I find the will to lift a slate of either roof has vanished!' (*WH*, 323). The narrative mode is commonly labelled a system of Chinese boxes or Russian dolls, a 'concentric' system of narratives.[16] But the structure is never 'concentric': it diffuses and exfoliates, rather than repeating a tidy system of enclosures. The two major narrators, male and female, southerner and northerner, outsider and insider, master and servant, narrate in a volatile rhythm, the one fading into the other, diffusing themselves in a neutral authorial voice, dividing again in recurrent dialogue. The term 'concentricity' is a spatial metaphor, not to be mistaken for a technical term.

Style varies from the poetic to the tersely casual; epithets are few and verbs forceful. The tellers use *thrust, pitch, fling* for *push* or *throw*; speech-acts *asseverate, vociferate, snap, sob, cry, shout, snarl*. A Latinate vocabulary is subtly grafted into a tough, lean telling, founded on Nelly's 'gossip's' style – that of an oral witness telling a 'yarn', with its dialect flavour ('My history is *dree*, as we say') and brusquely neutralising scepticism amidst emotional furore. The dogs of Yorkshire idiom savage the vacuities of southern politeness. Whenever Joseph appears or is quoted (in all but one chapter), wit sounds its comic bass. Joseph's rancid pharisaical humour and peaty idiom sends up the standard English of gentry and readers. 'Mim! mim! mim!' he mimics Isabella. 'Did iver Christian body hear owt like it? Minching un' munching! Hah can Aw say whet ye say?' (*WH*, 138).

The 'hermeneutic promise' of *Wuthering Heights* is said to lead towards empty space: 'one dreams of finding its centre only to find that the centre is a dream'.[17] Yet the ghostly interplay between story and frame, reader and text leads, in the experience of generations of readers, not into the solipsistic realm of *trompe l'oeil* but out to heart and mind, in the natural world. The novel's dialogue resembles less a voyage to the 'empty' heart of darkness than a musical exploration of themes extending their logic to its limit, before yielding to reluctant, relieved composure of conflict in 'that quiet earth'.

NOTES

1. Letter to Elizabeth Branwell, 29 September 1841, in *CBL* 1, 268.
2. See Edward Chitham, *The Birth of 'Wuthering Heights': Emily Brontë at Work* (Basingstoke: Macmillan,1998).
3. 'Queen Bees or Working Bees?' *The Saturday Review* 8, 12 November 1859, 576.
4. *The Professor*, edited by Heather Glen (Harmondsworth: Penguin, 1989), 292, n.1.
5. Letters to Constantin Heger, 24 July 1844; 18 November 1845, in *CBL* 1, 358, 437. See Lyndall Gordon, *Charlotte Brontë: A Passionate Life* (London: Chatto & Windus, 1994), ch. 4.
6. 'I wake and feel the fell of dark, not day', in *Poems of Gerard Manley Hopkins*, edited by W. H. Gardner, 3rd edn. (Oxford University Press, 1964), 109.
7. Diary Paper 31 July 1845, in *CBL* 1 , 410. See also Edward Chitham, *A Life of Anne Brontë* (Oxford: Blackwell, 1991), ch. 3.
8. Howard E. Gruber, *Darwin on Man: A Psychological Study of Scientific Creativity, together with Darwin's Early and Unpublished Notebooks* (London: Wildwood House, 1974), 281.
9. See Elizabeth Langland, *Anne Brontë: The Other One* (Basingstoke: Macmillan, 1989), 120–3.
10. William Wordsworth, 'She dwelt among the untrodden ways', in *Poems*, 1, edited by J. O. Hayden (Harmondsworth: Penguin, 1977), 366.
11. J. Hillis Miller, *Fiction and Repetition: Seven English Novels* (Cambridge, Mass.: Harvard University Press, 1982), 51.
12. Translated by Stevie Davies in *Emily Bronte: Heretic* (London: Women's Press, 1994), 250 (appendix). See also *Charlotte and Emily Brontë, The Belgian Essays*, edited and translated by Sue Lonoff (New Haven: Yale University Press, 1996).
13. See J. T. Matthews, 'Framing in *Wuthering Heights*', *Texas Studies in Literature and Language* 27: 1 (Spring 1985), 25–61.
14. See, for example, G. W. Peck, review of *Wuthering Heights*, *American Review*, June 1848, in *CH*, 235–42.

15. For a fuller discussion of Emily Brontë's relation to German Romantic thought, see Stevie Davies: *Emily Brontë: Heretic*, chs. 1, 2, and 4; and *Emily Brontë* (Plymouth: Northcote House with The British Council, 1998), 37, 52–3, 71, 94–9.

16. On 'concentricity' in *Wuthering Heights*, see Patsy Stoneman, ed., *Wuthering Heights. A Reader's Guide to Essential Criticism* (Cambridge: Icon Books, 2000), 71–83.

17. Carol Jacobs, '*Wuthering Heights*: At the Threshold of Interpretation', *boundary* 27: 3 (Spring, 1979), 49.

5

JILL MATUS

'Strong family likeness': *Jane Eyre* and *The Tenant of Wildfell Hall*

Jane Eyre is today a classic, canonical text, beloved of generations of readers. A passionate, headstrong narrative of a young woman confronting the world with obstinate integrity, it treats of marginality and loneliness, of the desire for adventure, intimacy and independence. Its heroine confronts myriad dangers and oppressions but survives to tell a tale of triumph and even revenge. Advertising itself as an autobiography – the title-page of the first edition reads *Jane Eyre: An Autobiography* edited by Currer Bell – it draws generically also on romance and quest narrative, fairy tale, the gothic novel, and the Bildungsroman. Densely allusive, it reflects its author's familiarity with the Bible, Milton and Shakespeare, and with works as diverse as *Pilgrim's Progress* and *The Arabian Nights*. Anne Brontë's *The Tenant of Wildfell Hall* is by comparison an obscure text. Though recently it has claimed the interest of feminist scholars for its focus on marital abuse and child custody, it has, in the one-hundred-and-fifty years since its publication, been neither well known nor well loved. Its dual narrative – the heroine's private diary framed by letters from her second husband to his brother-in-law – is often considered clumsy; its subject – a bad marriage and its consequences – depressing or uncongenial. The novel's frame of reference is religious rather than psychological; the Bible its most frequently quoted text. The heroine of *The Tenant* endures the degrading ordeal of her first marriage with piety and stoicism, trying to remain focused on doing her duty as she worries about her abusive husband's tainting and corruptive influence, even on herself. Only when she judges that maternal supersedes wifely duty does she flee him, abducting her child and hiding out in a distant county. The temperature of these texts, metaphorically speaking, is very different. *Jane Eyre* is hot: angry, aggrieved, clamorous, exhilarated; by comparison *The Tenant* is cool: reasoned, ironic, cautionary, sceptical. *Jane Eyre* is about injustice redeemed, *The Tenant* about keeping faith while living with error and mistakes. One makes demands on life, the other withstands them. One is about quest and passage, the other about aftermath. Yet for all these differences, the texts are clearly related. Each concerns a woman earning her own living and resisting threats to her personal integrity, at the same time, however, as countenancing the force of desire and sexual attraction. Each draws in its depiction of male characters on the tradition of the rake and opposes the nineteenth-century myth that it is the duty of women to save dissolute men from themselves. Both novels treasure the culture of the mind and imagination, and place a high value on the visual arts and the pleasures of literature. These two texts are also closely related to the Brontë novels that preceded them. It is as if each Brontë sister broke off a piece of the same large clump of creative clay and set to kneading and shaping it in her own way. That clay is what we may call the common matrix of the Brontë texts. It produced novels of great individuality that are also closely akin.

On the face of it, *Jane Eyre* looks like the eldest literary sibling because it was the first novel by a Bell brother (that is, Brontë sister) to appear in print. It was published in October 1847 by Smith, Elder & Company. *Agnes Grey* and *Wuthering Heights* appeared shortly thereafter in December 1847, published by Thomas Newby. Having bound Ellis and Acton Bell to an option on their second novels, Newby also published *The Tenant of Wildfell Hall* in June 1848, unscrupulously advertising it as by the author of the new bestseller *Jane Eyre*. The publication dates of these novels, as we know, do not correlate with the order in which they were written. For that, we must look to the history of their composition, which tells a story of overlapping productions and concurrent or closely serial activities. *Jane Eyre* was begun in the summer of 1846 and completed about a year later. Most critics believe that *The Tenant* was being written around this time too. 'It is not possible to discover exactly when she began it', says Juliet Barker, 'but the likelihood is that it had been prompted by the sudden unexpected visit to the parsonage in April of Mrs Collins, the long-suffering wife of the former curate of Keighley.'[1] If Anne did begin her novel in the autumn of 1846, as Edward Chitham suggests, *Jane Eyre* and *The Tenant* are especially close siblings in that they share roughly the same period of composition.[2] Reviewers frequently discussed the two novels in conjunction with each other, and on several occasions treated them as if the two came from the same pen. 'Here we have the same rigid, direct, compressed tone of narrating, which, with its undercurrents of humour and wayward pathos, was so striking in *Jane Eyre*', wrote the reviewer for the *Manchester Examiner* of *The Tenant of Wildfell Hall*.[3] Another declared that the two novels were 'strikingly alike in sentiment, style, and general modes of thought' (*CH*, 266–7). That claim bears some qualification, but the early reviewers' sense of their 'strong family likeness' (*CH*, 259) is worth recalling because it allows us to grasp the unique purchase of each on a common matrix. I begin with *The Tenant*, the lesser known of the two. While the account of *Jane Eyre* that follows pays some attention to its singular characteristics and its resonances with *Agnes Grey* and *Wuthering Heights*, I have structured much of the discussion comparatively, drawing on *The Tenant of Wildfell Hall* in order to approach *Jane Eyre* in the context of family likeness.

In a preface that she wrote to the second edition of *The Tenant of Wildfell Hall*, Anne Brontë defended herself against the sharp criticism this work had drawn from reviewers. She responded spiritedly to the charges that the work was coarse and brutal, that it put an offensive subject in the worst light. Declaring boldly that she would rather whisper a few wholesome truths than much soft nonsense, she averred that it was better to depict vice and vicious characters as they really were 'than as they would wish to appear' (*TWH*, 4). The second edition of *Jane Eyre* was also accompanied by a preface in which Charlotte thanked her reviewers and dedicated the novel to Thackeray, whom she described as the high-priest of truth.[4] As their prefaces show, both sisters share the view that fiction should not shrink from telling the truth, however unpalatable it may be. In the light of this common conviction, Charlotte's criticism of *The Tenant of Wildfell Hall* seems rather harsh. For she judged the whole enterprise a mistake, and omitted Anne's second novel from the 1850 edition of her deceased sisters' works. In the Biographical Notice of her sisters, which prefaced that edition, she intimated that Anne was not cut out to shed light on disturbing realities; though her motives were 'pure,' they were also 'slightly morbid'. Earlier, she had written that 'the simple and natural – quiet description and simple pathos are, I think, Acton Bell's forte' (*CBL* 11, 94). It may be that Charlotte's discomfort with Anne's novel increased because it was so twinned with *Jane Eyre,* which, like *The Tenant of Wildfell Hall*, had been labelled coarse and vulgar. But despite unfavourable reviews (or perhaps because of the notoriety they gave the novel) *The Tenant of Wildfell Hall* sold well, a second edition being issued not long after the first. Indeed, 'the demand for it was second only to *Jane Eyre*'.[5]

Charlotte's Biographical Notice unfortunately set the tone for ensuing valuations of *The Tenant of Wildfell Hall*. There is little doubt that the novel articulates its author's dismay at her brother Branwell's dissolution, Mrs Collins' plight as wife of a profligate clergyman, and the immorality and hypocrisy which had sickened Anne in her years as a governess at Thorp Green. But it is surely a mistake to see *The Tenant* merely as a documentation of social vice, and to deny Anne Brontë's self-conscious artistry, imagination and enjoyment of her work.[6] Just as *Agnes Grey's* journey to the heart of governessing darkness is far more than a governess' sombre account of her job, so Anne's second novel is rather more than a cautionary and didactic tract about marriage and masculine vice.

One aspect of Anne Brontë's creativity is her response to literary antecedents and traditions. For example, her novel is linked to the gothic tradition through the tale of terror, varieties of which the Brontë children had read avidly in *Blackwoods Magazine*.[7] *The Tenant of Wildfell Hall* has some close affinities to Samuel Warren's 'A "Man about Town"' (1830), a doctor's tale of the demise of a dissolute man.[8] This tale of terror does not rely on brooding mystery or the supernatural accoutrements of the gothic tradition, but thrills and appals in its graphic realism, its descriptions of the decay and wastage of the patient as he pursues his own self-destruction through drink and drugs. Like Warren's story, *The Tenant* is a form of what we might call medico/religious gothic, and, indeed, both have antecedents in current medical and temperance literature describing the symptoms of dissolution and decay.[9] The debauched subject of 'A "Man about Town"' dies haunted by the thought that his body is hell-bent, but he still refuses religion and the clergyman. Like Huntingdon, he thinks he will recover; his intimate acquaintance deserts him and he dies in fear and defiance rather than repentance. The difference is that Arthur has Helen to minister to and pray for him, even though she insists that no one can be responsible for another's salvation. She cannot, however, bring herself to believe in everlasting damnation and writes to her brother that whatever fires may purge the 'erring spirit', it will not be lost to God, 'who hateth nothing that He hath made [and] will bless it in the end!' (*TWH*, 431). 'A "Man about Town"' is important as a literary predecessor of *The Tenant of Wildfell Hall* in that it counters the assumption that Anne Brontë's work was merely a transcription of observed reality. That assumption is further countered by recognising the novel's engagement with literary representations of the rake: the 'progress' of Arthur Huntingdon is the aristocratic roué's downward spiral to an agonising and fearful end. As we know, the juvenile chronicles of Gondal and Angria were greatly influenced by Moore's *Life of Byron* and other accounts of the world of Regency profligacy which fascinated all the young Brontës. As well as drawing on the first-hand evidence of Branwell's delinquencies, Huntingdon and his milieu certainly owe something to works such as Moore's.

The Tenant is shaped structurally and thematically by its responses to the earlier Brontë novels. 'Family likeness' here is evident in Anne Brontë's intense engagement with male socialisation and maturation. Like Charlotte Brontë's first novel, *The Professor*, *The Tenant* features a fully developed and complex male narrator and begins in the epistolary mode. Like that of *The Professor*, the first letter in the novel treats of friendship, intimacy, and reserve. Gilbert Markham's pretext for telling his tale is atonement. His

Figure 4 A young military man. Pencil drawing by Charlotte Brontë. Brontë
Parsonage Museum.

correspondent has chided him about his previous unwillingness to communicate. Whereas Charlotte abruptly abandoned the epistolary mode, leaving
her narrator's first letter unanswered, Anne continues with the nominal sense
of an interlocutor and the occasion of a sharing of life history.[10] So, for example, when Markham brings Helen Graham a book, he imagines Halford's
question: 'What, then had she and you got on so well together as to come

to the giving and receiving of presents?' – 'not precisely, old buck; this was my first experiment in that line; and I was very anxious to see the result of it' (*TWH*, 67). But if Anne attempts a riposte to *The Professor* in creating a socialised, unalienated narrator who is capable of intimacy with other men, she handles a double-edged sword. Gilbert's connection with Halford is restored at the cost of Helen's confidences. Though we may recognise that Markham's correspondence is simply the pretext for his and Helen's narratives, it may yet strike us as discomforting that Helen's husband now offers up her private and intimate journal for another's perusal. When Helen gives him the diary she tells him not to 'breathe a word of what it tells you to any living being – I trust to your honour' (*TWH*, 121). Yet on the next page Markham offers it to Halford saying, 'I know you would not be satisfied with an abbreviation of the contents and you shall have the whole' (*TWH*, 122). We may imagine that now, some years later, Gilbert would surely have gained Helen's consent. But we could also read these details as conveying the novel's scepticism or even pessimism about the authority and voice women retain in marriage.[11]

If *The Tenant of Wildfell Hall* responds formally to *The Professor* it also grasps a thematic baton passed on at the close of that novel. What is perhaps most startlingly suggestive in the relationship between the two works is the discourse of the intolerable husband, raised only as the former novel nears its end and then in the context of Crimsworth's happy marriage. 'Frances was then a good and dear wife to me, because I was to her a good, just and faithful husband. What she would have been had she married a harsh, envious, careless man – a profligate, a prodigal, a drunkard, or a tyrant, is another question...' (*P*, 235). If she had married such a man, says Frances, 'I should have tried to endure the evil or cure it for awhile: and when I found it intolerable and incurable, I should have left my torturer suddenly and silently.' She adds that 'if law or might' forced her back to 'a drunkard, a profligate, a selfish spendthrift, an unjust fool', she would have returned and 'again assured myself whether or not his vice and my misery were capable of remedy; and if not, have left him again' (*P*, 235). This conversation rehearses in large part the enterprise of Anne's second novel: a wronged wife's course of action in a situation of marital abuse and misery. At the close of *The Professor* Charlotte also introduces the (related) question of how a son is to be raised: 'They are disputing about Victor, of whom Hunsden affirms that his mother is making a milksop.' Mrs Crimsworth retaliates: 'Better a thousand times he should be a milksop than what he, Hunsden, calls 'a fine lad' (*P*, 242). The Crimsworths do see a streak of passion and waywardness in their son that needs the 'ordeal of merited and salutary suffering, out of which he will come...a wiser and better man' (*P*, 245). In a reversal of Mrs Crimsworth's previous sentiments about 'fine lads', they conclude that if 'merited and salutary suffering' means he has to be beaten into shape at school, then so be it. In its closing pages, then, *The Professor* sounds a theme that runs through the sisters' novels – the education, discipline, and upbringing of boys.

When Mrs Markham invites the new tenant and her young son to tea much of the conversation revolves around competing notions of how to raise a young man. Charged with turning her boy into a 'mere Miss Nancy' or a milksop, Helen gives vehement voice to her views:

> You would have us encourage our sons to prove all things by their own experience, while our daughters must not even profit by the experience of others. Now *I* would have both so to benefit by the experience of others, and the precepts of a higher authority, that they should know beforehand to refuse the evil and choose the good, and require no experimental proofs to teach them the evil of transgression . . . [A]s for my son – if I thought he would grow up to be what you call a man of the world – one that has '*seen life*', and glories in his experience, even though he should so far profit by it, as to sober down, at length, into a useful and respected member of society – I would rather that he died to-morrow! (*TWH*, 31)

While few readers today would concur with Helen's 'aversion therapy' for turning poor young Arthur off tippling, Anne Brontë is nevertheless perceptive about prevailing constructions of gender, especially the way in which discourses of 'manliness' produce men.[12]

The choice of a male narrator for much of *The Tenant* provides Anne with a sustained opportunity for further exploring constructions of masculinity. Yet critics of the novel have not sufficiently recognised the importance of Gilbert Markham in Anne's comparisons of male and female socialisation. The eldest son of a doting mother, he is used not only to having his own way, but to finding it smooth. Mrs Markham's speeches about male privilege and her daughter Rose's complaints about Gilbert's precedence provide grist for the novel's critique of the indulgence of sons. His first response to Helen's impassioned speech about 'men of the world' is numbingly insensitive. He bypasses what Helen is saying and views the conversation simply as a parlour wrestling match, peevishly responding: 'you ladies must always have the last word' (*TWH*, 32). Provoked by her speech, he calls her his 'fair antagonist,' and on leaving gives her hand a 'spiteful squeeze'. He is vexed because she seems to think less well of him than he does of himself, but concedes: 'Perhaps, too, I was a little bit spoiled by my mother and sister, and some other ladies of my acquaintance; – and yet, I was by no means a fop – of that I am fully convinced, whether you are or not' (*TWH*, 32). The vehemence of this disclaimer emphasises its untruth, for the Gilbert who first meets Helen is indeed immature and foppish.

In this regard, Gilbert Markham recalls Lockwood, the narrator of *Wuthering Heights*, and *The Tenant of Wildfell Hall* is closely akin to Emily's novel in its sophisticated use of narrative frames and multiple narrators. Both novels begin with the arrival of a tenant, though here they stand in a relation of chiasmus. The former starts out with a male narrator who is the new tenant at the Grange and hard put to divine the relationship among the strange inhabitants of Wuthering Heights. The latter begins with a male narrator responding to the mystique of a new tenant at neighbouring Wildfell Hall. Both narrators are foppish, though Gilbert undergoes some degree of transformation, whereas Lockwood does not.[13] In the case of both Lockwood and Markham, the male narrator frames the account of a female narrator. Lockwood works on the narrative, domesticating it. No matter what 'bitter herbs' Mrs Dean's narrative offers, he resolves to make of them wholesome medicine, wondering at the end 'how any one could ever imagine unquiet slumbers for the sleepers in that quiet earth' (*WH*, 338). Gilbert, on the other hand, is affected by Helen's narrative in a way that suggests a capacity for growth and maturity, if not perfectibility. Whereas Arthur is the means through which Anne explores the failure to improve or reform, Hattersley, Lowborough and even Markham himself provide more sanguine possibilities.

Critics have suggested that *The Tenant of Wildfell Hall* demythologises the violence and gothicism of *Wuthering Heights*: whereas *Wuthering Heights* is amoral, *The Tenant* is moral. The occasion of Heathcliff's violent treatment of Hindley bears comparison with that in which Gilbert Markham violently whips Lawrence, whom he misapprehends as Helen's suitor. The salient difference between the two, it has been suggested, is that Emily does not allow us to see the effects of violence from the perspective of the victim whereas Anne insists on making Gilbert Markham witness and own up to the consequences of his aggressive rage.[14] But are the two so different in their attitudes to violence? Heathcliff and Markham both attend to their victim's wounds after having inflicted them: 'Then [Heathcliff] tore off the sleeve of Earnshaw's coat, and bound up the wound with brutal roughness' (*WH*, 177). Similarly, Markham provides his victim with a handkerchief to staunch his wounds. Heathcliff, as we have come to expect, feels no remorse for wounding Hindley, but nor does Markham for having thrashed Lawrence; both simply do not wish their victims to die. Even though Markham's conscience makes him return to see that his victim is not bleeding to death, he is neither ministering nor repentant. When Lawrence refuses his help in remounting his horse or binding his hand, Markham leaves him with this parting shot: 'You may go to the d – l if you choose – and say I sent you' (*TWH*, 111). Nor is Markham's subsequent apology effusive: 'The truth is Lawrence...I have not acted quite correctly towards you of late.' After perfunctorily begging his pardon, he says 'If you don't choose to grant it...it's no matter – only, I've done *my* duty – that's all' (*TWH*, 392–3). Markham becomes a constant visitor not so much to make amends for his 'brutality' but because he is becoming attached to Lawrence, who reminds him very much of Helen. 'I loved him better for it than I liked to express; and I took a secret delight in pressing those slender, white fingers, so marvellously like her own, considering he was not a woman, and in watching the passing changes in his fair, pale features, and observing the intonations of his voice' (*TWH*, 399). Once enraged to discern young Arthur's likeness in Lawrence, and filled with dread suspicion that Lawrence is Arthur's father, he now responds almost erotically to Lawrence as Helen's double. Markham's behaviour after his beating of Lawrence confirms rather than corrects *Wuthering Heights*'s law of desire.

But there is a generic as well as a psychological reason for Gilbert's violence. Despite the fact that only fragments of Gondal survive, I would argue that Gilbert's ferocity and wilfulness, his spite and diabolic coolness may be in important ways a continuation of the Gondal world which Anne and Emily shared. His narration is at times closely related to the mode of passionate and even violent romance that derives from the imaginative childhood worlds of Angria and Gondal and is manifest in both *Wuthering Heights* and *Jane Eyre*. The reviewer who surmised that perhaps 'the hand that penned [the horsewhipping scene] was accustomed to the savage luxury of chastising an insolent foe' ought rather to have asked about the tradition of reading and writing out of which that hand developed.[15]

Apart from the whipping of Lawrence, Markham's passionate outbursts are, for the most part, occasions for a genial mockery of arrogant immaturity or romantic lovesickness. 'I can crush that bold spirit', thought I. But while I secretly exulted in my power, I felt disposed to dally with my victim like a cat'. (*TWH*, 118). This image is very similar to that which Nelly Dean uses to describe Edgar Linton, after Cathy has slapped him: 'he possessed the power to depart, as much as a cat possesses the power to leave a mouse half killed, or a bird half eaten' (*WH*, 72). The difference is that while Emily startles the reader with the ambiguous subject positions of victim and predator, Markham makes himself look foolish with his puffed-up sense of power and his conception of relationship as antagonism and power struggle. When he later experiences love as rapture or torment, the language he uses is remarkable for its high-flown sentimentalism and exaggerated romanticism: 'I need not dilate upon the feelings with which I approached the shrine of my former divinity – that spot teeming with a thousand delightful recollections and glorious dreams' (*TWH*, 117–18); 'You have blighted the freshness and promise of youth, and made my life a wilderness!' (*TWH*, 120–1). 'Cupid's arrows', he says, 'not only had been too sharp for me, but they were barbed and deep rooted, and I had not been able to wrench them from my heart' (*TWH*, 107). He suffers 'pangs of unutterable regret' (*TWH*, 121). Markham is a self-styled romantic hero, whose turbulent passions and excesses are at times made to seem slightly ridiculous. In the course of the novel, he occupies a variety of subject positions as Anne Brontë engages with the discourses that construct masculinity: youthful romanticism; foppishness; sexual jealousy, aggression and violence; sensitive, unthreatening manliness. He is never an idealised antidote to Arthur Huntingdon, but a means by which Anne Brontë puzzles over the question of masculine adequacy – what makes a worthwhile, redeemable, 'good enough' man.

That is an important question in the context of the male power and privilege that Anne Brontë sees everywhere. Specifically comparing the situations of men and women in marriage, the novel offers a sustained consideration of issues such as domestic abuse, and marriage and custody law. The only way to end a marriage before 1857 was by ecclesiastical annulment or private act of Parliament. And even under the act of 1857, which provided for civil divorce, adultery was not sufficient grounds for a woman to sue. She could only do so if a husband was physically cruel, incestuous, or bestial as well. If she left him without first obtaining a divorce she was guilty of desertion and forfeited all claim to a share of property (even that which she might have brought into the marriage) and to custody of their children.[16] In *The Tenant of Wildfell Hall* Lord Lowborough eventually obtains a divorce from the adulterous Annabella, though initially they simply separate without public scandal. She lives a gay life in London, he stays in strict seclusion at his old castle, with the two children 'both of whom he keeps under his own protection' (*TWH*, 333). But after Annabella's second misdemeanour, an elopement to the continent, Lord Lowborough 'sought and obtained a divorce' and subsequently remarried a woman of sense and integrity, who would keep him from his own worst tendencies and be a fine mother to his children (*TWH*, 439). When he discovers his wife's duplicity, Helen assures him that '. . . two years hence you will be as calm as I am now, – and far, far happier, I trust, for you are a man and free to act as you please' (*TWH*, 328). Helen, however, cannot divorce Arthur because she has neither sufficient grounds nor funds, and a yet more pressing barrier in the shape of her young son.

By setting her novel prior to 1839, Anne Brontë ensures that the first minimal reforms in custody law would not be available to her heroine. At this time, 'fathers were by law the custodial parents of their children'.[17] During the 1830s, agitation for reform met with some success in the Custody of Infants Act, which was passed in 1839. This act provided that a mother could petition in the equity courts for custody of her children up to the age of seven, and for periodic access to children aged seven or older. A mother could not avail herself of even these limited rights if she had been found guilty of adultery either in an action for criminal conversation or in an ecclesiastical court. And, of course, the woman had to be rich enough to enter a suit in Chancery. No other statuary modification of the common law affecting custody was made for eighteen years. In *The Tenant of Wildfell Hall* Helen has no custodial right to her young son. Therefore she must hide, which is why she is now the secretive tenant of Wildfell Hall. When she returns voluntarily to care for Arthur, she attempts to make her husband sign a waiver of his custodial rights to the child, in the presence of Rachel, as witness: 'You will not see him till you have promised to leave him entirely under my care and protection and to let me take him away whenever and wherever I please, if I should hereafter judge it necessary to remove him again' (*TWH*, 410). He protests but eventually manages to hold a pen and 'ratify the agreement'. Though Helen confidently uses the language and authority of the law here, the legitimacy of the contract, obtained by putting Arthur under duress, is surely questionable. The incident shows, however, that Helen has moved a long way from her early zeal in saving her husband from his self-indulgence; she opts now instead to secure her maternal relationship and her son.

Brontë's grasp of the legal and practical inequities that women suffer in marriage leads her to the question of what kind of marriage might be possible for a woman who values her independence and integrity. For all the novel believes in the reality of heaven and hell and the absolute contrast between them, it suggests that on earth there are no absolutes and we live with compromise and imperfection. Brontë cautiously proposes for her heroine a second match that is far from perfect, but at least not oppressive. The union of Helen and Gilbert resists the familiar romantic scenario of the rich and masterful hero, who is the means of raising the heroine to a social station her beauty deserves. Rather, Helen is superior to Gilbert in almost all respects. Indeed, she raises him, not only in rank, but in moral and spiritual status as well. Whereas in *Jane Eyre*, Charlotte Brontë invests male dominance and mastery with allure, men are least attractive when most commanding in *The Tenant of Wildfell Hall*. Far from equalising the disparities between Gilbert and Helen at the close of the novel, Anne Brontë increases them by making Helen the heir of her uncle, generally a 'worthless' man but responsive in this instance to his wife's insistence that their niece inherit the estate. Helen is in fact indirectly inheriting her aunt's property, a detail that suggests both how marriage diminishes a woman's power – her aunt's property brought to the marriage became her uncle's – and how women may help to empower each other in spite of the inescapable and pervasive institutions of patriarchy.

Like *The Tenant of Wildfell Hall, Jane Eyre* bears the stamp of its author's personal experiences and observations of the world. In the shocking conditions that young Jane endures at Lowood, for example, we can see the transmutation of Charlotte's traumatic experiences at the School for Clergy Daughters at Cowan Bridge. Biographers have also suggested that through her narrator Brontë was able to express 'the pent-up emotion that had been fermenting in her soul' since her years in Brussels and her thwarted passion for her married teacher, Monsieur Heger.[18] But autobiographical details are only one element of Brontë's complex creativity, which blends experience, observation and invention. In *Jane Eyre* literary realism, with its emphasis on verisimilitude and the ordinary and everyday, is wedded to romance with its tendencies towards strong contrasts, repetitive patterns, and use of the supernatural and symbolic. The mix produces an extraordinary work that is both historically specific and imaginatively rich. Having been told that her first novel was 'deficient in startling incident' Brontë strove to impart to her second a 'more vivid interest' (*CBL* I, 535) only to find critics such as George Henry Lewes warning her to 'beware of Melodrame' [*sic*] and 'to adhere to the real'. Writing back to Lewes, Charlotte defended most eloquently her trust in the imagination:

> But, dear Sir, is not the real experience of each individual very limited? and if a writer dwells upon that solely or principally, is he not in danger of repeating himself, and also of becoming an egotist?
> Then too, imagination is a strong, restless faculty which claims to be heard and exercised: are we to be quite deaf to her cry, and insensate to her struggles? When she shows us bright pictures are we never to look at them and try to reproduce them? – And when she is eloquent and speaks rapidly and urgently in our ear are we not to write to her dictation?' (*CBL* I, 599)

Jane Eyre is indeed packed with startling incident of a melodramatic sort, but its 'vivid interest' also arises from the way the first-person narrator communicates the dramatic complexity of her inner life. Shifts and changes in feeling acquire themselves the status of incidents and are often expressed in powerful, emotive images and, on occasion, the language of melodrama. Commenting on her younger self's 'fierce speaking', the narrator says 'A ridge of lighted heath, alive, glancing, devouring, would have been a meet emblem of my mind when I accused and menaced Mrs Reed.' The after effect of such mutiny is 'the same ridge, black and blasted after the flames are dead' (*JE*, 37–8). Describing her attempts to suppress her love for Rochester, her fear that he is to marry Blanche Ingram, she has recourse to a disturbing image of infanticide: 'And then I strangled a newborn agony – a deformed thing that I could not persuade myself to own and rear – and ran on' (*JE*, 244). When St John proposes marriage, she responds, 'my mind is at this moment like a rayless dungeon, with one shrinking fear fettered in its depths'. As he presses his suit, she continues, melodramatically: 'My iron shroud contracted around me' (*JE*, 403–4). Brontë here echoes a tale of terror called 'The Iron Shroud' by William Mudford, which like Warren's 'A "Man about Town"' was published in 1830 in *Blackwood's Magazine*. Mudford's tale concerns a prisoner in a cell, whose walls of smooth, black iron slowly contract around him and crush him. His funeral bier is this iron shroud. The literal becomes metaphoric as Charlotte Brontë develops from this tale of terror a language of the self: the rayless dungeon and the contracting iron shroud image the collapse of Jane's mind and will under St John's pressure. But the novel uses terror and the gothic in a variety of ways. Brontë draws on the staple atmospherics and accoutrements of gothic fiction to arouse mystery and intensify fear. But even as she exploits gothic trappings and conventions, she also parodies them. The demonic laughter that Jane Eyre hears and is encouraged to attribute to Grace Poole does indeed emanate from a raving maniac; the horrific scene in which Rochester's bed is set alight by Bertha is leavened with humour as Jane pours cold water over her master.[19] Critics have suggested that the gothic characteristically literalises the internal, or projects an internalised state of mind onto the external. Such ideas might fruitfully be applied to *Jane Eyre*, particularly in thinking about Bertha as Jane's double, her avatar or agent, or an extreme form of aspects of herself.[20] The gothic is bent in *Jane Eyre* to express the 'darker side of feeling and personality'.[21]

The urgent and insistent expression of feeling has long been seen as this novel's hallmark. In *The Common Reader*, Virginia Woolf wrote: '[Brontë] does not attempt to solve the problems of human life; she is even unaware that such problems exist: all her force, and it is the more tremendous for being constricted, goes into the assertion, "I love", "I hate," "I suffer."'[22] This is in part true of Jane, whom Woolf here conflates with her creator. But Brontë's depiction of whom Jane Eyre loves, why she hates, and how she suffers draws us into a consideration of the problems of human life as a young woman in the early nineteenth century may have found them. Her encounters with the life-denying attitudes of Evangelical clergy, her experience of the marginal options available to a woman without class or wealth produce a novel that is historically specific about human problems even as it focuses on one individual's experience. So, in her oft-quoted outcry against stultification, her desire for travel and scope, Jane Eyre articulates more than a purely personal problem:

> Women feel just as men feel: they need exercise for their faculties, and a field for their efforts as much as their brothers do; they suffer from too rigid a restraint, too absolute a stagnation, precisely as men would suffer. (*JE*, 109)

Even where the novel does not self-consciously raise problematic issues, it encodes them through its focus on the heroine's inner world. For example, Brontë represents Jane's antithesis (and also *alter ego*) as a sexually overblown Creole from Jamaica, a vicious madwoman, the germs of whose hereditary insanity are nurtured by self-indulgence. The representation of Bertha draws on a range of specifically Victorian discourses for demarcating otherness: gendered notions of inherited insanity; racially inflected ideas about self-indulgence and excess; constructions of colonial identity and England's relations with her colonies in the early to mid 1800s. Bertha's fire-setting and insurrection may recall the slave riots in Jamaica; Jane's uncle Eyre is connected to the Mason family through the channels of colonial enterprise. These references to Jamaica and the colonies signal the novel's imaginative engagement with the reality of empire. This may not be what Woolf meant by 'the problems of human life', but they are arguably just that if we think of problems as historically specific. Though its focus is undoubtedly personal and emotional, *Jane Eyre* is a novel of vast scope, strongly connected to the problems of its day.

Of the Brontë novels that preceded *Jane Eyre*, *Agnes Grey* is, in some respects, its closest kin. *Jane Eyre*, too, is the first-person narrative of a governess, poor, plain and obscure. Turning to novel writing after their childhood collaborations, the Brontë sisters continued to involve each other in their work. In her biography of Charlotte Brontë, Elizabeth Gaskell writes:

> Once or twice a week, each read to the others what she had written, and heard what they had to say about it. Charlotte told me, that the remarks made had seldom any effect in inducing her to alter her work, so possessed was she with the feeling that she had described reality; but the readings were of great and stirring interest to all, taking them out of the gnawing pressure of daily-recurring cares, and setting them in a free place. It was on one of these occasions that Charlotte determined to make her heroine plain, small, and unattractive, in defiance of the accepted canon.[23]

Gaskell's account captures a sense of Charlotte's fierce, creative conviction – she could seldom be induced to alter her work – and of her under-acknowledged debt to Anne's first novel. Charlotte may have decided to make Jane Eyre plain and small in defiance of the accepted canon, but Anne

Brontë had already attempted just this in *Agnes Grey*. In *Agnes Grey* a young woman keen to try her talents and help her family's financial situation goes out with excitement and anticipation to earn a living as a governess. *Jane Eyre* develops a similar idea, though Jane's yearning for scope and adventure is more passionately avowed. Whereas Agnes believes she will find a certain liberty in servitude, Jane Eyre, yearning to escape 'the routine of eight years' at Lowood, distinguishes the two:

> I desired liberty; for liberty I gasped; for liberty I uttered a prayer; it seemed scattered on the wind then faintly blowing. I abandoned it, and framed a humbler supplication; for change, stimulus: that petition, too, seemed swept off into a vague space; 'Then,' I cried, half desperate, 'Grant me at least a new servitude!' (*JE*, 85)

Jane Eyre also follows *Agnes Grey* on the question of beauty and its social valuation. Agnes meditates on the fact that those judged not beautiful are likely to find little consolation in the conventional wisdom that beauty is only skin deep. Beauty elicits approbation; ugliness is unlovable. Thus a little girl will love her pretty bird, Agnes reasons, but not a toad, though it 'likewise, lives and feels' (*AG*, 138). Anne's literal is Charlotte's metaphoric toad: the servants at Gateshead agree that 'if [Jane] were a nice, pretty child, one might compassionate her forlornness; but one really cannot care for such a little toad as that' (*JE*, 26). Whereas Agnes communes philosophically with herself on the subject of beauty, Jane speaks out for all those who are judged 'soulless and heartless' because they are plain and poor. 'If God had gifted me with some beauty, and much wealth', she erupts, imagining that Rochester is about to marry Blanche Ingram, 'I should have made it as hard for you to leave me, as it is now for me to leave you' (*JE*, 253).

Jane Eyre shares with *Wuthering Heights* the use of several romance strategies. In both novels, for example, nature, landscape and weather carry strong symbolic significance. On the night when Rochester proposes to Jane, a storm rages and lightning strikes the great chestnut tree in the orchard; nature alerts us that all is not right with the union (*JE*, 259). But although place names in *Jane Eyre* have symbolic reverberations, and journeys from one place to another are important in plotting Jane's progress, the novel has none of the sense of rootedness or feeling for place to be found in *Wuthering Heights*. Nor does nature in *Jane Eyre* offer succour from the cruelties of human interactions and social arrangements. Fleeing from Rochester, Jane almost perishes out on the moors. *Wuthering Heights* opposes the freedom of nature to the repressions of culture, but *Jane Eyre* sets great store by acculturation and accomplishment; indoors, here, is often preferable to out. In the famous opening lines of the novel, Jane is glad to stay inside, curled up with a book about nature, protected from the 'cold winter wind' and 'penetrating rain'. In *Wuthering Heights*, Lockwood's first waking dream or nightmare of the fantastical waif Catherine, whose wrist he rubs against the jagged edge of a broken window pane, indicates how easily the thin veneer of civilised behaviour is stripped away, and makes Heathcliff's haunting real. *Jane Eyre* too makes use of dreams and supernatural occurrences. But Charlotte Brontë is less concerned to indicate a world beyond the real than to delineate Jane's psychic space through the use of dreams. Jane's several dreams of children perform an obvious foreshadowing function – dreams of children always mean trouble, Bessie has told her – but their main effect is to give form to Jane's subterranean fears and remind her of the parts of herself still unmothered and unnurtured.[24] Similarly, the supernatural occurrences in the novel can be understood as external manifestations of internal processes. Jane's experience of supernatural guidance in the form of the maternal moon's injunction to 'flee temptation' gives external form and authority to her inner convictions. Rochester's voice, heard over long distance summoning Jane to his side and releasing her from St John's inexorable control, is uncanny in its telepathic power, but functions too as a way of legitimating Jane's longing to return to him. The voice, says Jane, 'seemed in *me* – not in the external world' (*JE*, 421).

A keen understanding of childhood hurt and loss drives both *Wuthering Heights* and *Jane Eyre*, though the latter is unique among the Brontë novels in its focus on the solitary, suffering child. Charlotte Brontë writes particularly perceptively about the effects of the psychic shock that Jane suffers as a result of the red-room episode. The trauma vitiates affect and appetite. Jane is weakened and nervous, unable to enjoy what would once have given keen pleasure. She cannot read *Gulliver's Travels* with the same imaginative gusto, or relish a tart, or respond to the beauty of the 'brightly painted China plate' that she has always admired. Jane at Gateshead is a discord, 'an interloper not of [Mrs Reeds's] race'; again at Lowood Brocklehurst brands her an 'interloper'. Heathcliff too is described as an 'interloper' and a 'cuckoo'. Both novels focus on the way in which the marginal and spurned outsider comes to exert power and to triumph over oppressors. Heathcliff's revenge on his oppressors or rivals is overt, extreme and demonic. It is also ultimately ironic, for once Heathcliff has monopolised the property of Heights and Grange through gambling and coerced marriages, he lacks the will, he says, 'to lift a slate off either roof' (*WH*, 323). With the union of Catherine and Hareton, the 'cuckoo's' usurpations and dynastic control are over. Jane's triumph and revenge are less overtly acknowledged in the text because they are acted out by others (Bertha, for example) or enacted at the level of the plot. But all those who cross, thwart or oppress Jane Eyre – the Reeds, Rochester and St John – suffer punishment or die.

Both *Wuthering Heights* and *Jane Eyre* are concerned fundamentally with rebellion against the accepted order of things. Emily Brontë uses one stormy generation to plumb the extremes of a set of irreconcilable oppositions – Heights and Grange, nature and culture, social identity and individual integrity – and then a milder second to assess the possibility and costs of reconciling those oppositions. But rebellion and reconciliation are more problematically bound up in one central consciousness in *Jane Eyre*. From the first, reviewers commented on the fire-breathing quality of its almost vanquished but also vanquishing heroine. It fosters the spirit of Chartism, one reviewer pronounced; it murmurs against accepting one's place in the world. Never was there such a complainer, such an aggrieved soul.[25] (This of course is exactly what generations of readers have cherished in *Jane Eyre*.) But, as some critics have noticed, although Jane begins as a slave in revolt, a rebel questioning dominant ideological assumptions, she becomes part of the very order she was resisting and indeed ends up underwriting what she originally sought to oppose.[26]

An early reviewer, drawing out the similarities between *Jane Eyre* and *The Tenant of Wildfell Hall*, observed that, when troubles gather, the heroines of both novels 'take to open country under an assumed name...where they keep themselves concealed, and suffer hardships' (CH, 260). Helen Huntingdon, however, is helped by her brother; Jane, alone, almost perishes from exposure and hunger and is reduced to begging for a mess of cold porridge destined for the pigs' trough. This salient difference points to the fact that Charlotte Brontë creates a heroine thoroughly alone in a threatening world. What distinguishes Jane's narrative, then, is its urgent sense of the perilousness of existence. 'You must be tenacious of life', says Rochester, on hearing of Jane's survival of Lowood (*JE*, 121). This is not simply to say that more dangerous and exciting obstacles threaten Jane, though indeed they do, in the form of a nervous fit in the red-room; privations and disease at Lowood; a fire, a madwoman; death by starvation on the moors; and St John's urgings to go to India. Her battle is often against death itself, and her triumph is to stay alive. Jane is a survivor against a fairly constant threat of annihilation, detectable even in the 'happy ending' which finds her living at Ferndean, whose insalubrious climate she has survived for a decade at the time of writing her story. And this was the place that Rochester thought unfit for Bertha! Helen experiences marital abuse, incarceration, and the status of fugitive. Never, however, does she feel herself to be in mortal danger in a hostile and threatening world.[27]

Helen Huntingdon is also sustained by a strong religious faith that Arthur can never threaten. His view is that 'a woman's religion ought not to lessen her devotion to her earthly lord' (*TWH*, 193). She counters that she will give her heart and soul to her Maker, and 'not one atom more of it to you than He allows. What are *you*, sir, that you should set yourself up as a god, and presume to dispute possession of my heart with Him to whom I owe all I have and all I am' (*TWH*, 193). Both *Jane Eyre* and *The Tenant of Wildfell Hall* strongly endorse that no love should be entertained that threatens individual integrity.[28] Whereas Arthur sets himself up as a god, Jane makes one of Rochester, an apostasy that portends disaster: 'My future husband was becoming to me my whole world...He stood between me and every thought of religion...I could not, in those days, see God for his creature: of whom I had made an idol' (*JE*, 274). It is debatable, however, whether this idolisation eclipses Jane's relationship to her maker or to herself. Although Jane's narrative follows a familiar pattern of apostasy, from doubts about the reality of heaven to replacing God with Rochester, we never witness, as we would in a narrative about crisis and conversion, Jane's assumption of a secure faith. This is taken for granted in the retrospective tone of the narrative: when Jane says that 'in those days' she could not 'see God for his creature' she implies that now she can. And yet her final words about earthly bliss with Rochester are still framed in what contemporary readers would understand as a discourse of idolatry. The uncertain nature of Jane's faith is further underlined in her refusal of St John and God's work in India, and the triumph of romantic over religious love that the close of the novel suggests.[29] There is no such ambiguity in *The Tenant of Wildfell Hall*.

Like *The Tenant of Wildfell Hall*, *Jane Eyre* focuses on marriage as a tie that binds rather than sustains. Rochester is, like Helen, a spouse shackled to a failed marriage and burdened by an inadequate and degrading partner. Their rights are, however, very different, as are their responses to their respective situations. Both novels raise questions about the state of family and divorce law in the 1840s when the Brontës were writing, and in the period in which they are set. Rochester specifically addresses the question of legal proceedings when he eventually tells Jane the story of his marriage to Bertha:

> My brother in the interval was dead; and at the end of the four years my father died too. I was rich enough now – yet poor to hideous indigence: a nature the most gross, impure, depraved, I ever saw, was associated with mine, and called by the law and by society a part of me. And I could not rid myself of it by legal proceedings; for the doctors now discovered that *my wife* was mad – her excesses had prematurely developed the germs of insanity   (*JE*, 306)

Rochester implies here that because Bertha is mad, he cannot divorce her. Later he says, categorically: 'I knew that while she lived I could never be the husband of another and better wife.' The point here is not so much to ask why the law would not allow Rochester to divorce Bertha, but that in the terms of the novel it is necessary for him to be saddled with an immovable burden. This way, Rochester is guilty of error, dissipation and attempted bigamy, but he is also redeemable and forgivable, especially since he attempts to rescue Bertha from herself even at his own peril.

Rochester's capacity for redemption is intimated in a letter that Brontë wrote to W. S. Williams denying the similarity between *The Tenant of Wildfell Hall*'s Huntingdon and the hero of *Jane Eyre*:

> You say Mr Huntingdon reminds you of Mr Rochester – does he? Yet there is no likeness between the two; the foundation of each character is entirely different. Huntingdon is a specimen of the naturally selfish sensual, superficial man, whose one merit of a joyful temperament only avails him while he is young and healthy, whose best days are his earliest, who never profits by experience, who is sure to grow worse, the older he grows. Mr Rochester has a thoughtful nature and a very feeling heart; he is neither selfish nor self-indulgent; he is ill-educated, mis-guided, errs, when he does err, though rashness and inexperience: he lives for a time as too many other men live – but being radically better than most men, he does not like that degraded life, and is never happy in it. He is taught the severe lessons of Experience and has sense to learn from them – years improve him; the effervescence of youth foamed away, what is really good in him still remains.   (*CBL* 11, 99)

Charlotte Brontë's decided 'yet there is no likeness between the two' attempts to dispose of the matter. What the perceptive Williams may have been suggesting, however, is that both Charlotte and Anne Brontë are responding to the tradition of the rake and his progress. Whereas Anne treats 'progress' ironically as a steady decline, Charlotte redeems Rochester, who, embittered at being the dupe of his father and brother, became dissolute, but only for a time. In pleading with Jane to stay at Thornfield, he acknowledges his past: 'you must regard me as a plotting profligate – a base and low rake who has been simulating disinterested love in order to draw you into a snare...' (*JE*, 299). He admits to having tried 'dissipation' but 'never debauchery' (*JE*, 311). The rake truly progresses in Charlotte's terms to redemption through suffering and repentance, a movement that shows Rochester's Byronism to be 'external and reformable'.[30] The attempt to enlist Jane in that reform provokes one of the novel's most intense crises as Rochester pleads with her to be his 'comforter and rescuer'. Both *Jane Eyre* and *The Tenant of Wildfell Hall* oppose the contemporary notion that women can be agents of moral reform and spiritual salvation, though Helen Huntingdon, echoing Richardson's Clarissa, surely begins by subscribing to it: 'If he is now exposed to the baneful influence of corrupting and wicked companions, what glory to deliver him from them! – Oh! If I could but believe that Heaven has designed me for this!' (*TWH*, 275). She will later come to insist, however, that no one can be responsible for another's salvation. Even more strongly than Helen, Jane asserts her independence of the prevailing idea that it is the duty of woman to sacrifice herself in improving or protecting a sinning man. With a self-preservatory eye on the history of Rochester's past mistresses, Jane refuses to be compromised by staying with him after his attempt at a bigamous marriage, though she wrestles with 'Feeling', which begs her 'think of his misery; think of his danger – look at his state when left alone… soothe him, save him; love him…' (*JE*, 317).

The fantasised space of the hero at the end of both *The Tenant* and *Jane Eyre* is one of humility and reduced power. Gilbert Markham's sense of disentitlement corresponds to the humbling of Rochester, though here the loss of power comes not from disparity in rank and fortune but from Rochester's physical disempowerment and new-found Christian humility. Whereas Gilbert Markham talks of the folly of his cherished hopes, Rochester murmurs regretfully of his 'seared vision' and his 'crippled strength' (*JE*, 444). Both men feel that their wives will make sacrifices in marrying them. Both are brought to a position where they cannot behave masterfully and must rely on the woman to orchestrate and script the proposal scene. The Samson images that Brontë earlier invested in Rochester are cashed now by reference to his sightless eyes and reduced strength. It is Jane who has all power and control on her return, though the text remains ambivalent about the seductiveness of dominant male personalities; Jane continues to refer to Rochester as 'Sir' and 'my master' (*JE*, 444). While Rochester humbly thanks God for returning Jane to him, she makes no disclosure of the fact that she heard and answered his cry to her. In addition to supervising what is best for him to know, Jane enjoys teasing Rochester about her recent suitor, inciting her blackened Vulcan to jealousy of the fair Apollo who has not only made her a schoolmistress, and taught her Hindostanee but offered her marriage as well. With a sizeable inheritance from her Uncle Eyre, which she shares among her Rivers cousins, she is now anything but poor, obscure and friendless.[31]

The conclusion of *The Tenant of Wildfell Hall* has, at first sight, much in common with that of *Jane Eyre*. In each a second marriage takes place, which affects the fate of a young, dependent child; the happy couple live a secluded, anti-metropolitan life in the country, their children growing up around them; there are annual visits from extended family. But if the close of

The Tenant of Wildfell Hall is social, expansive and inclusive, the ending of *Jane Eyre* creates a sense of the opposite. Jane and Rochester seem isolated, exclusive, and in some way still under threat. Gilbert adopts young Arthur, Helen's son; Jane seems similarly to care for Adèle, whom she brings home from school, but she finds that she needs all her time for her husband. Adèle is sent away again to another, better, school, whose sound English education helps to iron out her 'French defects' (*JE*, 450). Helen and Markham live in pastoral comfort on their ordered estate with its fine lands, far from the 'dusty, smoking, noisy, striving, toiling city'. At the close of Gilbert's letter, he looks forward to the annual visit of his sister and her husband, which 'draws nigh' and promises the visitors 'invigorating relaxation and social retirement' (*TWH*, 471). Although Jane and Rochester too have alternate annual visits from Diana and Mary and their husbands, what 'draws nigh' at the end of *Jane Eyre* is not a visit, but a death. As St John Rivers anticipates his sure reward in Heaven, Jane, ever resolutely a survivor, and of this world, insists on hers here below. But while she and Rochester live in the manor-house at Ferndean, an unrentable building with 'dank, green walls' and a narrow front entrance, situated in a 'desolate spot', which lies 'deep buried' in a 'gloomy wood', that reward seems somewhat precarious. Though we have moved from the 'discord' that was Jane at Gateshead to her ' perfect concord' with Rochester, the novel's romantic apotheosis is still riven with tensions and contradictions. These are evident even in St John's imagined last words, scripted by Jane, which both undermine the status of her earthly happiness with their emphasis on death, and confirm her survival in opposing her heart's choice to his.

Indeed, both *Jane Eyre* and *The Tenant of Wildfell Hall* provoke some disquiet in their 'happy endings'. Although the mysterious tenant of Wildfell Hall becomes the proper mistress of Staningsley and finds happier accommodation in the social order, that order is still patriarchal and threatening to female voice; Helen seems silenced and distanced from the reader in Gilbert's closing retrospective. By the end of *Jane Eyre* we see how the narrator's will to power allows her to own and write her story. Yet despite the sense of Jane's ascendancy and power, and the fact that the unloved orphan finds kin, inheritance, personal refuge and marital joy, the novel still encodes a sense of the precariousness and fragility of human happiness.

NOTES

1. Juliet Barker, *The Brontës* (London: Weidenfeld & Nicolson, 1994), 530.
2. Edward Chitham, *A Life of Anne Brontë* (Oxford: Blackwell, 1991), 141.
3. *The Manchester Examiner* (supplement, 8 July 1848), 4.

4. See Barker, *The Brontës*, 541, for further explanation of the circumstances around this notorious dedication.

5. Lyndall Gordon, *Charlotte Brontë: A Passionate Life* (London: Chatto & Windus, 1994), 167.

6. Barker, for example, notes that 'though Charlotte suggested that Anne wrote her book out of a sense of duty and a distasteful one at that, the tone of much of *The Tenant of Wildfell Hall* belies this' (*The Brontës*, 532).

7. On the relationship of *The Tenant of Wildfell Hall* to the gothic tradition, see Jan Gordon, 'Gossip, Diary, Letter, Text: Anne Brontë's Narrative *Tenant* and the Problematic of the Gothic Sequel', *English Literary History* 51: 4 (1984), 720. For the most part, Anne's novel has been seen as opposed to the gothic; see, for example, Stevie Davies' introduction to *The Tenant of Wildfell Hall* (Harmondsworth: Penguin, 1996), x–xi.

8. Reprinted in Robert Morrison and Chris Baldick, eds, *Tales of Terror from Blackwoods Magazine* (Oxford: World's Classics, 1995), 181–214. Morrison and Baldick note that 'certain parts of this tale may have been used as the basis for the deathbed scene of Arthur Huntingdon' (293).

9. Marianne Thormählen, 'The Villain of *Wildfell Hall*: Aspects and Prospects of Arthur Huntingdon', *Modern Language Review* 88 (1993), 831–41, argues that Huntingdon is a 'textbook case' from John Graham's *Modern Domestic Medicine*, which was the Brontë's medical Bible (838).

10. Heather Glen, in her introduction to *The Professor* (Harmondsworth: Penguin, 1989) suggests that the abrupt cessation of the epistolary mode points to Crimsworth's alienation (12–13).

11. See Laura C. Berry, 'Acts of Custody and Incarceration in *Wuthering Heights* and *The Tenant of Wildfell Hall*', *Novel* 30: 1 (1996), 32–55.

12. Helen's methods were recommended by several temperance writers of the period. See Thormählen, 'The Villain of Wildfell Hall', 833; and the discussion of Helen's need for control in Russell Poole, 'Cultural Reformation and Cultural Reproduction in Anne Brontë's *The Tenant of Wildfell Hall*', *Studies in English Literature 1500–1900* 33 (1993), 860.

13. Elizabeth Langland, in *Anne Brontë: The Other One* (Basingstoke: Macmillan, 1989) observes that Anne uses Gilbert's enclosure – Helen's diary – to effect his transformation (135). Russell Poole, however, disputes that Gilbert Markham changes much in the course of the novel 'Culture Reformation' 860, and Rachel Carnell, in 'Feminism and the Public Sphere in Anne Brontë's *The Tenant of Wildfell Hall*', *Nineteenth-Century Literature* 53: 1 (1998), 1–24, continues the line of criticism which sees Helen as silenced by Gilbert's narration.

14. Edward Chitham suggests that *The Tenant* parodies and challenges *Wuthering Heights* both in its array of characters whose names begin with 'H' and in scenes showing the implications and consequences of violence (*Life of Anne Brontë*, 151–2).

15. *The Manchester Examiner* (supplement, 8 July 1848), 4.

16. See Mary Poovey, *Uneven Developments: The Ideological Work of Gender in Mid-Victorian England* (Chicago University Press, 1988), 55–57.

17. See Mary Lyndon Shanley, *Feminism, Marriage and the Law in Victorian England, 1850–1895* (Princeton University Press, 1989), 136.

18. Barker, *The Brontës*, 510.

19. See Robert Heilman's discussion of comic palliatives in 'Charlotte Brontë's "New Gothic"', in *From Jane Austen to Joseph Conrad*, edited by Robert C. Rathburn and Martin Steinmann, Jr (Minneapolis: University of Minnesota Press, 1958), 118–32.

20. On the gothic's literalisation see Margaret Homans, *Bearing the Word: Language and Female Experience in Nineteenth-century Women's Writing* (Chicago University Press, 1986), 84–99. On Bertha as Jane's atavar or double see Sandra Gilbert and Susan Gubar, *The Madwoman in the Attic: The Woman Writer and the Nineteenth-Century Literary Imagination* (New Haven: Yale University Press, 1979), 359–62.

21. See Heilman, 'Charlotte Brontë's "New Gothic"', 118–19.

22. Virginia Woolf, '*Jane Eyre* and *Wuthering Heights*' in *The Common Reader* (London: Hogarth Press, 1925), 199.

23. Elizabeth Gaskell, *The Life of Charlotte Brontë* [1857], edited by Alan Shelston (Harmondsworth: Penguin, 1975), 307–8.

24. On the dreams in *Jane Eyre*, see Homans, *Bearing the Word*, 84–99.

25. '*Vanity Fair, Jane Eyre* and the Governesses' Benevolent Institution Report for 1847', unsigned review by Elizabeth Rigby, *Quarterly Review* 84 (December 1848), 153–85 and unsigned review, *The Christian Remembrancer* 15 (April 1848), 396–409.

26. See, for example, Penny Boumelha, *Charlotte Brontë* (Hemel Hempstead: Harvester Wheatsheaf, 1990) and Terry Eagleton, *Myths of Power: A Marxist Study of the Brontës* (Basingstoke: Macmillan, 1975).

27. I am indebted to Heather Glen's study, *Charlotte Brontë: The Imagination in History* (Oxford University Press, 2002), which teases out these contrasting and irreconcilable aspects of the novel – Jane's sense of triumph and a corresponding, contradictory sense of the proximity of annihilation.

28. See Marianne Thormählen, *The Brontës and Religion* (Cambridge University Press, 1999).

29. I am here summarising Peter Allan Dale's thoughtful argument in 'Charlotte Brontë's 'Tale Half-Told': The Disruption of Narrative Structure in *Jane Eyre*', *Modern Language Quarterly* 47 (1986), 108–29.

30. Margaret Smith, introduction to *JE*, viii.

31. Although Jane Eyre does not betray Rochester's confidences in the same way as Markham does Helen's, the question of intimacy and confidantes is also a troubling one in *Jane Eyre*. See Lisa Sternlieb, 'Jane Eyre: Hazarding Confidences', *Nineteenth-Century Literature* 53: 4 (1999), 452–79.

6

HEATHER GLEN

Shirley and *Villette*

Shirley was written in circumstances very different from any of the Brontës' previous works. It was not merely that its writing was interrupted by the deaths of Branwell, of Emily, of Anne; that this was the first of the extraordinary productions of that extraordinary family to be completed outside of that intimate circle of excited, hopeful discussion of which Charlotte Brontë's first biographer was to tell. Less striking, in retrospect, but perhaps no less significant is the fact that *Shirley* was the first of the Brontë novels to be written by a famous author. Charlotte's long apprenticeship in literature had culminated in success. One, at least, of those youthful 'scribblemaniacs' now had an established place amongst the writers of the day.

'There has been no higher point in the whole history of English fiction' writes Raymond Williams of the year in which *Shirley* was conceived.[1] Dickens' *Dombey and Son*, Thackeray's *Vanity Fair* and Kingsley's *Yeast* were all appearing in parts; Mrs Gaskell's *Mary Barton* was to be published before *Shirley* was complete. And it was against her famous contemporaries that its author measured herself. 'Mr Thackeray, Mr Dickens, Mrs Marsh, & c., doubtless enjoyed facilities for observation such as I have not', Charlotte Brontë had written to her publisher just before the appearance of *Jane Eyre*. 'Certainly they possess a knowledge of the world, whether intuitive or acquired, such as I can lay no claim to – and this gives their writings an importance and a variety greatly beyond what I can offer the public.'[2] If the next novel she was to write is markedly different from *The Professor* and *Jane Eyre*, the difference might seem to bespeak an attempt to give her own work something of this 'importance' and 'variety'. *Shirley* is set, like *Vanity Fair*, in the period of the Napoleonic wars; concerned, like *Dombey and Son*, with technological change, like *Mary Barton* with the workers' 'starvation', and like *Yeast* with schemes for progress and for social reform. Its panoramic scope and its pronouncements on public issues seem to suggest that for this one at least of the Brontës that 'talking over' with her sisters of 'the stories they were engaged upon'[3] had been replaced by a different kind of dialogue with the eminent novelists of the day. Yet much that is most distinctive in *Shirley* has its origins in Haworth Parsonage: not in that 'consultation about plan, subject, characters or incidents' which its author had so recently enjoyed with Ellis and Acton Bell,[4] but in the more distant time of their shared literary apprenticeship, when four excited children had declared themselves powerful Genii and created the fictional world of Verdopolis, or Glass Town.

When *Shirley* was two-thirds completed, Charlotte Brontë wrote again to her publisher: 'Currer Bell – even if he had no let or hindrance and if his path were quite smooth, could never march with the tread of a Scott, a Bulwer, a Thackeray or a Dickens...calculate low when you calculate on me.'[5] *Shirley* has none of the easy authority of Thackeray, or the moral eloquence of Kingsley; nothing like Dickens' imaginative vision of social systems and institutions, or Mrs Gaskell's detailed knowledge of the living conditions of the poor. That 'making of connections between fragmentary and divided experiences' which Williams (speaking of *Dombey and Son*) calls 'the achievement, in the novel, of a new dimension of social consciousness' is notably absent here.[6] One finds instead a peculiar pot-pourri of subjects – the curates and their absurdities; Robert Moore's entrepreneurial ambitions; the dispute between masters and men; the story of Caroline Helstone's lonely decline, and of the aristocratic heiress, Shirley; the Yorke family and their concerns – interspersed with extended reflections upon such themes as the effects of the war with France and the sufferings of old maids. 'In *Shirley* all unity is wanting...It is not a picture; but a portfolio of random sketches', declared one contemporary review.[7] There are chunks of text in foreign languages, old ballads, hymns, poems, even a school essay. The first-person narrators of *The Professor* and *Jane Eyre* have here been replaced by a host of sharply characterised voices, whose divisive cacophony is emphatically evoked. This novel appears to have none of the strong imaginative coherence of the great diagnoses of the state of English society being produced by Charlotte Brontë's contemporaries in these years.

Thackeray's urbane ironies, Gaskell's moral earnestness are notably absent here. Instead, there is a more awkwardly intrusive narrator, who invites the reader 'back to the beginning of this century' with the distinctly deflationary image of an after-dinner snooze. 'Do you anticipate sentiment, and poetry, and reverie? Do you expect passion, and stimulus, and melodrama?' this voice demands on the opening page: 'twice in succession they are not good for you', reads a cancelled portion of manuscript here, in perhaps too-explicit reference to *Jane Eyre*.[8] Of course, this disclaimer is to be disproved, as the novel proceeds to tell of its dreaming, desiring heroines. In the stories of these, there is sentiment a-plenty, passion requited and not, poetry, reverie, even the melodramatic figures of a long-lost mother and a father who has tried to murder his child. Yet the feeling here is quite different from the passionate urgency of *Jane Eyre*. 'That music stirs my soul', says Shirley, listening to the 'martial tunes' played on the Sunday-school procession. 'I almost long for danger; for a faith – a land – or, at least, a lover to defend.' But the grandeur of this aspiration is punctured by the nature of the occasion which inspires it. 'No foe or tyrant is questioning or threatening our liberty', says Helstone, laughing at her. 'There is nothing to be done: we are only taking a walk' (*S*, 302).

Much of *Shirley* seems lacking in the sobriety which its subject-matter might appear to demand. Religious and political differences are here seen with a peculiar, 'jesting' irony; a tone which was, indeed, judged 'unseemly' by those accustomed to a rather different treatment of such themes.[9] It is thus that the novel opens, with a flippant allusion to the expansion of the church, and a sharply satirical view of those 'present successors of the apostles' who in other novels of the period were far more solemnly portrayed.[10] 'Why should religious distinctions and denominations be dragged in with a coarseness and vulgarity which would disgrace the pages of a pugnacious newspaper?' asked one reviewer at the time.[11] Throughout the novel, biblical texts are bandied about as counters in ignoble arguments; political disputes diminished into personal animosities. Theological disagreement becomes burlesque in the mock-heroic battle of the Sunday-school Whitsuntide feast. Even the story of class against class which lies at the novel's centre is presented with ironic detachment. 'You never heard that sound, perhaps, reader?' demands the obtrusive narrator, as he tells, at the climax of that story, of the 'West-Riding-clothing-district-of-Yorkshire rioters' yell':

> So much the better for your ears – perhaps for your heart; since, if it rends the air in hate to yourself, or to the men or principles you approve, the interests to which you wish well, Wrath wakens to the cry of Hate: the Lion shakes his mane, and rises to the howl of the Hyaena: Caste stands up, ireful, against Caste; and the indignant, wronged spirit of the Middle Rank bears down in zeal and scorn on the famished and furious mass of the Operative Class. It is difficult to be tolerant – difficult to be just – in such moments.   (*S*, 343)

And the distancing personifications, the alienating challenge to the 'reader', the relativising gesture at 'the principles you approve, the interests to which you wish well', all bespeak a view of the situation, and of the prospects for 'judgment' it affords, very different from those being articulated in the 'condition-of-England' novels of these years. The 'reader' is half taunted, half implicated – awkwardly detached from the 'tolerance' to which writers such as Gaskell appeal. Indeed, this peculiar irony seems, a little later in the novel, to be explicitly directed at the fictional expectations which *Mary Barton* had raised:

> I doubt not a justice-loving public will have remarked, ere this, that I have thus far shewn a criminal remissness in pursuing, catching, and bringing to condign punishment the would-be assassin of Mr Robert Moore: here was a fine opening to lead my willing readers a dance, at once decorous and exciting: a dance of law and gospel, of the dungeon, the dock, and the 'dead-thraw'. You might have liked it, reader, but *I* should not: I and my subject would presently have quarrelled, and then I should have broken down: I was happy to find that facts perfectly exonerated me from the attempt. The murderer was never punished; for the good reason, that he was never caught; the result of the further circumstance, that he was never pursued. (*S*, 725)

This kind of reflection on fictionality is very different from the dramatic immediacy of those distinctive first-person narrators, William Crimsworth and Jane Eyre.

Yet this peculiar abrasiveness is in Charlotte Brontë's writings by no means unprecedented. *Shirley* was completed, as she lamented, without 'the gentle spur of family discussion';[12] by the time it was published, all her fellow Genii were dead. But of all the novels of the Brontës' maturity, this is the one which is closest to the 'plays' of their early years. The debunking irony, the abrupt shifts of scene and character, the disconcerting reflections on narrative strategies which set this novel apart from *The Professor* and *Jane Eyre* are all prominent features of the writings of Glass Town. There, as here, romantic expectations are mocked, and heroic passions depicted in less than heroic guise. There, too, the reader is presented with a variety of points of view – points of view which are countered and challenged, and ironically or humorously portrayed. Not merely do the two principal narrators of Glass Town, Captain Tree and Lord Charles Wellesley, each offer markedly differing versions of events. From the 'anecdotes', the 'Conversations' and the correspondence columns of the early *Young Men's Magazine* to 'the talk of coffee-houses...the gossip of news-rooms... the speculations of public-prints...the chit-chat & scandal...respecting the characters, ongoings & probable destinies of eminent men'[13] evoked in Charlotte Brontë's later Angrian novelettes, the fictional world appears as a place of verbal controversy. And the joking play between the writing children includes a humorous emphasis on the narrative activity itself: 'A novel can scarcely be called a novel unless it ends in a marriage, therefore I herewith tack to, add, and communicate the following *postscriptum*.'[14] Throughout, the sense is less of feeling uncritically indulged than of a cool, critical, sometimes sardonic observation of feeling; less of an expressive outpouring of emotion than of a self-conscious play with fictionality – a play which points forward to *Shirley*'s ironic, distancing, self-referential narrative stance.

But in *Shirley* this stance seems to have become part of a much more coherent narrative enterprise than it is in the loosely structured fictions of its author's formative years. The banter with the reader on the opening page ('If you think, from this prelude, that anything like a romance is preparing for you, reader, you never were more mistaken') has an echo in the novel's closing words:

> The story is told. I think I now see the judicious reader putting on his spectacles to look for the moral. It would be an insult to his sagacity to offer directions. I only say, God speed him in the quest!

The family jokes of Glass Town have here been replaced by a deliberate, framing emphasis on the resistance of this 'story' to the kinds of interpretation its 'reader' is likely to attempt. And that passionate youthful interest in the contestatory voices of early nineteenth-century 'print culture', the imitation of that culture in the creation of Glass Town,[15] has become an elaborated fictional reflection upon the ways in which words both written and spoken construct the social world.

In the course of planning *Shirley*, Mrs Gaskell reports, Charlotte Brontë consulted the files of the *Leeds Mercury* for 1812–14.[16] Sometimes, this has been taken as evidence of her desire to acquire more detailed information about the historic events with which her novel was to be concerned. Yet from childhood the author of *Shirley* had been far more canny than this. 'We take 2 and see three Newspapers as such we take the Leeds Inteligencer party Tory and the Leeds Mercury Whig': thus wrote the thirteen-year old Charlotte in 1829.[17] And it seems that the impulse which led her, twenty years later, to turn once again to the *Mercury* 'in order to understand the spirit' of the times of which she was to write was not a naive desire to acquaint herself with the 'issues of the day', but a far more sophisticated sense that such 'issues' are refracted, always, through contesting voices and perspectives; that calm objectivity, or even simple fidelity to fact, are perhaps chimerical. Such a sense is prominent in *Shirley*. 'Sich paragraphs as we could contrive for t'papers!' cries Mr Yorke, fantasising a victory over 'these starved ragamuffins of frame-breakers'. 'Briarfield suld be famous; but we'se hev a column and a half i'th' *Stilbro' Courier* ower this job, as it is, I daresay: I'se expect no less.' 'And I'll promise you no less, Mr Yorke, for I'll write the article myself', the militant Helstone replies (*S*, 41). Joe Scott, Moore's foreman, tells him that 'I like reading, and I'm curious to knaw what them that reckons to govern us aims to do for us and wi' us' (S, 59). 'Lord Wellington's own despatches in the columns of the newspapers' are perused in the very different ways by the 'warlike' high Tory, Helstone and the 'bitter Whig', Robert Moore (S, 38, 102, 168). When Moore and Helstone quarrel at a public meeting, their dispute is continued in 'some pungent letters in the newspapers' (S, 168). Moore, visiting Shirley, brings with him 'a batch of newspapers, containing... accounts of proceedings in Nottingham, Manchester, and elsewhere' (S, 248). 'I should think you read the marriages, probably, Miss', says Joe Scott, patronisingly, as Shirley boasts of her newspaper-reading (S, 368): and the novel's account of its heroines' marriages is in the language of newspaper report. But the concern is not merely with 'print culture'. 'This was known at Briarfield: the newspapers had reported it: the "Stillbro' Courier" had given every particular, with amplifications', the narrator reports of the sentence on the attackers of Moore's mill:

> Disaffection, however, was still heard muttering to himself... One report affirmed that Moore *dared* not come to Yorkshire... 'I'll tell him that,' said Mr Yorke, when his foreman mentioned the rumour, 'and if *that* does not bring him home full gallop – nothing will'. (S, 528)

From the opening portrait of the curates, with their Babel-ish 'confusion of tongues' (S, 13), to the legends and reminiscences of the 'old housekeeper' at its close, there is in this novel a marked and distinctive emphasis – very different from anything in either *The Professor* or *Jane Eyre* – on that constant verbal interaction which constitutes the social world. 'Talking a bit! Just like you!' says Shirley, good-humouredly, to the crowd of 'milk-fetchers' at Fieldhead, on the morning after the attack on the mill. 'It is a queer thing that all the world is so fond of *talking* over events: you *talk* if anybody dies suddenly; you *talk* if a fire breaks out; you *talk* if a mill-owner fails; you *talk* if he's murdered' (S, 355). Even that question of the fate of single women which calls up Caroline's most intimate fears (and in dealing with which, perhaps, the narrative voice comes closest to the author's own) appears not just as a subject for private reflection, but as a theme of public talk. The rector's daughter's solitary musings, and indeed, the more spirited Shirley's pronouncements, are shot through with an awareness of that which others are wont to say: 'other people solve it by saying, "your place is to do good to others..." ' (S, 174); 'hard labour and learned professions, they say, make women masculine, coarse, unwomanly' (S, 229); 'Lucretia... and Solomon's virtuous woman, are often quoted as patterns of what "the sex" (as they say) ought to be' (S, 391). Indeed, the novel does not merely portray but itself appears to participate in such verbal controversy. Some of what 'they say' is directly reproduced in its verbatim quotation of passages from the hostile review which *Jane Eyre* had received two years previously in the *Quarterly Review*.[18] It seems that *Shirley*'s refusal of the authoritative voice of a Dickens, a Thackeray or a Kingsley is less symptomatic of its author's ineptitude in handling those public subjects with which they were concerned than indicative of a sense which she had been developing in fiction since childhood that the social world is a place of Babel dissension, which different voices configure in radically different ways.

Where other novelists of the mid-century appeal to a common humanity, *Shirley* insists on division. Where they make ethical judgements of their characters' actions and choices, there is a quite different emphasis in *Shirley* on that which the protagonists are impotent to change. And in this respect, too, Brontë's difference from her contemporaries appears to have its origins in the writings of Glass Town. For even in the very earliest of the Brontës' recorded 'plays' there is a constant, ironic emphasis on the limitations of those who inhabit the fictional world. It is an emphasis which owes a great deal to the lampoons of *Blackwood's* and of *Fraser's*. But it is not entirely or simply a debunking, satiric one. Informing the presentation of the early Glass Town characters is the (usually joking) awareness that these are relative creatures, dependent for their existence upon the mighty Genii, and not the independent subjects they believe themselves to be. 'It seemed as if I was a non-existent shadow, that I neither spoke, eat, imagined or lived of myself, but I was the mere idea of some other creature's brain,' confesses the usually confident Lord Charles Wellesley in one early story, as he tells of being lifted by 'a hand wide enough almost to grasp the Tower of all Nations' – that of the Genius who has created him.[19] The characters of *Shirley* are not disconcerted thus. But they are closer to the denizens of Glass Town than they are to the first-person narrators of *The Professor* or *Jane Eyre*. Emphatically objectified by a distancing narrative voice, their aspirations countered by the recalcitrance of 'events' – 'the cloth we can't sell, the hands we can't employ, the mills we can't run, the perverse course of events generally, which we cannot alter' (S, 23) – they are also suggestively different from the moral agents who inhabit those 'condition-of-England' novels with which *Shirley* is so often compared.

Robert Moore, the mill-owner, figure of thrusting ambition, is portrayed not through the prism of that ethical judgement which informs Gaskell's portrait of Carson in *Mary Barton*, but in language expressive of rather different concerns. The shaping interest is less in 'whether his advance was or was not prejudicial to others' than in a wholly different kind of challenge to that ambivalently seen 'advance':

At the time this history commences, Robert Moore had lived but two years in the district, during which period he had at least proved himself possessed of the *quality of activity*. (*S*, 29, my italics)

The energy which drives Moore forward is figured, strikingly, as a noun – a passive attribute, rather than an active force. And that which is foregrounded here is implicit in the description as a whole. Moore enters the narrative less as a free agent than as one who is subject to a causality beyond his control. Throughout the paragraphs which introduce him, the striving entrepreneur, 'keen o' making brass, and getting forrards', exponent of individualist competition and free trade, is presented in terms which emphasise passivity and unfreedom – as the inheritor of traits which (probably) determine his actions ('He came of a foreign ancestry by the mother's side ... A hybrid in nature, it is probable he had a hybrid's feeling on many points ...'); as one for whom 'Trade' is not a chosen occupation but a 'hereditary calling'; and as the victim of a whole constellation of 'bypast circumstances' not of his own making, of a shadowed childhood and a 'manhood drenched and blighted by the descent of the storm' (*S*, 27–8).

What is inscribed in this description of Moore is writ large in the novel's plot. For this 'man of determined spirit' (the ambiguity is surely intended) is portrayed less as a powerful agent than as one who is a prey to the 'cankering calculations' of trade (*S*, 540), 'baffled at every turn' (*S*, 25) by his own lack of capital and by a political situation beyond his control:

Moore ever wanted to push on: 'Forward' was the device stamped upon his soul; but poverty curbed him: sometimes (figuratively) he foamed at the mouth when the reins were drawn very tight. (*S*, 29)

His most urgent desire appears, indeed, as something quite other than free aspiration: 'straitened on all sides as I am, I have nothing for it but to push on' (*S*, 162–3). His most defiant assertion – 'Here I stay; and by this mill I stand' – carries a darker, more desolate charge:

Suppose that building was a ruin and I was a corpse, what then? ... would that stop invention or exhaust science? – Not for the fraction of a second of time! Another and better gig-mill would rise on the ruins of this, and perhaps a more enterprising owner come in my place ... (*S*, 136)

Moore is known in the district as a 'man of note and action'; he has 'breasted the storm of unpopularity with gallant bearing and soul elate' (*S*, 529). But he is here figured less as heroic subject than as replaceable object, a mere cog in a process of technological advance which continues heedless of his, or any individual's, agency, and regardless of his, or any individual's, fate.

If Moore is no more able to bend the world to his will than are the starving workers who threaten his mill, his powerlessness has its counterpart in the private, feminine sphere. If he is 'curbed' by poverty, Caroline's feelings are 'curbed and kept down' (S, 347). His ambition and his impotence are paralleled by her aching desire and enforced passivity. 'I see no more light than if I were sealed in a rock', says he, of his business prospects (S, 163); her life calls up the image of 'the toad's, buried in marble... for ever shut up in that glebe-house – a place... like a windowed grave' (S, 399). Both are constrained, of course, by economic necessity. But the wealthy Shirley's story takes the same shape as theirs. Hers is an 'independence' more romantic than the entrepreneur's, more defiant than Caroline's of conventional 'womanliness'. Where Caroline's dreams are filled, simply, with 'images of Moore' (S, 173), hers have the 'genii-life' of a more transcendent desire (S, 387). Yet if, to the reader familiar with Glass Town, this image is bound to recall the 'bright fresh' world of those plays, it carries too a more chilling reminder of promise blasted and hopes destroyed. 'She does not know', the narrator says, 'her dreams are rare, her feelings peculiar: she does not know, has never known, *and will die without knowing*, the full value of that spring whose bright fresh bubbling in her heart keeps it green' (S, 388, my italics). There is nothing, here, of that glamour of distant horizons, that sense of opening possibility, which shapes the young Jane Eyre's story: the future is not unknown, but all too decisively foretold.

This 'tale of the perfect tense'[20] is punctuated throughout by desolate images of futurity. Robert Moore's 'What then?' is answered in Caroline's bleak soliloquy: 'every path trod by human feet terminates in one bourne – the grave' (S, 175). Even the 'physically fearless' Shirley remarks, 'we have none of us long to live' (S, 266, 267). And the movement which relegates aspiration into the completed past is repeated throughout the novel. Twice, indeed, in the midst of a lively social scene, the novel looks forward to the death of one of the most vital participants, little Jessie Yorke. Here, the fictive illusion that the narrated present is progressing towards an open future is abandoned with disconcerting suddenness. But the feeling is less of a change in narrative perspective than of a more expansive, more explicit confrontation of a sense which has been shaping the telling throughout. Powerful longings, energetic strivings, 'merry and social' banter are displaced by the stark immediacy of an image of rain beating on a grave (S, 407).

The final chapter of *Shirley* tells of the resolution of many of the characters' dilemmas. The paralysis imposed by the Orders in Council is ended; Caroline's romantic desires are fulfilled; Robert Moore's 'day-dreams' are realised; the workers are employed. But the chapter title, 'The Winding Up' is suggestive of the feeling. 'Stocks, which had been accumulating for years, now went off in a moment, in the twinkling of an eye; warehouses were lightened, ships were laden; work abounded, wages rose: the good time seemed come' (*S*, 637). This surrealistic, speeded-up picture of unpredictable economic process underwrites rather than answers to that disquieting sense of human powerlessness inscribed in the novel's presentation of the public world. And there is a similar perfunctoriness in the following account of the weddings in which its two love-stories culminate. In a striking reversal of Jane Eyre's unconventional insistence on her agency as a bride – 'Reader, I married him' – both heroines are objectified here by the language of public report.

> This morning there were two marriages solemnized in Briarfield church, – Louis Gérard Moore, Esq. late of Antwerp, to Shirley, daughter of the late Charles Cave Keeldar, Esq. of Fieldhead: Robert Gérard Moore, Esq. of Hollow's mill, to Caroline, niece of the Rev. Matthewson Helstone, M. A., Rector of Briarfield.
>
> (*S*, 645)

The sense is of the sudden disappearance of those vivid, aspiring subjects of which the narrative has told.

'I suppose', says the narrator, in conclusion, 'Robert Moore's prophecies were, partially, at least, fulfilled' (*S*, 645). The Hollow has become a mill town. Yet the sense is less of achievement than of extinction and desolation. There is no sign, here, of that succour once promised for 'the houseless, the starving, the unemployed': the manufacturer's 'day-dreams' are 'embodied' not in bread, but in stone. The 'unmolested trees' of the place where Caroline and her mother walked (*S*, 372) have been replaced by 'a mighty mill, and a chimney, ambitious as the tower of Babel'; a 'cinder-black highway' runs through the Hollow which now only 'tradition' recalls as 'once green, and lone, and wild' (*S*, 645). Progress is figured as loss. And this sense is underwritten in the closing paragraphs of the novel, where the future to which the characters looked becomes the completed past, and the narrating voice gives way to the housekeeper's longer view. Those who have occupied the foreground become mere vanishing memories, as the process of 'alteration' moves imperviously on.

'Worse than useless did it seem to attempt to write what there no longer lived an "Ellis Bell" to read', Charlotte Brontë said of her efforts to finish *Shirley*. 'The whole book, with every hope founded on it, faded to vanity and vexation of spirit.'[21] Just so, at the end of the novel, the hopes and desires of the characters are 'faded' into the distance of an irretrievable past. Indeed, in *Shirley*'s closing pages one might perhaps trace a sombre rejoinder to the vanished 'Ellis Bell'. Here, as in *Wuthering Heights*, the narrative time becomes that of 'the other day', and the narrator-figure enters the narrative, listening, like Lockwood, to the stories his 'old housekeeper' has to tell. But the revenant dead, the perhaps unquiet graves, of that earlier novel are in *Shirley* replaced by a brisk 'winding-up' and the speeded-up time of modernity. The emphasis is not on regeneration and growth, but on despoilation and loss: not on possibility, but on a process of disenchantment. Memory is not collective, but individual, and disappearing. As the narrator's obtrusive glosses on the old housekeeper's words insist, even language is an obsolescent thing. And the voices that have filled the novel are replaced by a silent 'chimney, ambitious as the tower of Babel', monument to a single man's dreams.

Yet the ending of *Shirley* discloses not merely a haunting dialogue with the dead, but a sharp sense of a living audience, and of the difference of what this novel offers from what that audience might expect. This account of the 'altered' Hollow is succeeded by a closing image of the reader 'putting on his spectacles to look for the moral', and a taunt reminiscent of the Glass Town fictions – 'I can only say, God speed him in the quest!' She who feared she could not 'march with the tread of . . . a Thackeray or a Dickens' offers an assured, mocking rejoinder to the expectations aroused by these her contemporaries. 'Come children, let us shut up the box and the puppets, for our play is played out', Thackeray had pronounced, at the ending of *Vanity Fair*. If the 'winding-up' of *Shirley* might seem to echo this, its final challenge to the reader is quite different from the genial first-person plural of Thackerayan commonality. It is even less like the endings of those 'social problem' novels – *Yeast*, *Mary Barton*, and *Dombey and Son* – which had appeared in 1848. Dickens' and Gaskell's novels each end with muted optimism, images of a future which in some way repairs the past; each has a clear moral project, 'to make the world a better place!' (*Dombey and Son*, ch. 47). Kingsley's concludes with a striking vision of a 'nobler, more chivalrous, more godlike' England – of 'railroads, electric telegraphs, associate lodging-houses, club-houses, sanitary reforms, experimental schools, chemical agriculture, a matchless school of inductive science, an equally matchless school of naturalist painters, – and all this in the very workshop of the world!'[22] But the personal and social solutions proposed by Dickens and Gaskell seem curiously empty in *Shirley*; certainly impotent. Kingsley's confidence in effective human agency is countered here by a darker sense of the limits within which all such agency is framed; his vision of a transformed England by a bleaker picture, of a landscape irrevocably despoiled. Indeed, it is hard not to see, in Brontë's choice of the title of *Yeast*'s final chapter – 'The Valley of the Shadow of Death' – for that of the opening chapter of *Shirley*'s third volume, something in the nature of a conscious riposte. The issue of *Fraser's* in which the final instalment of Kingsley's novel appeared was received and read in the parsonage, as the writing of *Shirley* was halted by grief at the end of the second volume, in the dark December of 1848. It must have been a pored-over journal. For it contains a poignant reminder of the all-too-brief moment when the three sisters seemed at last to be seizing and sharing the triumph of public authorship. On the reverse of the page on which the novel concluded is a poem by Acton Bell.[23]

The peculiarities of *Shirley* – its sense of social cacophony, its informing bleak determinism – are not artlessly expressive of the darkness of personal despair. They offer a quite distinctive vision of the nature and fate of a society, worked out in the fabric of the fiction in ways which its author had been pondering for nearly twenty years. Even in 1849, it seems, Glass Town for Charlotte Brontë was not simply a memory. Its strategies were still shaping the way she imagined her world. And her debt to that 'play' is acknowledged as *Shirley* draws to a close. The image of 'a chimney, ambitious as the tower of Babel' looming in the once-green hollow is not just a telling reminder of the novel's central concerns – the heterogeneous voices, the antagonisms and divisions, which fracture its social world; the powerful yet doomed aspirations which drive the characters forward. It also speaks quite directly of that vanished childhood dream.

For the Tower of Babel was a potent symbol to the Brontë children in the framing of their 'plays'. Perhaps partly in acknowledgement of the fact that the excitement with which they constructed their imaginary world was like the ambitious energy which had fired the builders of that Tower, early in the plays 'the Tower of Babylon' – later called the Tower of All Nations – appeared as the mightiest of the buildings of Glass Town.[24] To the admiring denizens of Glass Town, the Tower seems a 'peerless' achievement.[25] Yet as that image of Lord Charles Wellesley, lifted by 'a hand wide enough almost to grasp the Tower of all Nations', suggests, the Tower speaks also of the irony which informs these youthful plays: their constant undercutting awareness not merely of the aspiring energies but also of the ultimate impotence of those whom the Genii have made. For the young creators of Glass Town were sharply aware of the darker meanings of the Tower. In the years of the building of Glass Town a mezzotint of *Belshazzar's Feast* – perhaps the most famous of John Martin's apocalyptic paintings – hung in Haworth Parsonage. In the background of that mezzotint looms the image of the Tower of Babel which the Brontë children knew best. Lightning playing about it, it hovers on the brink of destruction, above the fleeing Babylonians, the lavish interrupted feast; a doomed, ambiguous pointer to the mightiness of human aspirations, the futility of human schemes. It is an image which finds a ghostly echo in the closing pages of *Shirley*. There, the Tower has become

Figure 5 John Martin, *Belshazzar's Feast. Mezzotint* (1830).

a mill-chimney, familiar emblem of that 'progress' which was transforming the Pennine landscape in the years in which the Brontës grew up. Appearing in the 'altered' hollow, it offers a bleak, enigmatic comment on the England of 1849; pointing back at the 'Babel' world of controversy and aspiration which the novel has portrayed, and suggesting, against those closing images of peace concluded and marriages made, that differences and divisions will never be reconciled. Like that narrating voice throughout, it speaks of the vanity of human wishes, the frailty of that which they construct. Yet it testifies, paradoxically, to the continuing life of Glass Town.

If *Shirley* looks back to that shared childhood 'play', *Villette*'s is a narrative of isolation. The voice that speaks at the end of the novel is that of one who survives in a disenchanted world. This is the constricted first-person of one whose position is 'exceptional' (*V*, 273), unimaginable by those about her, invisible to the 'common gaze' (*V*, 179). 'The most autobiographical of all Charlotte's novels', one editor calls it.[26] 'The raging yet silent centre': this is what, in *Villette*, is heard. It is lonely, unexpressed feeling, 'that has now found a voice'.[27] Yet implicit in this praise by Raymond Williams is a judgement which others have also made. This is a narrative of private feeling and marginal experience, 'less concerned with the problems of society' than many others being written in these years.[28]

For *Villette*, like *Shirley*, was published at a time of extraordinary fictional achievement. *David Copperfield* and *Pendennis*, *Henry Esmond* and *Bleak House*, *Alton Locke* and *Ruth* had all appeared during the preceding three years. All offered panoramic views of a far wider range of social experience; even the last-named's domestic story had (as Charlotte Brontë put it) 'a philanthropic purpose – a social use' to which *Villette* did not pretend.[29] Beside these, *Villette*, with its peculiar, tormented narrator, might well appear concerned merely with subjective 'pain'.

Yet if most criticism of the novel has focused on the character of Lucy Snowe, *Villette* is not simply offered as a psychological narrative. More directly, indeed, than any of Brontë's previous protagonists, this one insists that hers is a lot which others share. 'I see that *a great many men, and more women*, hold their span of life on conditions of denial and deprivation', she declares, as she thinks of the probable loneliness of her future; and, later, as she contrasts her 'cloud' with the 'sunshine' of Graham and Paulina, 'Dark through the wilderness of this world stretches the way for *most of us*' (*V*, 361, 438, my italics). If hers is a story obscured from 'the strong and prosperous' (*S*, 427), it is, she suggests, more representative than theirs. Unlike Charlotte Brontë's two previous first-person novels, this bears neither the narrator's name nor that of her profession. Its title signals a central concern not merely with her peculiar viewpoint but with what that viewpoint reveals about the world through which she moves.

The ambitions portrayed in *Shirley* ended in a ravaged landscape and a chimney like 'the tower of Babel'. But *Villette* opens with images of 'peaceful' material well-being and confident purposeful life; of solid achievement and future promise; of security, prosperity, felicity; of effectiveness in the world. Instead of the 'stone, brick and ashes' of Robert Moore's mill town there are 'large peaceful rooms', with 'well-arranged furniture'; instead of his 'cinder-black highway', a 'clean pavement' and a 'fine antique street' (*V*, 5). This is not *Shirley*'s 'Monday morning' world of aspiration and striving, but a place where 'Sundays and holidays seemed always to abide' (*V*, 5). And those for whom it is home are thriving, flourishing figures; their authority and 'vivacity' are by no means ironically seen (*V*, 5). Indeed, they seem strangely impervious to that which threatens in *Shirley*. The 'clarity and power of five-and-twenty still breathed from her and around her', Lucy writes of Louisa Bretton; at fifty, 'good health and an excellent temperament' keep her 'green as in her spring' (*V*, 180, 173). Such troubles as come to John Bretton and his wife are easily surmounted. 'Doubtless they knew crosses, disappointments, difficulties; but these were well borne.' By such as these, it seems, even death can be transcended: 'others sprang healthy and blooming to replace the lost' (*V*, 436). For Dr John is very different from the 'baffled' Robert Moore. Buoyant in face of reversal, 'a man of luck – a man of success' (*V*, 318), he is emphatically not a figure of aspiration checked. 'I was going to write *mortal*', says Lucy, as she tells of his courtship of Paulina, 'but such words ill apply to one all living like him' (*V*, 433).

If Lucy is 'well habituated to be passed by as a shadow' (*V*, 334), those others of whom her narrative tells are confident and successful. They have connections and resources, and clearly defined identities; their stories have known beginnings and ends; they are at home in their world. For her, 'Fate' is a 'permanent foe, never to be conciliated' (*V*, 157), but they are effective and capable, can command and influence events. Things are arranged in Bretton so that 'time always flows smoothly' (*V*, 6); things are equally smoothly managed in the Villette to which Lucy goes. The 'long and difficult' lessons, the severity and austerity which Jane Eyre found at Lowood (*JE*, 53) are unknown in Madame Beck's school; it is a place of 'life, movement and variety' (*V*, 75) rather than of monotony, confinement and death. 'No minds were overtasked; the lessons were well distributed and made incomparably easy to the learner; there was a liberty of amusement, and a provision for exercise which kept the girls healthy; the food was abundant and good' (*V*, 73); 'the Catholic fête-days brought a succession of holidays all the year round' (*V*, 75). The pupils of Lowood are warned against the evils of curls and braids, but here a 'coiffeur' is summoned to arrange the young ladies' hair (*V*, 130). Jane Eyre was sickened at Lowood by the nauseous fumes of burnt porridge; but at Madame Beck's Lucy is tempted by the 'fragrance of baked apples' cooked with 'a little spice, sugar, and a glass or two of vin blanc' (*V*, 355). Doors 'revolve noiselessly on well-oiled hinges' (*V*, 118); 'glowing stoves' bring 'a sense of comfort' in winter (*V*, 231), while in summer, 'the broad folding-doors and the two-leaved casements' stand 'wide open' all day long (*V*, 128). 'How pleasant it was in its air of perfect domestic comfort!' Lucy recalls of the drawing room at La Terrasse (*V*, 173). The home of the Brettons in Labassecour is 'amply' curtained (*V*, 166, 168), cushioned (*V*, 173, 175, 182) and carpeted (*V*, 166, 279); one hears 'housemaid steps on the stairs' (*V*, 181). When Lucy arrives at the concert she finds 'a majestic staircase wide and easy of ascent, deeply and softly carpeted', and doors which 'roll back' as if 'by magic' to disclose a 'vast and dazzling, but warm and cheerful hall' (*V*, 209–10).

Here, the visual metaphors which shape each of Charlotte Brontë's earlier novels take on a different inflection: Crimsworth's self-defensive spying, Jane Eyre's transformative vision, *Shirley*'s cool observation have been replaced by a quite new emphasis on spectacle and display. At Madame Beck's fête, 'the long vista of the school-rooms' discloses 'a thronging, undulating, murmuring, waving, streaming multitude, all rose, and blue, and half-translucent white' (*V*, 137). 'How brilliant seemed the shops! How glad, gay, and abundant flowed the tide of life along the broad pavement! . . . a great illuminated building blazed before us' Lucy tells, of her drive to the concert (*V*, 208–9); when she flees by night from the Pensionnat Beck, 'Villette is one blaze, one broad illumination . . . the town, by her own flambeaux, beholds her own splendour – gay dresses, grand equipages, fine horses and gallant riders throng the bright streets' (*V*, 452). And if the 'splendours' and 'pleasures' of Villette appear before Lucy 'as a spectacle' (*V*, 142), so does the domestic life of her fortunate English friends. 'The blue saloon seemed to me gorgeous. In its Christmas-like fire alone there was a clear and crimson splendour which quite dazzled me', she says of the drawing-room at La Terrasse (*V*, 274). Paulina's bedroom at the Hotel Crécy is 'shadowy with pale-blue hangings, vaporous with curtainings and veilings of muslin'; the bed is 'like snow-drift and mist' (*V*, 263). Such metaphors and moments are writ large in a series of longer descriptions of spectacles, exhibitions and shows. The concert, the theatre, the public lecture, the galleries, the fêtes of Villette are prominent in the novel. Dr John takes Lucy to every 'object worth seeing', 'every museum . . . every hall sacred to art or science' (*V*, 196); when, later, he writes to her, it is of 'scenes which had passed before his eyes and mine' (*V*, 244).

Even examinations – the prelude to 'the distribution of prizes' – are at the Pensionnat Beck an occasion for display: 'a showy demonstration – a telling exhibition – must be got up for public view (*V*, 153). The lure of Rome is displayed in 'flowers and tinsel…wax-lights and embroidery' (*V*, 421): a crisis in the history of *Villette* is marked by 'spectacles, decorations, and illuminations' in the park (*V*, 453).

It seems that *Villette* is configuring not merely a peculiar protagonist but a quite distinctive social world; a world which is very different from that of any of the Brontës' other works. *Shirley*'s mill-chimneys and counting-houses are here replaced by images of leisure and enjoyment, of labour agreeably concealed. Here, instead of conflict, there is unobtrusive order; instead of economic uncertainty and actual starvation, ostentatious affluence. For if the Yorkshire depicted in *Shirley* would have been quite familiar to Ellis and Acton Bell, their sister's final novel speaks of something which they had scarcely known – that mid-nineteenth-century burgeoning of middle-class prosperity and confidence with which Charlotte Brontë was beginning to see in the years in which she wrote *Villette*.

Villette was conceived and written in unprecedented isolation. 'I can hardly tell you how I hunger to have some opinion besides my own, and how I have sometimes desponded and almost despaired because there was no one to whom to read a line – or of whom to ask a counsel,' Charlotte Brontë confessed to her publisher in October 1852. '*Jane Eyre* was not written under such circumstances, nor were two-thirds of *Shirley*.'[30] But Brontë was also now a celebrated literary figure. She was paying visits to London, and being taken about to 'sights', to the theatre, to public lectures, and to galleries. She was being entertained in the comfortable homes of kindly and prosperous friends. Indeed, if the once lively parsonage had become a place of 'hush and gloom',[31] it too was acquiring comforts and embellishments – carpets, curtains, furniture – of a kind hitherto unknown. When Elizabeth Gaskell – a keen observer of such things – visited for the first time in September 1853, she observed that 'the parlour has been evidently refurnished within the last few years, since Miss Brontë's success has enabled her to have a little more money to spend'.[32] Charlotte Brontë's own letters from this time are full of her new concern with fashions and with furnishings. And as the novel which she was writing suggests, this intimate personal experience points towards a larger social fact.

For the middle years of the nineteenth century saw a remarkable transformation in English society. John Stores Smith, who in 1850 admiringly presented Charlotte Brontë with a copy of his *Social Aspects* (and received an approbatory letter in reply),[33] speaks in that work of 'an entire change in the whole aspect of middle-class life'.

Figure 6 Mrs Gaskell's drawing-room, 84 Plymouth Grove, Manchester.

[The middle-class] house is no longer a cottage, but a comparative mansion; and a Manchester manufacturer, a Liverpool speculator, or a London merchant, oftentimes dwells in an every way more princely dwelling than many a continental prince of British nobleman…a house replete with elegancies, with plate, pier glasses, pictures, and all the paraphenalia of a drawing-room of fashion…[34]

The proliferation and increasing variety of manufactured goods meant a steady improvement in the material conditions of life for the middle classes. If the cult was of home as a private place, separate from the outside world,[35] 'home' was beginning to be well-appointed with luxuries. It was cushioned, curtained, carpeted, upholstered; more fully furnished, more brightly lit; its walls were covered with wallpaper, its tables with ornaments; its fires burned now in re-designed grates; it was crowded with comforts and gadgets of hitherto unknown kinds. The landscape of public life was likewise being dramatically changed. Prosperity was now far more visible than ever before. Great public buildings – railway stations, department stores, exhibition halls – 'massive monuments to wealth, imperial glory and commercial supremacy…self-important spectacle productions in real…brick…iron, and glass' – were appearing in English and, indeed, continental towns.[36]

Shopkeepers were beginning to try the new 'expedient of giving brilliancy and apparent vastness by clothing wall and ceiling with looking-glass, and causing these to reflect the light from the rich cut-glass chandelier'.[37] Dress, especially for women, became more ostentatious. If the woman of the 1830s and 40s had been slender, unobtrusive and delicate, the fashionable woman of the 1850s was imposing, colourful, difficult to overlook. And these gorgeously clad figures moved, in the middle years of the century, through a bright new world of pleasure, of luxury, of ease. This, as John Stores Smith remarked, was 'an age of . . . brilliant and fashionable . . . show'; of 'épergnes, ottomans, chandeliers, pier glasses, and champagne'.[38]

This is the world which Lucy confronts in *Villette* : the 'perfect domestic comfort', the 'stuffed and cushioned' chairs of La Terrasse (*V*, 173); the 'brightly lit' streets and 'brilliant . . . shops' of Villette (*V*, 208), the 'vast and dazzling' hall of the concert to which she goes (*V*, 210). It is a world not merely of spectacle, but one which is filled with things – 'crochet, guard-chains, cookery, and dress', a contemporary reviewer remarked disapprovingly[39] – minutely particularised, copiously described. Where Jane Eyre painted visionary watercolours, Lucy makes 'handscreens' decorated with 'elaborate pencil-drawings finished like line-engravings' (*V*, 166), a 'pin-cushion . . . of crimson satin, ornamented with gold beads and frilled with thread-lace' (*V*, 169), a watchguard 'glossy with silk and sparkling with beads' (*V*, 346), which she encloses in 'a small box I had bought for its brilliancy, made of some tropic shell of the colour called "nacarat", and decked with a little coronal of sparkling blue stones' (*V*, 334). As Lucy's story unfolds, articles such as a trunk, a pink dress, a watchguard, a paletot (or short overcoat), a pair of spectacles take on an almost fetishistic significance. 'Some object drop[s] prone at [her] feet' as she walks in the garden at evening (*V*, 110): things 'magically grow' in her desk, presents from M. Paul (*V*, 343). Repeatedly, her narrative tells of things displaced from their contexts, from the pots and pans littering the foreground in the painting of Cleopatra to the 'sky-blue turban' his mother places on the sleeping Dr John. And such moments reach a climax at the opening of the second volume, where the narrator returns to consciousness after an extremity of suffering, and 'all the paraphenalia of a drawing-room of fashion' meet her bewildered gaze.

The scene is one which encapsulates the novel's concern not merely with what Raymond Williams calls 'lonely, unexpressed experience', but also with a recalcitrant and quite material world. Here, that 'calm and decorated' drawing-room (*V*, 29), that quiet bedroom in Bretton, of which the opening chapters of the novel speak appear before Lucy ten years later and in a foreign land. And they come into focus, suddenly, as rooms crowded with furniture, every surface 'covered', every article abundantly 'finished' and 'adorned'. Things in these rooms are loaded with ornament, 'myriad gold leaves and tendrils'; 'bordered with . . . foliage', or 'frilled with thread-lace', 'worked with groups of brilliant flowers'; 'curtained', 'cushioned', 'smooth', 'shiny', 'polished', 'foliated', 'carved' (*V*, 166–70). If the splendours of *Jane Eyre*'s Thornfield – its 'Tyrian-dyed curtains' and 'Parian mantelpiece', its 'general blending of snow and fire' (*JE*, 104) – evoke an exotic world of romance, familiar from the sub-Byronic annuals, these are the too too solid objects of the high Victorian drawing room. Here, there is a thickness of description unlike anything in Brontë's earlier fiction; a superfluity akin to the superfluities of high Victorian design. This is not the voice of autobiographical experience, but a highly sophisticated art. And here, as in *Shirley*, it is an art charged with memories of Glass Town – though in a very different way.

'Had a Genius . . . borne me over land and ocean, and laid me down quietly beside a hearth of Old England?' Lucy asks wildly, as she gazes at 'the little pictures, the ornaments, the screens, the worked chair' (*V*, 167). The moment is reminiscent of those peculiar moments in Glass Town when the characters intuit that they are mere creatures of the Genii, and the 'reality' they inhabit suddenly becomes estranged. Yet if this exclamation carries a poignant private echo of a 'play' which now no others remained to share, it signals also a quite distinctive perspective on a familiar mid-nineteenth-century world. There is nothing, here, of the satirical assurance of Thackeray's description of the high Victorian drawing-room (in *Pendennis*, ch. 37); nothing of Mrs Gaskell's sharp sense of the social significance of a Manchester drawing-room's aggressive display:

> Every corner seemed filled up with ornament, until it became a weariness to the eye, and presented a strange contrast to the bald ugliness of the look-out into the great mill-yard . . .   (*North and South* (1854–5), ch. 20)

The things Lucy sees in this 'unknown room' (*V*, 166) are not, like the things in those other fictional drawing rooms, imbued with obvious social meaning. Rather, it is their refusal to yield up their meanings which is the centre of narrative concern. The confidence with which Gaskell or Thackeray read rooms is here replaced by a different narrative perspective; this is not a judging, but emphatically an impotent gaze. Here, verbal agency belongs not to the viewer, but to the objects she confronts. Chairs 'dawn' upon her, an armchair 'grows' familiar, 'a whole shining [tea]-service glance[s] at her familiarly' (*V*, 173): things obtrude upon her even as she tries to turn away (*V*, 170). 'Obliged to know', 'compelled to recognize' that which 'hovers before' her 'distempered vision' (*V*, 169), she seems to herself less subject than object – 'laid . . . on a sofa', reflected in a mirror, 'bewildered', 'harassed', 'alarmed'.

Peculiar as Lucy's viewpoint is, it speaks of much wider social experience. The scene is of things displaced from their contexts, 'well lighted, clearly seen'; the elaborately decorated evidence of bourgeois prosperity on display. Here, the familiar is defamiliarised, even objects the viewer has made. Here, 'home' appears, strangely, as a spectacle, in an unexpected place. And if in these ways this passage recalls the uncanny moments of those long-ago childish 'plays', it is also sharply evocative of a public contemporary fact: the Great Exhibition of 1851, which Charlotte Brontë visited five times as she began to conceive of *Villette*.

To the surviving creator of Glass Town, the exhibition, in its palace of glass, must have been a suggestive sight.[40] Even its official title – the Great Exhibition of the Works of Art and Industry of all Nations – could hardly have failed to prompt poignant memories of that Tower of All Nations which had dominated Verdopolis. 'It is such a bazaar or fair as Eastern genii might have created', she wrote of it to her father; and she may have well expected him to catch her allusion to the 'plays'.[41] But this was a Glass Town stripped of its aura: one which many saw quite simply as a bewildering collection of things. 'I came back quite dead beat and my head really bewildered by the myriads of beautiful and wonderful things, which now quite dazzle one's eyes', declared Queen Victoria, in her Exhibition Journal.[42] He 'stands agape and wondering' in 'pure vacant bewilderment', wrote *Tallis's History and Description of the Crystal Palace* of the characteristic behaviour of the plebeian visitor on a 'shilling day'. 'The eastern sun is flashing through the long avenues of glittering industry and art . . . and [he] stands petrified in the midst of elaborated chaos.'[43] 'I find I am "used up" by the Exhibition', Dickens confessed. 'I don't say there is nothing in it – there's too much. I have only been twice; so many things bewildered me.'[44] 'After some three or four hours' peregrination', wrote Charlotte Brontë, 'you come out very sufficiently bleached and broken in bits.'[45]

Such accounts are suggestively different from that exhilarated pride in achievement, that nationalistic triumphalism, which the Great Exhibition of all Nations was intended to promote. Yet they are arguably more representative of the average visitor's response. The more dazzlingly the exhibition displayed its phantasmagoria of commodities, the more strenuously it insisted on prosperity and progress, the more overwhelmed the spectator tended to be. Such 'bedazzlement' might be seen, indeed, as indicative of a much more general experience of what Arnold called, in the year of the novel's publication, 'the bewildering confusion of our times'.[46] It is this experience – in which authority and confidence were challenged, rather than confirmed – which is reflected, and reflected upon, in *Villette*.

'It is not a mere picture of things which are found standing together that we have had presented to us; the great achievement was the bringing them together', one of the most eloquent of the Great Exhibition's eulogists, William Whewell, was to declare:

> By annihilating the space which separates different nations, we produce a spectacle in which is also annihilated the time which separates one stage of a nation's progress from another ... How great and unexampled is the opportunity thus given to us, of taking a survey of the existing state of art in every part of the world.[47]

And his first-person plurals signify a confident identification with 'progress', with the power to 'produce' and to 'survey'; in this, his is characteristic of many such accounts. Yet there is no such identification in *Villette*. 'Of what are these things the signs and tokens?' Lucy had asked, as a girl in Bretton, finding, as she entered her bedroom, 'an unexpected change':

> In addition to my own French bed in its shady recess, appeared in a corner a small crib, draped with white; and in addition to my mahogany chest of drawers, I saw a tiny rosewood chest.   (*V*, 6)

It is not she, but others, who act, decide, effect: the results of their actions embodied before her in visible, material shape. Just so, in the scene of her awakening at La Terrasse, rooms full of inexplicable objects appear as the 'signs and tokens' of a world which she does not control. The sense is not of confirmation and recognition, but of 'baffled', blank dislocation. For her, as for Whewell, 'time and space' seem annihilated: 'Where was I? Not only in what spot of the world, but in what year of our Lord?' (*V*, 166–7). But for her, the experience speaks less of the 'magic' of generalised human achievement than of her own singular powerlessness, less of presence than of absence, less of 'taking ... survey' of a multifarious world than of helpless bewilderment.

Villette is indeed very different from those authoritative 'surveys' of society which 'men of large views and solid attainments' were attempting in other novels in these years.[48] It is not an artless rendition of narrowly personal experience, but a carefully crafted configuration of a different kind of relation to a sharply realised social world. Indeed, there appears to be something like a questioning of the contemporary impulse to novelistic overview in those images of limited, disturbed, bedazzled, occluded vision which recur throughout Lucy's narrative. In *Villette*, the eye does not organise but simply receives impressions; this is a world which baffles, bewilders, dazzles, strikes.

Where Jane actively 'traced the general points' of Rochester's appearance (*JE*, 113), this narrator tells that her 'eyes printed upon [her] brain the picture of M. Paul' (*V*, 480). The sense, is indeed, often, of an aggressive assault on the eye. 'This cabinet dazzled me, it was so full of light', says Lucy of the classroom-turned-dressing-room in which she prepares for her part in the play (*V*, 138); her eye is 'transfixed through its very pupil' when she tries to peep unseen at M. Paul (*V*, 325). Vashti's overpowering genius is 'a rushing, red cometary light – hot on vision and to sensation' (*V*, 259). And Lucy's narrative is punctuated by two recurring images of deranged or defective vision – the 'optical illusion' (as she and others term it) of the nun which appears to haunt her (*V*, 257) – 'the vision of the garret, the apparition of the alley' (*V*, 463); more banal, but no less prominent, the metonymic detail by which the man she comes to love is figured – those terrifying, vulnerable 'lunettes'.

'Pendant from the dome, flamed a mass that dazzled me, sparkling with facets, streaming with drops, ablaze with stars', Lucy tells of her arrival at the concert in Villette. If her words recall the young Jane Eyre's first sight of the drawing-room at Thornfield – 'I thought I caught a glimpse of a fairy place: so bright to my novice-eyes appeared the view beyond' ((*JE*, 109) – they lead, as Jane's artless wonder does not, to an irony akin to the ironies of Glass Town. 'It was only the chandelier, reader, but for me it seemed the work of eastern genii. I almost looked to see if a huge, dark cloudy hand – that of the Slave of the Lamp – were not hovering in the lustrous and perfumed atmosphere of the cupola' (*V*, 209). The prismatic refraction of colours ('gorgeously tinted with dews of gems dissolved, or fragments of rainbows shivered') becomes a figure not merely for a world magically, kaleidoscopically defamiliarised – the 'varying light and shade and gradation' which greets Lucy's gaze in this 'vast and dazzling...hall' – but also for that decentring of the viewing subject writ large in the image which 'flashes upon her' from a mirror immediately after this – a momentary, inadvertently 'received' 'impression' of self as object, estranged (*V*, 209). 'The world is a looking glass', Thackeray had observed in *Vanity Fair*, 'and gives back to every man the reflection of his own face' (ch. 2). But *Villette* has no such confidence in a morally meaningful universe. That which this narrator confronts is less instructive than disconcerting. She appears to herself not in the first but as 'a third person', 'in a black lace mantle and pink dress': an object in a world of dazzling surfaces, which she does not recognise as herself. The scene makes a sardonic riposte not merely to Thackeray's saw, but also to those for whom the point of such narratives as hers lies in their revelation of the heroine's moral growth.

In one sense, Lucy is not at all dazzled by the glamour of bourgeois life. She notes the vanities of the Pensionnat Beck, the obtuseness of the Brettons and Homes. She anatomises the defects even of her beloved Dr John. Yet she has none of the satiric or moralising distance of a Thackeray or a Dickens from the privilege and prosperity she surveys. The Brettons, the Homes, the Pensionnat Beck – these dominate her story: even the flirt Ginevra becomes 'a sort of heroine' to her. Almost, it seems, against her will, she is compelled and preoccupied by 'sunshine'. And this 'bedazzled' perspective is not merely recreated in *Villette*: its implications are pondered in a quite distinctive way.

Lucy tries to 'exclude' that bewildering room at La Terrasse by turning her face to the wall. But even as she 'arranges her position in this hope', she finds herself confronted by a picture, enshrined between 'looped-up curtains', displayed in a 'gilded frame'. It is the portrait of a handsome youth, 'with hair of a sunny sheen': an image which speaks, alluringly, of that privilege, happiness, confidence, which she – disoriented, baffled, powerless – is condemned merely to look upon. 'On the whole a most pleasant face to look at', Lucy decides; yet the qualification which follows – 'especially for those claiming a right to that youth's affections' – evokes the more painful perspective of one for whom to 'look' might be a more dangerous thing (*V*, 170). For as Lucy is later to admit, in a rare self-revealing exchange, one is not indifferent to that which one is dazzled by. The fortunate Paulina, beloved by the subject of that portrait – her 'native clear sight' now 'dazzled' by 'cloudless happiness' – begins to discuss her love in an exquisitely painful way. 'Do other people see him with my eyes?' she asks, importunately. '*I never see him*', is Lucy's strange and emphatic reply. 'I looked at him twice or thrice about a year ago, before he recognized me, and then I shut my eyes.' 'Lucy, what do you mean?' asks her friend. 'I mean that I value vision, and dread being struck stone blind' (*V*, 425).

When the sun came out at the Great Exhibition's opening, it was seen as a sign of God's blessing on those who had inherited the earth. 'He was born victor, as some are born vanquished', says Lucy, of Graham Bretton; and again and again in the novel this 'man of luck', this 'man of success' (*V*, 318) is likened to the sun. But he appears within Lucy's narrative not merely as a figure of all that she lacks and longs for – beauty, confidence, felicity, prosperity, emotional assurance – but also as the dazzling object of annihilating unreturned desire. 'The book is almost intolerably painful', Harriet Martineau wrote in her review (*CH*, 172). In bringing together those two most charged, most embarrassing of subjects in mid-nineteenth-century England – the pain of those excluded from its official narratives of happiness and success, and the more intimate, more unspeakable pain of a woman's unrequited longing – *Villette* speaks of rather more than mere lonely subjective feeling. That long apprenticeship in writing which began in a fictional play with the subject positions of the powerless culminates in this novel in a powerful, 'painful' challenge to that national story of prosperity and contentment being publically celebrated, ostentatiously proclaimed in the England in which it was conceived.

NOTES

1. Raymond Williams, Introduction to Charles Dickens, *Dombey and Son*, edited by Peter Fairclough (Harmondsworth: Penguin, 1970), 11.
2. To W. S. Williams, 4 October 1847, *CBL* I, 546. 'Mrs Marsh' was the author of the bestselling *Emilia Wyndham* (1845) and of *The Protestant Revolution in France, or, The History of the Huguenots* (1847).
3. Elizabeth Gaskell, *The Life of Charlotte Brontë* [1857], edited by Alan Shelston (Harmondsworth: Penguin, 1975), 307.
4. To W. S. Williams, 17 September 1849, *CBL* II, 255.
5. To W. S. Williams, 8 May 1849, *CBL* II, 207. 'Bulwer' is Edward George Earle Lytton Bulwer, later Bulwer-Lytton, reforming politician and prolific novelist.
6. Raymond Williams, Introduction to *Dombey and Son*, 20.
7. George Henry Lewes, unsigned review, *Edinburgh Review* 41, January 1850, *CH*, 164–5.
8. Herbert Rosengarten and Margaret Smith, eds., *Shirley* (Oxford: Clarendon, 1979), 7n.
9. These epithets are taken from the review in the *Atlas*, 3 November 1849, *CH*, 121.
10. See Kathleen Tillotson, *Novels of the Eighteen-Forties* (Oxford: Clarendon, 1985), 128–37, for a discussion of such works.
11. Mrs Sarah Ellis, in *The Morning Call* 1, 1850, 35.
12. Charlotte Brontë to W. S. Williams, c. 19 November 1850, *CBL* II, 513.
13. 'Passing Events', in Charlotte Brontë, *Five Novelettes*, edited by Winifred Gérin (London: Folio Press, 1971), 54.
14. Charlotte Brontë, *The Spell: An Extravaganza*. edited by George Edwin MacLean (Oxford University Press, 1931), 143.
15. See Carol Bock, ' "Our plays": *the Brontë Juvenilia*', 34–52, above.
16. Gaskell, *Life*, 378.
17. 'The history of the year', 12 March 1829, in Juliet Barker, ed., *Charlotte Brontë: Juvenilia 1829–1835* (Harmondsworth: Penguin, 1996), 2.
18. *S*, 375–7 and notes.
19. 'Strange Events' (1830), *EEW* I, 257.
20. This was the subtitle of Charlotte Bronte's *The Green Dwarf*, written in 1833 at the age of seventeen, which opens with a description of the 'dark halls' and 'desolate chambers' of the inn once kept by 'the four Chief Genii, Tallii, Brani, Emi and Anni' in Verdopolis 'twenty years since' (*EEW*, II. I, 132).
21. To W. S. Williams, 16 April 1849, *CBL* II, 203.
22. *Yeast, Fraser's Magazine* 38 (1848), 708–9.
23. Anne Bronte published two poems in *Fraser's* during this period, the first in the August issue, where it is printed immediately before the second instalment of *Yeast*, and the second, 'The Narrow Way', in that for December, printed on the reverse of the novel's closing chapter.
24. It is described as 'the Tower of Babylon' amongst the Advertisements in *Blackwood's Young Men's Magazine* for December 1829 (*EEW* I, 95), and

as 'Babel' in the *Conversations* reported in the August 1830 number (*EEW* 1, 224).

25. *Blackwood's Young Men's Magazine*, August 1830, *EEW* 1, 224.
26. Herbert Rosengarten, introduction to Margaret Smith and Herbert Rosengarten, eds., *Villette* (Oxford: Clarendon, 1984), xi.
27. Raymond Williams, *The English Novel From Dickens to Lawrence* (London: Chatto & Windus, 1973), 71.
28. Raymond Williams, *The Long Revolution* (Harmondsworth: Penguin, 1965), 84.
29. Charlotte Brontë to Elizabeth Gaskell, 12 January 1853, quoted in Barker, *The Brontës*, 714–5.
30. Charlotte Brontë to George Smith, 30 October 1852, quoted in Barker, *The Brontës*, 705.
31. Charlotte Brontë to W. S. Williams, 26 July 1849, *CBL* 11, 232.
32. Gaskell, *Life*, 506.
33. Charlotte Brontë to John Stores Smith, 25 July 1850.
34. John Stores Smith, *Social Aspects* (London: Chapman, 1850), 40, 45.
35. On the cult and the actualities of the middle-class 'home' in this period, see Leonore Davidoff and Catherine Hall, *Family Fortunes: Men and Women of the English Middle Class 1780–1850* (London: Hutchinson, 1987), 375–95.
36. Michael R. Booth, *Victorian Spectacular Theatre 1850–1910* (London: Routledge & Kegan Paul, 1981), 3.
37. Charles Knight, ed., *Cyclopaedia of London* (London: Charles Knight, 1851), 761.
38. Smith, *Social Aspects*, 52, 55.
39. *Eclectic Review*, March 1853, *CH*, 196.
40. For a suggestive discussion of Glass Town as a 'proleptic vision' of the Crystal Palace, and of *Villette*'s relation to this, see Isobel Armstrong, 'Charlotte Brontë's City of Glass', the Hilda Hulme Memorial Lecture, 2 December 1992 (University of London, 1993).
41. 7 June 1851, *CBL* 11, 631. For Patrick Brontë's 'lively interest' in his children's amusements, see Barker, *The Brontës*, 109.
42. The Queen's Exhibition Journal, 29 April 1851, quoted in C. R. Fay, *Palace of Industry, 1851: A Study of the Great Exhibition and Its Fruits* (Cambridge University Press, 1951), 45.
43. *Tallis's History and Description of the Crystal Palace and the Exhibition of the World's Industry in 1851*, 3 vols. (London: John Tallis & Co., 1851), 3, 54.
44. Dickens to the Hon. Mrs Richard Watson, 11 July 1851, in *The Letters of Charles Dickens*, Pilgrim Edition, vol. 6, edited by Graham Storey, Kathleen Tillotson and Nina Burgis (Oxford: Clarendon, 1988), 327.
45. Charlotte Brontë to Amelia Taylor, 7 June 1851, *CBL* 11, 633.
46. Matthew Arnold, Preface to *Poems*, edition of 1853, in Lionel Trilling, ed., *The Portable Matthew Arnold* (New York: Viking, 1966), 201.
47. William Whewell, *The General Bearing of the Great Exhibition on the Progress of Art and Science*, Inaugural Lecture as Master of Trinity College, Cambridge, 26 November 1851, 6, 4.
48. Charlotte Brontë to W. S. Williams, 28 October 1847, *CBL* 1, 554.

7

RICK RYLANCE

'Getting on': ideology, personality and the Brontë characters

This chapter places the Brontë narratives in three intersecting contexts: the changing social circumstances in which their work appeared, the changing literary context in which works of narrative were created and understood by Victorian people, and certain ideological factors which unite these two. The key term is 'character', and here we need to distinguish two quite separate meanings. There is, first, the modern sense of character as the literary depiction of psychologically complex personalities. But there is also a Victorian sense of character (hereafter designated 'character') as a desirable moral quality. I will argue that the Brontë novels were written at a point in literary history when the modern 'psychological' understanding of character emerged as a significant criterion in the judgement of fiction, and a more open enquiry into the nature of human behaviour contested moral orthodoxies. The tussle between the two engages key issues: what is the private cost of public image? What pressure does the ideological environment exert on personal behaviour? How can writers of fiction represent the contest between them?

To be thought to be 'of good character' was, in most circles of the literate population of Victorian Britain, an absolute requirement of those entering employment. It was also essential for those entering respectable marriage. These goals – 'getting on' in the world, and/or getting married – represent the two pivots of the Brontë narratives, and the points at which personality and ideology, private feeling and public image, intersect. In this, the sisters shared interests with others in the emerging generation of young 'realist' novelists: Dickens, Thackeray and George Eliot.

The phrase 'getting on' became established usage in the 1840s. It meant making a success of one's life, building a career, finding a place in the mainstream of society, often from beginnings that were disadvantaged or isolated. Charlotte Brontë used the expression 'to get on' in this sense several times in *Shirley* (1849). The thwarted factory owner Robert Moore early exclaims: 'I cannot get on. I cannot execute my plans' (*S*, 25). The fact that this, like other uses of the phrase in *Shirley*, is a cry of frustration is important. Moore's career is obstructed, he believes, by the government's conduct of the war against republican France, in particular the imposition of trading restrictions as a response to Napoleon's blockade; he is shortly to discover it is obstructed, too, by industrial sabotage by textile workers badly affected by factory mechanisation. Thus, *Shirley* opens with Moore's complaints about government, and the criminal destruction of a shipment of machinery. Moore blames government for his woes, and blames his workers too. He is a recognisable type today.

But his career is also frustrated by his position in Yorkshire society. Partly of Belgian extraction, and from a family for whom business is an 'hereditary calling' (*S*, 28), Moore's isolation is produced by his hybrid nationality and ambiguous social standing as a representative of 'trade'. The novel thus dramatises important divisions in British culture as plangent in the 1840s, when the book was written, as they were in 1812, when it is set. Moore's situation is the predicament of one interest in a fractious national community. Battling (as he sees it) against entrenched interests, his 'I cannot get on' is a familiar cry for the release of frustrated energies and the competitive spirit. By the mid nineteenth century, 'getting on' had become an established motif not only for personal ambition, but a whole class of (as they saw themselves) economically dynamic and socially mobile entrepreneurs. According to the *Oxford English Dictionary*, the use of the phrase 'to get on' in this sense was amplified by novelists like Charlotte Brontë, Dickens, Harriet Martineau and Thomas Hughes who put it in general currency.

The opportunity for the phrase to circulate widely was created by Britain's increasing economic prosperity. More people were talking about 'getting on' because more people were doing it – and, in turn, even more were *hoping* to do it. 'Getting on' expressed an imaginative aspiration as well as an economic opportunity. It articulated a new cultural norm in a freshly mobile society and, as for Robert Moore, it was often shadowed by bitter complaints about obstructions and the haunting prospect of failure. The desire to 'get on', as Moore's situation illustrates, was a high-cost activity in personal terms.

So what kind of person was it whom the Victorians thought would 'get on'? The typical person would be young, energetic and male. He would also possess that most nebulous of Victorian personal attributes 'character', which, as Stefan Collini demonstrates, increasingly dominated the discourse of Victorian economics, politics and morality at the mid century.[1] In one sense, ideas of respectable 'character' regulated movement in a newly mobile, expanding population. Thus, the idea of being 'of good character' was prominent in the assessment of social reputations, and was closely identified with the idea of the gentleman. It was crucial too in the conduct of employer–employee relations through the 'character reference' which applicants for posts were asked to supply. The greater use of the 'character reference' reveals an economy increasingly dependent upon written communication, and patterns of recruitment conducted more and more between strangers rather than intimates in a known community. It also signifies the distrustful moral and political invigilation of one social group by another.

The cultivation and projection of 'character', and its importance to social, economic and, indeed, romantic relations, was crucial to much Victorian thinking. Hundreds – perhaps thousands – of books on 'character' were consumed by mass readerships. These exhorted the moral necessity of being 'of good character' for its own sake, of course, but they also provided advice on how to project it. The vehement citation of countless instances of exemplary behaviour, which is the staple tactic of these volumes, was no doubt intended to be encouraging; but it also provided readers with a catalogue of roles to play and postures to assume. These books on 'character' present a dictionary of behaviour, a script for a public image, and were a key component in the fantasy life of the times.

Probably the most successful author of such works, of course, was Samuel Smiles who, in 1871, published a bestseller simply called *Character*. But Smiles gleamed at the tip of an iceberg, and probably more important than any individually successful volume were the thousands of books used for instruction in schools and distributed through churches and worker's educational organisations like the Mechanics' Institute. Volumes broadcast in this way, written by authors of less celebrity than Smiles, are still found in second-hand bookshops, often with prize-labels attached. Smiles' *Self-Help*, whose runaway success began on publication in 1859, ranges widely, but contains a chapter on 'Character':

> Character is human nature in its best form. It is moral order embodied in the individual. Men of character are not only the conscience of society, but in every well-governed State they are its best motive power; for it is moral qualities which rule the world. Even in war, Napoleon said that the moral is to the physical as ten to one. The strength, the industry, the civilisation of nations – all depend upon individual character; and the very foundations of civil security seat upon it. Laws and institutions are but its outgrowth. In the just balance of nature, individuals, nations, and races will obtain just as much as they deserve, and no more. And as effect finds its cause, so surely does quality of character among a people produce its befitting results.[2]

'Character' represents the moral and psychological condition to which readers should aspire; it is the motor of industry and civilisation, for to be civilised is to be industrious. Not only does the 'strength, the industry, the civilisation of nations' depend upon 'character', but 'civil security' also. This thread in the argument implies an undertow of anxiety no doubt derived from its composition – like Charlotte Brontë's drama of industrial unrest in *Shirley* – during the politically uncertain 1840s. Finally, this vision of 'character' is a distinctly *male* discourse. Smiles writes exclusively of 'men of character', and the examples he provides underscore the gendering of the argument. The chapter is entitled 'Character – the true gentleman'.

Psychologically and ideologically, this is supremely confident. 'Character' is exhibited largely by assertive temperaments, and there is little interest in psychological nuance. This is a discourse of types, not personalities, and its psychological crudity was objectionable to liberal psychologists doubting that complex personalities were so easily construed.[3] A key issue concerned the will, for behind much of the discourse of 'character' is an untroubled faith in the power of the will to enable one to 'get on'. The will suppresses self-doubt, as well as the distractions of what the Victorians euphemistically called 'the lower self'. It also, for men, served to repress those aspects of behaviour negatively associated with femininity, such as tenderness, ease or sensuality.[4] The man of 'character' was not feckless; he rarely surrendered self-control or subjected himself to doubt; and he despised those he judged incompetent in the business of life. At the end of the 1850s, George Eliot in *The Mill on the Floss* (1860) created a critique of such personalities in the figure of Tom Tulliver whose self-denying authoritarianism is tellingly related by Eliot not to worldly success, but, on the contrary, to failure, both personal and economic. According to Eliot, Tom's personality is a type: 'a character . . . that performs what it intends, subdues every counteracting impulse and has no visions beyond the distinctly possible, [it] is strong by its very negations.'[5] The key clause is the last. The most important critique of this vision of 'character' is that it is based on denial, and novelists and others increasingly explored not only the ideological limits of popular perceptions of 'character', but also the psychological consequences of trying to live in this way. In so doing, they were reporting on the mental condition of the 'getting on' generation.

Heather Glen convincingly argues that *The Professor*, Charlotte Brontë's first novel, is a psychological exposure of a man, Crimsworth, subjecting himself to a regime of 'character'-building.[6] Similarly, in *Shirley*, the battle within Robert Moore between the 'character' who wants to 'get on' and the man of feeling, is observed by Caroline Helstone, who loves him but whom Moore rejects because he needs to concentrate on 'getting on'. The novel's focus on Caroline's silent desperation heightens the poignancy, and exposes the potential heartlessness of male 'character' posited on a belief in self-determination and the irrelevance of others.

In *The Professor*, one of Crimsworth's favourite images for his own psychological condition is that of a soldier whose armour is secure: 'In less than five minutes', he remarks complacently of new acquaintances, 'they had thus revealed to me their characters, and in less than five minutes I had buckled on a breastplate of steely indifference, and let down a visor of impassable austerity' (*P*, 77). Crimsworth's self-congratulation makes a point about the instinctive distrustfulness and negativity of the posture. This is a fearful and not a buoyantly successful mental regime. Here is a 'character' who is playing the 'character' game, but who is not 'getting on' at all. In *Shirley* the analysis is made more explicit as Moore realises how mechanised he has become. Trapped by his own aspirations, he glimpses internal explosion. When asked 'What has gone wrong?' by a male friend, Moore replies: 'The machinery of all my nature; the whole enginery [*sic*] of this human mill: the boiler, which I take to be the heart, is fit to burst'(*S*, 532). Eventually, softening his free-market attitudes on labour questions, and relinquishing the steely defiance of his own heart, he acknowledges his repressed love for Caroline, and – dear reader – marries her. Like *The Professor*, which also rewards its hero with domestic happiness, the romantic plot of *Shirley* offers an anatomy of the rigid personality structures of 'character', a criticism of the ideological conditions which sponsor them, and a weighing of the costs of such behaviour.

However, both novels are ambiguous in their final attitudes. *The Professor* rewards Crimsworth with love and modest success in business, but his postures of suspicion and vigilance, though relaxed, are not forsaken. The novel continues to picture a world of intense inter-personal competition, and Brontë's portrait of the psychological environment is bleak. *The Professor* ends with an account of the war between spontaneity and self-control in the personality of Crimsworth's son. Crimsworth observes this with a disturbing mixture of anxiety and relish:

> She [his wife] sees, as I also see, a something in Victor's temper – a kind of electrical ardour and power – which emits, now and then, ominous sparks; Hunsden [the child's godfather] calls it his spirit, and says it should not be curbed. I call it the leaven of the offending Adam, and consider that it should be, if not *whipped* out of him, at least soundly disciplined; and that he will be cheap of [i.e. he will get off lightly with] any amount of either bodily or mental suffering which will ground him radically in the art of self-control.
>
> (*P*, 245)

The child's name is Victor, but it is difficult to see who, here, is victorious, or, indeed, whether this name is in fact ironic. The uncertainty suggests that Charlotte Brontë herself is trapped by this vision. She can see what is wrong with it but also – as a self-perceived outsider herself – why it comes into being and stays there.

Shirley, too, ends with the romantic contentment of two couples who represent an ideologically satisfying intermingling of partners from different social spheres: the landed Shirley with Moore's déclassé younger brother Louis, who is a private tutor, and the trader Robert with the Tory parson's niece Caroline. The matrimonial distribution suggests social reconciliation in divided times. However the novel pointedly ends not only with their contentment and success (the Moore brothers prove to be an accomplished squire and successful businessman respectively), but with what appears to some a gratuitous ecological lament for the spoiling of a natural habitat by industrialisation. An old woman, Martha, remembers the 'bonnie spot' of years past now destroyed and vanished (*S*, 646). *Jane Eyre* uses the same tactic: the novel actually ends with the dying St John Rivers rather than with the married bliss of Jane and Rochester. It is as if both novels are suspicious of their own resolutions and eager to note costs as well as benefits. At one level, they recognise severe social tensions, the costs of 'character' and 'getting on' and the spoliations of industrial capitalism. But, as a solution, they appear to get not much further than a softening of the personal and public rigours of these things. The result is an undertow of contrary messages.

That it is not the job of literature to solve ideological dilemmas was emphasised by Charlotte Brontë herself, who concluded *Shirley* thus: 'The story is told. I think I now see the judicious reader putting on his spectacles to look for the moral. It would be an insult to his sagacity to offer directions. I only say, God speed him in the quest!' (*S*, 646). Good literature deals with conundrums in 'the moral', and the importance of Charlotte Brontë's pointed openness is best measured against absolutist doctrines of 'character'. Hers is a disposition to enquiry rather than advocacy, and in this spirit she challenged the mores of 'getting on'. But it is important to recognise that what was attractive in ideas of 'character' for Victorian readers is not a matter of mere doctrine. The appeal is an imaginative one: an expression of hope, a sense of self-respect and independence for the aspirant reader, and a language with which to legitimate behaviour. Somewhat contrary to our sense of the repressive psychological cost of 'character' building, what Victorian theorists delivered was, at least in principle, a vision of freedom and opportunity. After all, 'getting on' did make strong, meritocratic claims for personal worth, and substituted attainable personal qualities for genuinely inaccessible ones of birth and patronage. 'Good character' in your individual sphere was something after which all could – and should – strive, and this had an appeal across a political spectrum. The socialist Robert Owen – himself as much a product of industrial culture as Smiles – produced similar arguments about the self-determination of character, but he aimed these at political purposes remote from the free-market liberalism of the entrepreneurs.[7] What this indicates, in relation to the Brontës, is a widely circulating, unresolved debate, to which, at home and elsewhere, they attended with considerable interest.

Though a graph of the growing number of books published on the theme of 'character' and 'getting on' would show a rising curve following the success of *Self-Help* after 1859, it would be wrong to see this as historically beyond the Brontë sisters, the last of whom, Charlotte, died in 1855. *Self-Help* itself started life as series of lectures delivered in nearby Leeds in 1845. In any case, the language of 'character' and 'getting on' was a familiar part of the ideological scenery of the Brontë household. Their father's life, indeed, might itself have been written-up as an exemplary narrative, as he 'rose' from Irish farmer's boy to Cambridge-educated clergyman. In fact, Patrick himself presented things this way in the occasional self-descriptions he prepared as he 'got on' in his career.

Juliet Barker (who has done much to rescue Patrick from his reputation as a patriarchal monster) makes clear how the career path of a Victorian clergyman depended on his ability to present a plausibly solid 'character' to potential employers and parishioners. Patrick therefore collected testimonials which offered encomiums on his 'character' in order to furnish moral recommendations and professional guarantees: 'For the character of the man', wrote his patron Henry Martyn, a Cambridge don, 'I can safely vouch as I know him to be studious, clever, & pious'.[8] In the ecclesiastical power struggle that confused his initial appointment to the Haworth ministry in 1819, Patrick, the local candidate, recommended himself on these grounds: 'believe me, the character and conduct of a man out of the pulpit is as much to be considered as his character and conduct in, and we are likely to know those best who live nearest to us'.[9] The habit of thinking in this way penetrated deep. The epistolary courtship of his future wife, Maria Branwell, was conducted in similar terms by both parties: 'I will frankly confess', she wrote in her first letter in 1812, 'that your behaviour and what I have seen and heard of your character has excited my esteem and regard'.[10] 'Excited' adds a faint morally flavoured eroticism, but the deeper point is that romantic interests are ethical as well as sexual, and communal as well as individual. Maria's interest in Patrick is not only a matter of personal observation; just as important is what she has heard from others. In other words, this is a public and not a private management of a reputation.

Much later, when asked about his family in Ireland by Mrs Gaskell for her biography of Charlotte, Patrick presented his life as a familiar Victorian tale. He had not, he wrote, troubled to discover his family's origins because his father's 'lot in life, as well as mine, depended under providence, not on family descent, but our own exertions.'[11] This is a recognisable story of 'getting on'. But, as Barker points out, it does not present the whole picture. Though little is known for certain, it is reasonable to suppose that the Irish Brontës were not, in fact, subsistence farmers, near to the peasantry. Had they been so, it is unlikely that Patrick would have had a basic education at a fee-paying school, or the opportunity to advance: an Irish family farm, existing on the economic margins, would have required its eldest son to work the land. The wider point is clear in this minor instance. It is a part of the myth of 'character' in the Victorian period that those who succeed are 'self-made'. Many of those who purportedly 'got on' under their own steam suppressed the advantage of their origins to enhance their own achievements and to confirm a popular, self-legitimating fantasy. This Dickens knew when he created that monster of 'getting on' hypocrisy, Josiah Bounderby in *Hard Times*, in 1854, the year before Patrick offered his own mild, personal version of the myth of lack of origins. The vision of the man 'of character' entailed a vision of man alone and self-determined. Indeed, men 'of character' seeking to 'get on' were likely to perceive themselves to be violently opposed by the world in general, as Robert Moore does in *Shirley*.

The main lineaments of the story of Patrick's 'character' are very recognisable and would have been clearly understood by his children, his parishioners, and his wife. 'Character', it seems, is a matter of public performance. In Patrick's life, as in those of most literate Victorian people, professional and romantic advancement (as well as issues of personal image and sense of self-worth) were negotiated around the sense of the 'character' you were able to sustain. The 'character reference' and the love letter appear to have shared the same language. This mental habit penetrated deep. In Anne's *Agnes Grey*, the solitary, self-communing heroine, in order to cheer herself up when she feels herself 'degraded by the life I led' as an isolated governess, addresses herself as though she were composing her own 'character reference'. In a private soliloquy, she consoles herself with a public form of praise. The soliloquy allows us to glimpse the internal, imaginative world produced by the discourse of 'character'. Agnes negotiates between defiant self-definition, pride, residual guilt, insecurity and the imposed forms of public judgement and professional estimation:

> Miss Grey was a queer creature: she never flattered, and did not praise [the children] half enough; but whenever she did speak favourably of them, or anything belonging to them, they could be quite sure her approbation was sincere. She was very quiet, obliging and peaceable in the main, but there were some things that put her out of temper . . . She had her own opinions on every subject, and kept steadily to them – very tiresome opinions they often were; as

> she was always thinking of what was right and what was wrong, and had a
> strange reverence for matters connected with religion, and an unaccountable
> liking to good people. (*AG*, 69–70)

It is sometimes said of Anne that her novels are flat and conventional by comparison with her more daring sisters. But in passages such as this (and there are plenty of them) something subtle is occurring. The style of the book – so repressed, so formal, so apparently stilted in phrase and static in rhythm – would appear to have all the eloquence of a letter of application. But this plodding syntax and formula phrasing represents, in the manner of a dramatic monologue, a representative state of mind. What energy there is emerges in the battle between compliance and self-justification: composure and rage coexist. It is bleak because it reminds one of an obituary.

That Anne was significantly interested in the collision between self-image and public image is clear. *The Tenant of Wildfell Hall* takes this as its central theme by contrasting the private causes of Helen Huntingdon's reclusiveness (she is the victim of an abusive marriage) with a public reputation that even darkens her true lover's suspicions. His relief, when he finds her innocent, reveals the tangled moral, social and psychological reflexes of the mid-century generation. Gilbert declares: 'through the noisome vapours of the world's aspersions and my own fancied convictions, her character shone bright, and clear, and stainless as that sun I could not bear to look upon', and he feels 'shame and deep remorse for my own conduct' (*TWH*, 382). The language is torpid with cliché, but that does not mean that it lacks interest or literary skill. Anne Brontë is, I think, an accomplished ventriloquist of character in all senses: it is 'character' which pre-occupies characters (in the modern sense) in a book which not only scandalously exposes cosy Victorian images of marriage (as *Agnes Grey* exposes images of child-rearing in bourgeois families), but is equally intelligent about the pressures of reputation.

So the discourses of 'getting on' and the establishment of 'character' formed an important part of the mental life of the Brontë household. But, when one reflects on it, it is probable that the sisters felt some discomfort with this for at least two reasons. There is, first of all, the fact of their womanhood. We have noted that the discourse of 'getting on', in the economic sphere particularly, was a characteristically male discourse. Interestingly, the *Oxford English Dictionary* detects an alternative use of the phrase from around 1816 (the year in which Charlotte was born) when women, particularly, seem to have used it to signify not the values of entrepreneurial competition, but a more relaxed range of meanings in which 'to get on with' someone signifies spontaneous ease and comradeship. The tension between embattled competition and friendly intimacy encapsulated in these rival usages of the phrase is representative of larger conflicts. Here again, how-ever, is a complication, for, notoriously, the Brontë children (including the self-destructive Branwell) seem to have found it difficult to 'get on' in *either* sense. Love and friendship seems to have been a spikey affair for Charlotte, and a constitutive absence for Emily and Anne. At the same time, the sisters' professional efforts as governesses, their entrepreneurial attempts to found their own school, and Branwell's hapless employment record, were all spec-tacularly unsuccessful. Their fiction incorporates a sustained critique of the idea of 'getting on' which proceeds from – but does not resolve – some of these ambivalences.

The second major reason for the Brontë children's discomfort with the idea of entrepreneurial 'getting-on' lies in their historical situation. Before them, on their doorstep, they saw vividly the effects of the industrial revolution on the craft-based wool industries of West Yorkshire, including vicious cy-cles of growth, slump and unemployment. Haworth was not the wild, rural backwater of popular fantasy, but a place in which the clergyman's daugh-ters witnessed very visible distress. Poverty, poor health and outraged indus-trial militancy were as evident here as in larger towns such as neighbouring Keighley. It is important to note that the sisters' lives did not coincide with the classic period of Victorian prosperity during which many people did, in-deed, 'get on'. Charlotte, the longest lived, died in 1855, Anne in 1849, Emily in 1848. Their work was written (with the exception of *Villette*, 1853) prior to the Great Exhibition of 1851, which is often considered the symbolic threshold of Britain's legendary Victorian prosperity. Economic historians have sometimes used the metaphor of an aeroplane taking off to describe the economy's success. After 1851, the argument goes, the British econ-omy was airborne.[12] Before this, however, it was in an uneasy, uncertain state, bumping along the runway searching for buoyancy, something we can see reflected in the Brontë fiction, preoccupied as it is with debates about uncertain values and priorities. The exploration of these areas of uncertain values is probably a better reflection of the turbulence of the times than the partial, somewhat prejudicial representation of specific class-based troubles in a novel like *Shirley*. The abiding direction of the enquiry concerns what it means to 'get on' in these circumstances, and here issues of gender and related disadvantages are much to the fore.

Jane Eyre (1848) might be read as the story of a woman who succeeds in 'getting on'. She strikes out courageously and independently and forges her own career, first as governess, then as an independent schoolmistress with her own business (thus imaginatively rectifying the sisters' own failings in these respects). Eventually, she becomes a woman of independent means and finds love and rest in the middle rank of landed society. She has 'got on' very far, struggling against poverty and adversity for most of her early life, enjoying immediately none of the benefits of birth or patronage – indeed her nearest relatives have both abused and rejected her. She, like Patrick Brontë, has to a degree made her own origins.

But in this distinctive, virtually exclusive focus on a *woman's* achievements, *Jane Eyre* is quite unlike the mass of narratives which circulated stories of approved achievement to Victorian people. Most of the case studies and exemplary instances in Smiles' books, for example, are male. In fact, the lengthy summaries of each chapter given in the contents list to *Self-Help* cites 306 men and two women, one of whom – Lady Peel – is there because she was the Prime Minister's mother. In *Character*, the 1871 volume Smiles himself described as a 'supplement' to the chapter on 'character' in *Self-Help*, women are included, but largely confined to a section on 'Companionship in Marriage'. Their stories run beneath titles like 'Great Wives' and 'Splendid Helpmates'.

There are therefore straightforward points to be made about the contrast between *Jane Eyre* and the ways in which women figured in the exemplary narratives. Smiles is tart about women's occupations. According to him, working women (for example those working in the factories of the industrial north) produce 'in many cases, an entire subversion of family order, of domestic discipline, and of home rule'.[13] The exclusion of women from Smilesian narratives of 'character' is therefore of a piece with their exclusion from the worlds of work, capital and 'getting on'. 'Character is property. It is the noblest of possessions. It is an estate in the general goodwill and respect of men', Smiles declared with thumping gender specificity, 'and they who invest in it... will find their reward in esteem and reputation fairly and honourably won. And it is right that in life good qualities should tell... and that the really best men should be foremost' (*Character*, 16–17). Legislation reflected attitudes such as these. Until the Married Women's Property Act of 1882, married women were excluded from owning any property of their own, and Charlotte Brontë herself much resented the transfer of the copyrights in her work to her husband on their marriage in 1854.

But if male narratives excluded such women as the self-reliant Jane Eyre, so too did classic female tales. The sort of role models offered to women in the ever-popular 'conduct' books (which offered advice and example of a conventional kind for women, and were often, though by no means always, written by women) largely confirmed the passive, secondary roles assumed in Smilesian stories. An example of such popular and influential early nineteenth-century writing is *Female Scripture Characters Exemplifying Female Virtues* by Mrs Elizabeth King, a clergyman's wife writing initially for her husband's parishioners, which went through numerous editions during the Brontës' childhood. Focusing each chapter on one biblical woman or another (Eve, Jezebel, Ruth, the Virgin Mary and so forth), King read lessons of constancy, obedience and home-making.[14]

The Victorians were fond of images of life as a path or journey, usually to a known destination. Sometimes, as in Dickens for instance, this image appears as Christian sentiment when worthy, hard-done-by souls like the young Paul Dombey journey to death, their lives imagined as a river journey to the eternal sea.[15] Such metaphors clearly captured Victorian people's attention – otherwise Dickens, who was highly market-sensitive, would have smartly dropped them. Instead, he used them laboriously across his career, for they resonated to those 'getting on' on life's journey. It is therefore interesting to conceptualise *Jane Eyre* in these terms. The diagram is loosely modelled on the famous London tube map. In it, the central line schematically represents Jane's career and the stations her stopping-off points.

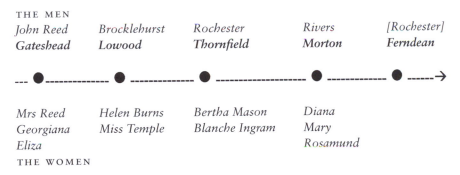

THE MEN

| John Reed | Brocklehurst | Rochester | Rivers | [Rochester] |
| Gateshead | Lowood | Thornfield | Morton | Ferndean |

Mrs Reed	Helen Burns	Bertha Mason	Diana	
Georgiana	Miss Temple	Blanche Ingram	Mary	
Eliza			Rosamund	

THE WOMEN

The diagram represents Jane's progress from place to place. It also, schematically, represents the social hierarchy with the patriarchal men at the top and, below the line, the women.

To some extent, the diagram misrepresents Jane's career. It pictures it as dead-level progress, whereas it actually consists in huge alterations in fortune and an exposure to poverty and abuse. Hers is a life without, initially, the protective armour of family, patrons or champions. Jane has to get herself along, and the central line should, strictly, be a swooping switchback. Nevertheless, if the novel emphasises the proximity of plenty and want, and the ever-present possibility of a plunge into de-classed poverty, a correlated message is that life is a matter of self-determination, and in this Jane's is, if hardly arrow-straight, at least an exemplary progress.

The diagram also represents important features of the social structure. Above Jane's lifeline are the exemplary males. Below it are various studies in female roles and behaviour which offer to Jane potential models for existence. To a man, the men exhibit modes of domination: John Reed's spiteful cruelty, Brocklehurst's religious and institutionally sanctioned sadism, St John Rivers' cold manipulation of the claims of faith and duty to achieve chilly sexual ends. Rivers recommends himself to Jane as if he were a creature stepped from a book on 'character' to be earnestly admired. He is an absolutist for duty who searches for an exemplary career in the ministry in which, he tells Jane, 'the best qualifications of soldier, statesman, and orator' are all needed (*JE*, 362). His is the mode of psychological bullying which complements the physical brutality of Reed and Brocklehurst. Male behaviour in *Jane Eyre* is a sequence of studies in dominion.

In this respect, the figure of Rochester is interesting. Forceful and romantically alluring, he like Jane is rewarded with love at the close. But his earlier behaviour hardly shows to advantage. Reed, Brocklehurst and Rivers to a lesser extent, exercise powers of status, wealth and institution. Rochester's persuasions have the fascination of sexual allure and energy, but also the captivating (in all senses) authority of wealth. He offers to present Jane with the family jewels:

> I will myself put the diamond chain around your neck, and the circlet on your forehead, – which it will become: for nature, at least, has stamped her patent of nobility on this brow, Jane; and I will clasp the bracelets on these fine wrists, and load these fairy-like fingers with rings.　　　　　　(*JE*, 259)

Despite the protestation of 'natural nobility', this is a clear reminder of the social inequality of which Rochester is always at least half-conscious. The imagery clearly suggests, in gender and class terms, the imposed, imprisoning drag on her free mobility entailed in this unequal relationship. Jane's own alarming image for the fear and fascination exerted by the charisma of wealth is that of Danae, the Greek princess raped by the god Zeus in the form of a shower of gold: 'I can never bear being dressed like a doll by Mr Rochester, or sitting like a second Danae with the golden shower falling around me' (*JE*, 268). It is because of this that she determines to re-contact her lost relatives in the hope that some sort of future inheritance will offset her dependency: 'I will write to Madeira', she continues directly, '... and tell my uncle John I am going to be married, and to whom; if I had but the prospect of one day bringing Mr Rochester an accession of fortune, I could better endure to be kept by him now' (*JE*, 268). The fortune, of course, eventually arrives, and her independence is secure before her marriage. The frank improbability of the event only underlines the size of the symbolic stakes. In the end, in a situation that can be read as having equal symbolic force, Rochester, blind, maimed, disgraced and represented in Jane's life-diagram in brackets, is dependent upon *her*; the balances of power are re-tilted.

If the men in *Jane Eyre* compose a sorry set, what of the women? Mrs Reed is a study in female subjection to the authority of the patriarchal family. She is enthralled by her brutish, insolent, young son and the imprisoning disdain of caste-consciousness. Blanche Ingram is the manipulative beauty operating the sexual markets. The insane creole Bertha Mason is, as is often said, the suffering emblem of all the results of Victorian patriarchy and racism. But again, the more interesting figures are probably those attracting more ambiguous judgements. Helen Burns offers Jane a model of martyrish heroism: hers is an exemplary tale of subjection to authority whose reward is moral advantage and posthumous compensation. But hers is not an example Jane can follow in its pious passivity and unresisting compliance. The case of Miss Temple is more intriguing still. As her name suggests, Jane worships her: 'to her instruction I owed the best part of my acquirements; her friendship and society had been my continual solace; she had stood me in the stead of mother, governess, and latterly, companion' (*JE*, 84). Mother, governess and companion – it is a catalogue of potential destinies for Victorian anywoman, to which might be added a career as 'superintendent of the seminary', Miss Temple's post. Jane rejects all of these for herself. Miss Temple leaves to become a wife (another potential destiny); but Jane, who might follow her career route and vocational example, rebels. It is freedom, independence and movement she wants, not stationary moral authority and the province of limited good works:

> I desired liberty; for liberty I gasped; for liberty I uttered a prayer; it seemed scattered on the wind then faintly blowing. I abandoned it and framed a humbler supplication; for change, stimulus: that petition too seemed swept off into vague space; 'Then,' I cried, half desperate, 'grant me at least a new servitude!'
> (*JE*, 85)

Praying to the empty spaces of nature is an eloquent symbol of her actual predicament, but it is equally eloquent as protest.

Jane's attitudes to Miss Temple are complex. Emotions of reverence and gratitude mingle with resistance. She remarks of Miss Temple's influence that

> I had imbibed from her something of her nature and much of her habits: more harmonious thoughts: what seemed better-regulated feelings had become the inmates of my mind. I had given in allegiance to duty and order; I was quiet; I believed I was content: to the eyes of others, usually even to my own, I appeared a disciplined and subdued character.
> (*JE*, 84)

The emphasis on appearance here is very marked, and the word signifies two things. First, it distinguishes the surface from the depth, the seeming from the reality, as is apparent when Jane speaks here of 'what *seemed* better regulated feelings' (my italics). But, second, appearance is partly a matter of seeing yourself through others' eyes, of projecting an image, of being conscious of an audience, just as actors 'appear' on stage, and again this passage illustrates the point. Jane projects the appearance of 'a disciplined and subdued character', a model 'inmate', as she revealingly puts it, in her own thoughts. What we see in this passage is a reluctance to accept the co-ercion of an approved 'character', a public image, an identity manufactured however tenderly from loving example. By this stage, Miss Temple embodies the authority of a person from a text on 'character' or 'conduct'.

Early critics despised the politics implied by Jane's urgent calls for in-dependence and self-expression and her heterodox attitudes to authority – what one, Lady Eastlake, described as the novel's general 'murmuring against God's appointment... [and] proud and perpetual assertion of the rights of man' (*CH*, 106). But the whole question of her 'character' was an issue be-cause it appeared to dramatise the same issues of conformity and obedience to example that were so generally pressing in the revolutionary decade of the 1840s. Lady Eastlake suspected Charlotte Brontë of revolutionary sym-pathies and directly connected *Jane Eyre* with 'the tone of mind and thought which has overthrown authority and violated every code human and divine abroad, and fostered Chartism and rebellion at home' (*CH*, 105). But she was particularly vehement on the question of Jane's character, which she found disgusting: 'As to Jane's characterisation – there is none of that har-monious unity about it which made little Becky so grateful a subject for analysis – nor are any of the discrepancies of that kind which have their ex-cuse and their response in our nature' (*CH*, 107). The assumptions are worth inspecting.

The comparison is with Becky Sharp in Thackeray's recently concluded novel *Vanity Fair* (1847–8), a comparison Charlotte Brontë in a sense invited by dedicating *Jane Eyre* to Thackeray. Becky Sharp is a duplicitous, amoral adventuress so the comparison is scarcely flattering. But the attitudes im-plied by these remarks are more revealing than the specific judgement. Lady Eastlake desires a smooth and harmonious 'character'; she wishes too for one that is quiescent under inspection (which will be 'grateful... for anal-ysis' is her way of putting it). The 'character' of Jane will not accommo-date itself to such scrutiny, any more than her personality will lie dormant under Miss Temple's exemplary tutelage. Her very unpredictability, which Rochester finds piquant, is furiously resisted by Lady Eastlake, who is savage as a result. Jane and Rochester, she finds, behave like 'animals in their native state' (*CH*, 111). Jane, meanwhile, is a 'flippant, fifth-rate, plebeian actress', 'the personification of an unregenerate and undisciplined spirit', and a 'mere heathen mind which is a law unto itself' (*CH*, 108–9). The outraged splutter reveals an anxiety about character (in both senses) that runs deep.

It is striking how many early reviewers of *Jane Eyre* remark that it is a novel of character, meaning now not Victorian 'character' but the more modern idea that a novel should present a psychologically probing portrait of a personality. Several reviewers were clearly unsettled by this, not least because the book so signally offended exemplary codes and models. The *North British Review* protested against its portraits of – in the moral sense – 'vigorous dwarfs' whose faults were 'deformity, not weakness' (*CH*, 116). Likewise, the *Spectator* thought the book's characterisation 'unnatural' and 'narrow' (*CH*, 74, 75). The *Christian Remembrancer* commented that 'all the power is shown and all the interest lies in the characters', and condemned the book for its 'moral Jacobinism' (*CH*, 90). The more liberal-minded *Atlas* noted that the novel 'depends not upon incident, but on the development of a character' (*CH*, 68). *The Examiner* saluted the book's 'impressive analysis of a single mind' (*CH*, 77). The book's powers in this respect appealed to the *North American Review* too, though its reviewer was troubled by the sex: 'the exhibition of mere animal appetite, and courtship after the manner of kangaroos' (*CH*, 99).

Jane Eyre, then, was not only popular but controversial, a fact easily now overlooked, sweetened as it is by Hollywood and TV. Possibly the most re-vealing response came from G. H. Lewes, an early champion of Charlotte Brontë, and one of the nineteenth century's most distinguished psychologists. In a positive review in *Fraser's Magazine* in 1847, he saluted the 'percep-tion of character and power of delineating it' as its special distinction (*CH*, 83). Lewes' partner, of course, was George Eliot, and in 1859 she praised Charlotte's psychological acuity and the way her stories grew from 'the psy-chological conception of the dramatis personae' rather than external action or convention.[16] Informed opinion, therefore, saw in Charlotte's work a new style of novel: one based on a serious interest in psychological portraiture. In a piece for *Blackwood's* in 1859, Lewes commented that the substitution of 'psychological justification' for general 'models of composition' or 'the representation of abstract types' was an especially welcome and distinctive feature of contemporary fiction.[17] By this time, Lewes had cooled a little in his enthusiasm for Charlotte's work, but these comments identify the mood in which the new realist fiction was being received. According to the literary historian Richard Stang, the novel began to be widely accepted by literary theorists and reviewers as a serious artistic form in the 1840s. But it was in the next decade that the claims of plausible psychological representation rather than 'the representation of abstract types' (as Lewes put it) became a major criterion guiding responses to new work.[18] By 1859, Lewes' expectations of psychological realism had increased, and his reservations about Charlotte's work focused on the fact that, twelve years after *Jane Eyre*, her characters appeared 'very vigorous sketches, but the reader observes them from the *outside*, he does not penetrate their souls, he does not know them'.[19] When he first encountered *Jane Eyre*, he was not so demanding. Then he found praise for Helen Burns as 'a character at once eminently ideal and accurately real' (*CH*, 86). The remark – balancing exemplary ideality and psychological reality – neatly illustrates the cusp on which the Brontë fiction was poised.

One might argue that by the time Charlotte came to write *Villette*, she too had become more exacting in her need for intensity in psychological observation. In that novel the outward action reduces nearly to stasis as the novel turns relentlessly inwards. A diagram of it, constructed on the same basis as that for *Jane Eyre*, would soon look like a train strike. And the tastes of the reviewers had changed too. *The Spectator*, for instance, had 'nothing but praise to bestow upon the characterisation of this book' (*CH*, 182). Though some – like the *Christian Remembrancer* – were still offended by the 'outrages on decorum, the moral perversity, the tolerance, nay, indifference to vice' which was the 'dangerous' legacy of *Jane Eyre*, for most the characterisation (in its modern sense) had become the principal point of critical entry into the work (*CH*, 203).

Villette, indeed, was written even more explicitly against the tradition of homilised, ideologically freighted lives than its predecessors, and, like *Jane Eyre*, consciously undertook to offend conventional understanding and exemplary portraiture. M. Paul sarcastically accuses Lucy Snowe of having the potential to become 'an useful, perhaps an exemplary character', and the novel forthrightly stresses the power and authority of exceptionality, and a disapproval of major aspects of conventional expectations of behaviour (*V*, 332). Chapter 17 begins:

> These struggles with the natural character, the strong native bent of the heart, may seem futile and fruitless, but in the end they do good. They tend, however slightly, to give the actions, the conduct, that turn which Reason approves, and which Feeling, perhaps, too often opposes: they certainly make a difference in the general tenor of a life, and enable it to be better regulated, more equable, quieter on the surface; and it is on the surface only that the common gaze will fall.
> (*V*, 179)

The passage contains significant assumptions, including the fact that a life should, outwardly, be apparently placid and certainly 'regulated'. But it is the assumption that 'a life' should deliver a message which is most notice-able, and the quoted passage is followed by an extended mediation on the religious import of this. Lucy (and Charlotte) know that lives are supposed to be exemplary, but that exemplary ambitions demand both falsification and severe inward combat.

Later, the tradition of enforcing orthodoxy by the representation of exemplary lives is turned in more liberal directions. Lucy remarks that she hopes that the confession of what might be perceived as her own aberrant experience will extend tolerance and alleviate prejudice and ignorance. It is self-repression, she argues, that fuels intolerance. Her example is that of those who go 'mad from solitary confinement' and she (and her creator) attack the attempt to brush extreme and distressing experience beneath the crude carpet of failure in 'character':

> The world can understand well enough the process of perishing for want of food: perhaps few persons can enter into or follow out that of going mad from solitary confinement. They see the long-buried prisoner disinterred, a maniac or an idiot! – how his senses left him – how his nerves first inflamed, underwent nameless agony, and then sunk to palsy – is a subject too intricate for examination, too abstract for popular comprehension. Speak of it! you might almost as well stand up in an European market-place, and propound dark sayings in that language and mood wherein Nebuchadnezzar, the imperial hypochondriac, communed with the baffled Chaldeans. (V, 273–4)

This demand for openness, psychological liberalism and enlarged understanding is enacted in the novel's frank account of Lucy's breakdown which is described with a strikingly modern inwardness and immediacy. The description represents, among other things, a strong advance on Charlotte's own grotesque, pot-boiling confirmation of stereotypes of the insane found in the portrait of Bertha Mason in *Jane Eyre*.[20] In this, *Villette* was companionable with the endeavours of liberal psychiatrists in the 1850s who emphasised the importance of the sympathetic understanding of depression and psycho-somatic illness.[21]

And what of Emily? *Wuthering Heights* attracted odium on first publication of a kind more comprehensive and severe even than that handed out to *Jane Eyre*. Most readers were baffled – and angry. *Wuthering Heights* was offensive and incomprehensible to most, like the reviewer in the *Examiner* who could detect no purpose or moral in it, or that in the *Spectator* who found it 'coarse and disagreeable' (*CH*, 221, 217). Gratuitousness, moral offensiveness and artistic incompetence were reproaches amplified by the social and ideological needs of the late 1840s. *Wuthering Heights* not only relished moral monstrosity, claimed the *Examiner*, it failed to tell a positive tale in troubled times: 'Never was there a period in our history of Society when we English could so ill-afford to dispense with sunshine.' This want of good weather was shared by a reviewer in the *Atlas* who also regretted the novel's 'few glimpses' of symbolic sunshine (*CH*, 218–9, 231).

A good deal of the anxiety *Wuthering Heights* provoked was caused by Heathcliff. The *Examiner* was not alone in feeling outraged by the mixture of affection and loathing he inspires (*CH*, 221). Charlotte Brontë, too, felt there was a charge to answer. When she came to write her memorial of her sisters in 1850, and again in her 'Editor's Preface' to the novel in the same year, she was clearly hard put to justify Heathcliff's 'repulsiveness' and was forced onto the defensive. The creation of Heathcliff, she conceded, may not have been 'advisable'. She excused Emily's want of judgement by her immaturity as an artist, her deployment of the gothic (the novel's 'storm-heated and electrical atmosphere'), her inexperienced provincialism (she was a 'homebred country girl'), and her quasi-anthropological interest in 'rude', 'unlettered', 'remote and unreclaimed' cultures – all of which must merely have confirmed prejudices.[22] She also stressed Emily's personal piety, and pointed in the novel to Nelly Dean as 'a specimen of true benevolence and homely fidelity', the 'constancy and tenderness' of Edgar, and the 'grace and gaiety' of the younger Catherine.[23] The smooth alliteration of the last of these is a clue to the public task of this rhetoric. Charlotte accepts the terms of the current critical conversation about 'character', and tries to justify the novel on grounds of a ready-reckoned balance of exemplary types to offset the 'inadvisable' elements. It is unlikely that this sort of ethical accountancy much detained Charlotte herself when she created her own work, but it was her natural line of defence when battle was engaged over Emily's. It reveals very clearly the context in which fiction was created and assessed in the period.

In its sharpest form, the problem revolves, as it always has done, around the moral ambiguity, glamour and degradation that is Heathcliff. But it is striking – bearing in mind the offence caused to Victorian readers – that, if Heathcliff is a 'type' in a world of typological writing, he is a gothic version of the self-made man. Here is a dark stray, picked off the streets of Liverpool by a quirky act of benevolence; perhaps, commentators have speculated, he was black (Liverpool was a slave port); perhaps, like Patrick Brontë, he was Irish. But, the point is, he rises and rises. Degraded and abused as a child and adolescent, he becomes, by his own efforts, a man of property, interest, local influence, wealth, success, iron willpower, even cultivation. The spin-doctors of 'character' could have done much with such a tale. One way of reading *Wuthering Heights*, therefore, is as a novel which implies an oblique, but nonetheless savage, attack on the narrative of exemplary Smilesean man. If, in the creation of Bounderby in *Hard Times*, Dickens took this type and revealed an ignominious base of hypocrisy and bluster, *Wuthering Heights* exposes violence, moral corruption, deceit and rapacity – but also that notorious, appealing glamour. It is the genius of the story that the creation retains its ambiguous fascination. What the novel touches are equivocal areas of judgement and assessment where standard judgements crumble. In a sustained way, it emphasises a relativity of values corrosive of the certainties that, amongst other things, underpin Victorian visions of excellent 'character'. The real discomfort the novel creates, of course, is not so much that Heathcliff is atrocious, but that he is not, after all, entirely despicable.

The clearest evidence for the view that the novel is an exercise in relativism is the narrative structure, where the celebrated 'Chinese box' format of stories within stories emphasises relativity of perception. Pointedly, the novel tells and re-tells stories from different perspectives. A particular example is the episode of the drunken Hindley's attempt to murder Heathcliff told first by Isabella in chapter 17, and then by Heathcliff himself in chapter 29. The retelling reveals as much about the teller as the event. So too do the rival accounts of their courtship given by Isabella and Heathcliff: her infatuation with his Byronic version of the 'self-made' outsider is contrasted with his cynical manipulation of this. The novel very much sees story-telling, and the matter of public image, as self-interested acts: 'he minded little what tale was told', remarks Nelly of the boy Heathcliff when he gains advantage over Hindley in the use of a horse, 'since he had what he wanted' (*WH*, 38). In a similar way, the novel dramatises divisions of culture as well as personality. Charlotte, in apologising for *Wuthering Heights*, excused it by reference to the distance between Emily's naïveté and the sophistication required by metropolitan critics. But actually the novel dramatises exactly this problem in its juxtaposition of the worlds of Heights and Grange, and especially in its portrait of Lockwood, whose patronising assumptions about his supposed bumpkin neighbours lead him into self-revealing difficulties both comic and gothic. Emily knew more about the relativity of cultural values than Charlotte, tactically, allowed in her defence.

So *Wuthering Heights* chooses a radical instability of behaviour, judgement and point-of-view rather than the pieties of stable 'character'. The social mobility which doctrines of 'character' were supposed to enable and anchor in consensual values, is both depicted and resisted. 'What new phase of his character is this?', exclaims the elder Catherine, as Heathcliff's plots unroll on his re-appearance as a man of substance (*WH*, 112). Character appears in *Wuthering Heights* as simultaneously both mobile and intensely fixated; as a sequence of pretences and role-plays occuring above a substratum of permanent obsessions like the 'eternal rocks beneath – as a source of little visible delight, but necessary', as Catherine famously puts it (*WH*, 82). Both Heathcliff and Catherine, in their different ways, achieve goals of social advancement, but they do so with no secure benefit. Instead of the psychologically stable world of 'character', based on the authority of the will and the security of agreed values, *Wuthering Heights* depicts a world, psychologically, of compulsion, obsession, sadism, fanaticism, self-harm and addiction. The very sources of this behaviour are as obscure as they are powerful.

The novel has, at its core, a set of psychological and behavioural enigmas that were, for Victorian readers, simultaneously recognisable and inexplicable. The depiction of these gives *Wuthering Heights* its power and its opportunity, like much of the Brontë fiction, to inspect and resist the stereotypes of the age and thus unsettle values and readers. Relentlessly, it takes shibboleths of Victorian ideological custom and exposes them: the family is revealed as an unstable and in some respects vicious unit; categories of consistent behaviour and secure moral codes crumble; acts of moral benevolence are shown to have enormously disruptive consequences; violence overrides charity and tolerance; the apparently clear psychological opposites of pleasure and pain, love and hate, aggression and affection, are hopelessly tangled; boundary experiences between living and dying, health and illness, consciousness and unconsciousness, dream and waking, are perturbed; even biological species, in this strange, volatile world, seem uncertain: 'he gnashed at me, and groaned like a mad dog, and gathered [Catherine] to him with greedy jealousy', says Nelly of Heathcliff. 'I did not feel as if I was in the company of a creature of my own species; it appeared that he would not understand, though I spoke to him; so, I stood off, and held my tongue, in great perplexity' (*WH*, 160–1).

All cultures have their areas of 'great perplexity', and literature, if it is to be worth much, explores them. What is significant about the work of the Brontë sisters is its appetite to conduct this exploration in the face of the contrary conditions in mid-Victorian Britain. In particular, in the context of narratives of psychological and behavioural orthodoxy, their novels opened questions of penetrating social significance and, in so doing, they pushed forward the developing range of nineteenth-century fiction. They maintain their challenge today.

NOTES

1. Stefan Collini, *Public Moralists: Political Thought and Intellectual Life in Britain 1850–1930* (Oxford University Press, 1991).
2. Samuel Smiles, *Self-Help; with Illustrations of Conduct and Perseverance*, 2nd edn (London: John Murray, 1866), 383.

3. Rick Rylance, *Victorian Psychology and British Culture 1850–1880* (Oxford University Press, 2000), esp. 131–4, 158–9, 170.
4. Collini, *Public Moralists*, 97, 103.
5. George Eliot, *The Mill on the Floss* [1860], edited by A. S. Byatt (London: Penguin, 1979), 407.
6. Heather Glen, Introduction to Charlotte Brontë, *The Professor* (Harmondsworth: Penguin, 1989). See also, Sally Shuttleworth, *Charlotte Brontë and Victorian Psychology* (Cambridge University Press, 1996), ch. 7.
7. Robert Owen, *Essays on the Formation of the Human Character* (1813–14) in *A New View of Society and Other Writings*, edited by John Butt (London: Everyman, 1972).
8. Quoted in Juliet Barker, *The Brontës* (London: Weidenfeld & Nicolson, 1994), 11.
9. *Ibid.*, 83.
10. *Ibid.*, 52.
11. *Ibid.*, 2.
12. E. J. Hobsbawm, *Industry and Empire: The Pelican Economic History of Britain*, vol. III: *From 1750 to the Present Day* (Harmondsworth: Pelican, 1969).
13. Samuel Smiles, *Character* [1871] (London: John Murray, 1931), 59.
14. Elizabeth King, *Female Scripture Characters Exemplifying Female Virtues*, 11th edn (London: C. & J. Rivington, 1828).
15. Charles Dickens, *Dombey and Son*, [1846–8], edited by Peter Fairclough (Harmondsworth: Penguin, 1970), ch. 16.
16. George Eliot to John Blackwood, *The George Eliot Letters*, edited by Gordon S. Haight, 9 vols. (London: Yale University Press, 1954–6, 1978), 2, 299.
17. G. H. Lewes, 'The Novels of Jane Austen', *Blackwood's Magazine*, 86 (July 1859), 108, 102.
18. Richard Stang, *The Theory of the Novel in England 1850–1870* (London: Routledge & Kegan Paul, 1959), Part 2, Section III, ch. 4 'Plot and Character'.
19. Lewes, 'Jane Austen', 108.
20. Shuttleworth, *Charlotte Brontë and Victorian Psychology*, ch. 8.
21. Such a one was Sir Henry Holland, the celebrated cousin of Charlotte's friend and biographer Elizabeth Gaskell, whose *Chapters in Mental Physiology* was published in 1852, the year before *Villette*. One tactic Sir Henry employed was the confession of his own disposition to these things. See Rylance, *Victorian Psychology*, ch. 4.
22. Charlotte Brontë, 'Biographical Notice of Ellis and Acton Bell' and 'Editor's Preface to the New Edition of *Wuthering Heights*' (both 1850), in WH, 361–71.
23. *Ibid.*, 369.

8

KATE FLINT

Women writers, women's issues

In chapter 9 of *Shirley*, Charlotte Brontë gives us a brief, vivid description of the Yorke family's domestic life. Among the six children, the twelve-year-old Rose stands out for her strength of character. Although her strong-minded, dour mother would like to turn Rose into a copy of herself, 'a woman of dark and dreary duties', the girl is of a very different, independent mould. She has 'a mind full-set, thick-sown with the germs of ideas her mother never knew' and it 'is agony to her often to have these ideas trampled on and repressed' (*S*, 148). Later, Rose shares her impressions of Ann Radcliffe's *The Italian* with Caroline Helstone: the gothic romance, she says, feeds her longings to travel, and she expansively gestures to the breadth of her hunger for experience:

> 'The whole world is not very large compared with creation: I must see the outside of our own round planet at least.'
> 'How much of its outside?'
> 'First this hemisphere where we live; then the other. I am resolved that my life shall be a life: not a black trance like the toad's buried in marble; nor a long, slow death like yours in Briarfield Rectory.' (*S*, 399)

A few paragraphs later, she voices her principles again: 'Better to try all things and find them all empty, than to try nothing and leave your life a blank (*S*, 400). The latter course is a suicidal one in the author's mind: as she wrote to W. S. Williams in 1851: 'depend upon it, it is better to be worn out with work in a thronged community, than to perish of inaction in a stagnant solitude' (*CBL* 11, 668).

Yet Charlotte Brontë does not leave Rose's spirited optimism unqualified. Not only does she have the considerably more cautious and conservative Caroline express her fears that 'a wanderer's life, for me at least, would end like that tale you are reading, – in disappointment, vanity, and vexation of spirit' (*S*, 400) – an interpretation of *The Italian*, it must be said, which tacitly serves to demonstrate Brontë's recognition of the degree of subjectivity which people project onto their reading material – but she has already pointed

170

forwards to Rose's future. In one of those sudden, bold shifts of temporal perspective which characterises *Shirley*, we have already seen Rose twenty years hence, pensive in wild, luxuriant countryside, 'a lonely emigrant in some region of the southern hemisphere. Will she ever come back?' (*S*, 150).

The figure of Rose encapsulates a theme which runs through the fiction of all three Brontës: the problems faced by an independent-minded woman, determined on expanding the emotional, intellectual, and on occasion the geographical boundaries of her immediate sphere, and yet forced to consider how far she is prepared to accommodate to societal norms. Sometimes this accommodation is directly addressed, indeed opposed, by the woman in question, as when Shirley replies to what she sees as her despotic uncle's insistent matchmaking, employing terms which link women's struggles to far broader possibilities for resistance against the powerful: 'Were Britain a serfdom, and you the Czar, you could not *compel* me to this step' (*S*, 473). Elsewhere, as we shall see, the dialogue between independence and forms of compromise is set up by the plots of the novels themselves. This topic is, moreover, an issue which directly relates to the very profession of the woman writer in the mid nineteenth century: a profession, or perhaps it would be fairer to say an activity, which was not necessarily condemned in itself, but which was commonly expected to be conducted with attention to women's primary social functions, and was often assessed in relation to strongly gendered norms.

When Charlotte Brontë sent copies of some of her poems to the Poet Laureate, Robert Southey, late in 1836, and asked his opinion of her work, she famously received his advice against indulging in daydreaming, and his dictum that 'Literature cannot be the business of a woman's life: & it ought not to be. The more she is engaged in her proper duties, the less leisure will she have for it, even as an accomplishment & a recreation.' His advice is not entirely negative, however, since he recommends that she writes poetry for its own sake, and not with a view to celebrity, and advocates it as a means of disciplining and strengthening 'your best thoughts & your wisest feelings' (*CBL* 1, 166–7). In her grateful and measured reply, Brontë repudiates any suggestion of frivolity, explaining her social situation, her dedication to duty, and, indeed, her obedient womanliness: 'I have endeavoured not only attentively to observe all the duties a woman ought to fulfil, but to feel deeply interested in them. I don't always succeed, for sometimes when I'm teaching or sewing I would rather be reading or writing; but I try to deny myself; and my Father's approbation amply rewarded me for the privation' (*CBL* 1, 169). The desire for dutiful propriety co-exists uneasily with the imaginative impulse: that 'creative gift of which [the writer] is not always master – something that at times strangely wills and works for itself', as Charlotte Brontë put it, attempting to explain and excuse her sister's creation of Heathcliff, in her Preface to *Wuthering Heights* (WH, 370).

Southey's caution against seeking celebrity through writing is a pointer to the publishing options that had been increasingly opening up to women. Although he was addressing himself to Charlotte's poetry, the expansion of women's writing was particularly noticeable in the field of fiction, whether appearing in volume form, in cheap part publication, or in the growing number of periodicals. Writing, as the feminist literary historian Dorothy Mermin explains, was one of the few means by which a middle-class woman could 'earn a living or enjoy the satisfactions of work outside her home or the unpaid, unprofessional rounds of church and charity'; it 'required no training or special skills', nor 'money or materials beyond the books and paper that would be available in most middle-class homes'.[1] 'Never was there greater scope for the literary talents of women than in England in the present day', wrote Mary Stodart in *Female Writers* (1842).[2] But she and others among the Brontës' contemporaries were also quick to point out that the very numbers of women who were joining the ranks of the published, and the inadvisable alacrity with which some of them rushed into print, resulted in extremely variable quality. This, inevitably, ensured a backlash against the presumed shallowness of women's minds, their thoughtless verbiage, the superficial reading pleasures which their texts offered, and their perceived unseemly desire for fame. Writing her obituary notice of Charlotte Brontë, Harriet Martineau noted approvingly that although she 'had every inducement that could have availed with one less high-minded to publish two or three novels a year', and that 'she might have enriched herself by very slight exertion', her 'steady conviction was that the publication of a book is a solemn act of conscience'.[3]

This yoking of seriousness with moral responsibility characterised those who set out to defend women as writers, whether the cautious and sanctimonious Stodart, or Marion Evans – soon to adopt the name 'George Eliot' – in her 1856 piece on 'Silly Novels by Lady Novelists'. It must be plain, writes Eliot, 'to every one who looks impartially and extensively into feminine literature, that its greatest deficiencies are due hardly more to the want of intellectual power than to the want of those moral qualities that contribute to literary excellence – patient diligence, a sense of the responsibility involved in publication, and an appreciation of the sacredness of the writer's art'.[4] Mary Stodart and George Eliot's remarks frame the adult writing careers of the Brontë sisters. As well as emphasising the desirability of taking one's writing seriously, especially if aimed at publication, they provide a context for the critical reception of women's writing, indicating some of the criteria to which, ideally, women were expected to conform. Stodart describes what she takes to be the characteristics of women's minds, indicating that for her, woman's 'keen and exquisite tact' (*Female Writers*, 19), 'facility in the association of ideas' (20), 'quickness of sympathy' and 'elegance of taste' (21) are facts of nature. But womanly susceptibility to impressions is also a liability, and to stop her fluttering like a butterfly on the flowers of Parnassus, her reasoning capacities need to be developed by education. Stodart protests, as many other women were to do, against their being taught too many frivolous things, which means the mind is lying 'unemployed and inert'(33), and against the lack of system in women's education. Less positively, however, she indicates that there should be limits to women's literary efforts: limits which bear a direct relation to the presumed desirability of the separation of the spheres. Home – as ordained by the scriptures – 'is and ever must be the true sphere for women' (9); 'Man is fitted for the rough struggles of public life; woman for the calm and dignified repose, the gentle duties of private life' (15). With this in mind, Stodart would have her readers believe that 'there must always be chasms in a literature where women are sedulously excluded from the expression of thought and sentiment' (9). This ambiguous 'where' – which can be read as 'when', signifying a critique of cultural norms, or as 'in which', suggesting a desirable segregation of women from certain subject matter and modes of writing – was to consolidate, in the comments of certain influential critics in the coming decades, into a voiced certainty that women not only should not, but cannot write about certain things. The topographical motif of Stodart's phrase was to be more fully mapped in the language employed by W. R. Greg in his 1859 article, 'False Morality of Lady Novelists', when, after claiming with relief that 'many of the saddest and deepest truths in the strange science of sexual affection' are to women 'mysteriously and mercifully veiled', he goes on to state that if woman treats of this science, she labours at a disadvantage. 'She is describing a country of which she knows only the more frequented and the safer roads...the rockier and loftier mountains, and the more rugged tracts, the more sombre valleys, and the darker and more dangerous chasms, are never trodden by her feet, and scarcely ever dreamed of by her fancy.'[5] The suggestive physicality with which the landscape of the mind is here delineated connects, if only by analogy, with the biological assumptions about what was, at the time, considered to constitute the 'natural': the assumptions which led G. H. Lewes to comment, notoriously, when reviewing *Shirley*, that 'The grand function of woman, it must always be recollected, is, and ever must be, Maternity' (*CH*, 161). In this climate, it is unsurprising that Charlotte Brontë felt obliged to defend the 'rude and strange' qualities of *Wuthering Heights* by explaining her sister's work as a product of social isolation and, indeed, rugged environment. Elizabeth Gaskell, in her *Life of Charlotte Brontë*, played up, in her turn, her subject's social and moral orthodoxy, her devotion to the 'sacred pious charge' of looking after her father, her literary, and by extension her personal purity, protesting how 'utterly unconscious she was of what was, by some, esteemed coarse in her writings', and her 'womanly seeking after protection on every occasion, when there was no moral duty involved in asserting her independence'.[6]

George Eliot's comments about the want of moral qualities exhibited by contemporary fiction follow directly from her scathing observations about the type of critical attention meted out to women writers. She claims that journalistic approval is in an inverted relationship to the literary merits of novels, at boiling pitch 'when a woman's talent is at zero...and if ever she reaches excellence, critical enthusiasm drops to the freezing point. Harriet Martineau, Currer Bell, and Mrs Gaskell have been treated as cavalierly as if they had been men.'[7] To be judged by masculine criteria was, of course, Eliot's intention with regards her own fiction, and a similar desire lay behind the Brontë sisters' choice of nomenclature. Charlotte Brontë explained, in the Biographical Notice of Ellis and Acton Bell which prefaced the 1850 edition of *Wuthering Heights* and *Agnes Grey*, how the sisters had cherished, from a very young age, the dream of becoming authors: a dream which crystallised into a resolve:

> We agreed to arrange a small selection of our poems, and, if possible, get them printed. Averse to personal publicity, we veiled our own names under those of Currer, Ellis, and Acton Bell; the ambiguous choice being dictated by a sort of conscientious scruple at assuming Christian names positively masculine, while we did not like to declare ourselves women, because – without at that time suspecting that our mode of writing and thinking was not what is called 'feminine' – we had a vague impression that authoresses are liable to be looked on with prejudice; we had noticed how critics sometimes use for their chastisement the weapon of personality, and for their reward, a flattery, which is not true praise. (WH, 362)

Mary Stodart reminded her readers of Letitia Landon (the poet L. E. L.)'s gloomy remark that 'a literary life is not a happy one for a woman' (*Female Writers*, 95), and some of the reviews which the Brontës' work received completely confirm this judgement. Criticism was unarguably gendered. If the sex of the authors was not immediately apparent, this only seemed to give added propulsion to critics' desires to lift the pseudonymous veil. Lewes, equivocating somewhat over the issue of authorial gender, but suspecting a female hand, complained against *Jane Eyre* that 'a more masculine book, in the sense of vigour, was never written. Indeed that vigour often amounts to coarseness, – and is certainly the very antipode to "lady like." This same over-masculine vigour is even more prominent in *Shirley*, and does not increase the pleasantness of the book' (*CH*, 163). On the other hand, the reviewer in the *Morning Chronicle* was glad to see the style of this second novel, since it enabled him to settle the authorial question: whilst many 'sagacious critics' had declared that *Jane Eyre* could only be the product of a female author, it now appears that they were mistaken. This new novel, 'totally free from cant, whining, affectation, or conventional tinsel of any kind', is characterised by the 'independence and uprightness' of its thought, its 'purity of heart and feeling', and is 'genuine English in the masculine vigour or rough originality of its conception of character'.[8] But even before they were unequivocally unmasked as being by women, the Bells' novels were attacked for their 'ill-chosen subjects, alike singular and coarse. This defect is visible enough in the poems', too, according to the *Spectator*'s reviewer (*CH*, 65). Anxiety focuses on consumer as well as producer. 'The fault of the book is coarseness', complained *Fraser's Magazine* of *The Tenant of Wildfell Hall* – not so much coarseness of subject matter, though this, it believes, will 'be the stumbling-block of most readers, and which makes it utterly unfit to be put into the hands of girls' – but coarseness of language. The writer of this review refers throughout to the novel's author as 'she', and explains this choice in a footnote: 'a woman's pen seems to us indisputably discernible in every page. The very coarseness and vulgarity is just such as a woman, trying to write as a man, would invent.'[9] Somehow, Acton Bell had managed to damn herself twice over.

The intensity of expression which is given to anger and desire, the vivid metaphors of violence and repression, and the frequent directness of expression in the narrative voices of the Brontës were considered unwomanly by some. Moreover, this intensity could be thought to equate with personal revelation on the part of the author: witness Matthew Arnold's famously pettish question, in a private letter: 'Why is *Villette* disagreeable? Because the writer's mind contains nothing but hunger, rebellion, and rage, and therefore that is all she can, in fact, put into her book' (*CH*, 201). What he detected was precisely the kind of unseemly display against which Stodart had warned in a vivid image:

> . . . in this laying bare of the workings of the inward heart, there is a peculiar inconvenience for a delicate and sensitive woman. It is like proclaiming to the public that which passes within her own breast. It is more – it is placing a glass window in her bosom, that every passer-by may look in and see the workings of her heart. (*Female Writers*, 134–5)

Yet impassioned tones were not automatically condemned. When G. H. Lewes commented that in *Villette* 'we read the actual thoughts and feelings of a strong, struggling soul; we hear the cry of pain from one who has loved passionately, and who has sorrowed sorely' (*CH*, 211), he was praising precisely the emotional directness which, both in the Victorian period and for later readers, has most notably accounted for the popularity of the Brontë's works.

Not all readers, however, have responded positively to the forthright way with which Charlotte and Anne Brontë, in particular, addressed women's issues. Virginia Woolf, in her essay 'Women and Fiction' (1929), argued that in *Jane Eyre* 'we are conscious not merely of the writer's character...but we are conscious of a woman's presence – of someone resenting the treatment of her sex and pleading for its rights' – a tactic which she condemns as being too self-assertive, too 'masculine', even.[10] Woolf had sympathy with the 'temptation to anger', but praises Emily Brontë for – unlike her sister – having a mind powerful enough to resist it. And yet in its way, *Wuthering Heights* may be seen as constituting something of a feminist protest: not in the direct way that Emily Brontë's sisters' novels were – as we shall see – to raise issues of opportunity, expectation and education, but in its subversion of the conventions of romantic fiction, a genre invariably associated with women's composition and consumption.

Wuthering Heights is, ultimately, a novel about desire, not fulfilment. Its structure suggests Emily Brontë's own impetus to transcend the socialised boundaries of the woman's novel at this period, with its habitual, if not inevitable stress on engagement or marriage being the most desirable of conclusions. In terms of its plot, *Wuthering Heights* does indeed end, more or less, with a betrothal: that of the second Cathy to Hareton. But this is not where the emphasis falls at the end of the narrative. In the final paragraph Lockwood wonders 'how any one could ever imagine unquiet slumbers for the sleepers in that quiet earth' (*WH*, 338). Whilst Catherine and Heathcliff's passion for each other was thwarted during the course of the novel by social factors, and by the self-righteous, moralising manoeuverings of Nelly Dean, here it is finally laid to rest by the voice of one who cannot bear human emotions to escape their orthodox boundaries. The impossibility of attempting to live rigorously by such social orthodoxy has been exposed much earlier in the novel, with Lockwood's reaction to the dream-apparition of Catherine: the sadistic machinations of his unconscious suggest the fear and anger he feels in relation to women and sexuality.

Moreover, Lockwood's certitude is undermined by the alternative version offered in Nelly's closing account of the stories of 'the country folks' (*WH*, 336). In these, Catherine and Heathcliff continue to roam the moors as unquiet presences, their ghostliness standing for what they leave unresolved and unfulfilled in the reader's mind: an expression of romantic desire. This desire is characterised by a belief in the possibility of achieving fulfilment in some kind of spiritual unity with another person, and, in its turn, is predicated on a belief that one possesses a 'real', unsocialised self which can find Another who will complete and complement it. A self without a body, one might say, since to possess a body in Victorian life or literature, as at other times, is inevitably to manifest sexuality, and hence to be subject to social definitions, strictures, expectations. The live body is curiously unimportant in Catherine and Heathcliff's relationship. Even when Catherine clasps his neck, and he covers her with 'frantic caresses', and 'strain[s]' her 'closer', their 'faces washed by each other's tears' in their final encounter (WH, 161–2), these intense physical details serve to underline and demonstrate the extraordinary *emotional* pull between them.

The plot, in all its interlayered complexity, works to show us the impossibility of achieving one's desire for a spiritually complementary Other within the terms of social norms and conventions. The successful romance of the novel is deliberately low-key. Hareton and the younger Catherine's relationship is a triumph of civilised norms, of domesticity. Even so, it quietly challenges conventional power relations. It is Cathy who teaches Hareton to read, thus giving him the key to unlock literature: the very thing which, the novel demonstrates by its own existence, has the potential to unsettle norms, to pose questions rather than provide answers. Nonetheless, after the passion of Heathcliff and Catherine, this is but a whimsical romance. Its lasting image is that of Cathy sidling over to Hareton and putting a primrose, with calculated uselessness, into his bowl of porridge.

This relationship acts as a tame foil to that of Catherine and Heathcliff: it also serves, at the last, to point up Lockwood's embarrassed helplessness in the face of any kind of romance, as he feels 'irresistibly impelled' to escape the couple. This is an act of evasion which, in its turn, gives him the opportunity to sever the bond which seemed to have grown up between him and Nelly through her recounting of the story. To the last believing that monetary exchange can be a substitute for empathy and feeling, Lockwood leaves, 'pressing a remembrance into the hand of Mrs. Dean, and disregarding her expostulations at my rudeness' (WH, 337). The lack of empathic involvement on the part of both the novel's main narrators means that they are a foil, through which we learn *of* passion, and also a device by means of which readers are placed in a privileged position, as the ones with the capacity to recognise the presence and power of desire. This position is in itself ungendered: with no secure viewpoint from which to ground our responses, there is no obligation to accept or resist the expectations governing contemporary women's or men's habits of fictional consumption.

By contrast, the fiction of Emily Brontë's sisters draws explicit attention to the position of women within the society of their day. Anne Brontë's *Agnes Grey*, whilst not ultimately relinquishing the romance form, dramatises the exploitation of the governess/companion, a role which, as M. Jeanne Peterson, Mary Poovey and others have ably shown, occupied an uneasy, potentially destabilising position in mid-nineteenth-century society. As Poovey puts it,

> Because the governess was like the middle-class mother in the work she performed, but like both a working-class woman and man in the wages she received, the very figure who theoretically should have defended the naturalness of separate spheres threatened to collapse the difference between them.[11]

Agnes is rapidly disabused of her idealised expectations – 'how charming to be intrusted with the care and education of children!'(*AG*, 9) – when she finds that the reality is an unruly schoolroom, her charges precociously aware of their class superiority, and, in the case of the bullying, sadistic Tom, already practising an ugly form of masculinity. The impossibility of her position is made clear: responsible for the Bloomfield children, and expected to educate them, she is at the same time forbidden to discipline them. Her experience with the Murray family, if far less overtly painful, further reinforces class privilege; her valuation of love is pitted against the priorities of Rosalie, the elder girl, marrying for money and status. What emerges is the apparent necessity of forbearance, and the concealment and suppression of powerful feeling. Such behaviour meets its reward in the shape of marriage to the clergyman, Mr Weston. Small wonder that contemporary reviewers should find the novel 'more acceptable... though less powerful' than *Wuthering Heights*,[12] but the apparent conservatism of both story and moral stance does not quite muffle the protest it makes against the corrosive effects of social values based on acquisition and display on the institution of the family.

The Tenant of Wildfell Hall (1848) is, however, a more difficult novel to assess. It resists assimilation as either a conservative or a radical text in feminist terms, and, as with *Wuthering Heights*, the reason lies both with its subject matter and with its structure. Again, Charlotte felt uneasy about the content: 'The choice of subject was an entire mistake...' (*WH*, 364). The novel centres on a young woman who marries a philandering drunkard, removes herself and her little boy from his depraved circle of cronies and earns a living as an artist, returning to nurse him on his deathbed. Helen does not enter into her marriage completely blindly. Her aunt warns her to be watchful against male unprincipledness in general; advises her to accept the 'sensible, sober, respectable' Mr Boarham, despite the age gap between them (*TWH*, 131). But this is no rehashing of the plot of *Sense and*

Sensibility, with circumstances ensuring that Helen sees the error of her ways and escapes a fatal error of judgement. Huntingdon lacks Willoughby's more redeeming features, and this heroine believes too naively in woman's power of redemption, covering up unmistakable sexual attraction towards him with the fervour of religious zeal: 'There *is* essential goodness in him; – and what delight to unfold it! If he has wandered, what bliss to recall him!' (*TWH*, 143). This is not to say that the novel mocks religious sincerity: far from it, since one lesson Helen learns, which she preaches to her dying husband, is that redemption cannot come through human intervention, but is a matter of an individual's relationship with God through Christ's intercession. Even the uncertainty in her mind about whether penitence and pardon attend Arthur's soul's passage to the grave is a reminder of the power that an individual has over their own fate, whether spiritual or secular.

Yet an individual also has social responsibilities, to be based not on innocent idealism, or 'delusive vanity' (*TWH*, 270), but on education and environment. Early influence is presented as all-important. The novel is an indictment of the way in which coarse masculinity seeks to replicate itself – the four-year-old Arthur goes down every evening to entertain his father's friends, 'and learnt to tipple wine like papa, to swear like Mr Hattersley, and to have his own way like a man' (*TWH*, 335) – and yet fosters a system of education which would seek to shield young women from the realities of the world. Early in *The Tenant*, Helen forcefully articulates the educational philosophy which lies at the heart of the novel – and which simultaneously acts as a justification for writing about unconventional topics in a format likely to be read by women:

> You would have us encourage our sons to prove all things by their own experience, while our daughters must not even profit by the experience of others. Now *I* would have both so to benefit by the experience of others, and the precepts of a higher authority, that they should know beforehand to refuse the evil and choose the good, and require no experimental proofs to teach them the evil of transgression. I would not send a poor girl into the world, unarmed against her foes, and ignorant of the snares that beset her path: nor would I watch and guard her, till, deprived of self-respect and self-reliance, she lost the power, or the will to watch and guard herself; – and as for my son – if I thought he would grow up to be what you call a man of the world – one that has '*seen life*', and glories in his experience, even though he should so far profit by it, as to sober down, at length, into a useful and respected member of society – I would rather that he died to-morrow! (*TWH*, 31)

One of this novel's un-worked-through ironies, however, is that it is precisely Helen's experience that gives her the self-respect and self-reliance to make this vehement utterance. A further, and more troubling irony still is produced by the novel's organisation. In many ways, Helen's story is that of a woman who performs courageous acts of self-determination. But she does not tell her story directly: this speech is narrated by the man who is to become her second, and far more sympathetic husband, as part of a long letter to his friend and brother-in-law Halford. Moreover, that husband also sends Halford the journal in which Helen's own words are, privately, recorded. We are encouraged to read the scene where Huntingdon seizes the same journal as an appalling violation, and yet here, Helen's private thoughts are freely shared with another. Whilst this may indicate a complete bond of trust between wife and husband which extends lovingly outwards towards other family members, it also uncomfortably points to the way in which men continue to frame woman's existence.

The tension between female autonomy and masculine dominance – however benevolent its intentions – lies at the centre of Charlotte Brontë's writing, too. It is explored, above all, in relation to the topics of heterosexual romance and women's self-expression. In many ways, her first published novel, *Jane Eyre* (1847), employs a fairly orthodox romantic structure of attraction, impediment, and final marital resolution. In this, *Jane Eyre* laid itself open to accusations that for women readers, its plot had the power to raise false expectations and stir up dissatisfaction with their life in the real world. It fell readily into the genre against which Caroline is warned in *Shirley* by Mrs Pryor:

> 'My dear, romances are pernicious. You do not read them, I hope?'
> 'Sometimes – whenever I can get them, indeed; but romance-writers might know nothing of love, judging by the way in which they treat of it.'
> 'Nothing whatever, my dear!' assented Mrs Pryor, eagerly; 'nor of marriage; and the false pictures they give of those subjects cannot be too strongly condemned'. (*S*, 379)

Since women were popularly presumed to identify all too readily with what they read, the specifics of *Jane Eyre*'s plot contained particular dangers. An 1856 article in *Household Words* argued that Jane's governess experience, up to her flight from Thornfield was completely realistic. The writer claimed to have known parallel cases in which governesses, similarly tempted, had also fought painful battles against the blandishments of their employers – but without Jane's romantically successful outcome. Seduction by master or eldest son was statistically a far more likely fate than marrying one's employer. But even if the novel's conclusion that 'No woman was ever nearer to her mate than I am: ever more absolutely bone of his bone, and flesh of his flesh' (*JE*, 450) seems to be a domestic and physical realisation of

Catherine's tormented but unfulfillable wail, 'Nelly, I *am* Heathcliff' (*WH*, 82), Charlotte Brontë's romance is a vehicle for more complex themes than fantasies of wish-fulfilment. It provokes a number of questions about women's roles. Jane bitterly attacks people who would attempt to confine women to bland domesticity, 'to making puddings and knitting stockings, to playing on the piano and embroidering bags' (*JE*, 109), and the passage in which this challenge to stereotyping occurs explicitly links women's barely repressed desire for action – and hence for the power of self-determination – with other, wider political struggles. 'Millions', Jane claims, 'are in silent revolt against their lot': a comment which helped fuel some of the antagonism with which the novel was greeted. 'Moral Jacobinism', or extreme radicalism, was detected by the *Christian Remembrancer* in its pages (*CH*, 90); Lady Eastlake famously connected the author's mental impulses with those which embraced Chartism and continental revolutionary activity (*CH*, 110). The language of slavery permeates the novel, connecting female British powerlessness with other forms of exploitation and cruelty: Jane calls her cousin a slave-driver made in the model of Roman emperors; is humiliated by Rochester buying her presents as though she were a member of a sultan's harem; records his banter about wanting to attach her to a chain. Despite the complexity of these allusions in relation to the presentation of Bertha, and, indeed, to the Madeira (and hence undoubtedly slave-trade-tainted) source of Jane's eventual fortune, they extend the context in which Brontë locates issues of agency and individuality.

These two terms may usefully be employed, indeed, to interrogate Jane's final pairing with Rochester, and to note that the novel goes well beyond the romance convention which suggests that a heroine's identity is only confirmed, paradoxically, through being joined with another. Throughout the novel, Jane has been characterised by activity, rather than by a tendency to become passively absorbed in the life of others. 'Reader, I married him' (*JE*, 448) is, after all, an active construction. And the last few paragraphs of the book do not, in fact, describe Jane's wedded bliss, but move outwards, emphasising, despite the relatively secluded life which Jane and Rochester lead, that marriage here, as in a Jane Austen novel, is not unrelated to the desirability of broader social harmony. 'My Edward and I, then, are happy: and the more so, because those we love most are happy likewise' (*JE*, 451), Jane comments, before concluding with three paragraphs concerning St John Rivers' missionary career in India. This emphasis on St John at the novel's close allows us to surmise that not every aspect of Jane's life has been absorbed into marriage: that there is a surplus. It demonstrates that a strong interest remains in the spiritual, and in the fate of one whose life has touched on her's, not her husband's. Moreover, this emphasis is of her own making.

For Jane's marriage, rather than constricting her, may, given the first-person narrative form of the novel, be read as releasing her – releasing her into writing.

Throughout, *Jane Eyre* explores the relationship between texts (both verbal and visual), interpretation, and autonomy. It suggests that the imaginative sphere is one which allows scope both for re-writing, and re-possessing, existent formulations, and for independent endeavour. Early in the novel, we see Jane as reader: perched in the window seat, half inside, half outside, typifying her liminal position throughout much of the novel in relation to society. She is, nonetheless, 'happy' in perusing Thomas Bewick's *History of British Birds*, concentrating on gloomy vignettes of desolate scenes which offer a clear indication of how she defines her own isolated position within a hostile environment (*JE*, 9). Her actions and attitudes in childhood indicate her desire to arrive at judgements on her own terms: she refuses to accept Mrs Reed and Mr Brocklehurst's would-be definitive interpretations of scripture and the moral law. Reading can be escapist, too – whether it takes the form of Richardson's *Pamela*, in which a servant girl marries her master (uncertainty as to whether or not this plot formula is invoked ironically or proleptically is a further means of prompting the reader's curiosity), or involves the adventures of the solitary wanderer, Gulliver, or the safe displacement of sexual passion into the pages of Schiller's *The Robbers*. But Jane's imagination is most powerfully demonstrated not through her interaction with other cultural works, but in the extraordinary paintings she displays to Rochester:

> The third showed the pinnacle of an iceberg piercing a polar winter sky: a muster of northern lights reared their dim lances, close serried, along the horizon. Throwing these into distance, rose, in the foreground, a head, – a colossal head . . . two thin hands, joined under the forehead, and supporting it, drew up before the lower features a sable veil; a brow quite bloodless, white as bone, and an eye hollow and fixed, blank of meaning but for the glassiness of despair.
>
> (*JE*, 125–6)

Rochester's enquiry, whether Jane was happy when painting these, is woefully inadequate as a response to this resurfacing of childhood isolation: a textual gesture which asserts, relatively early in her relationship with him, the powerful autonomy of her imagination – something reinforced by the accounts that she gives of her dreams which, whilst highly suggestive of her internalised tensions concerning maternity and responsibility and selfhood, resist clear-cut interpretation. This assumption of the power to shape and emphasise is threaded throughout the text. At the beginning of chapter 10, for example, Jane writes that 'I am only bound to invoke memory where

I know her responses will possess some degree of interest; therefore I now pass a space of eight years almost in silence: a few lines only are necessary to keep up the links of connection' (*JE*, 83). Whilst the primary narrative drive comes from the twists in the romantic plot, such asides serve to remind us the story is being told for our benefit, and thus the crucial relationship is in fact that between narrator and reader, not Jane and Rochester. This is evidenced by her sharing her interest in St John Rivers with us at the close – to such an extent that the final message is one about the broad issue of fulfilling one's earthly purpose, rather than the narrower topic of the desirability of a happy marriage. Whether one sees the assumption of power in terms of Charlotte Brontë writing fiction, or of an imaginary woman telling and shaping her own story, the important point is that this role *was* one available to woman in Victorian England, whatever the cost.

When one examines Brontë's letters, one finds this ambivalence about the place which romantic fulfilment should occupy in a woman's life, re-duplicated. Corresponding in 1843 with Ellen Nussey, she stated firmly:

> Not that it is a crime to marry – or a crime to wish to be married – but it is an imbecility which I reject with contempt – for women [who] have neither fortune nor beauty – to make marriage the principal object of their wishes & hopes & the aim of all their actions – not to be able to convince themselves that they are unattractive – and that they had better be quiet and think of other things than wedlock. (*CBL* 1, 315)

Whatever the part played by marriage in her fictional resolutions, Brontë is quick, in her correspondence, to defend the spinster:

> there is no more respectable character on this earth than an unmarried woman who makes her own way through life quietly perseveringly – without support of husband or brother and who having attained the age of 45 or upwards – retains in her possession a well-regulated mind – a disposition to enjoy simple pleasures – fortitude to support inevitable pains, sympathy with the sufferings of others, & willingness to relieve want as far as her means extend. (*CBL* 1, 448)

The theme of 'old maids' runs through *Shirley*, even giving the title to one of its chapters. Caroline fears at one stage that the 'duties and affections of wife and mother' which she has assumed will be her 'ordinary destiny' may turn into a life of self-sacrifice, of 'hollowness, mockery, want, craving, in that existence which is given away to others, for want of something else of your own to bestow it on?' (*S*, 174). Spinsterhood is not, however, to be the fate of Caroline, nor of her friend Shirley Keeldar: in a neat pairing-off, Caroline is yoked to the mill-owner Robert Moore, Shirley to his brother Louis.

But such an outcome, whilst having the tidiness of romantic comedy, is placed against serious textual qualifications. Relatively early in the novel, Shirley comments that marrying would mean 'I could never be my own mistress more' (S, 217). When Caroline describes Shirley's attachment to Louis, she calls her a 'bondswoman', him a 'captor': 'Mistress she may be of all round her' – in terms of her ownership of land, at this point – 'but her own mistress she is not' (S, 605). On Shirley's acceptance of Louis, she calls him her keeper: she is, the narrator tells us, 'fettered to a fixed day: there she lay, conquered by love, and bound with a vow (S, 637): she is linguistically bound, too, into a circular form of existence, since 'Her captor only could cheer her; his society only could make amends for the lost privilege of liberty' (S, 637). The marriages and families we have earlier been offered in the book provide no tempting models: indeed, the Yorke household, as we have seen, gives disturbing portraits of young girls who rebel against the status quo, but who seem to face a future ending in exile, or death in a foreign country.

For the conclusion of the novel shows Shirley and Caroline swallowed up: swallowed first into the impersonal rhetoric in which matrimonial contracts are solemnised in formal phraseology: 'Louis Gérard Moore, Esq., late of Antwerp, to Shirley, daughter of the late Charles Cave Keeldar, Esq. of Fieldhead: Robert Gérard Moore, Esq., of Hollow's mill, to Caroline, niece of the Rev. Matthewson Helstone, M. A., Rector of Briarfield': the man defined in relation to place and property, the woman according to patriarchal relations. Then, even more ominously, they seem to have been engulfed by industrialism, their own places of escape and conversation destroyed: 'the other day' remarks the narrator, 'I passed up the Hollow, which tradition says was once green, and lone, and wild; and there I saw the manufacturer's day-dreams embodied in substantial stone and brick and ashes' (S, 645). This vision of the characters' future, the reader's present, moreover, is depressing not merely in what it implies about the condition of women. Famously, in *Shirley* Brontë parallels the powerlessness of workers under laissez-faire capitalism and the powerlessness of women under patriarchal relations. 'Old maids', remarks Caroline, 'like the houseless and unemployed poor, should not ask for a place and an occupation in the world: the demand disturbs the happy and the rich: it disturbs parents' (S, 391). Whilst at the moment of its articulation this is part of the composite bitterness against the label and function of the 'old maid', by analogy, it raises the married woman into nothing more than the position of a housed and employed worker. In a world where the work environment is characterised by cinder-black highways, mighty mills, and chimneys 'ambitious as the tower of Babel' (S, 645), the position of woman, on the last page of the novel, is left without a distinguishing voice rising above this babble of dissatisfied tongues.

In *Shirley*, the friendship between Caroline and Shirley herself – the closest friendship between women in all the Brontës' fiction – offers a tantalising suggestion that same-sex relationships may offer different, and perhaps more fulfilling forms of conversational intimacy than come with marriage. Sisterhood, in both a real and figurative sense, was of the utmost importance to Charlotte Brontë. 'As to married women', she wrote to W. S. Williams, 'I can well understand that they should be absorbed in their husbands and children – but single women often like each other much and derive great solace from their mutual regard' (*CBL* II, 323). Whilst she became friendly with several published writers – Julia Kavanagh, Harriet Martineau and, of course, Elizabeth Gaskell – her closest relationships were family ones. To quote her own Biographical Notice of Ellis and Acton Bell: 'Resident in a remote district where education had made little progress, and where, consequently, there was no inducement to seek social intercourse beyond our own domestic circle, we were wholly dependent on ourselves and each other, on books and study, for the enjoyments and occupations of life' (*WH*, 359). Not only did the sisters collaborate on the Glass Town tales of their childhood, but Charlotte acted as editor and assessor of Emily and Anne's work. Their deaths increased her loneliness at both a personal and a literary level: 'the two human beings who understood me and whom I understood', as she put it: 'loving each other as we did – well – it seemed as if – might we but have been spared to each other – we could have found complete happiness in our mutual society and affection' (*CBL* II, 192). Charlotte Brontë was a writer who dreaded going into society, who relished in seclusion and in what she termed the 'voice we hear in solitude' (*S*, 228) – and yet who felt, at other times, desperately lonely. These personal impulses are examined in her fiction as Brontë both explores a woman's need for self-sufficiency, and considers how isolation may play upon her.

The question of a woman's self-determination lies at the heart of *The Professor*, the first of Brontë's novels to be written, and one which approaches the issue somewhat obliquely, through employing a male narrator, Crimsworth. As with *The Tenant of Wildfell Hall*, a masculine voice becomes a device which shows the male anxieties surrounding control and convention which collide with women's desires to shape their own lives. Frances, the Belgian woman who is to become Crimsworth's wife, makes it clear to him that she wishes 'to retain [her] employment of teaching' after their marriage. 'You are laying plans to be independent of me', he observes, apprehensively. 'Yes, Monsieur; I must be no incumbrance to you – no burden in any way', she continues. 'Think of my marrying you to be kept by you, Monsieur! I could not do it; and how dull my days would be! You would be away teaching… and I should be lingering at home, unemployed and solitary; I should get depressed and sullen, and you would soon tire of me….' (P, 208). Crimsworth finally acknowledges the fact of Frances's need – like Jane Eyre's – for action: 'Duties she must have to fulfill, and important duties; work to do – and exciting, absorbing, profitable work; strong faculties stirred in her frame, and they demanded full nourishment' (P, 229), and thus, she comes to perform a joint role in the running of their school: they spend their days apart in professional efficiency, and re-unite, in the evenings, in domestic bliss. Yet Crimsworth can only cope with this pattern by constructing Frances as a split person: 'So different was she under different circumstances, I seemed to possess two wives' (P, 230). Firmness, activity, and enterprise characterise one of these wives; but when he describes how the 'flowers' of 'poetic feeling' and 'fervour' were still there, 'preserved pure and dewy under the umbrage of later growth and hardier nature', ready to 'yield an exquisite fragrance' (P, 230), it is clear that, despite his surface open-minded liberalism, Crimsworth retains a firm idea of what is 'natural' in gender terms.

Nowhere is this made more obvious than in the way in which he treats his son Victor, after he and Frances return to a kind of premature rural retirement in England. Whilst in Belgium, Frances retained an independent, professional identity, but, despite the fact that her lifetime's dream of fulfilling her maternal inheritance and living in England is now realised, quite how she responds to her husband's leisure as a land-owner is not clear. And if in her working life she had attempted to break down what were commonly recognised as dividing lines between male and female, Crimsworth supports no such dissolution of gender divisions in the next generation. He finds few signs of incipient masculinity in Victor: 'scant sparkles of the spirit which loves to flash over the wine cup, or which kindles the passions to a destroying fire' (surely ominous echoes of the deplorable Huntingdon's personality?), 'but I saw in the soil of his heart healthy and swelling germs of compassion, affection, fidelity' (P, 244). How useful will these admirable, but 'womanly' characteristics be to him, however? This is the question Crimsworth must ask himself, as he determines to send his son to Eton: he knows the first couple of years there will be painful to him, 'but emulation, thirst after knowledge – the glory of success' – the masculine values of early Victorian England – 'will stir and reward him in time' (P, 245). Frances may go on walks with this sensitive, interesting child: may reason with him, may reach his affections through her love; but, Crimsworth thinks, reason and love will be poor weapons with which to forge his way in the future. Notably, this future will, it is suggested, contain a number of possibilities and opportunities for the young Victor – son, as his name suggests, of the new monarch's reign: things would have been different for a young, non-royal Victoria.

Of all Charlotte Brontë's novels, the most subtle, yet most triumphant portrayal of a woman's growth into self-recognition and self-sufficiency is found in *Villette*. Lucy Snowe's active presence as a narrator is apparent from the first chapters. She works hard, first to absent herself from the active centre of the story, substituting the precociously self-contained, doll-like Paulina – and then, with suspicious over-emphasis, declaring her own lack of internal fire: 'I, Lucy Snowe, plead guiltless of that curse, an overheated and discursive imagination' (*V*, 12). Her characteristic role is for a long time that of passionless spectator: 'I, Lucy Snowe, was calm', she proudly announces (*V*, 22). This is a means of avoiding emotional participation, of retaining control over self and circumstances; and also, Lucy implicitly tells us, of evading her own 'womanly' capacities. Early on, she admires Polly's father, for 'Indisputably, Mr Home owned manly self-control, however he might secretly feel on some matters' (*V*, 14). Slowly, however, she reveals to us the combination of unconscious repression and conscious play-acting involved in this apparent calmness, whether explicitly, suggesting her reticent surface manner is no more than costume – 'I had a staid manner of my own which ere now had been as good to me as a cloak and hood of hodden grey' (*V*, 44) – or in passing reference to her exhilarated response to walking around the city of London, 'utterly alone' (*V*, 49).

But throughout the novel, Lucy shows herself to be less than perfect at ruling her own life with self-control: she struggles with her own consciousness of self-division. It takes an almost perverse effort to master her desires: the effort to control them is described as driving nails into her temples: 'they did not die: they were but transiently stunned, and at intervals would turn on the nail with a rebellious wrench; then did the temples bleed, and the brain thrill to its core' (*V*, 110). In command so long as she can look at others, Lucy is unprepared, dislocated when circumstances suddenly force her to look at herself. The dichotomy between her habits of external observation and inner assessment is clearly revealed by her sudden glimpse of a threesome at the theatre:

> A handsome middle-aged lady in dark velvet; a gentleman who might be her son – the best face, the finest figure, I thought, I had ever seen; a third person in a pink dress and black lace mantle.
>
> I noted them all – the third person as well as the other two – and for the fraction of a moment, believed them all strangers, thus receiving an impartial impression of their appearance. But the impression was hardly felt and not fixed, before the consciousness that I faced a great mirror, filling a compartment between two pillars, dispelled it: the party was our own party.   (*V*, 209–10)

Off her guard, Lucy perceives herself as a *presence* – and by actual and semantic juxtaposition, not an unattractive one at that. When she recognises herself, once more she takes refuge in hoping that she's a space, an absence, a compartment between two pillars.

Yet one must consider Lucy Snowe *not* as an absence, but, like Jane Eyre, as a shaper of her own fiction. Certainly she suffers insecurity throughout much of the novel, both at the hands of individuals and as a result of certain of her experiences. But she takes revenge for this suffering by making the reader, in turn, insecure. As we have seen, she directly challenges the reader with statements about her character which other remarks contradict. More than this, she conceals and misleads, whether suppressing her recognition of Dr John, or hiding her awareness of M. Paul's interest in her for a while, or manipulating fictional conventions and expectations: the ghostly nun turns out to be a living man. Above all, Lucy mocks the reader whose comfortable imagination tends to call up fair-weather images. 'I will permit the reader to picture me', she says of her early adolescence:

> for the next eight years, as a bark slumbering through halcyon weather, in a harbour still as glass – the steersman stretched on the little deck, his face up to heaven, his eyes closed: buried, if you will, in a long prayer. A great many women and girls are supposed to pass their lives something in that fashion; why not I with the rest?
>
> Picture me then idle, basking, plump, and happy, stretched on a cushioned deck, warmed with constant sunshine, rocked by breezes indolently soft. However, it cannot be concealed that, in that case, I must somehow have fallen over-board, or that there must have been a wreck at last. (V, 35)

'A wreck at last': the conclusion is anticipated through the imagery of storms and waves and sea passages that flows through the text.

Once again, the conventions of romance are disturbed by the ending of *Villette*. It is possible to read providentiality rather than catastrophe into M. Paul's assumed shipwreck: God's mysterious plan with regard to Lucy and her place on earth may well be for her to remain single. This consolation was offered to single women by a variety of contemporary commentators. Frances Power Cobbe, for example, wrote in 1863:

> it is an absurdity, peculiar to the treatment of women, to go on assuming that all of them *have* home duties, and tacitly treating those who have none as if they were wrongly placed on God's earth, and had nothing whatever to do in it. There must needs be a purpose for the lives of single women in the social order of Providence...[13]

And one can read a political vengeance into M. Paul's fate, too: his overseas trip is to the French Caribbean colony of Guadeloupe, where the slaves had been emancipated in 1848, to oversee an estate there. As Susan Meyer has put it, 'it may not be entirely a tragedy if M. Paul is indeed killed by a storm and does not return from dominating West Indian blacks to marry the Lucy he calls "sauvage"'.[14] Moreover, Lucy drops strong hints throughout the text that a romantic ending, even with such an unconventional hero as M. Paul, would hardly suit her personality. 'To "sit in sunshine calm and sweet" is said to be excellent for weak people; it gives them vital force' (*V*, 196), she says of her convalescence, but the distancing of 'is said to be' removes herself from the category of weakness, as though priding herself on strength which comes from more stormy, adverse conditions.

Lucy, in the final paragraphs of the novel, writes of the warm anticipation with which she prepared for M. Paul's return. The gifts she gathered for him link literature with careful nurturing. 'I have made him a little library, filled its shelves with the books he left in my care: I have cultivated out of love for him (I was naturally no florist) the plants he preferred, and some of them are yet in bloom' (*V*, 495). Yet in fact, like Jane Eyre, Lucy has also moved herself into a position where she can tell her own story, devotedly tend her own autobiographical seedling – as well, of course, as self-fulfillingly following her own career: her school, like her horticulture, 'flourishes' (*V*, 495). 'I thought I loved him when he went away'; she comments of M. Paul: 'I love him now in another degree; he is more my own' (*V*, 495). The physical presence of a husband is hardly necessary for her possession of the little foreigner: such ownership, such control, can be achieved through the act of writing. For Lucy, as for Jane, as, indeed, for Charlotte Brontë, writing is the ultimate expression of selfhood. But this novel is unlike Brontë's others, for as well as celebrating the act of woman's writing, it ends, one might say, with an implicit affirmation of the strength which may be found in isolation.

Or does it? For this reading is predicated on the belief that there is, indeed, a stable, independent self to be located and celebrated. But *Villette* may also be read as if it were structured through Lucy's unconscious desires as well as through deliberate strategy. Brontë has her, after all, writing out of her bereavement: the narrative, one may argue, is ultimately very much dependent on M. Paul's ghostly presence. The inundation of the text with reference to storms and shipwrecks, indicating an obsessive, repetitive concern with death by water, points to his continual presence in the workings of her imagination. In *Mourning and Melancholia*, Freud tells us that profound mourning involves not just a sense of pain, but a 'loss of interest in the outside world – in so far as it does not recall' the lost one, a 'loss of capacity to adopt any new object of love (which would mean replacing him) and the . . . turning away from any activity that is not connected with thoughts of him'.[15] Lucy's self-deprecation and desire for self-effacement may thus be seen as a reluctance to love – even fully accept – herself after M. Paul's death. Other theorists of mourning, however, allow a different reading. If Freud sees the melancholia which accompanies mourning as ultimately a narcissistic activity, in which what is being mourned is not another person, but a part of the self, for Melanie Klein mourning, especially as it is reflected within art, is an attempt to make whole again what has been destroyed: an act of reparation and recreation.[16]

Both these impulses may be found within *Villette*, as indeed in all the Brontës' writing. The pull on the one hand is towards absorption and accommodation. Ultimately, however, this is weaker than a drive – however circumstantially compromised this drive may be – towards active self-determination. This suggestion of some of the socially and psychologically imposed difficulties under which a self-defining woman might labour is intimately related to the pressures operating upon women writers in the 1840s. No writers prior to the Brontës had explored this theme so powerfully, and the startling nature of their intervention may be gauged by the remarks of the more conservative novelist, Margaret Oliphant, writing in 1867. She declared that:

> there can be no doubt that a singular change has passed upon our light literature.... The change perhaps began at the time when Jane Eyre made what advanced critics call her 'protest' against the conventionalities in which the world clothes itself... When the curate's daughter in 'Shirley' burst forth in passionate lamentation over her own position and absence of any man she could marry, it was a new sensation to the world in general... up to the present generation, most young women had been brought up in the belief that their own feelings on this subject should be religiously kept to themselves.[17]

Oliphant claimed, with distaste, that Charlotte Brontë's novels had made it possible for women writers to reveal 'the story of the feminine soul as it really exists under its conventional coverings...a very fleshly and unlovely record' (259). But it was precisely this laying open of the workings of the inward heart, which Stodart had warned against; the rejection of passivity and the recognition of woman's need of an active sphere, which distinguished the Brontës' works from those of their more cautious contemporaries, and which was to constitute their most powerful legacy.

NOTES

1. Dorothy Mermin, *Godiva's Ride. Women of Letters in England, 1830–1880* (Bloomington and Indianapolis: Indiana University Press, 1993), 45.
2. M. A. Stodart, *Female Writers: Thoughts on their Proper Sphere, and on their Power of Usefulness* (London: R. B. Seeley and W. Burnside, 1842), 10.

3. Martineau, Harriet, 'Death of Currer Bell', *Daily News*, 6 April 1855, CH, 301.
4. George Eliot, 'Silly Novels by Lady Novelists', in *Selected Essays, Poems and Other Writings*, edited by A. S. Byatt and Nicholas Warren (Harmondsworth: Penguin, 1990), 161.
5. W. R. Greg, 'The False Morality of Lady Novelists', *National Review*, 8 (1859), 144–67.
6. Elizabeth Gaskell, *The Life of Charlotte Brontë* [1857], edited by Alan Shelston (Harmondsworth: Penguin, 1975), 274, 495, 393.
7. Eliot, 'Silly Novels by Lady Novelists', 161.
8. *Morning Chronicle*, 25 December 1849, 7.
9. 'Recent Novels', *Fraser's Magazine* 39 (1849), 423, 426.
10. Virginia Woolf, *Women and Writing*, edited by Michèle Barrett (London: Women's Press, 1979), 47–8.
11. Mary Poovey, *Uneven Developments. The Ideological Work of Gender in Mid-Victorian England* (London: Virago, 1989), 127. See also M. Jeanne Petersen, 'The Victorian Governess: Status Incongruence in Family and Society', in Martha Vicinus ed., *Suffer and Be Still. Women in the Victorian Age* (London: Methuen, 1980), 3–19.
12. [H. F. Chorley], 'Review of *Wuthering Heights* and *Agnes Grey*', *Athenaeum*, 25 December 1847, 1325.
13. Frances Power Cobbe, 'Social Science Congresses, and Women's Part in Them' [1861], in *Essays on the Pursuits of Women* (London: Emily Faithfull, 1863), 25.
14. Susan Meyer, *Imperialism at Home: Race and Victorian Women's Fiction* (London and Ithaca: Cornell University Press, 1996), 61.
15. Sigmund Freud, 'Mourning and Melancholia', in Albert Dickson, ed., *The Penguin Freud Library* 11: *On Metapsychology* (Harmondsworth: Penguin, 1991), 252.
16. Melanie Klein, 'Mourning and its Relation to Manic-Depressive States', in *Love, Guilt and Reparation and Other Works* (London: Hogarth Press, 1985).
17. Margaret Oliphant, 'Novels', *Blackwood's Edinburgh Magazine* 102 (1867), 258–9.

9

JOHN MAYNARD

The Brontës and religion

Although the Brontës' lives are obviously inscribed within a world of Victorian religion from their births as daughters of a clergyman to the final death of survivor Charlotte in the loving arms of her curate husband, although their works are filled with striking and prominent religious characters and scenes turning on religious issues, critics of the twentieth century did not much view the Brontës within religious structures of understanding. Issues of psychology, sexuality, feminism, social power, even the apparently far-removed worlds of colonial and imperial England preoccupied us far more. Nor was this merely a matter of the good reasons, which I shall attempt to provide below, for not inscribing the Brontës into one or another simple religious construction, of their age or ours; and for not seeing their vision as ultimately focused, as say Christina Rossetti's was, on religion, especially not on religious ultimates. Even their world of death was not seen as the traditional one of death and the afterlife but, as with the Brontës' other contemporary Dickens, this world of the dead and dying.

On the whole, unless the religious issues were so central as to brook no avoidance – for instance in Tennyson's *In Memoriam*, the priest Hopkins' sonnets, Newman's *Apologia*, or the very different representations of Trollope's familiar world of Barsetshire clerical politics – we did not search with interest for religious themes. As the twentieth century turned away from those overstuffed Victorian memoirs of life and letters, they turned away from the obvious but rather unwelcome evidence of the age's obsession with religion. By contrast, nineteenth-century critics were obsessed with finding the religious meaning in works. No subject occupied the Victorians, certainly not identity politics, or sexuality, or the empire, or even politics, as much – in the privacy of their meditations and in the public outpouring of their endless works, sermons, tracts, confessions, spiritual autobiographies, interpretations and re-interpretations of every aspect of the Bible and the Church fathers – as religion.

To sort out the strands of these central preoccupations for any Victorian writer is almost a hopeless task. There is an enormous world, extending into an entire array of social practices, a myriad of different sects and distinctions, an overwhelming history of commentary and commentary on commentary. Religious texts were the central texts of the west and they begat the language of the west. One has only to see Brontë characters bandying replies from the Bible or Church tradition to see how much their language and ways of thought ride upon those of religious tradition.

The point here is not, as in some conservative works of the past century, to call attention to the Bible's importance in order to deplore the loss of a major area of former cultural literacy. Religion was central to our language and patterns of thought; it may still be but it is sharing the word-ways with an ever-more cosmopolitan culture that has released itself as a culture – whatever the faiths of individuals – from the control of its religious traditions. What I hope to suggest here are the many exciting ways in which the Brontës participate in the conversion and redeployment of personal and societal verbal energies originally entrapped in religion: a redeployment of course already substantially begun by their Romantic predecessors, but surprising given their immersion in those traditions, where, for instance, the largest cluster of family books was theological. They provide a major scene for the secularisation of culture (Dickens would be another, George Eliot another, Trollope another); and they, like Matthew Arnold, show ways in which a liberalising religion could also be reinscribed within a more secular culture, with inner experience replacing institution, ritual, and myth as the location of the sacred. To the students who still say they have no interest in religion even in its disappearance or reincarnation, I offer the pleasure of intricate literary moves, games of dialogic complexity that allow, as Mikhail Bakhtin was amazed to find in Dostoevsky, a little room for individuals to manoeuvre around ideologies.

Our essential ignorance of Victorian religion, our exclusion from such an impossibly dense world, makes it easy for me to specify the basic players in the game. The United Kingdom accommodated a diversity of Christian religions: Ireland was predominantly Catholic though with an Anglican (Church of England or outside of England, Episcopalian) ruling class and Scots Presbyterian middle class especially in Belfast; Scotland predominantly Presbyterian (Church of Scotland), but with some dissenter groups such as Baptists or Methodists; England very mixed, with an established Anglican Church claiming succession to the early Catholic Church, but beset on all sides by a great variety of dissenter churches, from the intellectual and prosperous Unitarians and Congregationalists to the often working-class Baptists or Methodists (originally a group within the Church of England but eventually a separate, dissenter group). Dissenters, sometimes glorying in their role – one journal, the *Monthly Repository*, billed itself as the dissidence of dissent and the protestantism of the Protestant religion – represented by mid century roughly half of the church-going population of England; and to them was added a large and growing number of Catholics, some by conversion but most by passage over from Ireland, before and during the great famine, and an ever-increasing number of Jews, first mainly Sephardic Jews, later large groups of Eastern European Ashkenazi Jews who fled to England as to the United States and Canada. Add to this a growing number of free thinkers and atheists some, like the Feuerbach whose *Essence of Christianity* George Eliot translated, or Francis Newman, whom Charlotte read and admired, offering seductive explanations of religion as the projection of human psychology (seductive especially to those who found religion within), and one has a most distinguished brew of various religions, opening major possibilities for further free thinking within and without established sects.

To this turmoil of various sects was further added the hubbub of controversy within each sect, though this is sometimes mistakenly seen as only a set of controversies in the established, Anglican Church. Major issues perhaps fulfil the pattern Cardinal Newman found from his secure refuge in Roman Catholic conversion: an increasing pressure on the middles from the extremes. One extreme was in fact scientific scepticism, which waged a century-long war of attrition on two fronts: science, symbolically highlighted by Darwin's striking work, kept casting doubt on traditional views of man's origins and place in the universe; and rigorous historical scholarship, typified by the Higher (textual) Criticism of the Bible but continued in so many anthropological or archaeological or even psychological projects of the second half of the century, reconsidered the very nature of religious traditions and the religious experience. On the other side, and often in reaction, the famous – or notorious as it often appeared to Victorians – Oxford Movement, led by the earlier Anglican Newman and his tract-writing comrade in arms, Edward Pusey, challenged the moderates in the Church – especially identified with the Broad Church Movement of F. D. Maurice and Dr Thomas Arnold – who would accommodate to changing views. The Oxford Movement instead insisted upon all or nothing, a return to a secure source of authority in Church tradition just as other conservatives, especially in dissenter sects, might insist on a return to literal belief in every word of the Bible.

Where people care greatly – and religion, or anti-religion, seems to have been strongly interpellated into the very identity of most Victorians – they wrangle endlessly and sometimes fight bitterly. We cannot really understand the strength of their concern or the possible intensity of their battles on central issues such as Calvinist predestination versus justification by faith and/or works, eternal punishment versus the humane but rarely advocated universal salvation. We do recognise the variety and complexity that resulted from the continuous stirring of new issues within an already hopelessly complicated playing field of religious groups and types. And as religion was conceived of as central to so many matters we consider mainly secular – sexuality, health care, education, imperialism, social welfare, to name but a few – the always boiling pots of belief were forever spilling over into every aspect of society, its thought, and its self-representation.

That is the short story of religion as it confronted the Brontës in every aspect of their lives. Their own experiences with religion were perhaps typical of the age in their centrality and diversity, perhaps atypical but symbolic of others' in their intensity. I must again tell a very brief tale here where a full one could show the place of religion in every aspect of the Brontës' lives.[1] The Brontës, every one of the generation of famous writers, was afflicted with the same curse, to be born a child of a clergyman. Religion was not something they could choose to bring more or less into their lives: it was at the centre of concerns and livelihood. Patrick Brontë, their interesting and intelligent if sometimes irascible father, had moved from the Presbyterianism of his poor Northern Irish background to education at St John's College, Cambridge, an intellectual centre for a prominent low-church group within the Church of England, called Evangelicals, who were less interested in controversy over theological orthodoxy than in bringing Christian conviction into hearts and Christian morality into lives. There he was sponsored by the famous future missionary Henry Martyn and by the influential Charles Simeon, two prominent leaders in the low-church Anglican Evangelical group. He was promoted from various curacies to a comfortable permanent appointment at Haworth. He married Maria Branwell, who was connected to the by-then separate Wesleyan Methodist church, towards which he was tolerant and even sympathetic. When his wife died, she was replaced in practical and religious household management of the young children by her sister, Miss Elizabeth Branwell, who combined Methodist pietism with some degree of brimstone and hellfire, but probably not Calvinist, Christianity.

Patrick himself worked by and large within his Evangelical lineage, having more concern with reaching the poor, with good works, and with true inner spirit than with ritual or dogma. His children were perhaps more struck than he was by the disparities between his religious profession, on which of course the family welfare depended, and his vigour of mind and body, his interest in firearms, his youthful compositions of moralistic Evangelical poems and tales. His ministry was aided by curates, who were a vivid part of the Brontës' lives, often seen by them as satirical figures. The satire extended, on Charlotte's part, to the final one, Arthur Nicholls, who seemed to Charlotte bigoted, especially in his antithetical interest in the Puseyite Oxford High Church. Yet her life was to continue in clerical hands, with a relatively happy if brief marriage late in her life to none other than Nicholls himself.

Generally, the children could be said easily to side with their father in placing emphasis on religion as a living force within the individual, as a living connection between individuals, rather than as an institution or a set of beliefs or dogmas. Yet they must have felt him somehow complicit with the grimmer side of Evangelical Protestantism as the girls would experience it, through his use of hell as a threat to sinners in his sermons and above all through his decision to send the four eldest to the school for clergymen's daughters at Cowan Bridge, run by the grim Reverend Carus Wilson; there the two eldest died from fever and, Charlotte clearly felt, mismanagement and Christian sadism. Whatever the effect of this early hideous trauma on them, all the surviving children seem to have staked their own positions as primarily secular ones. As writers, from their abundant juvenile stories and magazines on, they followed their father's brief lead in his early creative work in bringing spiritual and moral issues into the secular discussion of literature rather than his career commitment to Church, ministry and belief. They might have identified themselves, as certainly Anne and Charlotte did, as members of the Church of England (Emily was a rare church-goer, brother Branwell early defiant). But their energies were devoted to a somewhat subversive project – the subversion sometimes acknowledged, sometimes not – of converting that tradition: most often into secular, usually psychological, tropes; but sometimes, as we will see, into alternative religious energies moving towards pagan, female, or pagan and female new religion.

Anne Brontë seems the easiest of the Brontës to situate in conventional views on religion and the marriage of religion and art. Youngest as she was, she seems nonetheless much the most severe of the sisters. She apparently took upon herself far more fully than the others the disaster of brother Branwell; her short life appears chastened and even disheartened by her early vision of the wages of sin. She brings religion into her novels with more directness and regularity than her sisters. And she does so with a dourness and seriousness not much present, as we shall see, in the rather fantastical, comic, or critical treatment of religious issues in her sisters' work.

The Tenant of Wildfell Hall has a love story and ends with the promise of a marriage. But within the Chinese-box structure of the story within a story is another marriage, used not as the usual happy ending of the domestic novel but as a memento for a serious vision of the entirety of life. Helen, the heroine who has escaped from her dreadful rake husband, is already deep in the midst of a dark forest of life when we, with hero Gilbert, meet her at rough Wildfell Hall. She has had her brief season of meeting and mating, has had her high time of life, borne a child to her rapidly deteriorating husband. It has been a disaster leading to massive disappointment, regret, resignation. She has failed to follow the sage and moral Christian counsel of her aunt in the choice of a husband and instead, following the urge of nature, has chosen a young and attractive but highly immoral mate. She finds herself growing ever more alienated from a hostile, abusive, drunkard and adulterous Arthur Huntingdon. Helen's perspective is now drastically altered, from that of an initiating young person (the central subject of Charlotte Brontë's work as of so much of the domestic fiction of the nineteenth century) to that of her religious aunt, awaiting the call of death.

The world of the novel is also very much one hedged in by a religious vision. We probably have a far more realistic representation of the speech of severe Evangelical Protestant upper- and upper-middle-class people of the Victorian period in this novel than we do with the other Brontës' far more wide-reaching and playful works. Helen and her aunt initiate the debate over her fatal decision by trading quotes from scripture. The plot will suggest that Helen is misled by her passion for pretty Arthur to a devil's abuse of scripture; but the more striking thing to a reader over a century-and-a-half later is the way in which life was read within the terms of biblical quotation. Scholarly notes in modern editions nail home the quotations; but one hardly needs an editor's knowledge of detail to understand that quotes are being bandied back and forth from a text foundational to the moral issues of the Brontës' time.

The plot of this inner story could be paralleled to that of another foundational text for the puritanical culture both within and without the Church of England in the first half of the nineteenth century, namely John Bunyan's *Pilgrim's Progress*. Arthur is Mr Worldly-Wiseman and Beelzebub all rolled into one. His way of the world, his outrageous vanity of drinking, revelling and adultery lead only down the slippery slope. Helen must detach herself from him, while still carefully following her wifely duties, and especially she must detach her son from the corrupting influence of his father. Suffer she will, but she suffers with the just who have a clear sight of the heavenly city to come after 'this dark and wicked world' (*TWH*, 313). And she has the distinct satisfaction of watching Arthur's pitiful attempts to find in her at the end a stay against damnation. Helen is careful to suggest, even somewhat heretically for a Protestant, that eventually he may be purged of his sins; but this hope seems driven more by a rhetorical need not to seem vindictive than by major conviction.

The focus is indeed on the powerful but also limited issue of whether religion can be a moral framework for life. Helen, like her aunt before her, tries to live her life by the light of her tradition's moral precepts; and she does so in a vague framework of supernatural sanctions for moral conduct. But there is not a strong sense of involvement in religion in other ways. The novel does not have much of a doctrinal message, other than the broad message that moral conduct married to religious belief saves in this life and the next. Helen finds little support from any version of organised religion nor is she, nominal member of the Church of England as we must think her, much concerned with varieties of the creeds or with any specifically religious practice, as opposed to the practice of the Christian life.

And this is odd because she does put her religious beliefs, even as she makes the mistake of her life, at the centre of her way of living – very much in the Evangelical tradition. Like a preacher who has seen the folly of his youthful ways, she is ready to offer her life, as her narrative effectively does, as a diary of a reformed sinner. She is not merely the wife whose goodness is worth more than gems or gold; she will be, as her aunt had attempted to be for her, a religious counsellor. We sense in her religious pedagogic relation to all she meets a desire on her part, and perhaps on the part of her author, for the tantalisingly near but, in her century, generally impossible role of female preacher – the role given to but then taken away from Dinah Morris in George Eliot's *Adam Bede*.

Religion thus is intricated in a web of other values, even in this most dour and conventional of Brontë novels. The betrayed wife accrues power from religion that compensates for her loss of power under husband Arthur's egregiously patriarchal control. And she is ultimately justified by religion, as so many English rebels had been, in taking a politically radical step: here, against patriarchal law that gives the husband authority over the persons of wife and children, she steals her own child, to save his soul, and absconds: a solution we easily applaud as an act of liberation, but she justifies by her religion.

Moreover, the novel is far from the monologic systematisation of religion that Bakhtin found in the pre-Dostoevskian novel. If Helen's narrative, imitating the single-minded textual rendition of the inner life so common in diaries and journals of the eighteenth and nineteenth centuries, inscribes a single Evangelical vision of the moral Christian life focused on hopes for heavenly reward, other structures in the novel speak quite contrary views of life. Helen's story is indeed framed as a more conventionally nineteenth-century novel of successful love and happiness ever after – in this world. This story is written by Gilbert, whose affinity to Helen is clear enough in his own obsession with preserving his tale, which he does for an otherwise shadowy friend, to whom he writes both his and Helen's tales. We of course find the Chinese boxes multiplied in the work of Anne Brontë's sisters, especially *Wuthering Heights*, with accompanying multiplying of point of view. But the effect is already clear enough here in that Gilbert, moral future mate for Helen as he is, nonetheless occupies a different view of life. He is even willing to pay lip-service to Helen's suggestion that they plan to meet in heaven since she, still married to her worthless husband, will not consider an extramarital arrangement. But he has an earthly love for Helen and finds this a very poor arrangement, which he only continues as he is deeply in love with her. Religion has for him a merely conventional place in his life.

What seems most interesting in this novel is the way in which Gilbert's personal relation to Helen and his position as her frame narrator keeps raising doubts about, or at least alternative perspectives on her studied religious morality. Even the rake her husband is given a number of strong lines in which, nearly to the last, he accuses her of excessive puritanism: driving him to drink by her coldness, spoiling the spirit of their boy, denying the attraction to his world of worldly joys that she has shown in falling in love with him, coming back to him in his final sickness in order to vaunt her charity and her belief in his damnation. The reader keeps wondering whether she isn't representing herself in her own narration in a way that conceals a life-denying and inhuman puritanism and whether the real issues, disguised by Helen's obsession with religious language, are not better couched in secular, psychological terms as those of emotional excess and restraint.

Gilbert, contradictorily, finds Helen both hard and cold and also seems to suspect the hypocrisy of hidden sensuality. Strongly attracted to her and her loving son, he easily persuades himself that she is conducting an affair with the Mr Lawrence who later will prove to be her brother. In a novel with no controlling voice, only those of the two more puritan characters, Helen and Gilbert, who are obviously feeling more sexual attraction than they dare admit, we are free to draw slantwise conclusions: not only that marital laws should be amended but that excessive concern with religious routes in life only violates a human nature closer to the earth. The frame novel of conventional worldly adjustment – love and money and social position – seems first to enshroud the inner religious tale with potential conflict and irony, then to claim the dominant view of life: one respectful of religious views but deeply secular.

When we turn to the less conventional representations of religious practice and belief in the work of Anne's two sisters, we will find such dissonances everywhere that religion enters their stories. This is perhaps most obvious where we would expect it to be most absent in the works of a clergyman's daughters, in the representation of the clergy themselves. Here Anne is once again closer to a fairly conventional perspective, weighted if anything in favour of organised religion. In her first published novel, *Agnes Grey*, Anne was already developing a sense of a female presence that settled moral and religious matters.

But here the ostensible focus is still on public figures of organised religion. Agnes is indeed herself a daughter of a clergyman, though family romance gives her a mother of the higher classes. The mother has married Agnes' father with respect for his calling as well as with personal love. Cut off from the gentry, her family is nonetheless the moral centre of things; the worst that the Brontës always had to fear, the death of their father and loss of his 'perpetual' living, happens, but Agnes (A like Anne) carries his religio-moral tradition out to the families she serves, where she sets up as the clergyman's daughter who shall judge all. While her foolish rich charges busy themselves robbing birds' nests or seeking prosperous marriage, she focuses rather on the local clergy. Her satirical eye is not closed to Mr Hatfield, rector of Horton, who is altogether too concerned with currying favour with the gentry. His agenda can be loosely associated with the Oxford Movement, although the usual tags of Puseyism, Newman, or Oxford Movement are not used. He seems to prefer Church fathers to the 'Apostles and Evangelists' (*AG*, 81) and strongly discourages independent thinking apart from church discipline and guidance.

His limitations are shown up as he fails a cottager who needs spiritual consolation while the new vicar, 'Maister Weston', is able to reach her with his conviction of God's love. Weston is described as an Evangelical Christian, one more concerned with inspiring conviction than with church governance, authority and rite. His sermons also please Agnes with the 'earnest simplicity of his manner, and the clearness and force of his style' (*AG*, 81). She indeed is so impressed with his style, as well as his warmth and humanity, that she marries him, reader, and finds he has rescued her dog and pleases her mother as well. This is certainly a very positive view of a good parson, one who would probably meet the approval of the entire Brontë family and follow Patrick's own concern, in verse and parish practice, with poor cottagers.

A clergyman as good man, as epitome of humanity, as Mr Knightley and Mr Rochester all wrapped up in one, whatever the incidence of such persons in real-life rural settings and romances, does not reappear in the Brontës' work. Far from it! In Charlotte's work clerical figures are much more negative and subject to tremendous imaginative accentuation. The least is perhaps the famous feast of the curates in her second published novel, *Shirley*. Here in the cool, representational world of this novel, which introduces itself as a move to social realism from the hot imaginative world of *Jane Eyre*, the religious gentlemen are presented with far grosser satire than Anne ever used. The narrator's opening refusal of romance is specifically an odd refusal of a romance of curates: 'Of late years an abundant shower of curates has fallen upon the north of England: they lie very thick on the hills' (S, 5). So opens chapter 1, entitled 'Levitical'. We may be dubious that such present times – the narrator's present – really offer a return to a biblical blessing of the earth by the priestly class. We suspect the narrator's tongue is in his cheek. Indeed the present 'romance' of curates falling only too abundantly from the air seems to morph easily into the anti-romantic realism of the novel's view of northern England undergoing industrial growing pains during the Napoleonic era. Then too, in the region in which the novel is set, there were too many curates; and there follows a memorable satirical look at three young, noisy, beery and generally useless ones. One, Malone, an Irish Protestant redolent of Patrick Brontë in his background and love of firearms, has spunk and gusto; another is a south-country fop, a kind of clerical Lockwood; the third is at least sweet tempered. None seems to do any good or offer the slightest positive image of religion. (A fourth, modelled on Charlotte's earlier view of her future husband, comes in for only limited praise at the end.)

Everyone remembers these bold and satirical scenes which open out to the themes *Shirley* is generally taken to be about: industrial problems and the role of women in this men's society. Yet it is the case that the novel looks at these matters for many chapters through the darkening glass of the country's priestly class. It seems implicitly to be asking: how have its spiritual leaders allowed England to slip into a situation where each man's hand is against his brother (Cain and Abel join the early biblical motifs as the condition of the novel's England, where Luddites and factory owners combat each other ferociously) and where men and women share only discord. The religious hierarchy over the curates, most apparent in the suffering heroine's uncle Helstone, seems equally embroiled in the perplexities and class/gender conflict of the time. Helstone uses his considerable religious learning to break up the curates' drinking party and command Malone to take revolvers and defend the mill – of the man who is already in the process of breaking his niece's heart. While Shirley, the eponymous epicene heroine, tries to heal social suffering by traditional gentry largesse, the clergy turn a Whitsuntide ceremony into a virtually military encounter between a troop of the established church and another of dissent. Again, representations of religious life only replicate the picture of the social strife everywhere. On a personal level, Helstone is a widower and confirmed misogynist. The curates offer a comic sub-plot of the sexual issues that will consume – or rewrite – the novel's issues of social strife: at tea with ladies, as at their private drinking party, they are broadly absurd, excellent satirical portraits by an author perhaps not given sufficient credit in this high low art. At Shirley's estate, the curates provide a low version of the mill-owner Moore's corruption of marital desire into mercenary deviousness, the diversion of affection that hurts Caroline so much and drives a wedge generally between the sexes. The curates' suit is itself wonderfully broken up by Shirley's big dog, who rightly singles them out for another hostile action.

Here and there are points of light in the massively unpleasant scene of religion in this truly unromantic post-lapsarian world – for instance the kindly if rather ineffectual vicar Hall, who comforts poor Caroline, or the Methodist mill-owner, Mr Yorke. But the very chapter titles – 'Levitical', 'Mr Donne's Exodus' – tell us this is modern burlesque of old-time religion. In 'Noah and Moses' we find that the central event of industrial violence that propels the novel has been itself caused by radical dissenter agitation by one Moses Barraclough, sectarian 'preacher of the Gospel' (S, 136). The progress of the novel is away from the strife of religion and politics and towards the pain and difficulty of interpersonal relations. In the conclusion, the clergy are comically summoned once more only to be dismissed as virtually irrelevant – Malone has disappeared, story not told, Donne has raised money for a merely ornamental, High Anglican Church. That true religious feeling might exist is not necessarily denied by the comic/satirical representation. But what progressive forces there are – especially Shirley herself, who most readers feel is, alas, neutralised in her instinct towards a new, female religion by the end of the novel – do not emanate from the religious world.

If the comic surface satire on religious officials runs deeper into the fabric of the social vision of *Shirley* than at first meets the eye, the satirical criticism in *Jane Eyre* is blatant and extremely bitter, a biting Juvenalian satire that should be better recognised. Jane Eyre, a grown-up and successful woman, joins the little Jane in her violent condemnation of the conservative religious philanthropist, Brocklehurst. His Lowood School is a charity foundation for orphan girls that uses religion, in the spirit of earlier religious conservatives such as Hannah More, to maintain the current social order. He is primarily presented as a person of authority; we know him as 'the black marble clergyman' (*JE*, 66), only secondarily. If he has all the power, Jane has all the right. His religious talk seems a running parody of religious cant. A pious reader like Jane's friend at Lowood, Helen Burns, may see him as a travesty of true religion; but the satire is often so strong and grotesquely abusive that other readers, in the rebellious spirit of Jane herself, may call into question his entire religious vision. Jane's instinct, which keeps being opposed to Brocklehurst's religious structures, is to opt out of the outrageous system entirely. Faced with the 'orthodox' view of punishment for liar girls, she prefers not: 'I must keep in good health and not die' (*JE*, 32). At Lowood, Brocklehurst quotes Jesus to justify burnt porridge; and he serves up as mortification of the 'lusts of the flesh' (*JE*, 64) his sadistic injustice to Jane. But

Jane is vindicated. Brocklehurst is proved to be a hypocrite, one of those whited sepulchres of the New Testament to whom Charlotte Brontë refers in her preface to the second edition. We had already seen that, as Brocklehurst was repeatedly likened to a marble pillar, rigid and phallic – black because of the clerical garb that is his hypocritical cover. The gross satire is indeed caricatural, as also in Dickens, but the preface is dedicated to the biting satirist of society, Thackeray. Brontë seems to make clear what is not entirely clear in the text, that she is attacking vanity fair's misuse of religion, not necessarily 'the world-redeeming creed of Christ' (*JE*, 4). The dedication is itself revealing: Thackeray's sceptical view of people living godlessly in a godless world does not make him an obvious candidate for sainthood.

Nor is Jane; her friend Helen Burns is burnt by the religion of hell and offers herself as a willing martyr (we recall Brontë's two older sisters were indeed martyred by the prototype of Lowood). Helen's religion arouses a very serious ambivalence in Jane and her reader. A loving and beloved figure, she seems nonetheless masochistic in her self-mortification. Jane would not be the icon of feminist activism that she is if her plan had been to turn the other cheek, as Helen does until her death. Yet Jane recognises a spiritual fire also burning in Helen. Inspired, 'her soul sat on her lips...the swelling spring of pure, full, fervid eloquence' (*JE*, 73). We may well think of the vapid eloquent words of Kurtz in Conrad's *Heart of Darkness*. Even Jane thinks of heaven and hell, the former of which at least Helen assures her exists, but finds her mind 'recoiled, baffled' (*JE*, 79). 'I questioned... "Where is that region? Does it exist?"' (*JE*, 82).

Religion in its institutional form seems hopeless; as a personal inspiration it can be attractive but then seems to challenge Jane's very secular, highly desired destiny. Miss Temple, the good headmistress at Lowood, raises the possibility that Anne Brontë flirted with, of a new female calling in religion. Her name suggests she is the true Church, if kept down by patriarchal power at the moment; her clear brow and modest but dignified bearing seem to confirm it. Her first name, Maria, however, condemns her to a relatively passive role, as failing intercessor with God for Helen's life and only moderately successful intercessor with Brocklehurst for the well being of all her charges. As with Helen, we share Jane's admiration and also her ambivalence. Shall Jane too devote her life to the merely relative autonomy of a female *aide-de-camp* in religious work, especially when the work itself seems so misdirected?

Miss Temple, in marrying Mr Nasmyth, chooses an unmythic destiny – to give herself away to a churchman rather than be a church. Jane opts for worldly activity, the only slightly religious work of governessing to a child of less than religiously respectable background, and ultimately for the worldly fleshpots of Rochester, whose wife so conveniently humbles him and frees him in one hysterical episode. But of course she confronts one more person of God, the dashing missionary St John Rivers, modelled on Patrick Brontë's real-life mentor, the Evangelical hero Henry Martyn. Rivers too is tagged with the odd marble pillar caricature: his handsomeness – far greater in obvious sex appeal than Rochester – is also phallically rigid, demanding submission of himself and the woman he marries to his religious causes. A hero for God! The idea bothers Jane, questioning as it does her own secular destiny. But it also isn't clear if the dashing role wouldn't be more attractive if Jane could have played first violin rather than St John's page turner. The novel inscribes this central ambivalence about Christianity and religious *men* on its final page, as Jane tells us, in language that may be, or may not be taken as ironic (irony being a trope in the eyes of the beholder), of the celibate missionary's assurance of 'his sure reward, his incorruptible crown' (*JE*, 452). 'No fear of death will darken St John's last hour; his mind will be unclouded; his heart will be undaunted; his hope will be sure.' Again, we may think of Kurtz's words, noble, empty, words, especially for this 'pioneer' missionary imperialist.

What positive religion the novel offers without much ambivalence is a very watered-down faith in the inner light (Wesley's 'inner witness', which leads Jane mainly into her secular destiny). As in Anne's work, true religion is mainly conduct; and cynical readers see Jane's rather conventional religious beliefs – namely those which condemn technical adultery with a man whose wife is legally insane – as less reverent than psychologically convenient. We have trouble, as we will in Emily Brontë, distinguishing an undoctrinaire Christian inner light of conscience from a pagan vitalism in which the universe seems full of the magic of our desires and needs. If the miracle of Rochester's call sounds like a patriarchal god's intervention, the monitory goddess who originally told Jane to flee temptation seems rather pagan. Jane certainly models her life story on the Bunyan-inspired tradition of puritan biography. But Jane's way, pursued with the combination of scepticism and hypocrisy that make her a secular pilgrim indeed, is to substitute a religion of romantic belief in the self and its journey of secular self-realisation for the negative religion she finds. And this threatens, as it does in the works of Thomas Carlyle, to emerge as a full-blown religion of personal will, where talk of God and use of traditional religious language merely cover a strongly asserted non-religious destiny. Jane continues to bother readers today, as she did on first publication, by her unresolved, opposing motives either to choose a secular life of human relation or to focus, as she perhaps tries to do as narrator, on dethroning masculine religion and creating a new female gospel, the life of Jane.

In Emily's poems and novel, the satirical critique of institutional religion is as strong, but the development of alternative religious possibilities is far more evident and much more fully articulated. The poems are of course a nest of problems in themselves: glorious fragments (most? some of them?) from the lost (never really attempted?) Gondal (childhood? young adult?) epic, they exist as disembodied arias from a great cycle of opera or, perhaps closer, monologues from an unseen Star Wars; they leave us groping for a context and a local meaning they forever deny us. They are lyric shadows of emotional magnitudes rather than coherent dramatic monologues. As such, they are not, like Browning's monologues, about reasons and motivations but about strong emotions generated out of moments of epic crisis; or they are deep breathings of ultimates from heroic characters whose fate has been fixed. The epical generality encourages existential focus. The speaker sums up not so much his life, as life itself. And whether he or she seems to be out of Gondal's heroic world or from Emily's own personal Haworth epic of moor and vacancy, the speaker welcomes the opposition of self and ultimates to proclaim/explore the nature of existence.

The typical monologue is perhaps that of a speaker from the depths, of dungeon, or solitude, or extremity. Facing loss of all externals, the speaker asserts internals, using an heroic/romantic language of spirit, soul, heart, breast. The same structure fits moments of capture, death, or loss of love. Against externals' failure, the soul uses a barrage of romantic modes to assert its power: memory, fancy, imagination, projection, apostrophe and appellation. Like some Romantic poets (Blake of the prophetic books, Wordsworth of the *Prelude*), Brontë's speakers find the power of something eternal in themselves. Like many Victorians (for example, Carlyle, Tennyson, Browning and Arnold), they sometimes connect this to something like belief: they find God within themselves certainly even if orthodox belief and institutional structures pale or fail. But the stress here is on the individual's private determination of religion. They know god in themselves rather than themselves in God. The key statement, a powerful combination of strong force of assertion and clear, sparse syntax, 'No coward soul is mine', asserts a vision of heaven's glories on strong feeling of 'God within my breast / Almighty ever-present Deity' (*EBP*, 182). The 'thousand creeds' are 'vain,' 'unutterably vain, / Worthless as withered weeds.' But the failure of institutional religion raises no issue of Victorian faith, only a stronger sense of true belief – in self.

If God begins in self, God may very well end in a world of spirits all manifestations of godhead, or indeed in a kind of pantheism or paganism. The world of the poems complements all those soul-asserting, *different* speakers, with frequent hints of other forces at work. In 'A Day Dream' (one of the poems published in Brontë's lifetime) a forlorn speaker finds a world of 'A thousand thousand gleaming fires,' 'little glittering spirits', assuring him of joy (*EBP*, 81); elsewhere spirits actually speak of human destiny or rescue a lost traveller. Generally religious orthodoxy is wished away or summoned in vain. Above all, powerful feeling in the souls of speakers finds answering power/powers in the universe as it pours its 'presence into all,' a forecasting of death as universal mingling:

> Thus truly when that breast is cold
> Thy prisoned soul shall rise
> The dungeon mingle with the mould –
> The captive with the skies. (*EBP*, 131)

Here, spirit assertion moves easily into a myth-making, personal religion of animated soul re-animating what had seemed a dead universe.

A similar rhetorical approach permeates the brilliant contrasting struc-tures within the encased multiple narratives of *Wuthering Heights*. Until we think of the way in which religion is brought into play in the novel we may think of the servant Joseph, a Methodist-inclined zealot who adjuncts the role of family preacher to his more menial duties, as merely a piece of comic relief; perhaps at best a negative contrast to the gentry characters to match the generally positive earthiness of narratrix Nelly. Another brilliant Brontë satire on male preachers, the more biting as his vocation is entirely self-assumed, Joseph also stands in for traditional religion, which is other-wise hardly represented (we hear only occasionally of regular clergymen in the neighbourhood). Joseph, who was old and sour even in the earlier time of Heathcliff and Cathy's childhood, and old as a patriarch when Lockwood meets him as a principal part of his strange introduction to the Heights in 1801, is given a very strong presence early in the novel. Even Lockwood is able to see through his tendency to pious ejaculation into his vinegary nature (*WH*, 2, 7). In his interaction with young Catherine, we are given some of the novel's strikingly powerful and naked exhibitions of difference of point of view. Catherine attacks the old Bible-mouthing, brimstone threatening, moralising pest directly: 'You scandalous old hypocrite.' He as directly tells Catherine she is damned to 'goa raight tuh t' divil, like yer mother afore ye!' (*WH*, 13).

With this clear opposition already before us, we are not surprised to find that the young Cathy's diary immediately singles out Joseph for abuse. It begins with a picture caricature and proceeds to describe the disgust the chil-dren felt in Joseph's attempts to break their spirits on his orthodox world. He performs a home service in which he assumes the role of preacher and drones on for three hours (three hours!). The rest of Sunday feels the force of his sabbatarian scruples as the children must not make a 'titter' but devote themselves to improving religious books, 'Th' Helmet uh Salvation' and 'T'Brooad Way to Destruction!', which they finally try to destroy, bringing on a major uproar, with Joseph assuring them that 'owd Nick' would soon fetch them (*WH*, 20–1). No opposition between fundamental forces, fundamentalism as it was arising in still Anglican Methodism and the fundamentals of these two children's brilliant lifeforce, could be more clear.

And it is then repeated, as if in a fantasy replay, in Lockwood's ensuing famous dream, in which he is forced to listen to the Pious Discourse of the Reverend Jabes Branderham[2] on Matthew's 'Seventy Times Seven' treated in the full four hundred and ninety parts, each equal to a separate sermon, each on another separate, generally odd sin. Here Lockwood himself, writhing, yawning, nodding, becomes the antagonist of Joseph's kind of fundamentalism. When he attempts to attack, using biblical language himself to accuse Jabes of the unforgivable sin (of boring him so), he is himself attacked by the pious puritans and in the mêlée he finds, as in *Shirley's* world, every hand against his neighbour. Lockwood's dream then attacks him from the other flank, with the seeming waking from this awful orthodoxy to the wraith/waif of dead Cathy.

This oppositional structure, thus repeated twice in the opening, patterns the metaphysical tentatives of the novel as a whole. In what might seem a grotesque combination of domestic and gothic novel, Emily brilliantly raises the novel to a dialogue about how to see humans' place in the universe. With some of Dostoevsky's intensity and with some of Nietzsche's brilliance, she will pit conventional and traditional religious and moral views against a kind of revived vitalist and pagan sensibility. Heathcliff, that 'wolfish man' (*WH*, 102) as Cathy fairly warns Isabella, is not a nice man; but he is somehow more in line with at least one powerful vision of the universe that the novel offers. That we may be of the side of the domestic conventionality of education of the second Cathy and Hareton's ending idyll, of the side of the unsettled spirits set loose in the natural world by the strong-souled passionate feelings of Heathcliff and Cathy, or really be drawn between these two visions, suggests how truly dialogic this novel is, a warring of opposing religious/moral views that would each alone too much conclude the forces still loose in the novel as we read it. By its opening satirical treatment of conventional religion, the novel succeeds in opening a space for metaphysical or spiritual invention beyond good and evil, pious and damned.

As in Emily's poems, we are led to identify with heroic figures – of course Cathy and Heathcliff – even as the novelistic context makes more problematic the moral issues raised by their focus on their strong-souled sense of identity and mutual merging. Values of domestic matrimonial morality, to take a modest instance, seem put into dispute by the protagonists' soul commitments. Conversely Heathcliff's apparently easily censured behaviour is momently revalued by our glimpses of the sublimity of his passion for long-dead Cathy. If conventional religion is here perhaps presented even more satirically than in the other Brontë novels, a seriously religious thinker would find this work the closest to raising ethical/religious questions as experiential realities. We seem not able even to interpret the novel – What has happened to Cathy and Heathcliff? What value does it have for us ? – without placing it in one or another large, religious outlook. This work insists on religion as experienced, not codified and turned into that most contemptuous quality to the protagonists: 'cant'.

I will leave the fortunate reader to explore the intensely upsetting/stirring issues raised by the soul-deep commitment of the protagonists: to speculate, as most readers have, as to whether this is a heroism (and a sexuality) of childhood carried into impossible maturity or a premonition, as Emily's poems would suggest, of the immortal longings all beings with souls should have as they sweep tragically across the stage of life, perhaps towards the wedding of love and death. More deeply, they may ask if a kind of Calvinism, no better than Joseph's, seeps into a work that seems intent upon forcing us to separate intensely souled goats who delight in the dangerous Heights from sheep who graze best in the domesticated world of the Grange. Certainly one can no more imagine a place for dainty and dull Lockwood, or even for good though conventionally worshipping and conniving Nelly in Cathy and Heathcliff's turbulent paradise than Joseph can a place for the protagonists in his. But that is to remind us that these are not just armchair ultimates: everything is at stake in where we stake our reading: indeed our choice of heavens and hells. And we may also note the tendency, apparent also in the other Brontë sisters' work, to replace patriarchal male testimony to the written traditions of religion by female inspiration about the nature of the universe; it is notably Cathy who is the new prophet and scribe, writing her new female tradition in the margins of works by males, and also oracle, sometimes even the divinity, at whose lamp the obsessed and dark pagan Heathcliff worships.

In a Victorian world still very much circumscribed within a conventionally Christian worldview and moral outlook, *Wuthering Heights* must seem a work of religious radicalism merely in its effective invention of a pagan, or often folkloric, religious alternative: a world of wraiths, apparitions, pagan afterlives in this world, heroic identifications with the violent animal world and with mother earth, and pagan agony at the reality of death (one thinks of Heathcliff's version of the agony in the garden – or immortal longings experiencing mortal life). And he is more directly the blood-splashed self-victim in the familiar woods of pagan myth. Charlotte has been routinely criticised for her pre-emptive condemnation of her sister's great novel as a 'rude and strange production' (WH, 367). But if that sounds patronising, her fuller reaction is close to terror at the story of 'natures so relentless and implacable, of spirits so lost and fallen' (WH, 369). Interestingly, she reaches for Genesis' 'a horror of great darkness' (WH, 369; Genesis 15:12) to convey the unsettling, unorthodox work that has emerged from her sister's 'creative gift'. The impression is correct: that the work has not only printed 'expletives' usually left unprinted in Christian publishing but offered a monster world of spiritual imagination.

Charlotte indeed may have been defending herself from the temptation also to let *her* creative gift go and discover the mythic new religion, 'grim or glorious, dread or divine' her inspiration would direct. In *Jane Eyre* she too had seemed to offer a new gospel; that novel also speaks of new things, if not with such violent oppositionality – especially of the social, linguistic and sexual empowerment of women – with the resonant language of the Bible. Her society's religious language saturates and activates this vision of woman's secular destiny. *Villette*, her last and greatest novel, continues to work within the language and culture of Christianity, even as it focuses more constantly on the secular destiny of one woman. Now the context of Christianity is even broader, a double world of Protestant and Catholic in which the symbols and resonances of both may be picked up and converted to secular use. To the author and character, both of whom are sobered in their view by the near experience of much shipwreck of death, including the death of that special troubled spirit Emily, the norms of religion with its confessions, its heavens and hells, seem not much relevant – no more than Joseph's were to the Heathcliff who lost Cathy. Lucy is precisely a heroine for a book of non-conversion, not a hero of Canterbury over Rome but a person finding and accepting her personal, worldly destiny. But she is also not much tempted, as Heathcliff and Cathy very much were (and as Jane Eyre was, though she called them Christian God) to find in her destiny a revitalization of pagan forces guiding the individual's life. She merely accepts, with Calvinist gloom but without Calvinist faith in God's ultimate plan, the clear non-appearance of any metaphysical order in the world. Charlotte's last novel thus shows her moving decisively, as much of her century would before its end, towards a secular vision of human destiny, a vision that takes away possibilities of life beyond the everyday to restore meaning to ordinary experience.

How can this be, in a novel that is also one of the century's richest evocations of the continuing power of biblical and other religious language?[3] The answer most often is that Charlotte uses her quiet narrator and modest heroine, who like Charlotte herself is deeply imbued with the tremendously rich culture of religion, here Protestant, Catholic and Old Testament Jewish, to perform a major conversion of religious language and values into secular ones: a great task also undertaken by other writers and thinkers of the nineteenth century from Matthew Arnold and George Eliot on to Jewish Freud and Christian Jung. Indeed in *Villette* the work is most often the work of recycling traditional religious mythic language into a language to describe not existence and metaphysics, the outside world, but psychology, the inside world. Jane might find her pilgrimage an affirmation of a kind of magical destiny that can compete with Christian martyrs' other road. Lucy will find only the magic of inner value, inner strength, without a new mythos – a new religion for the modern age – in which to set it. Lucy, who has come to Villette to put behind her the shipwreck of all who were dear to her in England and to begin to make her own way in the world, easily falls into biblical analogy (the Israelites in the desert) as a way of objectifying and controlling her emotional disturbance over disappointment in her first love interest. She commands 'a patient journeying through the wilderness of the present, enjoining a reliance on faith – a watching of the cloud and pillar which subdue while they guide, and awe while they illumine – hushing the impulse to fond idolatry, checking the longing out-look for a far-off promised land whose rivers are, perhaps, never to be reached save in dying dreams' (p. 289). The sentiment and language is religious, biblical and Bunyanesque; the story ultimately, even with the pledge of faith, a secular one: to endure suffering and deprivation, to keep to her path of perhaps hopeless hope.

The standard nineteenth-century use of typology – putting oneself into an archetypal story well known from religious tradition (Moses who will not quite make it to the promised land) – here serves only a psychological aim, of self-reserve and control. In desperation Lucy – Protestant though she is – goes into a Catholic confessional in her need; but she finds there that she had not been looking for a religious path, only for psychological support. People in Villette suffer from an entire range of psychological disturbances, which appear as a fairly new special vocabulary for fiction: highly nervous states, Hypochondria as a form of melancholy or depression, hysteria, or the kind of break-down experience (clearly indicated if still not here given a technical label) that Lucy endured. In such a world, religion is being re-seen as defined by systems of psychological pathology rather than, as in traditional culture, itself explaining such pathology (Joseph's sense that Cathy and Heathcliff are possessed). As do later thinkers on religion in the nineteenth century, outstandingly Freud himself and William James, Brontë in this novel looks at religious experience as a variety of psychological events. The most persistent is Lucy's own sense of isolation, deprivation, disempowerment.

Vashti is an actress bearing the name of a powerful queen in the Bible (see Esther 1 and 2), who defies her husband Ahasuerus; Lucy finds her 'torn by seven devils'; 'though a spirit, she was a spirit out of Tophet' (*V*, 258–9). But such biblical overlay is the kind of continuous draft Brontë makes upon the religious world as a large quarry for metaphors and analogies to describe inner qualities: Vashti is a strong force of heroic personal assertion and violence, much like Heathcliff, but she is a psychological portent, not an icon of a possible new paganism: she indeed brings down the house with her incendiary powers. Lucy likewise finds not conversion to Rome but access to her own nature and psychological powers as she slowly extricates herself from a great set of Catholic religious systems and vestiges. Although there has been much debate over Brontë's mixture of her anti-Popery and sympathy to Catholic ritual in this novel, the fact is that her heroine is not so much debating Catholicism as seeking herself – perhaps a last, secular outgrowth of her English Protestant upbringing. The negative treatment of most Catholic figures is very much in tune with the Brontë sisters' very negative representation of Protestant religious. The complicated gothic story of the nun with the cigar seems primarily to threaten Lucy with incarceration within the conventical structures of control and observation of Madame Beck's school, founded upon the site of a nun's immolation. The religious myth seems always already a secular force, a mere secular vehicle for espionage and restraint. In literally deconstructing the nun, Lucy not only exposes the system that would drug and waste her life, but also unfolds her own powers of perception, feeling and self-reliance. She abandons the Protestant denial of life before the vibrancy of the hissing but caring Professor Paul Emanuel: Paul because he does have a mission to preach and teach; Emanuel not because he is to serve as a type of Christ on earth but because he converts the saving work of a religion based on Christ to a caring work of interpersonal engagement in this world. The religious origins and language are as clear as they are later in, say, George Eliot's Portrait of Dorothea in *Middlemarch*; the force is similarly not towards founding new nunneries but to moral and affective secular activity. Emanuel is sacrificed to the nonsense of priestcraft and vows to dead nuns; his life is valued rather for his this-worldly commitment to Lucy's self-realization and to her human value. This personal connection, based on marriage of true minds, is her only, and only metaphorical, return to the first 'Great Garden'.

Emanuel can sound like a Heathcliff: 'His passions were strong, his aversions and attachments alike vivid' (*V*, 203); but this novel does not move us from an old religion to a new paganism of soul-force or passion. Nor does it propose, as Jane seems to want to, and so many other sceptical Victorian Christians did, a weak New Mythos of Christianity found within. Rather it makes its business with religion that of emptying out all religious theatre and turning its force only to better understanding of our personal and social life in this world.

Certainly the Brontës, like so many nineteenth-century thinkers who were gradually easing out of a religious and into a secular sensibility, were often prepared to avow a vague belief in a Creator and perhaps a world beyond this one. Anne and Charlotte clearly did and professed themselves members of the Church of England. But the *work* of all three Brontë sisters enacts especially a critique of a world founded on any kind of religious orthodoxy and a re-channelling of religious language and traditions into other, to them more compelling, secular issues. It is nonetheless centrally about religion both in its under-recognised focus on religious persons and institutions and in its concern with re-evaluating the pilgrimage of individual life. It testifies with great eloquence to the force of their culture's diverse religious traditions, as ritual, symbol and/or metaphor; and, sometimes, to some kind of lived sense of the sacred now experienced from within. It is built on the seismic fissure in the West, between religious and secular cultures. In a general way, the Brontës witness the novel replacing the Bible as the bright book of life where a culture sees and knows itself. In detail, in their works, as we have seen, the relation between older Book and new books, religion and novelistic literature, is strikingly dialectical and intertwined.

NOTES

1. For detailed accounts and further references concerning religion in the Brontës see Tom Winnifrith, *The Brontës and their Background, Romance and Reality*, second edn (Basingstoke: Macmillan, 1988), chs. 3, 4, and Marianne Thormählen's recent *The Brontës and Religion* (Cambridge University Press, 1999). Thormählen's account, more than my own, reads the Brontës as, by and large, orthodox supporters of the Evangelical wing of the Church of England; to do this she focuses rather heavily on issues of ordinary morality and conduct that she relates to Christian beliefs of the time. On the other hand, her full study offers a wider sense than I can here of the full texture of religious issues and ways of life in the nineteenth century.
2. Often given a source in Jabez Bunting, a Methodist preacher and anti-Luddite, friend of Patrick Brontë.
3. The reader is especially encouraged to look at the brilliant interfoliation of *Villette* and the Bible performed by Kathryn Bond Stockton, *God Between their Lips: Desire Between Women in Irigaray, Brontë, and Eliot* (Stanford University Press, 1994), ch. 5. Her training in theology allows her uniquely to experience how much of Lucy's text enacts a paradise lost, regained, and apocalypse by rich allusion to the Bible. Her larger argument parallels the one I make below, that religious types and symbols are used metaphorically to reveal psychology. As I have, she reads Lucy's narrative as itself a form of psychoanalysis; her extremely

interesting Irigarayan approach sees Lucy using language of religion (Paul as the Christ who, in departing, makes Lucy come to herself, in both senses) as a way of healing/accepting her personal and social sense of lack. I respect, without agreeing with her own desire to open out secular discourse into a religious framework (Jacques Lacan as material mystic and Luce Irigaray as 'feminist theologian of lack': p. 28). Stephen Prickett, *Origins of Narrative: the Romantic Appropriation of the Bible* (Cambridge University Press, 1996), ch. 3, argues broadly for the expropriation of the typological tradition by the novel for (mainly) psychological exploration.

10

PATSY STONEMAN

The Brontë myth

Pale Sisters! reared amid the purple sea
Of windy moorland, where, remote, ye plied
All household arts, meek, passion-taught and free,
Kinship your joy and Fantasy your guide!
Ah! Who again 'mid English heaths shall see
Such strength in frailest weakness, or so fierce
Behest on tender women laid, to pierce
The world's dull ear with burning poetry?
Whence was your spell? and at what magic spring,
Under what guardian Muse, drank ye so deep
That still ye call and we are listening;
That still ye plain to us and we must weep?
Ask of the winds that haunt the moors, what breath
Blows in their storms, outlasting life and death![1]

Myth or myths?

A sombre moor – a treeless expanse of barely inhabited upland swept by savage storms. Three solitary figures, struggling against the wind or, perhaps, sitting in the austere parsonage, reading, writing and eagerly conversing about life, and literature, and love. From their talk rise other figures in similar landscapes, suffering, even tragic, but likewise bold and eager in claiming their share of 'life, fire, incident'. Jane and Rochester, Catherine and Heathcliff are names that shape the dreams of the young and haunt the minds of the old.

'The Brontë Myth' is not a simple thing but a matrix of interlocking stories, pictures and emotional atmospheres. It might be easier to say that there are many Brontë myths, and indeed the rest of this chapter will move among them, trying to draw connections. Even this composite myth, moreover, does not remain static. From different perspectives the moorland, for instance, is seen as romantically inspirational or as uncouth or impractical. One sister is valued above the others and then sinks as public tastes change. The family, perceived as 'three sisters', expands to include a brother, a father, an aunt, schools, travels – and then contracts again to the psychology of a single mind. The novels are discussed by reviewers, by academics, by other writers, by the common reader, and these evaluations are swayed by current theories about aesthetics, or morals.

'Myth', of course, is a Protean word. It can mean a traditional story, passed down through a culture and available for endless re-working, such as the Greek myths or the legend of King Arthur. This is the sense in which I hope to consider 'the Brontë myth'. There is, however, a difference between mythical figures who had no historical existence (like the Greek gods), or whose origins are lost in time (like King Arthur), and relatively recent figures whose history can be defined by documentary evidence. For historians and biographers dealing with more detailed 'myths' about the Brontës, the word takes on a negative meaning, equivalent to 'falsehood'. Stories circulate, for instance, about Patrick Brontë, the father, eccentric and reclusive, barely moving from his room; or Emily Brontë, silent and devoted, helping her drunken brother into bed. Such often-repeated stories have now been matched against accumulated evidence, and much scholarly effort has been expended by researchers such as Tom Winnifrith and Juliet Barker to expel such 'myths' as these. By weighing the available evidence, we can now see that Aunt Branwell, for instance, was not a source of Calvinistic terror to the children she brought up and that Patrick Brontë was not only a kind and interested father, but a man of liberal sympathies, extensively involved in the social and intellectual movements of his day.

There are, however, social and psychological reasons why such 'myths' do not die. Calvinistic fears, for instance, may not have come from Aunt Branwell, but there is no doubt that Calvinism was an oppressive ideology which caused suffering to Anne, Branwell and Charlotte, along with many others of their time, when they encountered it from other sources. Although Patrick Brontë proves to have been an enlightened and encouraging father, there were plenty of repressive fathers in early Victorian society. And although the young Brontës may not have been so blighted by bereavement and bad treatment as early biographers suggested, the 'myth' of their sad, silent childhood was fed, in an age where orphans were commonplace, by contemporary readers' knowledge of other sad, silent children. So, although the precise stories told about the Brontës may have been falsehoods, these 'myths' often prove to have a historical validity.

The myths are also compounded by material from the Brontës' novels. Few readers of *Jane Eyre* are able to distinguish between Jane's experiences at Lowood and those of the young Brontës at Cowan Bridge, or even see the point of doing so. And here again, a 'fictionalised' version of the Brontë childhood takes on a generalised truth despite its inaccuracy in relation to dates and figures. Jane Eyre's childish cry: 'Unjust!–unjust!' (*JE*, 15) has voiced the anguish of generations of those who are, or have been, children, and thus, almost independently of specific data, invokes an 'archetypal' pattern based on the inevitable conflict between youth and age. In this 'mythical' system, it is easy for readers to slide from fiction to biography – from Jane Eyre to Charlotte Brontë, from Mr Brocklehurst to Carus Wilson, and even to Patrick Brontë.

This kind of mythologising, which confuses authors with their fictions and fictions with a personal source, seems very much out of step with the sophisticated literary theories which have declared 'the death of the author'. In fact, however, such theories give full weight to the part played by 'myths' in the way we read fiction. They do not deny the historical existence of the writer, but challenge the idea that the writer is the text's 'author' in the same sense that God is called the 'author of our being' – its 'only begetter'. In this new climate of literary criticism, the literary text which was once thought of as the fixed 'message' of the author to the reader is instead thought of as being recreated at each new reading as each reader brings to it their peculiar mix of previous knowledge, experience and desire. It is, moreover, not only individual readers who 'receive' the text differently according to 'reception theory'. Readers grouped by culture or historical period are likely to share responses, and a study of such shared readings forms part of 'cultural studies'. While such theories deny the author as absolute origin of the text, therefore, they recognise that personalised knowledge of the 'author' has been a dominant need in readers during the lifetime of the Brontë texts. Readers' construction of the Brontës *as authors* has thus been an important part of the Brontë myth.

'We are three sisters'

The autobiographical appearance of some of the Brontë novels – *Jane Eyre* and *Agnes Grey* in particular – is one reason why readers move easily between the Brontës' works and their lives. Charlotte made her heroines like herself – 'poor, obscure, plain, and little', so that Thackeray was not the only Victorian who spoke of meeting 'Jane Eyre' rather than 'Charlotte Brontë'.[2] Early readers were also confused by the pseudonymous publication, in 1847, of the first three Brontë novels, *Agnes Grey*, *Wuthering Heights* and *Jane Eyre*, which released a storm of speculation about the writers' identities. The discomfort of these readers can be tracked through reviews in the decades after publication, where an initial hostility to what appeared to be uncouth and uncivilized writings gave way to much more forgiving – not to say condescending – judgements when the writers were known to be three young daughters of a curate.[3]

Many early readers assumed that the novels had been written by one, or two, writers, not three, and Thomas Newby, the publisher of Emily's and Anne's less successful novels, encouraged this mistake by promoting *Wuthering Heights*, *Agnes Grey* and *The Tenant of Wildfell Hall* as by the same writer as *Jane Eyre*. Reviewers repeated this confusion, which has persisted ever since. In 1862 the entry for 'Charlotte Brontë' in Samuel Maundee's *Biographical Treasury* attributed *Wuthering Heights* to Anne and *Agnes Grey* to Emily.[4] In March, 1996, the *Yorkshire Post* announced the filming of *The Tenant of Wildfell Hall* for BBC television under a large photograph of Juliette Binoche and Ralph Fiennes as Catherine and Heathcliff. In October, 1997, the *New York Times* carried a review article on this adaptation of *The Tenant* which elaborated on public uncertainty about the sisters' identities. Stephen Henderson explains how Anne lived 'in the shadow of her elder sisters' and Tara Fitzgerald, who played the part of Helen Huntingdon, confirms that 'people in England know there are three Brontë sisters... but wouldn't be able to tell you the third one's name or what she'd written'. The article has an inset portrait labelled 'Anne Brontë' – but the portrait is of Charlotte.

The sisters originally agreed to conceal their identities because Emily refused public recognition, but the resulting confusion was repugnant to Charlotte, who soon revealed the truth – 'we are three Sisters'.[5] After the deaths of Emily and Anne in 1848 and 1849, Charlotte set herself to vindicate her sisters in the face of the hostile criticism which their writings had received. Her 'Biographical Notice', attached to the second edition of *Wuthering Heights* and *Agnes Grey* in 1850, was the first source of information about Emily and Anne; from this point onwards, readers were able to construct separate images of the three sisters. Charlotte added an 'Editor's Preface to the new edition of *Wuthering Heights*' in an effort to exculpate Emily from the charge of writing an immoral and violent book, and the phrases and images from this Preface have coloured readers' responses ever since. Charlotte stressed her sister's unworldly life, remote habitation and reclusive habits, setting in place the essential elements for the myth of Emily, the isolated genius. She also set out to explain, if not to vindicate, her sister Anne's 'mistaken' attempt to write realistically about 'the terrible effects of talents misused and faculties abused'. Charlotte presented Anne as 'sensitive, reserved, and dejected' in nature (*WH*, 364–5), and thus unsuited to the uncompromising social criticism which she attempted in her novels. Charlotte's well-intentioned eulogy began the myth of a diffident and unassertive third sister which prompted the ironic sub-title, The Other One, to a modern book on Anne.[6]

By 1850, when Charlotte offered her apologia for her sisters, she herself had begun to be recognised and even entertained by literary society.[7] Elizabeth Gaskell, who was to become Charlotte's first biographer in 1857, was enthralled by what appeared to her the 'novelistic' extremities of Charlotte's life, but her sympathy for Charlotte led to a persistent bias in later accounts of the family. In an effort to mitigate what reviewers had felt to be 'unladylike' elements in Charlotte's writing, Gaskell stressed Charlotte's dutiful attention to her role as elder sister and daughter, and in order to intensify this she represented Patrick as cold and domineering and Branwell as weaker and more dependent than he was. Charlotte's deferral to her father's unreasonable wishes, and her stoicism in living with a debauched and abandoned brother take their place with her pitiful experience of witnessing the early deaths not only of her mother and two elder sisters, but of all three of her remaining siblings within a year. The deaths of Branwell, Emily and Anne have themselves become part of Brontë mythology, and it is unlikely that any amount of historical reasoning will remove the cherished image of Emily dying on the sofa, refusing to take to her bed.

A literary shrine

During Charlotte's lifetime, visitors were already coming to Haworth. They came to feel the famed remoteness of the place, perhaps to catch a glimpse of Charlotte herself, or, after her death, of her father, or the house where he still lived. Even before Patrick's death in 1861, there were visitors from America who had read the cheap editions of the Brontë novels produced there in the days before international copyright agreements. Charles Hale, an American visiting the parsonage in the gap between Patrick's death and the entry of the new incumbent, carried away with him a parcel of glass from Charlotte's window, together with a quantity of moulded timber from her room, which he intended to use to frame the Brontë photographs which were already being sold by enterprising villagers. When informed that a Keighley–Haworth railway was planned, his reaction was that 'future worshippers will find their pilgrimage easier'. By 1868, W. H. Cooke could speak of places in Haworth 'made sacred through the habitual presence of these gifted beings'. Already the visitors' book in Haworth Church contained names 'from all quarters of the globe' and by the 1890s the notion of Haworth as a 'literary shrine' was well established.[8]

As well as visitors from a distance, there were fiercely local admirers who in 1893 formed themselves into the Brontë Society. The objects of the society were defined as 'to acquire literary, artistic and family memorials of the

Brontës' and 'to place the same at Haworth...for public examination'.[9] In 1928, the society was able to purchase the parsonage, which from that time became both museum and archive, repository of Brontë-related objects, manuscripts and books collected and authenticated by the society. This has been invaluable work; the society's stated emphasis on material relics has, however, had its own effect on the Brontë myth.

During two sunny days in August 1999, I stood outside the Parsonage Museum and asked the visitors why they had come there, and what they knew about the Brontës. Many of the visitors I spoke to were no longer 'worshippers at a shrine' but saw themselves as 'getting a sense of history'. Local visitors come because the Brontës 'represent Yorkshire to the outside world'. Americans come because 'this is our ancestry'. Oddly, the Brontë family is experienced as both unique and representative. Their novels are 'unusual' but also 'depict the life of the times'. The Brontë Society has played its part in fostering the focus on local history: its 'objects' give equal weight to the gathering of information on 'the Novels and the districts in which the Brontës resided'.[10] The society's heated debates concern the extension of buildings and the provenance of photographs; its annual competitive scholarship is given for research excluding literary criticism. Its journal, *Brontë Studies* (formerly *Brontë Society Transactions*) does carry literary articles but articles on biography and local history provoke livelier discussion. Its *Gazette* also reports visits to places with Brontë connections, whether historical, such as the Brontë birthplace or the home of one of Charlotte's friends, or fictional, such as North Lees Hall or Wycoller Hall, thought to have been models for Thornfield and Ferndean in *Jane Eyre*. This 'local history' aspect of the society contributes its own momentum to the general tendency to confuse fact and fiction, to slip between lives and works, so that a visitor at the parsonage was overheard to ask 'which sister was it married Heathcliff?'

The Brontë Society now has over 3,000 members, nearly a third of whom are from outside Great Britain, and the Parsonage Museum has 100,000 visitors a year. Present-day visitors still come to Haworth to recapture the atmosphere associated with the Brontës' home, despite the fact that the Brontës' bleak churchyard is now full of tall trees, a new church has been built over the one where the Brontës are buried, new wings have been attached to the parsonage, and signposts in Japanese stand at 'remote' spots on the moors. Haworth, in responding to this flood of visitors, has made itself prettier and more comfortable than the town the Brontës knew. Much of the tourist development which bears the Brontë names (the Branwell Tea Room, the Brontë Balti, Jane Hair, the Land of Gondal gift shop, Tabby's kitchenware, the Three Sisters Hotel, the Villette Coffee House) has no connection with the Brontës' writing and many visitors to Haworth see themselves as visiting primarily a *place* – 'part of our heritage'.

There are still Brontë enthusiasts, though they are outnumbered by casual visitors. Of the hundred people I spoke to in 1999, a quarter could be described as 'enthusiasts'. Three-quarters, however, had read at least one of the Brontë novels and half had read more than one. The range of different kinds of reader was both surprising and moving, and confirms the picture which Stevie Davies gives in her novel, *Four Dreamers and Emily*, where the Brontë enthusiasts include a rather desperate academic, an elderly widower with a romantic fondness for the landscape, a middle-aged woman with a brisk appreciation of 'passion' and a sad overweight waitress who identifies with Jane Eyre.[11] The enthusiasts I spoke to came to the parsonage because they wanted to feel the impact of the place which produced the writers and the writing – 'to have a place where it's all originated from is important'; they were intrigued by the family of writers – 'so much talent concentrated in one place'; and they were drawn by memories of the stories, of *Jane Eyre* and *Wuthering Heights* in particular. The 'Brontë myth' as filtered through these visitors seemed to collect around the landscape, the family of writers, and the stories about love, and I have arranged the rest of this chapter to take account of these perceptions.

'A Moorland village'

The Brontë Parsonage occupies a peculiar position in relation to the village of Haworth. When the Brontës lived there, the back of the house faced directly onto the moors, and this was the direction of most of their walks. If, however, they walked out of the front door and down the lane, a few yards would bring them to the main village 'square' and the head of the main street. The parsonage is thus pivotal between nature and culture, solitude and populousness, and the fact that we associate the sisters primarily with the moors is the result of deliberate or unconscious choices, on our part and theirs.

To be sure, early visitors to Haworth stressed the difficulty of arriving there. Many of them completed the journey, from Keighley or Bradford, on foot, and Elizabeth Gaskell, who arrived by horse-drawn vehicle, is minute in her description of the tediousness of the journey.[12] 'Remoteness' in this sense, however, is not the same as 'rusticity'. Visitors expecting a quaint or pastoral environment were, in the nineteenth century, surprised to find Haworth a flourishing town, with a population rapidly increasing from some 4,500 at the time of the Brontës' arrival to over 6,000 by the 1860s. Haworth was an important centre of the worsted trade; apart from a thousand hand-looms in the village itself, there were also thirteen textile mills (powered first by water and then by steam) at the time of the Brontës' arrival. The famed remoteness of the situation, moreover, did not cut the Brontës off from political and intellectual activities. Even Elizabeth Gaskell noted that the children were voracious readers of novels and poetry, newspapers and journals; Juliet Barker has now revealed the extent of Patrick Brontë's practical involvement in local politics and reform movements, resulting in frequent letters to the papers, and his unresting efforts to improve the water supply and sanitation of Haworth.[13]

Charlotte Brontë's 1849 novel, *Shirley*, did attempt to deal with these social movements, but her 1850 'Biographical Notice' on Anne and Emily turned the public eye away and up towards the moors. To the casual eye, she writes, 'the wild moors of the north of England can have no interest', but her defensiveness turns quickly to a kind of Romantic exclusiveness: 'it is only higher up, deep in among the ridges of the moors, that Imagination can find rest for the sole of her foot, and even if she finds it there, she must be a solitude-loving raven – no gentle dove' (*WH*, 371). In Gaskell's *Life*, too, Haworth is Janus-faced. The dreary description of the approach to Haworth is offset by the romantic sketch of the parsonage in which the churchyard becomes more picturesque, and the moors become higher and more looming. Ann Dinsdale's book, *Old Haworth*, encapsulates this duality.[14] The front cover shows industrial cottages and a mill with chimney, the church and parsonage figuring only on the distant sky-line. The back cover foregrounds the parsonage at dusk amid its gravestones and lit by a half-shrouded moon. This engraving was one of those prepared by E. M. Wimperis for the first illustrated edition of *The Life and Works of Charlotte Brontë and Her Sisters*, published in 1872–3, which drew all its illustrations from 'Brontë country'. The plate labelled 'Wuthering Heights' shows a solitary house high up on the moors which is recognisable as 'Top Withens', the now ruined farmhouse for ever associated with the novel, despite its bearing no resemblance to the house described in it.

It is worth remembering, then, that 'Haworth' did not have to mean 'the moors'. Both the Brontës and later visitors turned their backs on 'commonplace' Haworth somewhat wilfully, hoping to be taken for ravens rather than doves. Pre-eminent among the 'ravens' was Emily Brontë, whose poems show how, as Charlotte puts it, she could 'make an Eden' from 'a sullen hollow in a livid hill-side' (*WH*, 372). In *Wuthering Heights*, Catherine Earnshaw wakes 'sobbing for joy' after dreaming that angels had thrown her out of heaven into 'the middle of the heath on the top of Wuthering Heights' (*WH*, 80). All three sisters show vivid appreciation of wild landscape and the movement of the wind. Anne's response in 'My soul is awakened, my spirit is soaring' is near to pure enjoyment, while for Charlotte, locked away at school, the wind becomes a symbol of her frustration: 'a thousand wishes rose at its call which must die with me for they will never be fulfilled'.[15] In Emily's more famous poem the opposition of freedom to imprisonment becomes the condition of life itself:

> High waving heather 'neath stormy blasts bending
> Midnight and moonlight and bright shining stars
> Darkness and glory rejoicingly blending
> Earth rising to heaven and heaven descending
> Man's spirit away from its drear dungeon sending
> Bursting the fetters and breaking the bars.
>
> (*EBP*, 34)

Charlotte tells how Emily 'found in the bleak solitude many and dear delights; and not the least and best loved was – liberty' (*WH*, 372).

The Brontës, of course, did not invent this association of wild landscape with freedom. One of their favourite poets, Byron, wrote in the guise of Childe Harold, a man who loved to be alone and 'in Man's dwellings... Droop'd as a wild-born falcon with clipt wing'.[16] Sympathetic contemporary readers naturally placed the Brontë sisters in this Romantic tradition. Matthew Arnold's elegy, 'Haworth Churchyard',[17] ends with an 'Epilogue' in which the Brontës find resurrection through the physical life of the moors:

> Unquiet souls!
> – In the dark fermentation of earth,
> In the never idle workshop of nature,
> In the eternal movement,
> Ye shall find yourselves again.
>
> (lines 131–5)

Present-day visitors to Haworth also like to feel that we are rejecting the 'commonplace' aspects of social life to appreciate the stormy beauties of nature. Like Catherine and Heathcliff, we want to recapture the freedom of childhood which we associate with the moors. As a grown-up, Catherine Earnshaw laments, 'I wish I were a girl again, half savage and hardy, and free' (*WH*, 126), and Simone de Beauvoir argues that the romantic escape to nature has an especial appeal to girls. A girl may be hemmed in by the duties of domesticity, but 'seated on the hilltop, she is mistress of all the world's riches'.[18] Certainly most of the 'enthusiasts' I spoke to in Haworth were women, and almost half of these had read *Wuthering Heights* as girls. In Jean Barker's poem, 'Emily', the speaker seeks Emily's moors where 'her spirit walks, touches mine, and flies'.[19]

Despite their shared responses to nature, however, the Brontë sisters made very different uses of it in their mature writings. The wild pictures in Bewick's *British Birds* are an inspiration for Jane Eyre's painting, but she is glad to be looking at the book in the window seat, shut out from the wet weather. While Catherine Earnshaw in her last illness begs Nelly to open the window so that she can lean out into the storm, Jane Eyre looks longingly in at the window of Moor House, knowing that survival exists inside. Between Emily and Anne there is also a difference. Wuthering Heights, where 'one may guess the power of the north wind, blowing over the edge, by the excessive slant of a few, stunted firs' (*WH*, 2), is superficially similar to Wildfell Hall, 'only shielded from the war of wind and weather by a group of Scotch firs, themselves half-blighted with storms' (*TWH*, 23). The attitudes of their inhabitants, however, differ strikingly. For Helen Huntingdon, Wildfell Hall is an enforced retreat in which solitude and discomfort are the price she pays for independence. For Catherine and Heathcliff, however, Wuthering Heights means freedom and delight, and it is this image which has persisted as a prominent feature of the Brontë myth.

On the table as I write are three books and two videos about 'the Brontës'; all their covers show pictures of the moors, and four of them show Top Withens. Their promise is that 'the landscape which Emily knew is still there'.[20] Intellectually we may know that Top Withens is not Wuthering Heights, but we trek up there because it provides a focus for what would otherwise be desire without an object. Early visitors rejoiced in snowy weather when 'the wind blew . . . fiercely, coldly, but right gloriously' or 'a real northern snowstorm had been doing the honours of the moors'.[21] The first film version of *Wuthering Heights* was shot on location in Haworth in 1920,[22] despite the enormous difficulties of transporting the heavy cameras onto the moors, because the landscape and the weather were felt to be such intrinsic features of the story. The famous William Wyler film of 1939 opens with Mr Lockwood fighting his way to Wuthering Heights through an impressively orchestrated snow storm,[23] while the 1991 Peter Kosminsky film exploits its gothic staging to intensify the terrors of lightning and wind.[24]

Once again, moreover, the extreme example, *Wuthering Heights*, is allowed to impinge on the other novels. Robert Stevenson's film of *Jane Eyre* (1944)[25] is distinguished by its eery music deriving from the moorland wind, a motif which haunted its composer, Bernard Herrmann, until he was able to use it in an opera based on *Wuthering Heights*.[26] Delbert Mann's 1970 film of *Jane Eyre* ends with the camera drawing away from Ferndean to show the sheltered garden surrounded by a huge moor.[27] In such ways, the focus of films and plays for *all* the Brontë texts comes to rest on the iconography properly related to *Wuthering Heights*. Programmes for stage versions of

Jane Eyre in England and Japan feature Top Withens on the cover, like a 'sign' that this is a play about romantic isolation.[28]

Chris Baldick, in his book on *Frankenstein*, argues that the process by which stories become 'modern myths' involves reducing them 'to the simplest memorable patterns'.[29] Such simplicity, however, lays itself open to laughter as well as adulation. Monty Python's Flying Circus semaphore version of *Wuthering Heights* (1989) offers a minimalist representation of Catherine and Heathcliff on separate hill-tops, signalling their desire with semaphore flags. Noreen Kershaw's stage entertainment, *Withering Looks: A Slice of Life with the Brontë Sisters* (1988), finds its comic inspiration in the dual motivation which we have seen in present-day visitors to Haworth: a desire to recapture historical authenticity coexisting uneasily with a wish to leave 'society' behind. *Withering Looks* gives us a ramshackle stage parsonage, doubling as Wuthering Heights, which shelters an elaborately costumed Brontë/Earnshaw family who venture out to be blasted by stage winds and lightning, re-entering with dishevelled wigs and bonnets while recounting the deep and tragic events which are mostly happening off-stage.

The twentieth century has not, however, simply laughed off the Romantic excesses of the Brontë myth. For Lord David Cecil, *Wuthering Heights* is a 'myth' in the most sublime sense, in which Heathcliff 'is a manifestation of natural forces' in a system where characters are governed by 'the principle of storm' or 'the principle of calm'.[30] Throughout the century, serious poets have continued to work out the complex impact of the myth of the Brontë landscape. Sylvia Plath's poem, 'Wuthering Heights', registers mainly the inhumanity of the landscape and the ruin of (the unnamed) Top Withens. For her the myth is growing thin:

> Of people the air only
> Remembers a few syllables.
> It rehearses them moaningly:
> Black stone, black stone.[31]

The choice of words recalls Charlotte's 'Preface', in which she describes her sister Emily as 'a statuary' (sculptor) who 'found a granite block on a solitary moor: gazing thereon, he saw how from the crag might be elicited a head, savage, swart, sinister' (*WH*, 370). The association of Heathcliff with the 'swart' (black) rock derives directly from *Wuthering Heights*, where Catherine compares her love for Heathcliff to 'the eternal rocks' and his character to 'a wilderness of furze and whinstone' (*WH*, 82, 102). In *Changing Heaven*, the Canadian novelist Jane Urquhart questions Heathcliff's fascination as a lover who is part of the landscape. Just as Brontës and

Brontë enthusiasts chose to construct 'Haworth' as a Romantic wilderness, so Urquhart shows Emily's ghost claiming that she 'made' the landscape of *Wuthering Heights*: 'I did, I did! I invented, I built it all!...The rocks were particularly difficult, and that is what Mr Capital H was made out of – different shapes of black stone'.[32] In contrast, Urquhart's modern heroine comes to love a 'moor-edger', a man whose skill keeps at bay the charming dangers of the moor.

'Growing potatoes in a cellar': the family of writers

One of the reasons why the Brontë sisters were so attached to Haworth and 'home' was that while they were there together they could devote themselves to their shared fantasy worlds. While Elizabeth Gaskell was preparing her *Life of Charlotte Brontë*, she was shown the 'little books' – tiny hand-sewn volumes – which the children had written, and she included transcriptions from some of them in her biography,[33] but the script was so small that for most of the nineteenth century they were regarded as curiosities rather than literary productions, and were widely dispersed as keepsakes and mementoes.

Fannie Ratchford was the first scholar to transcribe the little books which have subsequently been edited and analysed by Christine Alexander, and the world she uncovered was a revelation.[34] The Brontë children had worked in pairs – Charlotte and Branwell, Emily and Anne – to develop the worlds of Angria and Gondal. One surprising feature is that these are not 'fairy-tale' or 'never-never' lands, but countries with a recognisable geography in West Africa and the North Pacific. The children had read of explorations in the journals their father encouraged them to discuss, and drew maps, wrote travel journals, newspaper accounts of settlements; eventually the 'little books' included examples of just about every printed *genre* of writing, from parliamentary debates to gossip columns and from personal diaries to epic poems.

Many of the visitors to the parsonage I spoke to were still intrigued by 'the phenomenon of the family of authors' which created a special kind of curiosity – 'they *all* wrote: if it had only been one it would have been different'. Fascination with the family of writers begins young, and several modern writers for children have used the Brontë family to explore the role of fantasy in relation to questions of identity and morality.[35] The 'little' books' themselves, however, have entered the Brontë myth only in the vaguest way. Although the junior branch of the Brontë Society calls itself 'the Angrians', their activities scarcely relate to the Brontë prototypes. Pauline Clarke's story,

The Twelve and the Genii (1962) is one of the few successful attempts to convey to modern children the excitement of 'bringing to life' creatures of the imagination.[36] One of the reasons for this may be that most of the Brontë 'juvenilia' has subject matter which is not at all childish. The precocious writers showed a thorough acquaintance not only with political and economic debates, but with affairs of the heart, including scandalous liaisons and tales of betrayal, exile and illegitimacy. For nineteenth-century readers, moreover, these qualities were startlingly evident in the published works, and early reviewers blamed the 'remote' location of Haworth and the sisters' lack of healthy social contacts, which forced them together and promoted a hothouse atmosphere. One of Charlotte's friends described her and her sisters as 'growing potatoes in a cellar' – morbidly aetiolated in their precocious growth.[37]

The link between secluded environment and artistic intensity was clear enough to Victorian visitors to Haworth,[38] but Virginia Woolf suggests the special fascination of a closed *feminine* group, so that we 'tremble slightly as we approach the curtain and catch glimpses of women behind it and even hear ripples of laughter and snatches of conversation'.[39] She compares the Brontë lives 'behind the curtain' with that of women in a harem, and while time has made the image merely 'romantic' for modern visitors, commentators in the nineteenth century were often reproving and in the early twentieth century often prurient. Lady Eastlake's 1848 review of *Jane Eyre* finds in the novel a 'pervading tone of ungodly discontent' (*CH*, 109). As for *Wuthering Heights*, Eastlake saw Catherine and Heathcliff as 'the Jane and Rochester animals in their native state', and as such, 'too odiously and abominably pagan to be palatable even to the most vitiated class of English readers' (*CH*, 111). An anonymous reviewer in the same year objected to all the male characters in *The Tenant of Wildfell Hall* as 'coarse, brutal, and contemptibly weak, at once disgusting and ridiculous' (*CH*, 265).

In the following decades it was *Jane Eyre* which continued to catch public attention, the vehement reviews only an alarmed indication of the extent of its popularity. Margaret Oliphant, in 1867, blames *Jane Eyre* for a new fashion in women's novels; heroines now, she says, 'give and receive burning kisses and frantic embraces, and live in a voluptuous dream, either waiting for or brooding over the inevitable lover' (*CH*, 391). The corollary of this disapproval is the secret delight of women readers and writers such as Dinah Craik, Julia Kavanagh, Rhoda Broughton and Mary Elizabeth Braddon, who felt liberated by *Jane Eyre* to speak of desires hitherto unspeakable. And whether with approval or reproof, Charlotte was attributed with all the feelings of Jane Eyre.

By 1912, the feminist writer May Sinclair was moved to defend Charlotte against Oliphant's 'horrible portrait' of Charlotte as 'a plain-faced, lachrymose, middle-aged spinster, dying, visibly, to be married, obsessed for ever with the idea, for ever whining over the frustration of her sex' (21). Sinclair's *The Three Brontës* (1912) presents the Brontë sisters as articulate heroines, escaping the prevalent repression of Victorian women by a combination of fortunate upbringing and heroic clearsightedness. In an odd contrast, her novel, *The Three Sisters* (1914), reads like a demonstration of Freud's comments on the difficulty, for women, of negotiating the Oedipus complex.[40] Mary achieves 'normal' femininity; the independent Gwendolen shows us a 'masculinity complex'; the fragile Alice resorts to defensive hysteria. All are condemned to less than full humanity by their repressive father. Together, Sinclair's two books demonstrate the contradictory need, in early twentieth-century feminists, on the one hand for rational analysis of women's psychological options, and, on the other, for feminist heroines who would rise triumphant above them.

The 'heroism' was all the more necessary because the new discipline of psychoanalysis reinforced the Victorian 'common-sense' view that women only wrote because they lacked 'normal' satisfactions. Thus Rosamond Langbridge's *Psychological Study* of Charlotte Brontë (1929) repeats all the sensational stories about Patrick Brontë's misogyny in order to argue that 'every agony she endured may be traced back directly to...her revered Papa' and that 'the three Brontës longed, in the sultry little closets of their corseted Victorian hearts for lovers, passionate, vehement, dark and brooding as their own Yorkshire moors'.[41] The idea of writing as sublimation was eagerly adopted by Emilie and Georges Romieu in their 1931 'biography' of the Brontë sisters:

> Their arms embrace only the void, and no form emerges for them to press frenziedly to their ripening breasts...
> Blessed misery!
> Deep within life will burn with an unexampled heat – unappeased. The white page is the needful outlet; thereupon in words of flame they will write an immortal utterance![42]

Although all the sisters were linked in this kind of analysis, Charlotte became the main focus for the idea of sexual frustration, while Emily was singled out as an example of sublimation.

Emily, who had been condemned, ignored or misunderstood by her immediate readers, came into prominence after 1883, when Mary Robinson published the first biography of Emily. If Charlotte had shown Emily as rustic recluse, Robinson showed her as a modern Joan of Arc, chaste, courageous and combative, whose writing has 'the purity of polished steel'.[43] Swinburne endorses Robinson, likening Emily's work to 'the splendour of lightning or the roll of a gathered wave' (*CH*, 443). His eulogy appropriates Emily Brontë for the aesthetic movement, where vividness in the representation of the moment as it passes is more important than moral earnestness. At the turn of the century, when the slogan 'votes for women and chastity for men' carried the coded warning of sexual disease, Emily's sexual 'purity' became heroic self-denial. When Charlotte Brontë said of Emily: 'her nature stood alone', she meant that she was unique. For Charlotte Mew in 1904 the statement becomes an 'awful fact – the tragedy of her life'.[44]

By the 1930s, it was easy for Emilie and Georges Romieu to present Emily as the lonely genius who courts the storm, 'bareheaded, her brow affronting the bite of the wind and the gash of the hail'. Strained sublimity topples into farce: 'when the farm people glimpse the weird form in the distance, they rush in and lock their doors and fold trembling hands in prayer' (*Brontë Sisters*, 11). It was this kind of Romantic excess which prompted Stella Gibbons to write *Cold Comfort Farm* (1932), whose heroine, Flora Poste, 'sorts out' the tragic cousins on a Wuthering Heights-like farm.[45] Virginia Woolf, in 1904, could already imagine wanting 'to exorcise the three famous ghosts',[46] and for Rachel Ferguson, in *The Brontës Went to Woolworth's* (1931), the Brontë sisters represented a haunting but alarming reminder of what life was like without £500 a year and a room of one's own.[47] Both Gibbons and Ferguson earned their livings as journalists, and one wonders whether Ferguson, who wrote for *Punch*, had a hand in the full-page doggerel cartoon, 'Christmas dinner at Haworth Parsonage', which appeared in that journal on Christmas Day, 1935. Upset by the absence of Branwell, Mr Brontë leaves the room and his dinner, whereupon the sisters respond in counterpoint:

ANNE: He's gone.
EMILY: Thank God!
CHARLOTTE: His dinner barely tasted.
EMILY: Just like our lives – hard, underdone and wasted.

Branwell Brontë only came to public attention with Gaskell's 1857 *Life of Charlotte Brontë*, which presented him as the cross born by the patient sisters, as the excuse for their otherwise unforgivable knowledge of base manhood and as the probable model for Heathcliff and for Arthur Huntingdon. Around Haworth, however, as early visitors discovered, Branwell's reputation was quite different. There was no lack of local people to attest to his brilliance in conversation and to his kindness.[48] Juliet Barker's *The Brontës*

Figure 7 'Christmas Dinner at Haworth Parsonage', *Punch*, 25 December 1935, 708.

more recently has shown that at the very time when Branwell was supposed to have abandoned himself to an unmanly orgy of grief over his unattainable Lydia, he was writing poems disciplined enough to be published, albeit in the local press.[49]

From the 1860s, moreover, supporters made a more audacious claim for Branwell: namely, that he had either written, or had a hand in writing, *Wuthering Heights*. This theory originated with William Deardon, who in 1867 claimed that Branwell, in 1842, had read him some sections of *Wuthering Heights*. It was revived in 1923 by Alice Law's biography of Branwell, which found it inconceivable that 'a young girl like Emily Brontë' could have written 'a book so marvellous in its strength'. Law's opinion of Emily's character was a common one during the interwar period. The diary papers, Law argues, show Emily to be 'one of the helpers of the world, a lifter of other people's burdens'.[50] Such a person might have laboured selflessly to give her brother's brilliant fragments a publishable form. The myth of Emily as selflessly devoting herself to Branwell is extravagantly expressed in J. A. Mackereth's long poem, *Storm-Wrack* (1927), in which 'She with frail enfolding arm / Shields that torn Brother-soul from harm'.[51] The Branwell ferment persisted for most of the interwar period, although the myth of devotion began to be challenged by that of sibling rivalry. The refreshing Flora Poste knows exactly what to think when she hears of a

> 'young fellow who wrote books, and then his sisters pretended *they* wrote them, and then they all died of consumption, poor young mommets'.
> 'Ha! A life of Branwell Brontë', thought Flora. 'I might have known it. There has been increasing discontent among the male intellectuals for some time at the thought that a woman wrote *Wuthering Heights*.'
> (Gibbons, *Cold Comfort Farm*, 75–6)

The flood of writing on the relationship between Branwell and Emily included plays by Clemence Dane (*Wild Decembers*, 1932) and Dan Totheroh (*Moor Born*, 1934) and E. T. Cook's novel, *They Lived* (1935), while Kathryn MacFarlane's 'biography', *Divide the Desolation* (1936), intensifies the myth of Emily's 'adoration' of her 'meteoric brother' (jacket blurb).[52] In Robert Buckner's film, *Devotion* (1946),[53] the sisters are thoroughly sanctified by their devotion to Branwell and to one another. Juliet Barker, in her 1994 biography, contests the myth rather sharply:

> all the evidence points to the fact that [Emily] was so absorbed in herself and her literary creations that she had little time for the genuine suffering of her family. Her attitude at [times] seems to have been brusque to the point of heartlessness.[54]

Whether we side with Branwell or with Emily, it seems that public intrigue with 'the family of writers' is insatiable. Recently Charlotte has appeared in the role of villain. In *The Crimes of Charlotte Brontë* (1999), James Tully sets out evidence to prove that Charlotte, together with her husband Arthur

Bell Nicholls, plotted to poison the other members of her family.[55] The novel
is no more than a clever piece of crime writing, but it is the very stuff that
myths are made of, and was reported in the press worldwide. For one of the
visitors I spoke to in 1999, it proved that 'everything we've been told about
the Brontë history is wrong'.

Meanwhile, the family of writers receives its due in academic circles.
Branwell's reputation is on its way to being restored not only by Juliet
Barker's biography but also by Victor Neufeldt's meticulous edition of his
writing. Feminists have drawn new attention not only to Charlotte but to
Anne, who is for the first time being seen as a sharp-eyed, tough-minded
critic of society. Feminists have been less easily able to appropriate Emily,
but by compensation *Wuthering Heights* has become the playground of every
literary theory from aestheticism to deconstruction.

'The world's greatest love stories'

Whatever the critical permutations, the novels are primarily perceived as love
stories. Visitors to the parsonage still think of it as a place of 'dark passion'
to which, as one of them told me, 'repression is the key; they disinhibited
themselves through the books'. While Victorian readers, however, especially
women, found the mere expression of emotion liberating, later women find
the Brontë models of love problematic. Flora Poste, in *Cold Comfort Farm*,
and the Carne sisters, in *The Brontës Went to Woolworth's*, are alarmed at
the prospect of being dragged back to a time when women lived in a steamy
confinement ruled by hopeless desire. More recently, feminists have offered
a more thorough *critique* of marriage as a goal and of the romance hero in
particular. In one recent rewriting of *Jane Eyre*, Jane discovers that she is to
be the latest in a whole series of wives each of whom has been locked up in
the attic and called mad.[56]

The 1996 televised version of *The Tenant of Wildfell Hall* was rated by the
Daily Mail as a contribution to the 'battle of the bodice-rippers' (6 December
1996). It is, however, *Jane Eyre* and *Wuthering Heights* which are generally
thought of as among 'the world's greatest love stories'. Although they tend to
be bracketed together, the two novels actually derive from different models of
'romantic love'. *Jane Eyre* at its simplest is a version of an ancient courtship-
and-marriage plot in which the lovers overcome obstacles and find true love
in the end. This pattern in turn matches Freud's Oedipus complex: Jane
yearns for the love of her 'master' Mr Rochester – a man who combines the
protective status of father with the thrill of sexual partnership – and earns
it by proving her own 'adult' status, taking her place as 'lady of the house'
instead of 'bad' older women like Aunt Reed and Bertha Mason. These

Figure 8 'Come to me – come to me entirely now': Jane and Rochester in the garden. Fritz Eichenberg, illustration to *Jane Eyre* (New York: Random House, 1943), facing p. 190.

reductive versions of *Jane Eyre*, however, fail to emphasise Jane's outspoken daring, which prompts her to 'talk back' to her aunt, and to claim equality with her older, richer lover. It is these qualities which keep *Jane Eyre* on the list of most-loved novels, and which, perhaps, explain its 'mythic' quality. For while some readers are thrilled by Jane's fiery independence, others find it threatening or offensive. The novel thus becomes a battleground, where lines of gender-tolerance are tested.

Critics and adaptors of novels, whether consciously or unconsciously, inevitably select and emphasise in accordance with ideological agendas.

Different Victorian stage versions of *Jane Eyre*, for instance, made some striking alterations to its plot which completely change our 'reading' of the story. Some purified 'Lord Rowland' Rochester, in his role as protector of widows and orphans, by making the grotesque madwoman the wife of his dead brother and the object of his charity. In other versions, however, Rochester embodied the potential sexual threat exposed by the debate over the Contagious Diseases Acts.[57] Modern dramatic reproductions can also be overtly polemical. In Charlotte Brontë's novel, it is important that Rochester loves Jane in spite of her being 'little, plain and insignificant'; she is explicitly contrasted with the heartless beauty, Blanche Ingram. A 1990s television sketch, however, showed an extremely ugly Jane who makes sure that Rochester stays blind by shooting the doctor who is about to restore his sight. This version, which produced screams of laughter from the studio audience, refuses the novel's validation of Jane's inner qualities, and re-locates the story within the dominant myth that beauty is all.[58]

Reproductions can also be subtly manipulative. Franco Zefirelli's 1996 film of *Jane Eyre*, for instance, heightens the rebelliousness of the young Jane at Lowood, but ends with Jane and Rochester frozen in the form of a conventional engraving such as might illustrate any Victorian romance.[59] On the other hand, versions of the myth which seem very conventional may not be so. The formula romances of the Mills and Boon type follow the *Jane Eyre* plot quite closely: young, unprotected heroine, older man with a dark secret, final bliss. After years of feminist debate about the effects of these novels on their readers, however, a consensus seems to be emerging that the point of the narrative for women readers is not the final marriage, with its loss of independence for the heroine, but the transformation of the hero into a softer, more feminised companion.[60]

As soon as *Wuthering Heights* began to be taken seriously, attempts were made to make it conform to the same kind of love-and-marriage model as *Jane Eyre*. It is hardly possible to overestimate the importance in the 'mythification' of *Wuthering Heights* of William Wyler's 1939 film version of the novel. Many features which have come to be accepted as part of the Brontë myth actually derive from this film, in which Laurence Olivier played Heathcliff. The characters of Catherine and Heathcliff are changed to emphasise Catherine's social climbing and Heathcliff's failure to rise to her ambition. Their childish 'scampering on the moors' is translated into an adult tryst. The plot is truncated to end with Catherine's death and the ghostly reunification of the lovers. Perhaps most significant of all is the prominence given to Penistone Crag, the place where the lovers meet as children, as adults, and finally, as ghosts. The film is full of dramatic and moving moments; its

Figure 9 Laurence Olivier and Merle Oberon as Catherine and Heathcliff on the hilltop, from the 1939 film *Wuthering Heights*, directed by William Wyler.

effect on what we might call the *Wuthering Heights* myth, however, has been to obscure the unique fascination of the novel.

I have argued that we can read *Jane Eyre* as showing – with some variations – what Freud saw as the 'normal' feminine path through the Oedipus complex, and most reproductions of *Wuthering Heights* try to make it conform to a similar pattern. The Wyler film, for instance, presents us with a pair of lovers who might have married, if only Heathcliff had behaved more like a potential husband. The atmosphere of the novel, however, is difficult to reduce to a plot of 'if only'. The second-generation love-and-marriage plot is a version of this story and most readers find it pale in comparison with the Catherine-and-Heathcliff love, which offers a 'something beyond'. It is significant that the most vivid scenes involving Catherine and Heathcliff take place when they are children, for in psychological terms, their relationship is like that of siblings who look to one another not for a sexual union, but for a confirmation of their identity in a mirror-image of themselves. This mirror-pattern can also be found in early nineteenth-century Romantic poems, in which male poets looked for ideal mirrors of themselves in semi-divine women, spirits of beauty or truth, sometimes conceived as sisters like Byron's half-sister Augusta or Shelley's 'twin-soul', Emilia Viviani. Because such lovers are held, as it were, in parallel, rather than converging, these stories do not end in happy marriage but are often tragic.

Wuthering Heights, however, offers a complication of this pattern. Catherine and Heathcliff act 'in parallel' as children, but because Catherine acts as a marriageable woman in relation to Edgar, the relationship can also be read in terms of what Denis de Rougemont calls the 'great European myth of adultery'.[61] In the novel, the scenes between Catherine and Heathcliff after Catherine's marriage give us a curious sense of dissonance; we cannot tell whether to interpret them in terms of their earlier, mirroring love, or in terms of an adult, adulterous triangle. Most modern reproductions try to incorporate the 'twin-soul' theme into an adulterous triangle. Luis Buñuel's film, *Abismos de Pasión* (1953), has no childhood scenes and the drama focuses on the quarrel between Edgar and Heathcliff for possession of the heavily pregnant Catherine.[62] Frank Dunlop's 1996 musical, *Heathcliff*,[63] also makes explicit the fact that in Catherine's death-scene, her pregnant body is an object of contention between the two men. Sir Cliff Richard, who was to play the part of Heathcliff, linked the story in a pre-production interview with that of *Romeo and Juliet* (*Daily Express*, 27 October 1995), while Buñuel invokes both Romeo and Juliet and Tristan and Isolde; in each of these cases, the 'twin soul' ideal becomes tragic because a potentially marital relationship is prevented by practical obstacles. This 'domestication' of *Wuthering Heights*, however, brings its own difficulties, since it requires Heathcliff to appear as a possible alternative husband, and thus ignores or recuperates his peculiar appeal as an imaginary twin rather than a reproductive mate. Anna L'Estrange's saga-novel, *Return to Wuthering Heights* (1978), is unusual among popular texts in gesturing towards this problem; by having successive generations of women fall in love with successive versions of Heathcliff, it suggests that his appeal can be neither fulfilled nor annihilated.[64]

The 'triangular' reading of *Wuthering Heights*, which brings it closer to the *Jane Eyre* model, contributes to confusion between the novels themselves. From early in the twentieth century, actors seem to have regarded the parts of Rochester and Heathcliff as a 'matching pair'. Milton Rosmer, who played Heathcliff in the 1920 silent film of *Wuthering Heights*, read the part of Rochester on the radio in the 1930s. Timothy Dalton, who played Heathcliff as a young man, played Rochester as an older one.[65] A reviewer of one *Jane Eyre* stage play used the title, 'Throbbing Heights' to relate the meaning of *Jane Eyre* to 'the strange repressed sexuality of the sisters' (*In Dublin*, 5 December 1990), while an advertisement for another shows a huge brooding face reminiscent of Fritz Eichenberg's woodcut of Heathcliff.[66] Lin Haire-Sargeant's novel, *Heathcliff*, literally amalgamates the two novels, so that

Heathcliff is prevented from returning to Wuthering Heights by his need to search for Jane Eyre.[67]

If Top Withens represents the idea of outdoor freedom in the Brontë myth, Penistone Crag represents romantic love. From the Wyler film through the Bernard Herrmann opera and in repeated stagings of the 1990s, including the Cliff Richard musical, the looming mass of Penistone Crag represents an escape from the problems of society and a promise of fulfilment, even if only after death. The Crag is not nearly so prominent in the novel, and it may be that the novel continues to fascinate readers precisely because it fails to offer any such focal point. Neither does it offer any image of a lovers' embrace except the fierce cleaving together on Catherine's deathbed. What the critic Jay Clayton calls 'the representational void' creates an intense need which film-makers and stage adapters have filled 'with a place – Penistone Crags, where the lovers meet even after their death – and with an action, a sexual embrace'.[68] Sensitive readers recognise that this promise of fulfilment is only ever a promise. In Sylvia Plath's poem, 'Wuthering Heights', the speaker is tempted by 'horizons' which 'Only dissolve and dissolve / Like a series of promises'. In 'Two Views of Withens', she recognises that such 'sites of passion' signify only what viewers bring to them. She finds 'the House of Eros / Low-lintelled, no palace'.[69] In Ted Hughes' 'Two Photographs of Top Withens', on the other hand, it is Plath who holds the hopeful pose while in her absence the ruin becomes 'a roofless / Pissoir for sheep and tourists'.[70]

Jane Eyre and *Wuthering Heights* are now unimaginably famous. After a hundred and fifty years they are still the third and fourth most borrowed books from British public libraries. Their titles and key images can be found in advertisements, pop songs and conversation. They are available in Britain in nearly thirty editions and have been translated into nearly thirty languages. In Japan Catherine and Heathcliff appear in the whole cultural span from Samurai tragedy to Disney-like whimsy. Jane Eyre has been a role model for girls from America to Africa.[71] In the last twenty years, a million copies of *Jane Eyre*, in eight different translations, have been sold in China.[72]

The very dominance of the world's greatest love stories has made them an object for revision. Those who have felt excluded from the myth have altered it to represent their point of view. As a heterosexual myth, *Jane Eyre* has been revised by Jeanette Winterson, who writes, 'I would cross seas and suffer sunstroke and give away all I have, but not for a man'.[73] As a European myth of happy endings, it has been challenged by Jean Rhys' novel, *Wide Sargasso Sea* (1966), which tells the story of the first Mrs Rochester, the gentle Antoinette, renamed 'Bertha' by the husband who brought her from her native Dominica to leap from the battlements of Thornfield.[74] This novel had an immediate impact on popular perceptions of *Jane Eyre*.

Figure 10 Catherine and Heathcliff's last embrace. Japanese picture-book edition of
Wuthering Heights (1989).

Delbert Mann's 1970 film, for instance, replaces the raging maniac of earlier
representations with a sweet-faced, vacant young woman. A further development of this position came in 1979 with Sandra M. Gilbert and Susan
Gubar's book, *The Madwoman in the Attic*, which argues that Bertha Mason
is a device for expressing the social and sexual rage which could not be tol-
erated in the decorous heroines of nineteenth-century writing by women.

Locked away in the attic, Bertha's tumult can be repudiated, but her presence in the text still serves to destabilise the apparently endorsed social order. While some critics rejoiced that the marginalised figure from the colonies was receiving due attention,[75] the postcolonial critic Gayatri Spivak replied by arguing that Rhys privileges the Creole Bertha/Antoinette at the expense of the black women of the Caribbean colonies, on whom Jane Eyre's wealth depends.[76] Ripples from post-colonial theory are felt in popular culture. Robbie Kydd's *The Quiet Stranger* and Maryse Condé's *Windward Heights* retell *Jane Eyre* and *Wuthering Heights* in different Caribbean contexts.[77] Peter Forster's illustrations for *Wuthering Heights* build on the novel's hints of Heathcliff's non-white origin to represent him as a full-lipped African.[78]

Turning from Forster's African Heathcliff to the Laurence Olivier version, or from the Victorian 'maniac' to Jean Rhys' Antoinette, we may long to recover the 'true', the 'original' stories. It may seem that the ephemera pursued by 'cultural studies' are no more than a sideshow, amusing or annoying, while 'real' literary criticism continues to elucidate texts which are acknowledged to be 'great' literature. This chapter has hardly glanced at academic interpretations of the Brontë texts; even a glance, however, reveals a plethora of readings. The conclusion we have to draw is that literary texts are unstable constructions – that there is no 'true' version independent of particular readings. In practice, moreover, a myriad of responses does not damage that sense of the text being 'special', but rather intensifies it. A literary 'myth' like the image of Catherine and Heathcliff embracing on Penistone Crag cannot be traced to a direct origin in the text, and has to be seen as the shared hallucination of a cultural group. It is, however, a response to indirect promptings which, when analysed, prove to be the very stuff on which literary criticism works – structure, vocabulary, metaphor – producing not an image but a need, which we fill with whatever comes to hand. The nature of myth is that it constantly changes, absorbing or rejecting whatever is needed by the moment. The Brontë myth has developed through time, shifting its focus, collapsing lives with works and landscape with fiction. Swelling to bombastic girth, it is deflated by satire or challenged from the margins. Such surging and seething is what keeps texts alive.

NOTES

1. Anon. Appended to Donald Hopewell, 'The Misses Brontë: Victorians', *Brontë Society Transactions* 10: 55 (1940), 3–11.
2. Juliet Barker, *The Brontës* (London: Weidenfeld & Nicolson, 1994), 675; Charles Lemon, ed., *Early Visitors to Haworth: From Ellen Nussey to Virginia Woolf* (Haworth: Brontë Society, 1996), 17 and 26.

3. See Patsy Stoneman, ed., *Emily Brontë: Wuthering Heights*, Icon Critical Guides (Cambridge: Icon Books, 1998), 11–24.
4. Samuel Maundee, *The Biographical Treasury* (London: Longman, Green, Longman and Roberts, 1862), 902–3.
5. Barker, *Brontës*, 557–63.
6. Elizabeth Langland, *Anne Brontë: The Other One* (Basingstoke: Macmillan, 1989).
7. Barker, *Brontës*, 660.
8. Lemon, ed., *Visitors*, 81, 74, 95, 60 and 124–5. Also J. A. Erskine Stuart, *The Literary Shrines of Yorkshire: the Literary Pilgrim in the Dales* (London: Longmans, Green & Co.: 1892).
9. Charles Lemon, *A Centenary History of the Brontë Society* (Haworth: Brontë Society, 1993), 4.
10. *Ibid.*, 4.
11. Stevie Davies, *Four Dreamers and Emily* (London: Women's Press, 1996).
12. Elizabeth Gaskell, *The Life of Charlotte Brontë* [1857] (Harmondsworth: Penguin, 1975).
13. Barker, *Brontës*, 635.
14. Ann Dinsdale, *Old Haworth* (Keighley: Hendon, 1999).
15. Barker, *Brontes*, 255–6.
16. George Gordon, Lord Byron, 'Childe Harold's Pilgrimage', canto III, stanza XV (1816).
17. 'Haworth Churchyard' was first published in *Fraser's Magazine* for May 1855. See Kathleen Tillotson, ' "Haworth Churchyard": the Making of Arnold's Elegy', *Brontë Society Transactions*, 15: 2 (1967), 105–22.
18. Simone de Beauvoir, *The Second Sex* [1949] (London: New English Library, 1970), 104.
19. Jean Barker, 'Emily', in Wendy Bardsley, ed., *An Enduring Flame: the Brontë Story in Poetry and Photographs* (Otley: Smith Settle, 1998), 97.
20. See F. B. Pinion, *A Reader's Companion to the Brontës* (Basingstoke: Macmillan, 1975); Arthur Pollard, *The Landscape of the Brontës*. Photographs by Simon McBride (London: Webb & Bower, 1988); and Brian Wilks, *The Brontës* (London: Hamlyn, 1975). The videos are *In the Shadows of the Brontës* (Bridlington: Rushton Studies, 1989) and *Wuthering Heights: a Critical Guide to the Novel* (Braceborough: Literary Images Ltd, 1992). The quotation is from *Wuthering Heights: a Critical Guide.*
21. Lemon, ed., *Visitors*, 97, 125.
22. A. V. Bramble (director), *Wuthering Heights* (London: Ideal Film Renting Co., 1920).
23. William Wyler (director), *Wuthering Heights* (Hollywood: United Artists: Samuel Goldwyn Productions, 1939).
24. Peter Kominsky (director), *Emily Brontë's Wuthering Heights* (Hollywood: Paramount, 1991).
25. Robert Stevenson (director), *Jane Eyre* (Hollywood: Twentieth Century Fox, 1944).
26. Bernard Herrmann, *Wuthering Heights* (opera). Vocal (piano) score (London: Novello, 1965).
27. Delbert Mann (director), *Jane Eyre* (British Lion Pictures, 1970).

28. Kazue Kontaibo (director), *Jane Eyre* (Japanese play 1978); Willis Hall (adaptation), *Jane Eyre* (Crucible Theatre, Sheffield, 1992).
29. Chris Baldick, *In Frankenstein's Shadow: Myth, Monstrosity and Nineteenth-Century Writing* (Oxford: Clarendon, 1987), 3.
30. Lord David Cecil, *Early Victorian Novelists: Essays in Revaluation* (London: Constable, 1934), 151–3, 164–5.
31. Sylvia Plath, 'Two Views of Withens', *Sylvia Plath: Collected Poems*, edited by Ted Hughes (London: Faber & Faber, 1981), 167.
32. Jane Urquhart, *Changing Heaven* (Sevenoaks: Hodder & Stoughton, 1990), 179–80.
33. Gaskell, *Life*, 112–23.
34. Fannie Elizabeth Ratchford, *The Brontës' Web of Childhood* (New York: Columbia University Press, 1941).
35. See Jane Gardam, *The Summer after the Funeral* [1973] (Harmondsworth: Puffin, 1983); Sheila Greenwald, *It all Began with Jane Eyre or the Secret Life of Franny Dillman* (Harmondsworth: Penguin, 1988); Garry Kilworth, *The Brontë Girls* (London: Methuen, 1995); and Robert Swindells, *Follow a Shadow* (Harmondsworth: Penguin, 1989).
36. Pauline Clarke, *The Twelve and the Genii* (London: Faber & Faber, 1962).
37. Gaskell, *Life*, 132.
38. Lemon, ed., *Visitors*, 62.
39. Virginia Woolf, *Women and Writing*, ed. Michèle Barrett (London: Women's Press, 1979), 75.
40. May Sinclair, *The Three Brontës* (London: Hutchinson, 1912); *The Three Sisters* (London: Macmillan, 1914).
41. Rosamond Langbridge, *Charlotte Brontë: a Psychological Study* (London: Heinemann, 1929), 5, 85.
42. Emilie and Georges Romieu, *The Brontë Sisters* (London: Skeffington, 1931), 10.
43. Mary Robinson, *Emily Brontë* [1883] (London: W. H. Allen, 1890), 164.
44. Charlotte Mew, 'The Poems of Emily Brontë' [1904], in V. Warner, ed., *Collected Poems and Prose of Charlotte Mew* (Manchester: Carcanet, 1981), 368.
45. Stella Gibbons, *Cold Comfort Farm* [1932] (Harmondsworth: Penguin, 1978).
46. Lemon, ed., *Visitors*, 127.
47. Rachel Ferguson, *The Brontës Went to Woolworth's* [1931] (London: Virago, 1988).
48. Lemon, ed., *Visitors*, 66, 76.
49. Barker, *Brontës*, 489–90.
50. Alice Law, *Patrick Branwell Brontë* (London: A. M. Philpot, 1923), 104, 121.
51. 'Storm-Wrack: A Night with the Brontës, 184–', in James Mackereth *Storm-Wrack and Other Poems* (London: Lane, 1927), 27.
52. Clemence Dane, *Wild Decembers* (London: Heinemann, 1932); Dan Totheroh, *Moor Born* (New York: Samuel French, 1934); E. T. Cook, *They Lived* (London: John Murray, 1935); and Kathryn MacFarlane, *Divide the Desolation* (New York: Simon & Schuster, 1936).
53. Robert Buckner (director), *Devotion* (Hollywood: Warner Brothers [1943], 1946).
54. Barker, *Brontës*, 455.

55. James Tully, *The Crimes of Charlotte Brontë: the Secret History of the Mysterious Events at Haworth* (London: Robinson, 1999).
56. Clare Boylan, 'Jane Eyre Revisited: An Alternative Ending', *Good Housekeeping*, January 1900, 136–40.
57. See Patsy Stoneman, *Brontë Transformations: the Cultural Dissemination of 'Jane Eyre' and 'Wuthering Heights'* (Hemel Hempstead: Harvester Wheatsheaf/ Prentice Hall, 1996), ch. 1.
58. 'The Russ Abbott Show', BBC 1, 18 October 1991.
59. Franco Zefirelli (director), *Jane Eyre* (New York: Miramax, 1996).
60. See Tania Modleski, *Loving with a Vengeance: Mass-Produced Fantasy for Women* (London: Routledge, 1982); Janice Radway, *Reading the Romance* (London: Verso, 1984).
61. Denis de Rougemont, *Love in the Western World* [1940] (Princeton University Press, 1983), 248, 18.
62. Luis Buñuel *et al.* (screenplay), Abelardo Rodriguez (director), *Abismos de Pasión* (Mexico: Producciones Tepeyac, 1953).
63. Frank Dunlop (director), *Heathcliff* (musical), VCI video, 1997.
64. Anna L' Estrange, *Return to Wuthering Heights* (London: Corgi, 1978).
65. See A. V. Bramble (director), *Wuthering Heights* (London: Ideal Film Renting, Co., 1920); Barbara Couper and Howard Rose (adaptations), *Jane Eyre* [play] (BBC Radio, 1931); Robert Fuest (director), *Wuthering Heights* (American International Pictures, 1970); and Julian Amyes (director), *Jane Eyre* [serial dramatised by Alexander Baron] (BBC TV, 1983).
66. Fritz Eichenberg (illus.), Emily Brontë, *Wuthering Heights* (New York: Random House, 1943), facing p. 80.
67. Lin Haire-Sargeant, *Heathcliff: the Return to Wuthering Heights* (London, Century, 1992).
68. Jay Clayton, *Romantic Vision and the Novel* (Cambridge University Press, 1987), 84.
69. Plath, *Poems*, 167, 72.
70. Bardsley, ed., *Enduring Flame*, 122.
71. See Stoneman, *Brontë Transformations*.
72. Shuyu Zhang, 'Brontë Research in China', *Brontë Society Transactions* 24: 2 (1999), 174–81, 180.
73. Jeanette Winterson, *Oranges Are Not the Only Fruit* (London: Pandora, 1985), 74.
74. Jean Rhys, *Wild Sargasso Sea* [1966] (Harmondsworth: Penguin, 1983).
75. For example, Dennis Porter, 'Of Heroines and Victims: Jean Rhys and *Jane Eyre*' *Massachusetts Review* 17: 3 (1976), 540–52.
76. Gayatri Chakravorty Spivak, 'Three Women's Texts and a Critique of Imperialism', *Critical Inquiry* 12 (1985), 243–61.
77. Robbie Kydd, *The Quiet Stranger* (Edinburgh: Mainstream, 1991); Maryse Condé, *Windward Heights* [1995]. Trans. Richard Philcox (London: Faber & Faber, 1998).
78. Peter Forster (illus.) Emily Bronte: *Wuthering Heights* (London: Folio Society, 1991).

FURTHER READING

There is a considerable amount of scholarly work on the Brontës. What follows is a necessarily incomplete listing of more important primary sources, and a selective list of critical studies, most of which have been published during the last thirty years.

A useful selection of early criticism may be found in Miriam Allott, ed. *The Brontës: The Critical Heritage*. Routledge & Kegan Paul, 1974.

Primary sources

Alexander, Christine (ed.), *An Edition of the Early Writings of Charlotte Brontë*. Oxford: Basil Blackwell, vol. I, *The Glass Town Saga 1826–1832*, 1987; vol. II, *The Rise of Angria 1833–1835*, part 1: *1833–4* and part 2: *1834–5*, 1991.

Alexander, Christine and Sellars, Jane, *The Art of the Brontës*. Cambridge University Press, 1995.

Barker, Juliet (ed.), *Charlotte Brontë: Juvenilia 1829–1835*. Harmondsworth: Penguin, 1996.

Poems by Currer, Ellis, and Acton Bell. Aylott and Jones, 1846; repr. London: A. & C. Black, 1985.

Brontë, Charlotte, *Unfinished Novels*. Stroud: Alan Sutton Publishing, 1993.

Chitham, Edward (ed.), *The Poems of Anne Brontë: A New Text and Commentary*. Basingstoke: Macmillan, 1979.

Gérin, Winifred (ed.), *Charlotte Brontë: Five Novelettes*. London: Folio Press, 1971.

Gezari, Janet (ed.), *Emily Jane Brontë: The Complete Poems*. Harmondsworth: Penguin, 1992.

Lonoff, Sue (ed. and trans.), *The Belgian Essays: Charlotte and Emily Brontë*. Yale University Press, 1996.

Winnifrith, Tom (ed.), *The Poems of Patrick Branwell Brontë: A New Annotated and Enlarged Edition of the Shakespeare Head Brontë*. Oxford: Blackwell, 1983.

The Poems of Charlotte Brontë: A New Annotated and Enlarged Edition of the Shakespeare Head Brontë. Oxford: Blackwell, 1984.

Biography

Most of the surviving letters of the Brontë family are reprinted in T. J. Wise, and J. A. Symington (eds.), *The Brontës: Their Lives, Friendships and Correspondence*,

4 vols. Shakespeare Head, 1932. This edition contains many inaccuracies: a new and definitive edition of Charlotte Brontë's letters is in the process of preparation by Margaret Smith.

Margaret Smith (ed.), *The Letters of Charlotte Brontë, with a selection of letters by family and friends*. 3 vols. Oxford: Clarendon, 1995, 2000 (vol. 3 forthcoming).

The classic biography is Elizabeth Gaskell, *The Life of Charlotte Brontë* [1857] rpt. Oxford University Press, 1974.

See also

Barker, Juliet, *The Brontës*. London: Weidenfeld & Nicolson, 1994.

Chitham, Edward, *The Brontës' Irish Background*. Basingstoke: Macmillan, 1986.

A Life of Emily Brontë. Oxford: Blackwell, 1987.

A Life of Anne Brontë. Oxford: Blackwell, 1991.

Gérin, Winifred, *Branwell Brontë*. London: Hutchinson, 1961.

Charlotte Brontë; The Evolution of Genius. Oxford: Clarendon Press, 1967.

Emily Brontë: A Biography. Oxford University Press, 1971.

Gordon, Lyndall, *Charlotte Brontë: A Passionate Life*. London: Chatto & Windus, 1994.

Lock, John and Dixon, Canon W. T., *A Man of Sorrow. The Life, Letters and Times of the Rev. Patrick Brontë 1771–1861*. London: Nelson, 1965.

Winnifrith, Tom, *The Brontës and Their Background. Romance and Reality*. Basingstoke: Macmillan, 1973.

Selected criticism

Poems

Donoghue, Denis, 'The Other Emily'. In Ian Gregor (ed.), *The Brontës: A Collection of Critical Essays*. Hemel Hempstead: Prentice Hall, 1970, 157–72.

Grove, Robin, 'It Would Not Do': Emily Brontë as Poet'. In Anne Smith (ed.), *The Art of Emily Brontë*. London: Vision Press, 1976, 33–68.

Homans, Margaret, *Women Writers and Poetic Identity: Dorothy Wordsworth, Emily Brontë, and Emily Dickinson*. Princeton University Press, 1980.

Lewis, C. Day, 'The Poetry of Emily Brontë', *Brontë Society Transactions* 13 (1965), 83–95.

Mew, Charlotte, 'The Poems of Emily Brontë' [1904]. In V. Warner (ed.), *Collected Poems and Prose of Charlotte Mew*. Manchester: Carcanet, 1981.

Myers, William, 'The Poems of Emily Brontë'. In William Myers (ed.), *The Presence of Persons: Essays on Literature, Science and Philosophy in the Nineteenth Century*. Aldershot: Ashgate, 1998, 155–176.

Wordsworth, Jonathan, 'Wordsworth and the Poetry of Emily Brontë', *Brontë Society Transactions* 16 (1972), 85–100.

Novels

Eagleton, Terry, *Myths of Power: A Marxist Study of the Brontës*. Basingstoke: Macmillan, 1975; 2nd edn, 1987.

Gilbert, Sandra M. and Gubar, Susan, *The Madwoman in the Attic: The Woman Writer and the Nineteenth-Century Literary Imagination*. Yale University Press, 1979.

Jack, Ian, 'Novels and those Necessary Evils: Annotating the Brontës', *Essays in Criticism* 32: 4 (1982), 321–37.

Jacobs, Naomi, 'Gender and Layered Narrative in *Wuthering Heights* and *The Tenant of Wildfell Hall*', *Journal of Narrative Technique* 16: 3 (1986), 204–19.

Meyer, Susan, *Imperialism at Home: Race and Victorian Women's Fiction*. London and Ithaca: Cornell University Press, 1996.

Michie, Elsie, 'From Simianized Irish to Oriental Despots: Heathcliff, Rochester, and Racial Difference', *Novel* 25 (1992), 125–40.

Qualls, Barry. *The Secular Pilgrims of Victorian Fiction: The Novel as Book of Life*. Cambridge University Press, 1981.

Stoneman, Patsy, *Brontë Transformations: the Cultural Dissemination of 'Jane Eyre' and 'Wuthering Heights'*. Hemel Hempstead: Harvester Wheatsheaf Prentice Hall, 1996.

Tayler, Irene, *Holy Ghosts: The Male Muses of Emily and Charlotte Brontë*. New York: Columbia University Press, 1990.

Thormählen, Marianne, *The Brontës and Religion*. Cambridge University Press, 1999.

Vargish, Thomas, *The Providential Aesthetic in Victorian Fiction*. University Press of Virginia, 1985.

Wheeler, Michael, *Death and the Future Life in Victorian Literature and Theology*. Cambridge University Press, 1990.

Williams, Raymond, *The English Novel from Dickens to Lawrence*. London: Chatto & Windus, 1973.

Anne Brontë

Frawley, Maria, *Anne Brontë*. New York: Twayne, 1996.

Jay, Betty, *Anne Brontë*. Plymouth: Northcote House with the British Council, 2000.

Langland, Elizabeth, *Anne Brontë: The Other One*. Basingstoke: Macmillan, 1989.
 'The Voicing of Desire in Anne Brontë's *The Tenant of Wildfell Hall*'. In Antony H. Harrison and Beverley Taylor (eds.), *Gender and Discourse in Victorian Literature and Art*. Northern Illinois University Press, 1992.

Matus, Jill, *Unstable Bodies: Victorian Representations of Sexuality and Maternity*. Manchester University Press, 1995, 89–156.

McMaster, Juliet, ' "Imbecile Laughter" and "Desperate Earnest" in *The Tenant of Wildfell Hall*', *Modern Language Quarterly* 43: 4 (1982), 352–68.

Meyer, Susan. 'Words on "Great Vulgar Sheets": Writing and Social Resistance in Anne Brontë's *Agnes Grey*'. In Barbara Lea Harman and Susan Meyer (eds.), *The New Nineteenth Century: Feminist Readings of Underread Victorian Fiction*. New York: Garland Publishing Inc., 1996.

Charlotte Brontë

Alexander, Christine, *The Early Writings of Charlotte Brontë*. Oxford: Blackwell, 1983.

Bock, Carol, *Charlotte Brontë and the Storyteller's Audience*. University of Iowa Press, 1992.

Boumelha, Penny, *Charlotte Brontë*. Hemel Hempstead: Harvester Wheatsheaf, 1990.

Brownstein, Rachel, *Becoming a Heroine: Reading About Women in Novels*. Harmondsworth: Penguin, 1984.

Carlisle, Janice, 'The Face in the Mirror: *Villette* and the Conventions of Autobiography', *English Literary History* 46 (1979), 262–89.

Chase, Karen, *Eros and Psyche. The Representation of Personality in Charlotte Brontë, Charles Dickens and George Eliot*. London: Methuen, 1984.

Dale, Peter Allan, 'Charlotte Brontë's "Tale Half-Told": the Disruption of Narrative Structure in *Jane Eyre*', *Modern Language Quarterly* 47 (1986), 108–29.

Dale, Peter Allan, 'Heretical Narration: Charlotte Brontë's Search for Endlessness', *Religion and Literature* 16: 3 (1984), 1–24.

David, Deirdre, *Rule Britannia: Women, Empire, and Victorian Writing*. Cornell University Press, 1995.

Gezari, Janet, *Charlotte Brontë and Defensive Conduct: the Author and the Body at Risk*. University of Pennsylvania Press, 1992.

Glen, Heather (ed.), *Jane Eyre: New Casebook*. Basingstoke: Macmillan, 1997.

Gounelas, Ruth, 'Charlotte Brontë and the Critics: Attitudes to the Female Qualities in her Writing', *Journal of the Australasian Universities Language and Literature Association* 62 (1984), 151–70.

Heilmann, Robert, 'Charlotte Brontë's "New" Gothic'. In Robert C. Rathburn and Martin Steinmann, Jr (eds.), *From Jane Austen to Joseph Conrad*. Mineappolis: University of Minnesota Press, 1958, 118–32.

Heilmann, Robert, 'Tuliphood, Streaks and Other Strange Bedfellows: Style in *Villette*', *Studies in the Novel* 14 (1982), 223–47.

Ingham, Patricia, *The Language of Gender and Class: Transformation in the Victorian Novel*. London: Routledge, 1996.

Jacobus, Mary, 'The Buried Letter: Feminism and Romanticism in *Villette*'. In Mary Jacobus (ed.), *Women Writing and Writing About Women*. London: Croom Helm, 1979.

Keefe, Robert, *Charlotte Brontë's World of Death*. University of Texas Press, 1979.

Kucich, John, *Repression in Victorian Fiction: Charlotte Brontë, George Eliot, and Charles Dickens*. University of California Press, 1987.

Lanser, Susan Sniader, *Fictions of Authority: Woman Writers and Narrative Voice*. Cornell University Press, 1992, 176–93.

Litvak, Joseph, *Caught in the Act: Theatricality in the Nineteenth-Century English Novel*. University of California Press, 1992.

Lodge, David, 'Fire and Eyre: Charlotte Brontë's War of Earthly Elements'. In *The Language of Fiction: Essays in Criticism and Verbal Analysis of the English Novel*. London: Routledge & Kegan Paul, 1966, 114–43.

Maynard, John, *Charlotte Brontë and Victorian Sexuality*. Cambridge University Press, 1984.

Nestor, Pauline (ed.), *Villette: New Casebook*. Basingstoke: Macmillan, 1992.

Newton, Judith Lowder, *Women, Power and Subversion: Social Strategies in British Fiction, 1778–1860*. University of Georgia Press, 1981.

Peters, Margot, *Charlotte Brontë: Style in the Novel*. University of Wisconsin Press, 1973.

Peterson, Carla L., *The Determined Reader: Gender and Culture in the Novel from Napoleon to Victoria*. Rutgers University Press, 1986, 82–131.

Rich, Adrienne, '*Jane Eyre*: The Temptations of a Motherless Woman'. In *On Lies, Secrets and Silence*. London: W. W. Norton & Co., 1979, 88–106.

Shaw, Margaret L., 'Narrative Surveillance and Social Control in *Villette*', *Studies in English Literature, 1500–1900* 34 (1994), 813–33.

Shuttleworth, Sally, *Charlotte Brontë and Victorian Psychology*. Cambridge University Press, 1996.

Silver, Brenda R., 'The Reflecting Reader in *Villette*'. In Elizabeth Abel, Marianne Hirsch and Elizabeth Langland (eds.), *The Voyage In: Fictions of Female Development*. University Press of New England, 1983, 90–111.

Tanner, Tony, Introduction to *Villette*. Harmondsworth: Penguin, 1979.

Tillotson, Kathleen, *Novels of the Eighteen-Forties*. Oxford University Press, 1954.

Tromly, Annette, *The Cover of the Mask: The Autobiographers in Charlotte Brontë's Fiction*. English Literary Studies, University of Victoria, 1982.

Warhol, Robyn R., 'Double Gender, Double Genre in *Jane Eyre* and *Villette*', *Studies in English Literature, 1500–1900* 36 (1996), 857–75.

West, Rebecca, 'Charlotte Brontë'. In H. J. and Hugh Massingham (eds.), *The Great Victorians*. London: Nicholson and Watson, 1932.

Wyatt, Jean, *Reconstructing Desire: The Role of the Unconscious in Women's Reading and Writing*. University of North Carolina Press, 1990, 23–40.

Emily Brontë

Chitham, Edward, *The Birth of 'Wuthering Heights': Emily Brontë at Work*. Basingstoke: Macmillan, 1998.

Davies, Stevie, *Emily Brontë: The Artist as a Free Woman*. Manchester: Carcanet Press; 1983.

Emily Bronte: Heretic. London: Women's Press, 1994.

Emily Brontë. Plymouth: Northcote House with The British Council, 1998.

Hewish, John, *Emily Brontë: A Critical and Biographical Study*. Basingstoke: Macmillan, 1969.

Hillis Miller, J., *Fiction and Repetition: Seven English Novels*. Harvard University Press, 1982.

Kermode, Frank, *The Classic*. London: Faber & Faber, 1975, 115–41.

Knopfelmacher, U. C., *Wuthering Heights*. Basingstoke: Macmillan, 1989.

Leavis, Q. D., 'A Fresh Approach to *Wuthering Heights*'. In G. Singh (ed.), *Collected Essays of Q. D. Leavis*. 3 vols. Cambridge University Press, 1983–9, vol. 1, 228–74.

Newman, Beth, 'The Situation of the Looker-On: Gender, Narration and Gaze in *Wuthering Heights*', *PMLA* 105: 5 (1990), 1029–41.

Parker, Patricia, 'The (Self-)Identity of the Literary Text: Property, Proper Place, and Proper Name in *Wuthering Heights*'. In *Literary Fat Ladies: Rhetoric, Gender, Property*. London: Methuen, 1987, 155–64.

Pykett, Lyn, *Emily Brontë*. Basingstoke: Macmillan, 1989.

Smith, Anne (ed.), *The Art of Emily Brontë*. London: Vision Press, 1976.

Stoneman, Patsy (ed.), *Wuthering Heights: New Casebook*. Basingstoke: Macmillan, 1993.

   Wuthering Heights. A Reader's Guide to Essential Criticism. Cambridge: Icon Books, 2000.

INDEX

Aesop, *Fables*, 44

Agnes Grey, 4, 5, 7, 8, 10, 72, 73, 75, 79, 90, 95, 96, 100, 101, 112, 113, 155–156, 178, 199–200, 216, 217

Alexander, Christine, 37, 225

Angrian saga, 4, 6, 36, 38, 44, 53–55, 57, 102, 125–126, 225

Arabian Nights' Entertainments, The, 44, 99

Arnold, Matthew, 142, 175, 193, 205, 210
  'Haworth Churchyard', 222

Arnold, Thomas, 194

Audubon, John James, 24

Austen, Jane, 1, 2, 179

Aykroyd, Tabitha, 28

Babbage, Benjamin Herschel, *Report on the Sanitary Condition of Haworth*, 17–19

Bakhtin, Mikhail, 193, 198

Baldick, Christopher, 223–224

Barker, Jean, 223

Barker, Juliet, 100, 154, 215, 221, 228, 230, 231

Bell, Currer, Ellis and Acton, 2, 4, 5, 7, 54, 84, 99, 100, 123–125, 131, 133, 138, 174, 175, 216, 217

Bewick, Thomas, 24, 29, 182, 223

Bible, 44, 72, 79, 80, 87–90, 99, 124, 158, 192–194, 197, 201, 209–212

Blackwood's Magazine, 23, 24, 35, 39, 41, 44–49, 52, 102, 111, 128, 163

Blackwood, William, 47–48

Blake, William, 205

Bonaparte, Napoleon, 35

Braddon, Mary Elizabeth, 226

Branwell, Elizabeth, 23, 49, 72, 73, 195, 215

Brontë family
  childhood writings, 3, 4, 6, 24, 28, 30, 34–53, 55, 77, 123, 125–126, 133, 142, 145, 196, 225–226
  education, 7, 29–30, 53–54, 72, 110, 196, 216
  reading, 3, 23, 24, 30, 35, 45, 77, 221, 225

Brontë, Anne
  Diary paper, 1845, 83
  poetry, 60–61, 63, 146, 222

Brontë, Charlotte
  Biographical Notice of Ellis and Acton Bell, 1, 54, 101, 174, 185, 217, 221
  Editor's Preface to *Wuthering Heights* and *Agnes Grey*, 2, 166, 167, 171–173, 178, 185, 209, 217–218, 224
  'History of the year', 3, 47, 58, 125–126
  later juvenilia, 38, 41, 42–43, 125–126, 130, 146
  poetry, 53–54, 58
  'Poetaster, The', 41–42, 46–47
  Prefatory Note to 'Selections from Poems by Ellis Bell', 222
  Roe Head journal, 34, 222

Brontë, Elizabeth, 18, 53

Brontë, Emily
  'Butterfly, The', 92
  poetry, 4, 10, 60–70, 92, 205–206, 221, 222

Brontë, Maria (née Branwell), 53–54, 154, 195

Brontë, Maria, 18, 53, 58, 61

Brontë, Revd Patrick, 7, 17–19, 21–27, 35, 37, 44, 51, 59, 72, 77, 154–155, 158, 166, 195, 204, 215, 216, 221, 227
  Mrs Gaskell on, 25, 30
  writings, 23–25, 44, 200

CAMBRIDGE COMPANIONS TO LITERATURE